ROYAL HISTORICAL SOCIETY

STUDIES IN HISTORY

New Series

FRENCH EXILE JOURNALISM AND
EUROPEAN POLITICS

1792–1814

Studies in History New Series
Editorial Board

Professor Martin Daunton (*Convenor*)
Professor David Eastwood
Dr Steven Gunn
Professor Colin Jones
Professor Peter Mandler
Dr Simon Walker
Professor Kathleen Burk (*Honorary Treasurer*)

FRENCH EXILE JOURNALISM AND EUROPEAN POLITICS

1792–1814

Simon Burrows

THE ROYAL HISTORICAL SOCIETY
THE BOYDELL PRESS

© Simon Burrows 2000

All Rights Reserved. Except as permitted under current legislation no part of this work may be photocopied, stored in a retrieval system, published, performed in public, adapted, broadcast, transmitted, recorded or reproduced in any form or by any means, without the prior permission of the copyright owner

First published 2000

A Royal Historical Society publication
Published by The Boydell Press
an imprint of Boydell & Brewer Ltd
PO Box 9, Woodbridge, Suffolk IP12 3DF, UK
and of Boydell & Brewer Inc.
PO Box 41026, Rochester, NY 14604–4126, USA
website: http://www.boydell.co.uk

ISBN 0 86193 249 8

ISSN 0269–2244

A catalogue record for this book is available
from the British Library

Library of Congress Cataloging-in-Publication Data
Burrows, Simon, 1966–
 French exile journalism and European politics, 1792–1814 / Simon Burrows.
  p. cm. – (The Royal Historical Society studies in history. New series, ISSN 0269–2244)
 Includes bibliographical references and index.
 ISBN 0–86193–249–8 (alk. paper)
  1. French newspapers – Europe – History – 19th century. 2. French newspapers – Europe – History – 18th century. 3. France – History – Revolution, 1789–1799. 4. French – Europe – Political activity. 5. Political refugees – Europe – History – 19th century. 6. Political refugees – Europe – History – 18th century. I. Title. II. Series.
PN5177.B87 2000
074'.09421'09033 – dc21   00–034196

This book is printed on acid-free paper

Printed in Great Britain by
St Edmundsbury Press, Bury St Edmunds, Suffolk

Jacques Mallet Du Pan, by Rigaud, from an engraving by J. Heath.

FOR MY PARENTS

Contents

		Page
List of illustrations		viii
List of tables		ix
Acknowledgements		xi
Abbreviations		xiii
Notes on names and terminology		xv
Introduction		1
1	Scripting counter-revolution? Emigré journals and journalists, 1792–1814	15
2	The business of counter-revolution	56
3	The propaganda war	95
4	Reactions to revolution, 1792–1799	143
5	The challenge of Bonaparte, 1799–1814	179
Conclusion		222
Appendices		
1.	Proprietorship of the *Courier de Londres*	231
2.	Profiles of émigré journals	232
Bibliography		237
Index		253

List of Illustrations

Frontispiece/jacket illustration: Jacques Mallet Du Pan, by Rigaud, from an engraving by J. Heath

1.	Jean-Gabriel Peltier	20
2.	Front page of the *Courier d'Angleterre*, vendredi le 16 février 1810	22
3.	Vignette of Bonaparte as a sphinx from *Ambigu* 1 (n.d. 1802)	123
4.	Cryptic vignette from *Ambigu* 10 (n.d. 1803)	210
5.	Vignette representing the massacre at Jaffa, from *Ambigu* 15 (n.d. 1803)	213
6.	Vignette (presumably) representing the poisoning of French soldiers at Jaffa, from *Ambigu* 14 (n.d. 1803)	216

Photographic Acknowledgements

The portrait of Jacques Mallet Du Pan is reproduced by kind permission of Victor Mallet. I am grateful to Cambridge University Library and to the University of Waikato Photographic Department for their assistance in reproducing material from the *Courier d'Angleterre* and *Ambigu*.

List of Tables

1.	Format, periodicity and content classification of émigré journals	18
2.	Contribution and counter-revolutionary political activity of minor journalists and collaborators	32
3.	Length of editorial service of major émigré journalists	38
4.	Social status of journalists and collaborators on the French exile press	39
5.	Nationalities of journalists and collaborators	40
6.	Social origins and professional backgrounds of major émigré journalists	41
7.	Key dates in the emigration of major journalists	47
8.	Marital status of journalists and collaborators	49
9.	Minimum, approximate or estimated circulation figures for émigré papers	79
10.	Robert Heron's circulation figures for leading English periodicals, 1805–6	85

Publication of this volume was aided by a grant from the Scouloudi Foundation, in association with the Institute of Historical Research.

Acknowledgements

The researching and writing of this book has been a global undertaking, begun in England in 1988 and completed in New Zealand in 1998. As a result, I have many debts to acknowledge to friends and colleagues in many countries. My biggest intellectual debts are to Hélène Maspero-Clerc who gave me her card indexes, offprints, copies of documents and hospitality, and to my doctoral supervisor, Laurence Brockliss. I am also grateful to Hannah Barker, Iain McCalman, Kirsty Carpenter, Michael Durey, Robert Griffiths and Jennifer Mori, for discussing my work, suggesting sources and providing samples of their unpublished work. Dominic Bellenger, the late Angus Macintyre, Bill Murray, Hugh Gough, Edward Ingram, Paul Kielstra, Tone Urstad, my brother Jeremy Burrows, Gawain Wilson and Paula Rainsborough of Boosey and Hawkes all suggested sources or helped me to refine my ideas. So did several anonymous referees who have commented on my work. My editor Colin Jones has been supportive and patient. Douglas Simes, Natalie Philippe, William Jennings, Jane Garnett, Cliff Davies, Annabelle Ritchie, Bede Harris and Ken Coates have commented on and/or proof-read some or all of the final manuscript or earlier versions. Kirstin Kennedy and Jo Lally helped me with texts in Spanish, Portuguese and German.

I would also like to thank the trustees and administrators of the various funding bodies which supported my doctoral research and travel: the British Academy, the Taylorean Institute, the Oxford University Graduate Studies Committee, Wadham College and the Faculty of Modern History at Oxford University. More recently, study leave and teaching arrangements at the University of Waikato have helped me to continue my work on the French émigrés and move on to new projects.

Among numerous librarians and archivists, I am particularly grateful to staff at the Bodleian Library, Cambridge University Library, the University of Waikato Library, the Archives Nationales, the Public Record Office, and the Archives du Ministère des Affaires Etrangères. My special thanks go to Philip and Mary Mallet for permission to consult their family papers and for opening their home to me, and to their son Victor Mallet for providing a copy of the print of Mallet Du Pan. The Mallet papers have recently been most generously deposited in the library of Balliol College, Oxford. I am also grateful to Sister Germaine Blais at Trois-Rivières and Dr Per-Gunnar Ottosson at the Riksarkivet in Stockholm for the papers and information they communicated concerning the abbé Calonne and Pierre-François Fauche respectively. The archivists at the Chapeltown Branch of the West Yorkshire District Archives, and Kari Holm, reference librarian at Uppsala Universitetsbibliotek, were also extremely helpful, providing me with useful materials and copies of documents, often at short notice.

In addition, I wish to thank the editors and publishers of the *International History Review*, the *Journal of European Studies*, *French History* and the *New Zealand Slavonic Journal* for permission to draw on or reproduce material which has appeared elsewhere.

Finally, my friends Hormuz Ebrahimnejad, Mohammad Hamdan, Marcus Akroyd, Susan Headicar, Ruth and Burton Kidd, and my colleagues at Waikato variously provided encouragement, support or accommodation. Above all, I thank my parents, who provided endless support, and my wife Andrea who has lived with Peltier *et al.* from the beginning, and always criticised my ideas with patience and rigour. She, Lepidus and Cleopatra made it all worthwhile. Any merit in this work is largely due to all these people: its faults, of course, are entirely my own responsibility.

Simon Burrows
Hamilton
New Zealand

Abbreviations

AAE	Archives du Ministère des Affaires Etrangères, Paris
ACC	Archives Condé, Chantilly
ADI	Archives Départementales d'Isère, Grenoble
ADLA	Archives Départementales de la Loire Atlantique, Nantes
ADS	Archives Départementales de la Seine, Paris
AHRF	*Annales historiques de la Révolution française*
AMN	Archives Municipales, Nantes
AN	Archives Nationales, Paris
AO	Audit Office papers
AP	Archives privées
APP	Archives de la Préfecture de Police, Paris
Arsenal	Bibliothèque de l'Arsenal, Paris
AUTR	Archives des Ursulines de Trois-Rivières
BHESRF	*Bulletin d'histoire économique et sociale de la révolution française*
BHVP	Bibliothèque Historique de la Ville de Paris
BL	British Library
BM	*British Mercury* (English language version of Mallet Du Pan's *Mercure britannique*)
BMN	Bibliothèque Municipale, Nantes
BN	Bibliothèque Nationale, Paris
BPN	Bibliothèque Publique de la Ville de Neuchâtel
BPUG	Bibliothèque Publique et Universitaire de Genève
BUCOP	British Union Catalogue of Periodicals.
CA	*Courier d'Angleterre*
CL	*Courier de Londres*
CP	*Correspondance politique*
CPA	Correspondance politique, Angleterre
CUL	Cambridge University Library
dos./dos	dossier/s
DTP	*Dernier Tableau de Paris*
DUL	Perkins Library, Duke University, Durham, NC
ECSTC	*Eighteenth-Century Short-Title Catalogue*
EHR	*English Historical Review*
FO	Foreign Office
GGB	*Gazette de la Grande-Bretagne*
HMC	Historical Manuscripts Commission
HO	Home Office
HR	*Histoire de la restauration de la monarchie française*

IHR	*International History Review*
JFA	*Journal de France et d'Angleterre*
JMH	*Journal of Modern History*
mem./docs	Mémoires et documents series
MF	*Mercure de France (London)*
MS Add.	Additional Manuscript
NRA	National Register of Archives, London
Paris	*Paris pendant l'année*
PC	Privy Council
PRO	Public Records Office, London
PRO 30/8	Public Records Office papers series, Chatham papers
RHLF	*Revue d'histoire littéraire de France*
SR	*Supplément au Rédacteur*
TE	*Tableau de l'Europe*
TS	Treasury Solicitor's papers
WO	War Office
WYDA	West Yorkshire District Archives, Leeds

Notes on Names and Terminology

Several names in this book could prove confusing. I have adopted the following conventions. The surname 'Calonne' standing alone indicates Charles Alexandre de Calonne. His brother is denoted in the text as the abbé Calonne, and in footnotes by his initials, J.-L.-J. As Jean-Louis Mallet anglicised his name to John Lewis when he became a British national in 1806 and his *Autobiographical retrospective* was published posthumously under that name, footnotes use both forms. Context should make abundantly clear whether the name 'Regnier' refers to the journalist Jacques Regnier or Napoleon's justice minister Claude Regnier.

This study also refers to two different periodicals entitled *Mercure de France*. One was published in London from April 1800 to April 1801, the other in Paris until 1794, and again after June 1800, when it was refounded by, among others, Chateaubriand and Fontanes. Where context does not make it clear, I will indicate to which I am referring.

Usage of the terms 'newspaper', 'gazette', 'journal', 'periodical' and 'paper' when describing the émigré organs, and where possible foreign publications, is very specific. The definitions of these terms involve function, format and periodicity:

'Journal' and 'paper' are used as inclusive terms comprising 'newspapers' and 'periodicals'. However, the terms 'newspaper' and 'periodical' are mutually exclusive.

'Newspaper' is used to indicate broadsheet publications appearing frequently (at least twice weekly in the case of the émigré newspapers produced in London) for the purpose of providing news information. Émigré 'newspapers' were printed on one or two loose folded sheets of paper, usually of at least quartavo size, to give four or eight pages. The émigré 'newspapers' are the *Courier de Londres*, the *Courier d'Angleterre*, the *Gazette de la Grande-Bretagne* and *Correspondance politique*.

'Periodical' indicates a publication appearing less frequently, comprising at least twenty-four pages sewn together, usually in octavo format, but possibly in quartavo or duodecimo. All the London émigré journals not listed as newspapers were periodicals.

Except in the case of court gazettes, I have used the term 'gazette' to indicate a 'newspaper' which is primarily a compilation from other newspaper sources, with little or no original analysis of its own.

Although there is technically a difference between 'émigrés', who leave their homeland by choice, and 'exiles', who are expelled, I have used the terms interchangeably in order to relieve the monotony of repetition.

All extensive quotations in this study, except those in verse, are given in

English. Translations from original documents are my own. Those from printed sources have been given from published English sources wherever these have been freely available to me while writing. In a few cases I have had to provide my own translations even though an English translation is available. The most notable example is A. Sayous, *Mémoires et correspondance de Mallet Du Pan*. Readers should also note that quotes from Mallet Du Pan's *Mercure britannique* are taken from the *British Mercury*, the official translation which appeared five days after the French edition. In citing the source I have given the date and page reference for the English translation.

Money equivalents: £1 sterling was roughly equivalent to twenty-five livres. The terms *livre* and *franc* were interchangeable.

$$480\ sous = 24\ livres = 24\ francs = 1\ louis$$

As is customary, French dates are not capitalised except to refer to specific events where the name of a month is commonly used as shorthand, notably the *coups* of 'Brumaire', 'Fructidor', 'Thermidor' and 'Vendémiaire'.

Introduction

> There remains a vast and still little explored area: that of the sources for the history of the revolution in the foreign press. . . . Historians must pay them all the more attention because they can find in them the echo of the passions of our enemies and the émigrés; other [foreign periodicals] were financed by the republican government and these are no less interesting.[1]

The French revolution was moulded and defined by the printed word, above all by journalistic texts. These texts include those produced abroad by French exiles and foreigners, yet, despite Maurice Tourneux's plea, this book is the first systematic published study of the newspaper and periodical press of the revolutionary émigrés.[2] It examines the political and commercial contexts in which the London-based émigré press functioned, and offers an assessment of its practical significance in political, literary and psychological terms. Moreover, because it locates the émigré press within the context of the emerging European public sphere, this book explores the rich and little studied interface between the printed word and international politics in the revolutionary and Napoleonic age. However, in order to understand the role of the émigré press, it is first necessary to examine the publishing world and émigré milieu in which it arose.

By the late eighteenth century western Europe was awash with print[3] and most historians agree that a functioning public sphere, at least partially independent of government but susceptible to regulation nevertheless, had emerged in most European states.[4] In theory, at least, old regime France had

---

[1] Maurice Tourneux, *Les Sources bibliographiques de l'histoire de la révolution française*, Paris 1898, cited in A. Caron, *Manuel pratique pour l'étude de la révolution française*, Paris 1947, 223.
[2] This study is based upon my doctoral thesis, Simon Burrows, 'The French exile press in London, 1789–1814', unpubl. DPhil. diss. Oxford 1992. The only previous work concerning the entire émigré press is Hélène Maspero-Clerc's bibliographical article, 'Journaux d'émigrés à Londres (1792–1818)', BHESRF années 1972–3 (1974), 67–79. See also Samuel Joseph Marino's again largely bibliographical study, 'The French-refugee newspapers and periodicals in the United States, 1789–1825', unpubl. PhD diss. Michigan 1962, which despite its title covers all French-language titles, most of which were not written primarily for or by émigrés.
[3] R. A. Houston, *Literacy in early modern Europe: culture and education, 1500–1800*, London 1988, 157, suggests that 1.5 billion books were produced in Europe during the eighteenth century. This total excludes pamphlets, newspapers and 'popular ephemera'.
[4] The classic treatment of the rise of the public sphere in Germany, France and Britain is Jürgen Habermas's *The structural transformation of the public sphere: an inquiry into a category of bourgeois society*, Cambridge, Mass. 1991. The original German edition appeared in 1962.

particularly tight controls on her domestic press and publishing industries, but this resulted in the development of a flourishing extra-territorial publishing industry and a vigorous trade in smuggled and illegal books.[5] However, early in the revolutionary crisis, the remaining apparatus of government control broke down and France was inundated by a tidal wave of print. In late 1788, after the ministry invited free discussion on the composition of the Estates-General, there was a flurry of pamphleteering activity and from July 1789, when the royal licensing system collapsed altogether, there was an explosion of newspaper titles and an exponential rise in the number of readers. By the end of the year the newspaper had supplanted the pamphlet as the main form of political publishing and contributed to the formation of a distinctive revolutionary political culture.[6] The journals published by and for the émigré community in London, the subject of this study, continued and drew on French press traditions, and resembled the revolutionary press far more than the British domestic press.[7] It is therefore worth exploring the development of the French publishing industry in some detail.

In the last twenty years cultural historians have increasingly argued that print culture should be envisaged as a process rather than a fixed phenomenon and that developments in the production, dissemination and use of printed texts are deeply implicated in the cultural origins and outcomes of the French revolution. The path-breaking work of Elizabeth Eisenstein has shown that the availability and form of printed texts, perhaps more than the

---

Roger Chartier, *The cultural origins of the French revolution*, Durham, NC 1991, ch. ii, provides an excellent summary and reinterpretation of this subtle and complex work, with regard to *ancien régime* France. For further discussions of Habermas's theories in a French context see Benjamin Nathans, 'Habermas's "public sphere" in the era of the French revolution', *French Historical Studies* xvi (1990), 620–44, and Dena Goodman, 'Public sphere and private life: towards a synthesis of current historical approaches to the old regime', *History and Theory* xxxi (1992), 1–20. Nathans concluded that Habermas's model was 'empirically weak' and requires some important modifications.

[5] On illegal extra-territorial publishing see Robert Darnton, *The literary underground of the old regime*, Cambridge, Mass. 1982, and *The forbidden best-sellers of pre-revolutionary France*, London–New York 1996; Elizabeth L. Eisenstein, *Grub Street abroad: aspects of the French cosmopolitan press from the age of Louis XIV to the French revolution*, Oxford 1992. For a statistical survey of illegal titles see Robert Darnton, *The corpus of clandestine literature in France, 1769–1789*, London–New York, 1995.

[6] The best accounts of this process are Jeremy D. Popkin, *Revolutionary news: the press in France, 1789–1799*, Durham, NC–London, 1990, 16–34, and 'The business of political enlightenment in France, 1770–1800', in John Brewer and Roy Porter (eds), *Consumption and the world of goods*, London 1993, 412–36.

[7] For the press and politics in late eighteenth-century England see Hannah Barker, *Press, politics and public opinion in late eighteenth-century England*, Oxford 1998; Jeremy Black, *The English press in the eighteenth century*, London 1987; Arthur Aspinall, *Politics and the press, c. 1780–1850*, Brighton 1973. See also Lucyle Werkmeister, *The London daily press, 1772–1792*, Lincoln, Neb. 1963. To compare developments in England and France see Bob Harris, *Politics and the rise of the press: Britain and France, 1620–1800*, London–New York 1996.

messages they contain, played a vital part in cultural transformation. In the centuries after the invention of the Gutenberg press, European readers had access to ever-growing numbers of texts, allowing them to compare, contrast, critically assess and process, organise and store vastly more information than had ever previously been possible. Faced with a multiplicity of conflicting texts, readers developed habits of critical reasoning, which led them to challenge received authority.[8] By the late eighteenth century, print was so accessible and cheap, and reading so habitual for a large section of the population, that, in Roger Chartier's words, 'A new relationship with the text was established. It was disrespectful of the authorities, alternately seduced and disappointed by novelty, and, most of all, little inclined to religious obedience or belief.' He thus argues that 'it was a new way of reading, rather than the content of philosophical books' that created a 'critical attitude' and undermined traditional values.[9]

Chartier's arguments draw strongly on the work of the German sociological theorist Jürgen Habermas. In *The structural transformation of the public sphere*, Habermas argued that the eighteenth century witnessed the development of a new cultural space, the political public sphere, which existed primarily through the medium of print. This public sphere was a space for political discussion and exchange of ideas separate from and autonomous of state power. In France it grew from the 'public literary sphere' in the periodicals, pamphlets and salons, where a growing élite audience of connoisseurs and consumers of high culture passed aesthetic judgement on art and literature. Thus the 'public literary sphere' wrested cultural power away from the court and academies, where the power to assess artistic products had traditionally resided. Similarly, the political public sphere was developed through print and the institutions of enlightenment sociability (cafés, salons, clubs, debating societies, masonic lodges etc.), and was critical of the actions of public authority. It was open to anyone with access to print and was essentially egalitarian. The judgements of the rational critical public differentiated between individuals and their arguments only on the quality of their critical reasoning, and ignored the hierarchical distinctions of old regime society. Nor was any sphere of human activity exempt from the scrutiny of this new rational critical public. The opinion of the public thus increasingly became a new legitimising tribunal which judged the acts of political authority.[10] In this new political culture authority was transferred from the person of the king, whose decisions had been reached alone in secrecy and were not subject

---

[8] See Elizabeth L. Eisenstein, *The printing press as an agent of change*, Cambridge 1979, abridged as *The printing revolution in early modern Europe*, Cambridge 1983.
[9] Roger Chartier, 'Book markets and reading in France at the end of the old regime', in Carol Armbruster (ed.), *Publishing and readership in revolutionary France and America*, Westport, Conn. 1993, 117–36 at p. 133. See also Chartier, *Cultural origins*.
[10] Mona Ozouf, 'Public opinion at the end of the *ancien régime*', *Journal of Modern History* lx, supplement (1988), S1–S21 stresses at S9 that 'the key word in contemporary evocations of public opinion was *tribunal*' [my italics].

to appeal, to 'the judgement of an entity embodied in no institution, which debated publicly and was more sovereign than the sovereign'.[11] According to Mona Ozouf the Enlightenment substituted judgements before the tribunal of opinion and posterity for judgement before God, and these judgements took on 'components of infallibility, externality and unity'.[12] However, the public sphere was not truly democratic. Habermas defined it as essentially 'bourgeois', sociologically separate both from the public power of the court and from the 'people' who lacked the skills and opportunity to make public use of their reason.[13] The literate 'public opinion' to which enlightened authors appealed was conceived as the antithesis of the opinion of the 'people'. The 'people' were inarticulate, ill-educated and liable to be driven by hunger: popular opinion was 'multiple, versatile, and inhabited by prejudice and passion'.[14] Public opinion, the product of rational critical discourse and 'final arbiter' of the great issues of the day, was necessarily 'stable, unified, and founded on reason'.[15] The 'people' were nevertheless represented by the public sphere, in that the citizens of the enlightened republic of letters could be seen as articulators of ideas they were incapable of formulating. It was thus essential to distinguish between 'popular opinion' and 'public opinion'; and between the opinion of faction and that of the unified public. Thus revolutionary political discourse was to be centred around rival claims to represent the public and allegations of faction.

Keith Michael Baker has located the first appeals to French public opinion in the 1750s in the controversy surrounding the decision of the archbishop of Paris to withhold the last sacraments from suspected Jansenists. Faced with an alliance between parlements, Jansenism and popular outrage, Louis XV's government accepted the necessity of appealing to and winning over 'public opinion' as the final arbiter of political legitimacy. But in the very act of attempting to justify its policies, the monarchy opened its actions to question and debate. However, the involvement of the monarchy in the public sphere indicates that it was not a space entirely separate from government, as Habermas suggested. Instead, the French public sphere was characterised, according to Baker, by the emergence of 'a politics of contestation' in which it became normal for competing groups and public authority to appeal to the tribunal of enlightened public opinion.[16]

Numerous recent studies have explored the emergence and construction of an increasingly hostile and critical public in France in the generations

---

[11] Chartier, *Cultural origins*, 30.
[12] Ozouf, 'Public opinion', S14.
[13] Chartier, *Cultural origins*, 21. However, as Nathans, 'Habermas's "public sphere" ', points out at p. 622n., Habermas's use of the term *bürgerliche Öffentlichkeit* is ambiguous, and can be translated as both 'bourgeois public sphere' and 'civil public sphere'.
[14] Chartier, *Cultural origins*, 27.
[15] Ibid.
[16] See Keith Michael Baker, *Inventing the French revolution: essays on French political culture in the eighteenth century*, Cambridge 1990.

prior to the revolution. They range from Arlette Farge's innovative study of Parisian gossip to Sara Maza's investigation of the published trial briefs in pre-revolutionary *causes célèbres*. Farge demonstrates convincingly how, in the course of the eighteenth century, ordinary men and women in the street began to express thoughts which increasingly challenged the legitimacy of absolutist government.[17] Maza shows that the development of the concept of a rational-critical 'public opinion' as an alternative and legitimate tribunal was both facilitated and reflected by the practice of opposing litigants in high-profile court cases publishing their trial briefs. Trial briefs sold in large quantities, dramatising the differences between sides and the issues involved, and cases were discussed at length. At the same time, the role of the public was elevated and existing authority called into question, especially in the sensational diamond necklace affair.[18]

Nevertheless, prior to the revolution, the French publishing industry was strictly supervised by the government. The newspaper and periodical press was carefully licensed and political news was subject to royal censorship.[19] Newspapers required a royal *privilège* (permit) to publish at all and, theoretically at least, the official *Gazette de France* held a monopoly over political news.[20] Until the 1750s the only newspapers published in France were the *Gazette* and its officially authorised reprints in the provinces.[21] Although independent periodicals called *Affiches* were permitted in provincial centres, they were primarily commercial in focus, and like all other publications their licences were costly and revocable.[22] Moreover, all journals had to pay an annual fee to the leading established paper in their field for infringement of privilege. Political newspapers paid the *Gazette*, literary and society papers paid the *Mercure galant* and journals covering science, history, theology or the fine arts paid the *Journal des savants*.[23] However, in the final decades of the old regime, a number of new Parisian titles were permitted to encroach on the *Gazette de France*'s privilege. These changes facilitated the appearance of the first Parisian daily, the *Journal de Paris*, in 1777 and the development of

---

[17] Arlette Farge, *Subversive words: public opinion in eighteenth-century France*, Cambridge 1994. As this edition mistranslates key terms, readers are advised to consult the original French edition, *Dire et mal dire: l'opinion publique au XVIIIe siècle*, Paris 1992.
[18] Sara Maza, *Private lives and public affairs: the causes célèbres of pre-revolutionary France*, Berkeley–Los Angeles 1993.
[19] The best treatment of the pre-revolutionary French press is Jack R. Censer, *The French press in the age of enlightenment*, London 1994. See also Jack R. Censer and Jeremy D. Popkin (eds), *Press and politics in pre-revolutionary France*, Berkeley–Los Angeles 1987.
[20] See Hugh Gough, *The newspaper press in the French revolution*, London 1988, 2–4; Censer, *French press*, 141–2; Anthony Smith, *The newspaper: an international history*, London 1979, 26–31.
[21] Popkin, 'Business of political enlightenment', 413. On relations of government and press see Censer, *French press*, 15, 138–83.
[22] Gough, *Newspaper press*, 3; Popkin, 'Business of political enlightenment', 413. On the *Affiches* see Censer, *French press*, ch. ii.
[23] Gough, *Newspaper press*, 3; Censer, *French press*, 141–2.

Charles Joseph Panckoucke's publishing empire, which owned the privileges of the *Mercure de France*, the *Journal de Bruxelles* and the *Gazette de France*.[24] By 1760 there were twenty-five established journals of all varieties published in France, and by 1785, on the eve of the revolutionary crisis, there were sixty.[25] Yet, due to strict censorship, the political news published in these papers tended to be drab and colourless, drawn from court circulars, official documents and foreign gazettes. Although the censorship regime could be subverted by suggestive juxtaposition of contradictory sources, publishing under a seemingly innocuous title, or placing news under a foreign dateline to dupe a careless censor, the desire for up-to-date political news and opinions under the old regime had to be met by other means.[26]

The gap was filled by foreign gazettes and pamphlet literature, much of it illegal. Unlike newspapers, which, because they appeared serially and had to circulate through the post, could not escape surveillance, pamphlet literature could generally avoid censorship. Although all printed matter theoretically required a censor's permission before it could be published, many pamphlets flouted the law and gave false publication details on their title pages. Many more were published beyond the French borders, in Holland, Switzerland or London, and circulated in large numbers 'under the cloak'. Moreover, Robert Darnton has shown that these clandestine pamphlets represented a substantial part of the eighteenth-century book trade. Many, such as Charles Théveneau de Morande's notorious *Gazetier cuirassé* (London 1771), which depicted sexual, political and pecuniary corruption at Louis XV's court, crossed modern genre boundaries, mixing philosophy, politics, gossip and pornography in endless permutations. Darnton contends that such scurrilous illegal works, produced by alienated literary hacks, played a central role in the desacralisation of the monarchy and began the political education of 'a public that could not assimilate the *Social contract* and would soon be reading *Le Père Duchesne*'.[27] As the revolution approached, sexual–political *libelles* (lampoons) aimed especially at the queen became more virulent and their pornography more explicit, licentious and obscene.[28] In these writings

---

[24] Popkin, 'Business of political enlightenment', 413.
[25] Censer, *French press*, 7. The compilation of such figures is problematic due to changes of title, mergers and categorisation. Censer therefore only counts papers published over a period of at least three years.
[26] The classic example of an innocuous-sounding title being used for political purposes is the *Journal des dames*. On this fascinating journal see the excellent study by Nina Rattner Gelbart, *Feminine and opposition journalism in old regime France: Le Journal des dames*, Berkeley 1987.
[27] Robert Darnton, 'The high enlightenment and the low-life of literature in pre-revolutionary France', *Past and Present* 1i (1971), 81–115, repr. in his *Literary underground* (all references are to this version) at pp. 1–40, where this quote appears on p. 35. On Charles Théveneau de Morande (1741–1805) see P. Robinquet, *Théveneau de Morande: étude sur le XVIIIe siecle*, Paris 1882, and Simon Burrows, 'A literary low life reassessed: Charles Théveneau de Morande in London, 1769–1791', *Eighteenth-Century Life* xxii (Feb. 1998), 76–94.
[28] On the development of the *libelle* tradition see Hector Flieschmann, *Marie-Antoinette*

Marie-Antoinette's public *persona* seems to have become inextricably linked to the character of another sort of public woman, the prostitute, preparing the way for the *coup de grâce* to her reputation in the diamond necklace affair.[29] Lynn Hunt has therefore persuasively linked this literature to the allegations of incest levelled at the queen's trial, and it seems fair to link it also to the sexual atrocities meted out to the queen's favourite (and putative fellow libertine and lesbian lover) the princesse de Lamballe in September 1792.[30] This *libelle* tradition also helped shape émigré journalism (see chapter 5).

However, Darnton's thesis has not gone unchallenged. Jeremy Popkin has pointed out that most Grub Street writers were either affluent or worked for aristocratic patrons;[31] Roger Chartier has argued that politico-pornographic publications were less influential than Darnton believes.[32] It is certainly possible that foreign gazettes, although requiring official consent to circulate in France, had a greater formative impact on French political culture in the years preceding the revolution than illegal books and pamphlets. By the 1780s there was a long tradition of French extra-territorial journalism. The first French exile journalists were Protestant Huguenots who fled from Louis XIV's France. The gazettes they established in Holland to oppose French-funded pamphleteers and support the European coalition established Europe-wide circulations, played a leading role in the propaganda battle against Louis XIV, and prospered long into the eighteenth century.[33] Moreover, the French government was unable to prevent Dutch-produced papers from circumventing border controls through smuggling or being secretly reprinted in Paris. Thus, in order to control the expansion of francophone publishing in Europe, and meet increasing public demand for news, from the 1750s French governments allowed foreign newspapers to enter

---

libertine, Paris 1911; Darnton, 'High enlightenment'; Lynn Hunt, 'The many bodies of Marie-Antoinette: political pornography and the problem of the feminine in the French revolution', in Lynn Hunt (ed.), *Eroticism and the body politic*, Baltimore–London 1991, 108–30; Peter Wagner, *Eros revived: erotica of the enlightenment in England and America*, London 1990, 91–100; Burrows, 'A literary low-life'.

[29] On the diamond necklace affair see Sara Maza, 'The diamond necklace affair revisited: the case of the missing queen', in Hunt, *Eroticism*, 63–89, and Frances Mossiker, *The queen's necklace*, London 1961. On 'public women' see Joan Landes, *Women and the public sphere in the age of the French revolution*, Ithaca, NY 1988.

[30] Hunt, 'Many bodies'.

[31] Jeremy Popkin, 'Pamphlet journalism at the end of the old regime', *Eighteenth-Century Studies* xxii (1989), 351–67.

[32] See Chartier, 'Book markets', and *Cultural origins*, 81–3 and passim. For critiques of other aspects of Darnton's thesis see Frederick A. de Luna, 'The Dean Street style of revolution: J.-P. Brissot, jeune philosophe', *French Historical Studies* xvii (1991), 159–90; Burrows, 'A literary low-life'.

[33] E. Hatin, *Les Gazettes de Hollande et la presse clandestine au xviie et xviiie siècles*, Paris 1865; Joseph Klaits, *Printed propaganda under Louis XIV: absolute monarchy and public opinion*, Princeton 1976.

France legally. By the early 1780s fifteen foreign political newspapers were permitted, among which the most influential were the *Gazette de Leyde*, the *Courier du Bas-Rhin*, the *Courier de l'Europe* and the *Courrier d'Avignon*: by 1789 this number had risen to twenty-nine.[34] The price of admission for these papers was submission to French censorship, but such censorship was necessarily more relaxed than for the domestic press, due to distance and time-constraints. Foreign-produced papers thus filled a significant gap in the demand for political news in late old regime France. Nevertheless, one exile journalist still complained that he was ordered to reprint seventeen issues of his twice-weekly newspaper in a single year,[35] and the prices of foreign printed gazettes remained three or four times higher than those of Parisian papers.[36]

Recent studies have suggested that these foreign gazettes played an important part in the political education of the French people, and this echoes the views of contemporaries.[37] Jack Censer has concluded that in the pages of foreign gazettes the French élite were 'bombarded . . . with beliefs about governing that were at variance with Bourbon proclamations'.[38] In particular, foreign papers helped to equip Frenchmen and women with the conceptual vocabulary of representative politics and familiarise them with the workings of the British political system.[39] Thus, for example, Gunnar and Mavis von Proschwitz have demonstrated that the *Courier de l'Europe* introduced the usage of the term 'opposition' in a political sense into the French language in the late 1770s.[40] Moreover, the foreign papers, especially the *Courier de l'Europe*, strongly influenced the appearance of the newspapers of the French revolution. This link between the pre-1789 exile press and the post-1789 French press is epitomised by Jacques-Pierre Brissot de Warville, pre-revolutionary journalist and Girondin leader. Brissot worked on the *Courier de l'Europe* in the late 1770s and took it as his model for the quarto format and news layout adopted by his influential *Patriote françois*, one of the first

---

34 Censer, *French press*, 8; Gough, *Newspaper press*, 5. Studies of individual papers include Jeremy D. Popkin, *News and politics in the age of revolution: Jean Luzac's 'Gazette de Leyde'*, Ithaca, NY 1989; Jack Censer, 'English politics in the *Courrier d'Avignon*', in Censer and Popkin, *Press and politics*, 170–203; Gunnar von Proschwitz and Mavis von Proschwitz, *Beaumarchais et le Courier de l'Europe: documents inédits ou peu connus*, Oxford 1990; Hélène Maspero-Clerc, 'Une Gazette anglo-française pendant la Guerre d'Amérique, *Le Courier de l'Europe*, 1776–1788', AHRF xliv (1976), 572–94. For profiles of individual papers see Jean Sgard (ed.), *Dictionnaire de journaux*, Paris 1991. See also Henri Duranton, Claude Labrosse and Pierre Rétat (eds), *Les Gazettes européennes de langue française (XVIIe et XVIIIe siècles)*, St Etienne 1992.
35 *Argus patriote*, prospectus (June 1791), 3.
36 Gough, *Newspaper press*, 5.
37 See, for example, Jean-Gabriel Peltier's comments in *Correspondance française* 1 (2 Nov. 1793).
38 Censer, 'English politics', at p. 200.
39 Proschwitz and Proschwitz, *Beaumarchais*, chs ii, vi; Censer, 'English politics', and *French press*, 49.
40 Proschwitz and Proschwitz, *Beaumarchais*, 22–3.

new newspapers to appear in revolutionary Paris. The main difference between the two papers was that, like most revolutionary papers, the *Patriote françois* concentrated almost exclusively on French domestic politics.[41]

The foreign gazettes formed part of a Europe-wide French publishing trade, which served both France and Europe's francophone élites. Thus, when French refugees began flooding into England in 1792, they found that a flourishing French-language publishing industry already existed. London was home to specialist French bookseller-publishers, French print shops and French journalists. The capital also boasted a well-established French newspaper, the *Courier de Londres* (formerly the *Courier de l'Europe*), which quickly became an émigré organ. It was soon joined by other émigré-edited titles. Indeed, from October 1792 to November 1814 thirteen different newspapers or periodicals were produced by or for the London émigré community. With only brief interludes, the French exile press – defined for the purposes of this study as those papers that were edited or owned by émigrés, and/or aimed at an émigré market – comprised between two and four titles at any one time.[42]

The analysis of the émigré press in this study comprises two parts. The first considers the structure of the press (chapters 1–3). It treats the journalists who worked on it, the journals they produced, their market, the problems they faced and their administrative and financial structures. It also provides an extensive treatment of the political constraints and patronage systems within which the journalists operated and analyses their role in the propaganda warfare of the age. A second section (chapters 4–5) considers the political content and campaigns of the émigré journals within a primarily thematic framework. It treats the responses of the émigré journalists to the revolution, their arguments and campaigns. It considers both the reporting of news and the presentation of information, together, as far as possible, with the selection of materials. This is no easy task. Newspapers and periodicals are deceptive and treacherous texts: the relationships between patron, editor, contributor and reader are often highly complex and frequently undetectable. It would therefore be naïve and superficial to suggest that the émigré journals were representative 'organs of opinion'. In fact, they were not representative of any one 'opinion' *per se*, not even in many cases that of their editors. However, it is my contention that in a looser sense these journals are

---

41 For Brissot's account of his role on the *Courier de l'Europe* see Jacques-Pierre Brissot de Warville, *Mémoires*, ed. Claude Perroud, Paris 1910, i. 154–79. However, Charles Théveneau de Morande, *Réplique de Charles Théveneau Morande à Jacques-Pierre Brissot sur les erreurs, les infidélités, et les calomnies de sa réponse*, Paris 1791, alleges that Brissot only worked as a foreman in the paper's printshop at Boulogne in 1778 and as a translator in 1783, and Maspero-Clerc, 'Gazette anglo-française', at pp. 587–9 offers strong evidence that Brissot's role did not include editorial duties.

42 This inclusive definition avoids the difficulties posed by editors who were Swiss, Haitian or Scots; émigré editors on English language-papers; and editors who were not technically émigrés.

indicative of the *mentalité* prevailing among a closely defined and, after 1803, increasingly homogeneous, group, which was to contribute to the élite and courtly circles of the restoration.

The émigré press has received scant attention from mainstream French or British press historians. In Claude Bellanger *et al.*'s monumental study of the French press, Jacques Godechot deals with émigré publications in a few lines and erroneously identifies Hamburg as the largest publishing centre.[43] Among at least nineteen titles published, or allegedly published, in London in French between 1789 and 1814, he mentions only the *Courier de Londres* and Mallet du Pan's *Mercure britannique*.[44] Although there are autobiographical and biographical sources for several émigré journalists, including Mallet Du Pan, Montlosier, the abbé Calonne and Jean-Gabriel Peltier, with the exception of Hélène Maspero-Clerc's informative study of Peltier, their exile journalism is presented as a footnote to their careers.[45] There is no study of the exile press in a broad context.

Until recently the French émigrés who arrived in England during the early 1790s had been marginalised by contemporaries and historians alike. The

---

[43] Claude Bellanger, Jacques Godechot, Pierre Guiral and Fernard Terrou (eds), *Histoire générale de la presse française*, Paris 1969, i. 542–3.

[44] Ibid. i. 543. The other titles besides the thirteen émigré journals discussed here were Serres de La Tour's short-lived *Journal de l'Europe* and *Journal de Londres* in 1789; the *Journal de Middlesex* in 1791; the *Phare politique et littéraire* (1790); the *Impartial ou Courier de Middlesex*, allegedly published in 1791, but which actually appeared in 1787; and Le Texier's *Ami des mères*, a monthly educational journal published in 1798–9. Since Le Texier was not an émigré, the paper's audience is not entirely clear, and no copies survive, it is not discussed in this book. On all these titles see Burrows, 'Exile press', ch. i.

[45] The only autobiographical source by a full-time émigré journalist is F.-D. Reynaud de Montlosier, *Souvenirs d'un émigré (1791–1798)*, ed. the comte de Larouzière-Montlosier and E. d'Hauterive, Paris 1951. This work supplements Montlosier's *Mémoires sur la révolution française, le consulat, l'empire, la restauration et les principaux événements qui l'ont suivie*, Paris 1829, which despite the title goes no further than 1792. For valuable information see also John-Lewis Mallet, *An autobiographical retrospective of the first twenty-five years of his life*, privately printed, Windsor 1890, and P. V. Malouet, *Mémoires de Malouet*, 2nd edn, Paris 1874, which reproduces correspondence between Mallet Du Pan and his son. The main biographical sources, excluding entries in biographical dictionaries, obituary notices and brief articles, are Hélène Maspero-Clerc, *Un Journaliste contre-révolutionnaire: Jean-Gabriel Peltier (1760–1825)*, Paris 1973; H. Miramon-Fitzjames, 'Le Comte de Montlosier pendant la révolution et l'empire', unpubl. PhD diss. Aix-en-Provence 1944; A. Brugerette, *Le Comte de Montlosier et son temps (1755–1838)*, Aurillac 1931; A. Bardoux, *Le Comte de Montlosier et les constitutionnels pendant l'émigration, d'après des documents inédits*, Paris 1879, and *Le Comte de Montlosier et le gallicanisme*, Paris 1881; Hélène Maspero-Clerc, 'Montlosier, journaliste de l'émigration', BHESRF année 1975 (1977), 81–103; Frances Acomb, *Mallet du Pan (1749–1800): a career in political journalism*, Durham, NC 1973; N. Matteuchi, *Jacques Mallet du Pan*, Naples 1957; Bernard Mallet, *Mallet Du Pan and the French revolution*, London 1892; A. Sayous (ed.), *Mémoires et correspondance de Mallet Du Pan pour servir à l'histoire de la révolution française*, Paris 1851 (English translation published in 1852). The only substantial biographical source treating the abbé Calonne is a hagiography: Sr Marguerite-Marie OSU (attrib.), *Vie de l'abbé Calonne: mort en odeur de sainteté aux Trois-Rivières (Octobre 1822)*, Trois-Rivières 1892.

bi-centennaire conferences and publications on England and the French revolution somehow overlooked the presence of 10,000 exiles on British soil. There is scarcely enough writing in English on the subject to merit a historiographical survey. As I write, the closest thing to a general history remains Margery Weiner's whimsical and uneven *The French exiles*, which relies heavily on the human interest of a true love story. E. M. Wilkinson's thesis on the émigrés' arrival, though comprehensively researched, is disorganised and lacks analysis; Donald Greer's statistical survey is flawed; while Dominic Bellenger's scholarly and erudite study of the clergy in exile has not attracted the interest it deserves.[46] The list of French works on the emigration is endless. General histories are many, but thematic studies few. In general, the émigré question has been seen in a French and royalist context, and disputed between Marxist scholars and right-wing amateurs.[47] A historian researching the émigrés is left with the impression that much has been written but little said. This is astonishing considering that the émigrés had such a pervasive influence on both their host communities and the development and course of the French revolution. However, in recent years there has been new interest in the émigrés, encouraged by the efforts of Philip Mansel and Kirsty Carpenter and the de-politicisation of revolutionary studies in the wake of the collapse of the Soviet Union and disintegration of the French communist party. Dr Carpenter's informative and engaging study of the London émigrés, which was published after the manuscript of this book was completed, was thus eagerly awaited, as were the proceedings she edited of a conference on 'The Emigrés in Europe' held in July 1997, which attracted more than twenty papers.[48] The conference both set the agenda for future émigré studies and revealed how much remains to be done.

It has thus been all too easy for Anglo-Saxon scholars to relegate the émigrés to an historical wasteland without challenging the popular images of the émigrés as the swaggering aristocrats of Coblenz. Chateaubriand's melodramatic portrayal of life in a damp garret, sucking a blanket to ward off star-

---

[46] See Dominic Aidan Bellenger, *The French exiled clergy in the British Isles after 1789: a historical introduction and working list*, Downside 1986; Donald Greer, *The incidence of the emigration during the French revolution*, Cambridge, Mass. 1951; Margery Weiner, *The French exiles, 1789–1815*, London 1960; E. M. Wilkinson, 'French émigrés in England, 1789–1802, their reception and impact on English life', unpubl. BLitt. diss. Oxford 1952.

[47] The best published study in French remains J. Vidalenc, *Les Emigrés français, 1789–1825*, Caen 1963, which contains a brief section on émigré journalists at pp. 302–7. R. G. M. de La Croix (duc de Castries), *Les Emigrés*, Paris 1962, is also useful. In addition I have drawn on two classic studies: E. Daudet *Histoire de l'émigration pendant la révolution française*, Paris 1905–7, and H. Forneron, *Histoire générale des émigrés*, Paris 1884–90.

[48] Kirsty Carpenter, *Refugees of the French revolution: émigrés in London, 1789–1799*, Basingstoke 1999; Kirsty Carpenter and Philip Mansel (eds), *The French émigrés in Europe and the struggle against the revolution, 1789–1814*, Basingstoke 1999. See also Kirsty Carpenter, 'Les Emigrés à Londres, 1793–1797', unpubl. doctorat du nouveau régime, Paris I 1993. There are also useful treatments of the politics of emigration in Jacques Godechot, *The counter-revolution: doctrine and action, 1789–1804*, trans. Salvator Athanasio, Princeton 1971, esp. ch. ix, and James Roberts, *The counter revolution in France, 1787–1830*, London 1990, ch. i.

vation, and the pathetic lamentations of William Wordsworth's 'Emigrant Mother' are useful correctives to the romanticised view, but equally unrepresentative.[49] Yet the migration of so many persons, many of them distinguished members of French society, could not fail to have had an impact upon their hosts. In Britain alone they influenced the reviving Catholic Church and the reintroduction of monasticism; published vast amounts of ephemeral literature; inspired a huge charity appeal followed by a major government relief effort; fought as British auxiliaries and inspired the government to introduce the first immigration control legislation. Thus in view of the paucity of literature on the subject available in English, it is necessary to say a little here about the emigration and its political leaders.

Donald Greer identified several waves of emigration, each provoked by political events inside France.[50] The first, in July and August 1789, responded to the fall of the Bastille and the great fear. It comprised members of the high court nobility, led by Louis XVI's youngest brother, the unpopular and frivolous comte d'Artois, and Marie-Antoinette's reviled favourites the Polignacs. They expected to be away just months, but they did not return to France for twenty-five years. While numerically insignificant, this 'émigration joyeuse' was of great political, social and psychological importance. A second wave of emigration in 1790 included much of the upper clergy, and a third wave in 1791 comprised the bulk of the pre-revolutionary officer corps, who hastened to join the princes' army at Coblenz. The final great wave of emigration began with the coming of war in April 1792 and continued beyond the overthrow of the monarchy on 10 August into 1793. Hitherto mainly confined to the nobility and clergy, in 1793 the emigration 'became democratic'.

The greater number of the French refugees who settled in England arrived in late 1792 and the early months of 1793, in the last of these waves. The arrival of secular émigrés in England peaked in the winter of 1792–3, galvanised by the beginning of the Terror. The main influx of clergy came slightly later. The law of 14 August 1792 ordered the expulsion from France of any priest who was denounced by six citizens, and on 23 March 1793 it was decreed that any priest who had not taken the civic oath was to be expelled. Between late August and December 1793 some 3,000 non-jurors arrived in England and another 3,400 in the Channel Islands.[51] Roman Catholic clergymen comprised about half of the total number of émigrés in Britain throughout the period.[52]

The émigrés, many of whom arrived in England destitute, were the benefi-

---

[49] François-René de Chateaubriand, *Mémoires d'outre-tombe*, Paris 1973 (Livre de Poche edn, Librairie générale française), i. 417; William Wordsworth, *The poems: volume one*, ed. John O. Hayden, London 1977, 518–21.
[50] Greer, *Incidence of emigration*, ch. ii.
[51] Bellenger, *French exiled clergy*, 2–3.
[52] Wilkinson, 'Émigrés in England', 596, cites BL, MS Add. 37,863, entitled 'L'Etat des émigrés français qui sont à present en Angleterre', which gives a figure of 5,240 priests and 5,731 lay *émigrés* in England of whom only 500 priests and 100 laypersons were not on the

ciaries of a massive charitable relief effort, soon taken over by the government, which provided financial assistance at the rate of 1s. per day for adults and 6d. for children and domestic servants. The distribution of relief was orchestrated by Jean-François de La Marche, bishop of St Pol de Léon, from an office in Golden Square, and was one reason why the lay émigré community was almost entirely concentrated in London. The relief lists are the major source for the demography of the emigration in England, providing Dominic Bellenger with the bulk of his working-list of over 5,000 clergy, and Kirsty Carpenter with most of the 4,500 lay émigrés she has been able to name.[53] In 1795 able-bodied émigré men on the relief lists were enlisted to serve in the Quiberon expedition and the execution of 640 of them, captured under arms by French forces, was a devastating blow to many émigré families. Most of the surviving émigrés returned to France within a few years of the establishment of the consulate. More than two-thirds of them left between the coup of Brumaire (9/10 November 1799) and the collapse of the peace of Amiens in May 1803. By the restoration, the relief lists enumerate only 701 lay émigrés, and approximately 490 clergy.[54]

While most émigrés had never been political activists, the successive waves of emigration included representatives of the various political groups who fled, or were proscribed, each in turn, by the revolution. The early waves mainly contained *pur* émigrés, those hard-line royalists who claimed to reject any compromise with the revolution and the changes it had introduced since 1789. Between 1790 and 1792 they were joined by the *monarchiens*, a term which for the purposes of this work indicates the small group of publicists and politicians associated with Malouet and Mounier. They played a leading role in the Constituent Assembly during the summer of 1789 until their plans for a bi-cameral legislature and absolute royal veto were defeated.[55] They were only a small group, but their spokesmen Montlosier and Mallet Du Pan produced some of the most significant émigré journals of the 1790s. Moreover, they came under heavy fire from *pur* publicists, who blamed them for giving the revolutionary bandwagon its first push. They were followed later by the Fayettiste *constitutionnels*, who played little part in émigré life and mostly returned to France after the fall of Robespierre (27 July 1794), and

---

government's relief registers in March 1797. The rounding off of the last figures suggests that they were estimated.
[53] This list forms an appendix to Carpenter, 'Les Emigrés à Londres'. I would like to thank Dr Carpenter for allowing me to consult drafts and statistical summaries of this list during her research.
[54] See AAE, CPA supplément 23, fos 10–20.
[55] Although the term *monarchien* was sometimes used as a catch-all term of abuse by *purs*, I use it throughout this work in the narrow sense indicated here, as do Griffiths, Godechot, Beik and Roberts. The phrase '*monarchien* journalists' refers specifically to Mallet Du Pan and Montlosier alone. For the sake of clarity and consistency, the abbé Calonne is not included, despite the convergence of his thinking with that of the *monarchiens* from 1795 onwards.

then by the victims of the Directorial purge of 18 fructidor V (4 September 1797), several of whom played leading roles on the émigré press.

The political leaders of the emigration were Louis XVI's brothers, the comte d'Artois, darling of the *purs*, and the comte de Provence. Initially they pursued a policy which opposed and compromised Louis XVI, especially when they began to gather and finance an émigré army in Coblenz and its neighbourhood. The army was commanded by the prince de Condé, and invaded France alongside Prussian and Austrian forces in the summer of 1792. After the disastrous retreat from Valmy, in September 1792, the army was financed by various allied powers. Before it disbanded in 1800, it had had Austrian, Russian and British paymasters. After the execution of the king on 21 January 1793, Provence declared himself regent for the imprisoned boy king Louis XVII. On news of Louis XVII's death in 1795, Provence 'succeeded' as Louis XVIII, but failed to gain formal recognition from the powers. He continued to be known in diplomatic circles as the comte de Lille [*sic*.]. After Valmy he led an unsettled life, shunted between Hamm, Verona, Blankenburg, Mittau in Latvia, Warsaw and Mittau again, by the politics of the powers. In 1807 he finally arrived in England, where he lived until the restoration, initially as a guest of the marquess of Buckingham and from April 1809 as tenant of Hartwell House in Buckinghamshire. The comte d'Artois landed in Britain after the failure of the expedition to the Ile d'Yeu in 1795, but had to remain in Edinburgh to avoid his English creditors until a settlement was reached in 1799 that allowed him to visit London. He returned to Edinburgh before the peace of Amiens, but eventually returned to London. Thus, throughout the 1790s the émigré press in London was operating at a great distance from its political leaders. This may in part explain the freedom and divisions which reigned within it throughout the 1790s, and which have affected historical perceptions of the émigrés ever since.

1

Scripting Counter-Revolution? Emigré Journals and Journalists, 1792–1814

The thirteen émigré papers published in London between 1792 and 1814 were heirs to the French revolutionary press. In revolutionary Paris newspapers offered many advantages over the pamphlets they superseded as the dominant form of political publication. They allowed writers to develop continuing relationships with their readers and to respond rapidly to events. Readers, who had been ill-served by the heavily censored pre-revolutionary press, began to feel a greater sense of engagement with events. For the first time they began to structure their lives around a regular staple of news-information and to view themselves as participants in great events rather than idle bystanders. The public sphere had become revolutionary: the sovereignty of the people found expression through the mediation of the newspaper text.[1]

Newspapers offered writers and publishers far greater opportunities for profit and political influence than pamphlets, with little financial risk. Subscriptions were collected in advance, so unsold stock was not a problem, and since technological constraints made printing costs relatively constant regardless of the size of print run, even small circulations could reap significant returns. A few hundred subscriptions was sufficient to break even, and one to two thousand would make a journalist rich in a short time.[2] Moreover, from July 1789 until August 1792 there were almost no legal restrictions over what could be published in France. The result was a free-for-all, in which hundreds of new titles appeared annually.[3] Few survived for more than a few months, but even short-lived titles could prove profitable and influential:

---

[1] Popkin, *Revolutionary news*, 1–15, 35–95 and passim. However, Popkin has been careful to argue that the break between the pre-revolutionary and revolutionary press should not be exaggerated. See, especially, Jeremy Popkin, 'The pre-revolutionary origins of political journalism', in Keith Michael Baker (ed.), *The political culture of the old regime*, Oxford 1987, 203–23. The same impression is given by the essays in Censer and Popkin, *Press and politics*.
[2] See the worked examples for the *Ami du roi* and *Gazette de Paris* in W. J. Murray, *The right-wing press in the French revolution*, Woodbridge 1986, 78–83, and J.-P. Bertaud, *Les Amis du roi: journaux et journalistes royalistes en France de 1789 à 1792*, Paris 1984, 49–56. For further information on production and distribution costs see Gilles Feyel, 'Les Frais d'impression et de diffusion de la presse Parisienne entre 1789 et 1792', in Pierre Rétat, *La Révolution du journal, 1788–1794*, Paris 1989, 77–99.
[3] For a checklist of French newspapers published in 1789 see Pierre Rétat, *Les Journaux de 1789: bibliographie critique*, Paris 1988.

many revolutionary leaders launched or promoted their careers by involvement in journalism, among them Mirabeau, Robespierre, Hébert, Marat, Brissot, Danton, Roederer and Camille Desmoulins.

Moreover, Jeremy Popkin has shown how newspapers scripted the revolution, by creating a nexus of political tensions, suspicions and excitement, which led to self-fulfilling expectations of direct action and political violence.[4] There were newspapers to represent almost every shade of opinion, a cacophony of discordant voices. Between 1789 and 1792 pro-revolutionary papers recommended policies to revolutionary governments, denounced enemies, directed Jacobin activities, and called for and orchestrated direct action.[5] Right-wing papers attacked the legislature and revolutionary policies, slandered revolutionary journalists, and called for pledges of loyalty to the king and armed resistance.[6] Such pronouncements simultaneously reflected, provoked and perpetuated tension, suspicion, fear and recrimination. Newspapers of all parties were often quick to allege that conspiracy, treason or venality lurked behind views expressed by their enemies. Such accusations always tend to polarise and destabilise a state, but in late eighteenth-century France they were particularly dangerous, due to the prevalence of ideological frameworks which made political pluralism almost unthinkable. Neither the sovereign people armed with the conceptual vocabulary and rhetoric of Rousseau's general will, nor the traditional Bourbon monarchy and Catholic Church whose power they sought to usurp, could accept a role for legitimate dissent within the state. The multiplication of newspaper texts during the revolution threatened the monolithic ideologies of both the divine right monarchy and the republic one and indivisible. Thus it was only natural that the Convention, Directory and Napoleon should seek to restore the apparatus of press control.[7]

The newspaper texts of revolutionary France were overwhelmingly political in focus. There was little, if any, advertising, and seldom any cultural content. Usually compiled by a single editor and a small staff, they tended to represent a single viewpoint. Lacking professional reporters and resources, news content was usually compiled from newspapers from other towns, merchants' letters, the editor's own network of correspondents, and the reports of travellers. Revolutionary papers lacked the visual markers which modern newspapers use to guide their readers around the text. There were no

---

[4] Popkin, *Revolutionary news*, 106–68.
[5] Ibid.; J. Censer, *Prelude to power: the Parisian radical press, 1789–1791*, Baltimore 1976; Harvey Chisick, 'Politics and journalism in the French revolution: the readership of the *Journal de la Montagne* and the Jacobin clubs', *French History* v (1991), 345–72.
[6] Murray, *Right-wing press*, 105–91; Bertaud, *Amis du roi*.
[7] On revolutionary censorship see Gough, *Newspaper press*, 83–159; Jeremy D. Popkin, *The right-wing press in France, 1792–1800*, Chapel Hill, NC 1980, 3–53. On Napoleon's censorship and use of the press see Robert B. Holtman, *Napoleonic propaganda*, Baton Rouge 1950, 44–75; André Cabanis, *La Presse sous le consulat et l'empire*, Paris 1975; A. Périvier, *Napoléon journaliste*, Paris 1918.

headlines, no illustrations, and conflicting sources were often juxtaposed suggestively but without comment. Even their formats bore more resemblance to books than to modern newspapers. Most newspapers and periodicals in the early revolution consisted of sixteen or more octavo pages. This is hardly surprising, as many of the newspapers founded in 1789 began life as successful news pamphlets recording a single event, which their publishers then extended into serials. However, newspapers published in the larger quarto size knew more success proportionate to their numbers, and became increasingly common as the revolution progressed. The octavo and even the duodecimo formats continued to be favoured for periodical literature, appearing less frequently than the news-sheets, such as the weekly *Mercure de France* and the thrice-monthly *Décade philosophique*, both of which offered their readers literary and cultural items as well as news content.[8]

The journals produced by and for émigrés in London from 1792 to 1814 resembled the Parisian press of 1789–92 in form, physical appearance and content. They also inherited several experienced Parisian editors. The exile journals, like their Parisian counterparts, lacked headlines and other means to steer readers around the text. However, readers familiar with a paper's layout would quickly be able to find the sections that interested them, for, like the Parisian papers, the émigré journals habitually arranged their material in a set order. Thus the *Courier de Londres* always began with its foreign news items, arranged under the town and dateline from which they were sourced, giving the most distant centres first. Then came French, followed by British, news under the title 'Bulletin de Londres' (or from 1805 'Affaires Publiques'), which included editorial comment. Extracts from the official government newspaper, the *London Gazette*, were published from time to time under the title 'Nouvelles Officielles', and when parliament was sitting important speeches and bills were summarised under the rubric 'Journal du Parlement'. Separate rubrics reported on 'Amérique', 'Indes Occidentales' and 'Indes Orientales' (which included India), but generally only reproduced official documents, accounts of speeches and extracts from newspapers. A subsequent section, in marked contrast to most revolutionary papers, offered literary morsels, general interest stories and miscellaneous information under the rubrics 'Variétés' and 'Articles Divers'. Finally, the paper gave shipping and commercial information, prices of public funds and currency exchange rates, and a stop-press 'Postscriptum'. The paper carried more advertising than any other émigré journal, but it never amounted to more than a handful of brief announcements.

Like the Parisian journals, the exile press experimented with paper size, style and periodicity (see table 1). Those which existed primarily to give news content, such as the bi-weekly *Courier de Londres* and *Courier d'Angleterre*, retained the quarto format or, in the unique case of Jean-Gabriel Peltier's

---

[8] On the presentation of revolutionary newspapers see Popkin, *Revolutionary news*, 97–105.

Table 1
Format, periodicity and content classification of émigré journals

Full Title	Format	Pages/issue	Periodicity	Content
Ambigu	nos 1–30 in 4vo nos 31–526 in 8vo	24pp. 64–c. 120pp.	3 per month	politics literature
Antidote	8vo pamphlet		1 or 2 nos only	politics
Correspondance politique	Folio	4pp.	3 per week	news etc.
Courier d'Angleterre	4vo	8pp.	2 per week	news etc.
Courier de Londres	4vo	8pp.	2 per week	news etc.
Dernier Tableau de Paris	8vo instalments composing 2 vols	varied	uncertain	recent history
Histoire de la restauration	8vo instalments	36pp.	weekly	politics
Journal de France et d'Angleterre	8vo	varied	nos 1–7 weekly 8–29 varied	politics literature
Mercure britannique	8vo	64pp.	2 per month	politics
Mercure de France	8vo	68pp. +	3 per month	politics literature
Paris pendant l'année	8vo	64pp. 120pp. + 48pp. 120pp. +	nos 1–99 weekly 100–93 per month 110–54 each 5 days 155–250 2 per month	politics literature
Supplément au Rédacteur	8vo	4pp.	4 nos only irregular	politics
Tableau de l'Europe	8vo by thematic instalments	Varied	varied 17 nos in theory every 8 days	politics history

Correspondance politique, which appeared every other day, adopted the folio format favoured by British newspapers. The ten other émigré periodicals, all of which appeared on a less frequent basis, adopted the octavo format, except for the first thirty numbers of Peltier's *Ambigu*.

The most successful and durable of the émigré papers was the *Courier de Londres*. It was founded in July 1776 as the *Courier de l'Europe* by a French exile called Alphonse-Joseph de Serres de La Tour and Samuel Swinton, a cynical Scottish speculator, and survived until 1826, successfully absorbing François-Dominique Reynaud de Montlosier's *Journal de France et d'Angleterre* in 1797 and Jacques Regnier's *Courier d'Angleterre* in 1815.[9] One of the

---

[9] On the early history of the *Courier de l'Europe* see Proschwitz and Proschwitz, *Beaumarchais*, and Maspero-Clerc, 'Gazette anglo-française'. On Swinton see Jean Sgard (ed.),

paper's chief strengths was its set formula, from which it only diverged between 1805 and 1807, when Robert Heron relaunched it as the *Gazette de la Grande-Bretagne ou Mercure Universel de l'Europe*. A second great strength was its commercial focus. The paper was a profit-making venture and succeeded beyond the wildest dreams of its founders. During the American Revolution it had 5–6,000 subscribers in Britain, France and Europe,[10] and Serres de La Tour was wont to boast that he made more money from journalism in a year than Rousseau earned from a life in letters.[11] The paper remained a viable commercial venture throughout the revolutionary and Napoleonic periods, but its circulation never again reached such dizzy heights. However, frequent changes of editor and market focus led to charges of inconsistency. *Frondeur* under Serres de La Tour (1776–83), the paper became a mouthpiece for patriotic reform and constitutional monarchy under the editorship of Théveneau de Morande (1784–91), Jacobin under his successors (1791–2), and then the organ of various émigré groups from 1793.[12] Moreover, from April 1789 the *Courier de Londres* also served as a mouthpiece for the disgraced former French finance minister Charles-Alexandre de Calonne, after he bought a 50 per cent stake in it, and in 1793 he installed a series of editors, the last of whom was his brother, the abbé Jacques-Ladislas-Joseph de Calonne.[13] It is hardly surprising therefore that the paper was considered inconsistent and mercenary. Swinton's cupidity was notorious: Morande claimed that but for his determined opposition 'Swinton's paper . . . would be as venal as his soul.'[14] Likewise, Peltier, who revelled in every opportunity to attack a rival, addressed Swinton thus:

> Monsieur, I have not read your paper in a long time. If you have felt the need to introduce continual variations into it in the different phases of the revolution; if you were a Jacobin under Mirabeau, a *constitutionnel* under La Fayette, and a Royalist in 1794, you have no doubt had your motives for

---

Dictionnaire des journalistes, 1st edn, Grenoble 1976, supplément iii (1984), 196–9; Hélène Maspero-Clerc, 'Samuel Swinton, éditeur du *Courier de l'Europe* à Boulogne-sur-Mer (1778–1783) et agent secret du gouvernement britannique', *AHRF* lvii (1985), 527–31; Proschwitz and Proschwitz, *Beaumarchais*, esp. i. 75–80. On Serres de La Tour see Sgard, *Dictionnaire des journalistes*, 230; supplément ii (1981) 106–12; supplément iii. 106, 149, 197–8. On Jacques Regnier see Simon Burrows, 'British propaganda for Russia in the Napoleonic wars: the *Courier d'Angleterre*', *New Zealand Slavonic Journal* (1993), 85–100.
[10] Bibliothèque de l'Institut de France, MS 1675, duc de Croy, 'Mémoires de ma vie', p. xxxv, cited in Maspero-Clerc 'Gazette anglo-française', at p. 590; AN, 446 AP/3, 'Mémoire pour J.-P. Brissot contre les sieurs Desforges, Swinton propriétaire du *Courier de l'Europe*, abbé Aubert censeur, comte d'Apremont', fos 28, 165.
[11] Ibid. fo. 28.
[12] On Morande's journalism see Robiquet, *Théveneau de Morande*, chs vi, viii; Proschwitz and Proschwitz, *Beaumarchais*; Burrows, 'Exile press', 271–80, and 'A literary low-life'. On his Jacobin successors see Burrows, 'Exile press', 81–5, 281–93.
[13] See AN, 297 AP/2, pièce 85, 'Contrat relative au *Courier de l'Europe*, 1806' [draft], and ch. 2 below.
[14] AAE, CPA 569, fos 332–3, Morande to Montmorin, 8 June 1789.

Plate 1. Jean-Gabriel Peltier

seeking to appeal to every taste successively, but I don't have any for reading you.[15]

After Swinton's death in 1797 his widow Felicité and son Richard and their co-proprietors seem to have intervened rarely in the paper's day-to-day affairs.[16] Yet the paper's facility for finding talented editors whose political leanings fitted the exigencies of the moment remained a third great strength,

[15] CP 77 (29 Apr. 1794).
[16] On the paper's proprietors see appendix 1.

even if it owed more to luck than judgement. Under its émigré editors the paper evolved with the phases of the emigration. The abbé Calonne's hardline *pur* attitude mellowed as the homesickness of his fellow émigrés began to grow, and his successor Montlosier supplied the news they wanted as they contemplated returning to France in the early consular period. Then, at the very moment that the émigré audience was reduced to a rump, Regnier took over and turned the paper into a vitriolic but readable satirical organ which appealed to both *pur* émigrés and vulgar British patriots. His tone was so objectionable that in April 1805, as the British government considered making peace with Napoleon, he was sacked under pressure from the ministry.[17] Thereafter Heron and Gérard bowdlerised the paper, purging it of vitriol and satire, to turn it into an informational gazette appropriate to the needs of commerce and British propaganda.

Versatility was also a key to Peltier's success and journalistic fecundity, which was unsurpassed by any of his émigré compatriots. In exile he produced over 100 volumes of newspapers, periodicals and other miscellaneous works, and experimented with content, title and format according to the nature of sources available and political and economic circumstances.

Peltier's journalistic debut was in Paris as editor of the notorious and widely read right-wing satirical *Actes des apôtres*. Its latitudinarian banner rallied contributors with a broad spectrum of right-wing opinions. Several of them later contributed to his exile journals. Others were important journalistic, literary or political figures in their own right. The content of their articles ranged from biting satire to Montlosier's 200–page treatment of the best constitution for France. But the paper's popular appeal lay rather with its humorous and satirical content than with the political theories of *monarchien* politicians such as Montlosier, Bergasse, Mounier or Malouet. In exile Peltier experimented with various styles, but in his most successful, long-running periodicals *Paris pendant l'année* (1795–1802) and *Ambigu* (1802–18), both of which were divided into political and literary sections, he resorted to a similar formula to that of the *Actes des apôtres*.[18]

Prior to *Paris pendant l'année*, Peltier produced four journals. The first, the *Dernier Tableau de Paris, ou récit historique de la révolution du 10 Août 1792, des causes qui lui ont produite, des événemens qui l'ont précédée, et des crimes qui l'ont suivie*, had a very specific purpose. Published between October 1792 and July 1793, it attempted to be the first account of the fall of the monarchy and September massacres not to be written 'under the influence of the dominant

---

17 PRO, FO 27/71, Regnier to [?Mulgrave], 25 Apr. 1805; FO 27/219, 'The humble petition of James Regnier' [to Castlereagh], Manchester, 15 June 1819. See also the *Annual Register* (1807), 566–7.
18 On the *Actes des apôtres* see Maspero-Clerc, *Peltier*, 26–55 and passim, and 'Vicissitudes des *Actes des apôtres*', AHRF xxxix (1967), 481–9; Bertaud, *Amis du roi*. Murray, *Right-wing press*, 52–5, offers a short but incisive treatment of the paper and bibliography of less accessible studies.

Courier d'Angleterre.

No. 502.] VENDREDI, LE 16 FEVRIER, 1810. [Prix 9d.

JOURNAL DU PARLEMENT.

CHAMBRE DES PAIRS.

Séance du Lundi, 12 Février.

Le Comte de Coningham présente une pétition des Catholiques Romains du comté de Clare.—On ordonne qu'elle soit mise sur la table.

Lord Holland présente une pétition des débiteurs détenus dans la prison de Marshalsea.

M. Lushington et plusieurs autres Membres de la Chambre des Communes présentent le Bill relatif au droit sur la drèche. On en fait la première lecture.

Le Comte Grosvenor annonce qu'il demandera, Vendredi prochain, la seconde lecture du Bill sur les survivances, et il espère que les Ministres se trouveront à la séance pour déclarer leurs sentimens. En conséquence, les Pairs sont convoqués pour Vendredi.

COMMERCE DES ESCLAVES.

Lord Holland désire connoître les démarches qu'ont faites les Ministres actuels pour effectuer l'objet de l'Adresse présentée il y a trois ans à Sa Majesté, dans laquelle la Chambre prioit le Roi de vouloir bien donner des instructions à ses Ministres près des Cours Etrangères pour engager ces Puissances à concourir avec l'Angleterre à abolir le commerce des esclaves. Les différends avec les Etats-Unis n'ont pas sans doute permis d'obtenir de ce Gouvernement rien de bien satisfaisant sur cet objet, mais nos relations actuelles avec le Portugal et l'Espagne nous mettoient à même d'user de toute notre influence pour les engager à cesser ce trafic infâme.

Lord Liverpool dit que les Ministres se sont occupés de l'objet de l'Adresse; qu'ils ont donné à cet effet des instructions aux Envoyés près la Cour du Bresil, mais que quant à l'Espagne, située comme elle l'étoit relativement à ses colonies, on ne pouvoit attendre aucun heureux résultat en lui faisant des communications sur cet objet.

Lord Holland ne trouve pas la réponse du Noble Secrétaire satisfaisante, et il annonce que, Jeudi en huit, il demandera que l'on fasse connoître à la Chambre les communications qui ont été faites aux Cours Etrangères relativement à l'abolition du commerce des esclaves.

Les Pairs sont convoqués pour Jeudi en huit.

La Chambre s'ajourne à demain.

CHAMBRE DES COMMUNES.

Séance du Lundi, 12 Février.

On fait la troisième lecture du Bill relatif au droit sur la drèche, et il passe.

M. *Rose* demande qu'il soit présenté à la Chambre un Etat des blés et des farines qu'on a importés d'Irlande et des autres pays depuis 1807.—*Ordonné*.

M. *Lushington* fait le rapport sur les ressources.—La Chambre agrée les Résolutions et ordonne qu'on dresse les Bills.

Colonel Wardle demande que l'on produise l'état des sommes employées pour le soutien de chaque colonie depuis le 5 Janvier, 1807, jusqu'au 5 de Février, 1808.—La motion est agréée.

M. *Ashley Cooper* présente l'état de la force effective de l'artillerie embarquée pour Walcheren, ainsi que celui des morts d'après les listes les plus récentes. On ordonne que cet état soit mis sur la table.

PLAN D'ANVERS.

M. *Hutchinson* demande que les Ministres produisent 1. le plan de la forteresse d'Anvers; 2. le plan du fort Lillo et d'un autre; 3. l'information relative à l'état des ouvrages d'Anvers. M. Hutchinson observe que si les Ministres ne peuvent point produire ces plans, ils sont coupables d'une négligence impardonable, et si après avoir connu la force de cette place ils se sont décidés néanmoins à envoyer l'expédition pour la prendre par un coup-de-main, ils sont également coupables. L'Honorable Membre pense qu'on ne peut s'opposer à sa motion vu qu'il ne demande point d'où les Ministres ont reçu leurs informations, mais si les Ministres en ont eu aucune et de quelle espèce elle étoit.

M. *Perceval* dit que cette production se fera s'il est nécessaire devant le Comité Sécret qui est saisi de cette affaire.

Divers Membres parlent ensuite pour et contre les motions qui sont rejetées sans partage.

On lit une première fois les Bills relatifs aux lois pénales et on en ordonne la seconde lecture pour Lundi.

PLACES SANS EMPLOI.—SINECURES.

M. *Fuller* se lève pour faire la motion qu'il avoit annoncée sur les places sans emploi. Il ne s'oppose point à l'influence de la Couronne qui doit nécessairement augmenter avec les richesses nationales et les dépenses de l'Etat. Il attaque l'avidité de cette partie de l'Aristocratie qui pourvoit de ces places ses plus jeunes enfans: M. Fuller calcule que le montant des places sans emploi et de celles dont les devoirs sont remplis par députés, est de 350,000 liv. st. Il suffiroit d'accorder 50,000 liv. st. pour le salaire des places qui exigent quelques devoirs, et en abolissant le reste, on épargneroit à la nation 300,000 liv. st. Ici M. Fuller fait l'éloge de Sa Majesté et conclut en demandant qu'il lui soit permis d'introduire un Bill pour abolir, après la mort des possesseurs actuels, les places sans emploi, et réduire les autres d'après les sommes payées aux députés.

M. *Thornton* ne s'oppose point à la motion, mais pense qu'il vaudroit mieux la différer jusqu'à ce que l'affaire fût portée devant la Chambre d'une manière plus régulière et plus étendue. Il seroit difficile actuellement de décider quelles sont les places qu'il faut laisser subsister et celles que l'on doit abolir; il y en avoit, en outre, quelques-unes qui n'avoient besoin que de réforme. Il conviendroit préalablement de nommer un comité, qui feroit son rapport sur ces divers objets.

M. *Ward* appuie la motion; mais ses motifs sont différens de ceux de l'Hon. Membre, qui avoit dit qu'il ne s'opposoit point à l'influence de la Couronne. C'est pour s'opposer à cette influence qu'il (M. Ward) appuie la motion. Il y a bien des années que la Chambre avoit adopte

Plate 2. Front page of the *Courier d'Angleterre*, vendredi le 16 février 1810

faction'.¹⁹ It promised graphic eyewitness accounts of the September massacres, and hoped that they would inspire avengers for the victims.²⁰ Drawing on the experiences of many of Peltier's émigré colleagues, including Louis de Noailles, Jourgniac de St Méard, Alexandre de Tilly and Royou,²¹ the work was a run away success and ran to several editions between 1793 and 1797.²² It remains one of the richest historical sources on the *journées* of August and September 1792.

Peltier's second émigré journal appeared in the spring of 1793 in weekly instalments. *L'Histoire de la restauration française, ou la campagne de 1793* purported to be an epistolary correspondence with an émigrée in America, but only ran for three numbers. Perhaps Peltier regretted the misplaced optimism of his title? It was also his least interesting journalistic product. Each number consisted of little more than a résumé of military events, although Peltier did append a handful of official documents, and offer a few martial songs and odes as light relief to rally émigré spirits. There are also bursts of vituperation attacking revolutionary leaders and generals, Orléanists, *parvenus* and *ingrats*, but these were few.

Peltier's next journal, the *Correspondance politique*, was launched on 2 November 1793, initially entitled *Correspondance française ou tableau de l'Europe*. It appeared every Tuesday, Thursday and Saturday, more frequently than any other émigré journal, and was aimed at a Europe-wide émigré audience. In layout it resembled the *Courier de Londres*. It usually began with foreign correspondence, finishing with France. The rubric 'Paris', often composed from newspaper reports, aspired to give a comprehensive list of executions in the capital, as well as political comment and other news. This

---

¹⁹ *DTP* i, avertissement, p. i. The paper's numbers were undated, but AAE, CPA supplément 29, fo. 274, Scipion Mourgues to Lebrun, London, 6 Oct. 1792, enclosed a prospectus, and CPA 583, fo. 12, Nöel to Lebrun, London, 18 Oct., referred to the first number. The last number, *DTP* ii. 410, refers to the recent assassination of Marat by Charlotte Corday (13 July 1793), and her execution.
²⁰ *DTP* i, pp. v–vi.
²¹ *Louis-Marie de Noailles* (1756–1804), veteran of the American revolution, brother-in-law of Lafayette, member of the National Assembly, emigrated in mid-1792. *Jourgniac de Saint-Méard*, royalist journalist, was a collaborator on Gautier's *Journal de la cour et de la ville*, and old friend of Peltier. *Comte Alexandre de Tilly* was a former *apôtre*. Royou's precise identity is unclear. AAE, CPA supplément 30, fo. 57, Dumas to Lebrun, 7 Mar. 1793, names him as a brother of right-wing journalist abbé Thomas-Marie Royou. Maspero-Clerc, *Peltier*, 339 (index) identifies him as Jacques-Corentin Royou, but Murray, *Right-wing press*, 198, 203, asserts that Jacques-Corentin was hiding in Rouen where he contributed to the clandestine *Véridique* (Oct. 1792–May 1793). He could be the journalist Louis Royou deported from France in 1799, named by Peltier, *Paris* 174 (31 Jan. 1799), 634.
²² Maspero-Clerc lists four separate editions, two further reprintings, an English translation of 1792–3, and a *Tableau des Massacres* (extracts) published in France in 1797. Wadham College Library, Oxford, contains a further reprint dated September 1793, distributed in London by Peltier and at Brussels through B. le Francq. PRO, PRO 30/8/165, Peltier to William Pitt, 4 Jan. 1796, mentions a further edition published at Paris in 1795 and promptly seized.

was followed by coverage of the British parliament and a 'Bulletin de Londres', including any late news. There was no advertising and little literary content. Only in the last few numbers did Peltier find sufficient space to cover the sittings of the Convention. Of all the émigré journals, the *Correspondance politique* appears to have been the most dependent upon a network of correspondents. Although none of his many correspondents is identifiable, Peltier's letters from émigrés in Belgium, Germany, Spain, Switzerland and northern Italy, as well as from Condé's army, seem to have been genuine.[23] Moreover, Peltier's account of the deeds of Charette and his followers in the Vendée rising was prepared in collaboration with Pierre de la Roberie, Charette's emissary to England, who was related to Peltier by marriage.[24] Peltier also received letters sporadically from Lyon, Paris and even Jamaica, and first-hand accounts of events in Toulon, Pondichery and Saint-Domingue (Haiti).[25] Although it attracted a wide readership, the paper's continental audience made it vulnerable to strategic circumstance. It collapsed after just nine months when the French over-ran Belgium. As a result Peltier was cut off from his continental readership, lost considerable sums of outstanding subscription revenue, and was imprisoned for debt.[26]

The *Correspondance politique* was followed by the *Tableau de l'Europe*, Peltier's most misleading title. Apart from a hastily compiled account of the sittings of the British parliament in lieu of a third volume, the emphasis was almost entirely on France and her politics, although the Polish insurrection receives a brief treatment.[27] Like the *Dernier Tableau de Paris*, it was a collection of accounts, *résumés* and narratives of events in France appearing in instalments, supposedly every eight days, rather than a periodical in the regular sense.[28] The ordering of materials is thematic, but the pagination is confused, and publication was not as regular as Peltier had intended. The

---

[23] For letters to the CP from Belgium see nos 3 (7 Nov. 1793), 30 (9 Jan. 1794), 103 (28 June 1794); from Switzerland see no. 62 (25 Mar. 1794); from Germany see no. 107 (8 July 1794); from Condé's army see no. 30 (9 Jan. 1794).
[24] CP 32–4 (14–18 Jan. 1794). *François-Athanase Charette de la Contrie* (1763–96) was a prominent Vendéan commander. De la Roberie is identified by C. de Sourdeval, 'Le Journal d'un Nantais à Londres pendant la Terreur', *Revue de Bretagne et de Vendée* xxv (1869), 5–25 at p. 10. Peltier mentions their collaboration and relationship: CP 44 (11 Feb. 1794), 32 (14 Jan. 1794).
[25] For information received directly from Lyon see CP 9 (21 Nov. 1793); from Paris no. 109 (12 July 1794); from Jamaica no. 59 (18 Mar. 1794); for accounts of Toulon see no. 45 (13 Feb. 1794), 53 (4 Mar. 1794); for the fall of Pondichery see no. 47 (18 Feb. 1794); for Saint-Domingue see nos. 59 (18 Mar. 1794), 113 (22 July 1794).
[26] See CP 118 (2 Aug. 1794); Jean-Gabriel Peltier, *Avis du rédacteur du Tableau de l'Europe à ses souscripteurs en Angleterre*, Fleet Prison, 2 June 1795, p. 1 (bound with *Paris*, vol. i, in Cambridge University Library); ACC, Z. tom. CXXV, fos 135–6, Peltier to Drouin, London, 17 Sept. 1794.
[27] See TE i, pt iii, 171–2; ii, pt i, 29–32, 71–4.
[28] TE i, pt ii, 'Avis aux souscripteurs', unnumbered page following p. 14; ACC, Z. tom. CXXV, fos 135–6, Peltier to Drouin, 17 Sept. 1794.

main subject matter was the Terror and the thermidorian reaction. Primarily a compilation from other sources, the *Tableau de l'Europe* generally offered neither eyewitness reports in the style of the *Dernier Tableau de Paris*, nor fresh news in the manner of the *Correspondance politique*. Original material is restricted primarily to Peltier's analysis in 'Tableaux Politiques', 'Situations de Paris', and his reflections on the proceedings of the Convention. Thus its historical interest save as a repository of documents, is limited. There are, however, a handful of materials on colonial affairs, mostly provided by Vénault de Charmilly, which attempted to justify British policy and defend the motives of the *colons*.[29] The work's main appeal was no doubt to the émigré community, eager for any news of France, and elucidation of the proceedings of the English parliament; and to British readers seeking comprehensive, though not necessarily fresh, materials on revolutionary politics. The journal's premature demise followed further losses caused by the French invasion of Holland, and led to Peltier's re-internment in the Fleet Prison.[30]

The Swiss bookseller Joseph De Boffe paid Peltier's debts in return for his labours on a new journal, *Paris pendant l'année*, but Peltier quickly bought him out. *Paris pendant l'année*, which appeared from 6 June 1795 to 15 June 1802, offered news from Paris and was divided into literary and political segments. Many of its political articles and reviews were copied from the Parisian press, both royalist and republican. The interest and variety of these pieces varied enormously according to the political situation. The paper lost much of its vitality and audience after the 18 fructidor *coup* (4 September 1797), when there was a clampdown on royalist journalists such as Adrien Lezay de Marnésia and Jean-Thomas Richer-Sérizy, and regained its vigour only after the *journée* of 30 prairial VII (18 June 1799).[31] Important articles gleaned from the Parisian press were generally preceded by a few words of comment from Peltier, and disclaimers often accompanied articles, speeches and official discourses containing views abhorrent to the émigré community. Such articles played an important role in informing the émigrés about political developments and the state of opinion in Paris, but Peltier's comments persistently denigrated revolutionary leaders, culture and literature.

Peltier's next journal, the *Ambigu*, launched in July 1802,[32] continued this

---

[29] See *TE* i, pt iii, 109–12; ii, pt i, 3–14, 41–2. On P.-F. Vénault de Charmilly, *colon* representative in London, commander of the *émigré* Légion britannique in Saint-Domingue 1793–4, see Robert Griffiths, 'Pierre-Victor Malouet and the *monarchiens* in the French revolution and counter-revolution', unpubl. PhD diss. British Columbia 1975, chs vi, vii; D. Geggus, *Slavery, war, and revolution: the British occupation of Saint Domingue, 1793–1798*, Oxford 1982.
[30] Peltier, *Avis du rédacteur du Tableau de l'Europe*.
[31] *Paris* 185 (31 July 1799), 5. On Lezay and Richer-Sérizy see Popkin, *Right-wing press*.
[32] Although the information against Peltier in Jean-Gabriel Peltier (ed.), *The Trial of John Peltier esq. for a libel against Napoleon Buonaparté . . .*, London 1803, 2, implies that the *Ambigu* first appeared on 16 Aug. 1802, AAE, CPA 597, fos 480–1, Otto to Talleyrand, 12 thermidor X (30 July 1802), indicates that it appeared in late July.

policy of denigration, concentrating on a single target: Napoleon Bonaparte. Peltier's attacks could take the form of polemic, information to counter Napoleonic control of the European press, or satire. If the polemic descended into personal vitriol, the information was occasionally fabricated, and the satire often contravened the bounds of good taste, all were grist to the mill. The *Ambigu* is the most comprehensive anthology of the anti-Napoleonic 'Black Legend' and an arsenal of anti-Napoleonic materials, many of which originated on Peltier's pages. Others he merely popularised, translated and disseminated to a Europe-wide audience, to bear endless repetition from the Black Legend pamphleteers of the restoration.

In the first thirty numbers of the *Ambigu* Peltier adopted a quartavo format with a wide mixture of anecdotes, essays, documents, poems, *jeux de mots*, letters, news reports and satires, and, for the first and last time in any émigré journal, offered cartoons and vignettes. The most significant was a sphinx with the head of Napoleon which adorned the title page of the first few numbers. There could be little doubt that this was the *Ambigu* of the journal's title, and when Peltier was summoned before a British court and charged with libelling Bonaparte, he retaliated by striking the head from the sphinx (see plate 3). From the thirty-first number Peltier reverted to the more practical octavo format: there were no more illustrations and no further changes of format.

The remaining émigré journals can be divided into three categories: political and literary periodicals; propaganda organs; newspapers. The first category includes Montlosier's *Journal de France et d'Angleterre*, which was founded in 1797 as the organ of the *monarchien* party,[33] together with Jacques Mallet Du Pan's *Mercure britannique*, and the *Mercure de France*. The *Mercure de France* was published in London between April 1800 and April 1801, modelled on its *ancien régime* namesake, and likewise edited by a 'society of men of letters', a shadowy committee of six. It comprised a literary section and a political section. The identities of five of the editors are unknown, but a large circle of perhaps ninety collaborators and contributors put names, initials or *noms de plume* to its articles, poems and *jeux de mots*. Such participation set it apart from the other émigré journals, and its wide constituency in the émigré community suggests that its contributors were more representative of the emigration as a whole. It might be seen perhaps as the 'school magazine' of the emigration, but a number of talented contributors ensured it was anything but mediocre. However, the timing of the journal's launch was unfortunate. By 1800 the market was contracting as the émigré community rallied to a more lenient régime inside France and despite all its *esprit*, a non-profit-making ethos and numerous contributors, the *Mercure de France* folded in April 1801.

Montlosier's *Journal de France et d'Angleterre* was also never a commercial

---

[33] Montlosier, *Souvenirs*, 247.

or political success and its author struggled to fulfil his commitments to subscribers. Initially the paper was published weekly, but after a few numbers its appearance became increasingly haphazard as Montlosier proved unequal to his task and began to struggle financially. The paper initially took Peltier's *Paris pendant l'année* as its model, but Montlosier rapidly decided that the market would not bear two such similar journals and began to write on English issues and general political matters. He also, unlike Peltier, wrote most of his own scant literary material. Yet despite the goodwill of his *monarchien* friends and the advantage of Mallet Du Pan's correspondence from Berne, the paper was clearly failing in July 1797 when Montlosier accepted the abbé Calonne's invitation to join him in the editorship of the *Courier de Londres*.[34] The *Journal de France et d'Angleterre* has attracted the attention of historians interested in *monarchien* ideology or Montlosier's subsequent career,[35] but it was nevertheless among the least consequential of the émigré journals. Although Montlosier revelled in the importance the paper seemed to confer on him, it never enjoyed widespread influence.

Mallet Du Pan's *Mercure britannique* was an altogether more successful venture. Its content was almost exclusively political, with a clear missionary purpose:

> This work is devoted to the purpose of reviving in every quarter the courage of governments and nations overwhelmed or menaced by the French Republic; of showing them the necessity of resistance, and inspiring the hope of success, if supported by united endeavours and the rectitude of intention.[36]

This was an ambitious manifesto, and in the hands of any lesser journalist it might easily be dismissed as mere hyperbole. However, Mallet was a political analyst who had advised princes and statesmen and expected to be heard. To ensure a wider audience, he commissioned an English translation, the *British Mercury*, and apparently an Italian one as well.[37] The *Mercure britannique* was launched in September 1798 and ran until 25 March 1800. The early numbers followed a clearly preconceived plan. After twelve issues Mallet had outlined the political situation of Europe, beginning with a case study to show how the revolution undermined the Swiss Confederation, analysed the revolution's dynamic and development, and finally prescribed the remedy of an anti-French crusade in the face of the pan-European revolutionary threat. This exposition does not take the form of a single tract, but rather a set of long-meditated political essays on related subjects. However, as Mallet's work progressed, more and more space was devoted to essays upon current affairs,

---

[34] Ibid.
[35] Notably Robert Griffiths, *Le Centre perdu: Malouet et les monarchiens dans la révolution française*, Grenoble 1988, 181–6; Maspero-Clerc, 'Montlosier'.
[36] BM 24 (15 Aug. 1799), 463.
[37] The Italian translation in the Bodleian Library, *Il Mercurio britannico*, purports to have been published in London in 1798–1800, but may have been unauthorised.

and occasional political pamphlets and publications. With the exception of one or two commissioned letters, Mallet's copy was entirely his own, and almost exclusively political. Gradually there was a decline in the quality of the journal. Mallet's health was deteriorating and his polemic became stale through repetition. However, in the last few issues Mallet's defence of the Napoleonic régime gave the journal a new polemical vigour, although Mallet still nursed a personal antipathy towards Bonaparte. The final number was completed by Malouet, shortly before Mallet's death.[38]

The propaganda journals, Nicolas Dutheil's *Supplément au Rédacteur* and François-David Kirwan's *Antidote* were produced entirely for British government subsidised distribution in France. Dutheil's declared aim was to give an accurate picture of the military situation in order to undermine the French government while sustaining *Chouan* morale. He also attempted other genres of propaganda, including the political biography 'so in vogue in France',[39] but as propaganda it was naive. Opting for a 'cloak-and-dagger' approach, which was all the more comical in the light of the paper's transparent counter-revolutionary sympathies, Dutheil advised Grenville:

> This journal will not be available in England, but only in the provinces of Normandy and Brittany, from whence it will circulate into the rest of the kingdom. This journal will lose its effect if it is not edited with skill and if it gives reason to suspect it is printed outside France.[40]

The paper's title attempted to call the reliability of the Directory's official organ, the *Rédacteur*, into question, but its failure to give a false place of publication, price or date would probably arouse rather than allay suspicions as to its sponsors. Grenville approved the project, and at least four numbers were produced at the British government's expense in June and July 1799.[41] Kirwan's *Antidote* was intended as a sporadic periodical, and probably appeared in December 1804 and January 1805. The editor's aim, according to his first number, was to enlighten the French on their true interests, and reveal to sovereigns the secret motives for French declamations against England. He contended that fear of British ambition was grounded in trifling commercial disputes, whereas French ambition consisted in the 'overthrow of empires'. He argued that conditions were right for a successful coalition of great powers, and that Bonaparte's power was largely based on bluff. He declared that Napoleon lacked a popular constituency, appealed only to sycophants, had insufficient revenues and lacked experienced veterans. The populace was indignant about conscription and the duc d'Enghien's judicial

---

[38] Mallet, *Retrospective*, 247.
[39] PRO, FO 27/54, pt ii, fo. 346, Dutheil to Frere, 19 July 1799.
[40] Ibid. fo. 249, Dutheil to Grenville, 10 June 1799.
[41] Ibid. fos 253–4, 348–9, 350–1, are the prospectus and the third and fourth issues respectively. A sample of the first number, enclosed in fo. 293, Dutheil to Frere 21 June 1799, is lost.

murder.⁴² He concluded that the time was finally ripe to rally Frenchmen by raising the Bourbon standard and called on the powers to unite with Britain to defeat the Napoleonic threat and secure peace and stability in Europe by restoring Louis XVIII.⁴³ Kirwan approached Hammond, under-secretary of state at the Foreign Office, in January 1805. He offered to distribute the journal inside France by clandestine means, and suggested that the government should distribute it elsewhere. The offer appears to have been declined, perhaps because the government would not give such blatant support to Bourbon pretensions. A second number, which Kirwan claimed was almost ready for the press, may have appeared, but no more is heard of him or the journal.⁴⁴

Regnier's *Courier d'Angleterre*, launched on 30 April 1805, was to prove an altogether more durable organ for British propaganda.⁴⁵ Within three weeks of Regnier's dismissal from the *Courier de Londres*, friends loaned him enough to buy a printshop,⁴⁶ and when more funding was required to keep the paper afloat,⁴⁷ Louis XVIII was among his sponsors.⁴⁸ However, in late 1806, following a request from the tsar, the paper was recruited by the British government as a propaganda organ for distribution on the continent (see chapter 3). The paper's success was due as much to British government sponsorship as to the journalistic skills of its editor-proprietor and his two remarkable collaborators, the comte d'Antraigues and Henri-Larivière. The former, a spy-master, provided essays and intelligence; the latter, a former president of the revolutionary Conseil de Cinq-cents, and Regnier's probable co-editor, anecdotes on French dignatories, analysis and epigrams.⁴⁹ The British government continued to subsidise the *Courier d'Angleterre* until December 1814, save for a brief interruption between October 1807 and March 1808. Thereafter Regnier's paper had outlived its usefulness. Finally, he arranged favourable terms to abandon it and cede his ownership to the proprietors of the *Courier de Londres* in May 1815.⁵⁰ Regnier's journalism differed in style

---

42 D'Enghien, Condé's grandson, was seized in Baden, taken to Paris, secretly tried and shot at Vincennes on 21 Mar. 1804. See ch. 5 below.
43 *Antidote* 1 (dated 1804), [?Dec.]. The only known copy is in PRO, FO 27/71.
44 See ibid. Kirwan to Mulgrave, 23, 25 Jan. 1805. Other possible reasons for Mulgrave's reluctance to employ Kirwan include fear that he was a double agent, or the possibility of peace negotiations.
45 See ibid. Regnier to [?Mulgrave], 25 Apr. 1805.
46 Ibid. and FO 27/124, Regnier to Castlereagh [memoir], 10 Mar. 1815, enclosed with letter of 23 Mar. 1815.
47 See PRO, FO 27/71, Regnier to De Boffe, 29 June 1805.
48 See George Canning papers, West Yorkshire District Archives, Chapeltown, bundle 54, d'Avaray to de La Châtre (copy), Gothenburg, 20 Oct. 1807.
49 On Regnier's desire to associate Henri-Larivière with the paper see ibid. bundle 59a, Regnier to Canning, Dec. 1807; bundle 56a, Regnier to Canning, 30 Dec. 1807.
50 PRO, FO 27/124, Regnier to [?Hamilton], 17 Mar. 1815, and Regnier to Castlereagh [memoir], 10 Mar. 1815, sent 23 Mar. implore the government to support a merged journal. The request was unsuccessful: *CL* lxxvii/35 (2 May 1815) informs subscribers to the *CA* that

and approach from other émigré newspapers and periodicals. Like his rivals, he covered the British parliament in a matter-of-fact manner, reproduced important documents, and gave foreign reports under the titles of 'Journaux de France' (etc.). But he also wrote lengthy but punchy articles of political analysis, which seldom over-ran from one number into the next, unlike the tortuous articles in which Montlosier or the abbé Calonne expounded their ideas in the *Courier de Londres*. The surviving collections of the *Courier d'Angleterre* contain the same vicious anti-Bonapartist invective and mordant irony that characterised Regnier's *Courier de Londres*,[51] and which, while frequently entertaining, often overstepped the bounds of taste and (ironically enough) allowed Peltier to brand him a 'Gazetier cuirassé'.[52]

Like their Parisian counterparts the thirteen émigré journals had very small editorial staffs. Most were single editor ventures, although there is evidence that most had at least one editorial assistant who might also serve as office manager. Thus, the journalistic texts of the London émigrés were primarily the product of a very select group. In all, only nine journalists are known or suspected to have served for over six months as controlling editors of the papers. Their names and the titles of the journals they edited are given in table 3. Although their length of service varied enormously, these men can be considered the 'major journalists' who shaped the émigré press. All, except Jean-Baptiste Couchery, were editors-in-charge or proprietors of their own papers. Although Couchery appears never to have had a paper of his own, he merits inclusion here because of his important role on both the *Courier de Londres* and the *Ambigu*. He edited the Paris column for the *Courier de Londres* from about 1802 to 1805,[53] and from about 1809–14 regularly filled in as editor of the *Ambigu* during the long spells when Peltier was sick or in prison.[54]

In addition to these nine 'major journalists', it is possible to identify positively four 'minor journalists', who had roles as executive editors, however briefly. Two of them, Dutheil and Kirwan, as we have seen, edited short-lived

---

henceforth they will receive the *CL*, 'which will be the only French journal published twice a week in London'.

[51] For surviving collections of the paper see appendix 2.

[52] *Ambigu* 201 (30 Oct. 1808), 224.

[53] Couchery is identified as author of the Paris column in J.-C.-H. Mehée de la Touche, *Alliance des Jacobins français avec le ministère anglais*, Paris germinal an XII (1804), 68. His collaboration probably ended in 1805. Several secret police files describe Couchery as 'principal collaborateur' on the *CL*, notably AN, F^7 3703, police bulletin of 8 floréal XI (27 Apr. 1803); F^7 4336^A, dos. 4 (year XII/1803–4), which mistakenly names him Eugène Couchery; AAE, mem./docs France 620, 'Couchery', and AN, AF^{IV*} 1710, p. 231, no. 447.

[54] AAE, mem./docs France 620, 'Couchery', alleges that Peltier paid Couchery £10 per month to edit the *Ambigu*, and he was almost certainly the 'foreign pen' whom Peltier employed during the illness mentioned in PRO, FO 27/94, Peltier to FO, 19 Jan. 1813. Couchery was the author of 72 articles satirising Napoleon and his court under the title 'Le Logographe ou le Moniteur secret', in *Ambigu* 281–397 (20 Jan. 1811–10 Apr. 1814). In 1813 and 1814 these articles were republished in 2 volumes and enjoyed a considerable vogue.

papers. A third, Velley, was sent to London by Calonne to edit the *Courier de Londres* in late 1791, and presumably briefly did so.[55] The final identifiable 'minor journalist' is the abbé Jean-Marie de Châteaugiron, an *anti-concordataire* polemicist, who identifies himself as one of the six editors of the *Mercure de France* of 30 July 1800.[56] The actual identities of the other five editors of the paper remain an enigma. However, they did reveal a little about themselves. They were all Catholics, Frenchmen and royalists, of whom 'several' (i.e. between two and four) were clergymen ('consacrés aux autels'), and 'several' were nobles ('gentilshommes').[57] Thus it is sometimes possible to talk of nine 'minor journalists' in the statistical tables which follow.

It is also possible to identify a further twenty-four individuals who seem to have made significant regular contributions of materials or efforts to the émigré press without being editors-in-charge (see table 2). For the purposes of this study they will all be known as 'collaborators', although their roles did not always involve journalism. Few of them were experienced journalists, and many only seem to have collaborated loosely or for a brief time. The group includes several persons who received a salary from the papers, but many who almost certainly did not. It also embraces Samuel Swinton and Charles-Alexandre de Calonne who, as proprietors of the *Courier de Londres*, occasionally intervened in editorial affairs. Salaried employees of the émigré press included Serani, Royou and Dallas, together with Montlosier's correspondents Butet, André de Montluel and Tromelin. It is probable that Pradel, Tilly and La Corbière were also paid for their work. Individuals involved in the routine business of production, binding, marketing or distribution, are not included.

The roles of these collaborators varied enormously. Royou, La Corbière, Serani, d'Auerweck and possibly Pradel served as sub-editors or office staff; Jean-Louis Mallet was a bi-lingual secretary and handled distribution for both his father and Montlosier. Others, notably Pichegru, Durfort-Boissières and d'Antraigues both submitted material regularly and supervised the political content of the papers. So, probably, did Henri-Larivière on the *Courier d'Angleterre*. Butet, André de Montluel and Tromelin corresponded with the *Courier de Londres* from Constantinople, Paris and the Near East respectively. Our twenty-four also include agents for the large-scale clandestine distribution of the *Courier d'Angleterre* (Pierre-François Fauche, Louis Fauche-Borel), and émigrés named as important 'collaborateurs' by the French secret police (the Bédées, Béhague). Although the term 'collaborateur' is problematic, and

---

[55] See PRO, PC 1/125, pieces 353, 356, 359, letters of Suleau to Calonne, samedi 15 [Nov. 1791], Neuwied, 3 Dec. 1791, and Brussels, 17 Dec. 1791. The first letter is misdated: the 15th was a Friday. Velley may be the dying editor referred to in PRO, PC 1/126, piece 677, J.-L.-J. de Calonne to Calonne, 28 Oct. [1793].
[56] MF 12 (30 July 1800), 385–7. On this occasion his name is given as J. M. Dechasteaugiron. Châteaugiron was born in Brittany, and died in London in 1802. The *Dictionnaire de biographie française*, viii, contains a brief entry on him.
[57] MF 1 (10 Apr. 1800), 4.

Table 2
Contribution and counter-revolutionary political activity of minor journalists and collaborators

Name	Abbreviated journal title	Dates (K = Known, P = Probable)	Role	Other counter-rev. activities
d'Antraigues, L.-A.	CA	1806–12 K	info., articles distribution	spy master, publicist
d'Auerweck, L.	TE	1794–5 K	assistant ?	spy
de Bédée, l'aîné	CL	c. 1810	articles, poems	counterfeiter, bandit?
de Bédée, jeune	Paris	c. 1802	uncertain	counterfeiter, bandit?
de Béhague, J. P. A.	Ambigu	c. 1810	articles	Chouan leader
Butet, [?]	CL	c. 1790s–1800s	Turkish corresp.	
de Calonne, C.-A.	CL	1789–98	co-proprietor, articles	princes' agent, publicist
de Châteaugiron, J.-M.	MF	1800 K–1801 P	co-editor	publicist
Dallas, R. C.	MB	1798–1800	translator	
Durfort-Boissières, A.	Ambigu	c. 1803–10	articles, supervision	princes' agent
Dutheil, N.	SR	1799	editor	princes' agent
Fauche, P.-F.	CA	1807–9	agent, Sweden	princes' agent
Fauche-Borel, L.	CA	c. 1807–9	info., articles ? distribution	spy master, propagandist
Henri-Larivière, P. F. J. de	Ambigu, CL, CA	c. 1802–7	poems, info., poss. edits CA	provided intelligence to British
Kirwan, F.-D.	Antidote	1804	editor	editor, Bordeaux
La Corbière [?]	CL	c. 1802	sub-editor	
Mallet, J.-L.	JFA, MB	1797–1800	bilingual secretary; distributor	
Malouet, P.-V.	MB	1799–1800	articles, help	*colon* leader
André de Montluel	CL	c. 1797–1802	Paris correspondent	spy ?
Pichegru, J. C.	CL	c. 1803–4	supervision	conspirator
Pradel, [?]	CL	c. 1798–1802	editorial assistant?	
Royou	DTP	1792–3	secretary	editor, Paris
Serani, [?]	CL	1791–3 +	assistant editor	
Swinton, S.	CL	1776–98	proprietor	
de Tilly, A.	DTP	1792	article +	
de Tinseau, C.-M.-T.-L.	Paris, CL	1801	articles	polemicist, intelligence
Tromelin, J.-J.-M. F. Boudin de	CL	1798–1801	Egypt & Syria correspondent	spy for Sidney Smith
Velley, [?]	CL	early 1793 P	editor	

can indicate a mere contributor to a paper, the very fact that the French secret police mentioned them probably implies a more substantial relationship in most cases. The list of collaborators does not include the authors of articles unless they seem to have been connected to either the administrative or editorial side of the journals. Collectively, 'journalists' and 'collaborators' are referred to as 'pressmen' in the text that follows.

The personalities of the nine 'major' journalists had a disproportionate influence in shaping the émigré press. As the longest serving journalist, Peltier set the tone. Irascible, jealous, vindictive and vituperative, he was quick to anger and to launch attacks on perceived political opponents and journalistic rivals, including Mallet Du Pan, Montlosier, Regnier and the abbé Calonne. Sooner or later almost all of Peltier's disputes descended into personal vitriol, and this was spectacularly true of his attacks on Mallet Du Pan in 1799–1800 (see chapter 3) and his dispute with Regnier from 1804. In the latter the apple, or rather, as Peltier pedantically pointed out, the carrot of discord, was a poisoned vegetable used in an attempt to assassinate Louis XVIII.[58] News of the attempt was brought to England by the turncoat propagandist Lewis Goldsmith, former editor of Napoleon's English-language organ *The Argus*, and given to Regnier. However, to Regnier's chagrin, Peltier broke the story to the British press before he could publish it. Regnier retaliated by attacking Peltier in the *Courier de Londres* and Peltier responded in two supplements to the *Ambigu*. Thereafter they traded racial, political and professional taunts based on their respective pasts and Peltier's service of Christophe of Haiti.[59] Disputes like these, and the manner in which they have been portrayed by the *monarchiens* in their memoir sources, seem to have distorted historical perspectives on the extent of division among the rank-and-file of the emigration. However, as Peltier's quarrel with Regnier suggests, professional jealousy, patronage and market share were probably at least as important as ideological factors as motives for these attacks. Among friends Peltier was a witty and amiable companion, capable of great loyalty and generosity. Chateaubriand, describing his first visit from Peltier, has left an enduring monument to his character:

> He was not exactly vice ridden, but he was devoured by a vermin of small faults which it was impossible to purge. [He was] a libertine, disloyal subject, earning much money and eating the same, simultaneously the servant of legitimacy and ambassador for the negro King Christophe [of Haiti] at the court of George III, diplomatic correspondent of the comte de *Limonade*, drinking in champagne the proceeds of appointments paid in sugar. This sort of M. Violet, playing the celebrated tunes of the revolution on a pocket violin came to see me and offer me his services as a fellow Breton. I told him of my plan [to write] the *Essai* [*sur les révolutions anciennes et modernes*]; he loudly approved of it . . . . My Gil Blas, tall, slender, escalabrous, with his hair powdered and bald forehead, always shouting and laughing, put his round hat on one ear, and took me to his printer Baylie [Baylis].[60]

---

[58] See *Ambigu* 323 (20 Mar. 1812), 684.

[59] The dispute can be followed in *Ambigu* 51 supplément (30 Aug. 1804); 52 supplément (10 Sept. 1804); 167 (20 Nov. 1807), 358–60; 201 (30 Oct. 1808), 219–26; 224 (20 Oct. 1809), 635–44; 305 (20 Sept. 1811), 621–36; 322 (10 Mar. 1812), 599–608; 323 (20 Mar. 1812), 673–88; *CL* lvi/20 (7 Sept. 1804); lvi/23 (18 Sept. 1804); *CA* 352 (9 Sept. 1808); 355 (20 Sept. 1808); 358 (30 Sept. 1808); 359 (4 Oct. 1808); 364 (21 Oct. 1808); 368 (4 Nov. 1808); 374 (25 Nov. 1808); 379 (13 Dec. 1808). Peltier claimed in *Ambigu* 323 that Regnier had attacked him on more than forty occasions since the carrot of discord was thrown, which is quite possible given the incompleteness of the surviving collections of the *CA*.

[60] François-René de Chateaubriand, *Mémoires*, i. 411–12. As this passage does not appear

And a little later, as Chateaubriand's funds ran out, he adds:

> Translating work no longer came my way. Pelletier [sic], a man of pleasure, bored of a prolonged obligingness. He would have given me all that he had, if he had not preferred to consume it himself; but to search out work here and there, to do good works patiently, were things impossible to him.[61]

The artist Henri-Pierre Danloux, less kind, recorded that 'Peltier is a man who we don't have to receive. These journalists in general are people who insinuate themselves everywhere and on whom the door should be closed.' Danloux also complains of factual inaccuracies in the *Dernier Tableau de Paris* and Peltier's laziness and asserts that the reputation of the *Actes des apôtres* was due to the wit, fertile imagination and style of Rivarol alone.[62]

Regnier, too, was agreeable company but considered unreliable by friend and foe alike. Several sources comment on his laziness.[63] R. A. Routledge, co-owner of the *Courier de Londres* and his former employer, thought him politically suspect, while the consular police labelled him a 'royaliste terroriste' in memory of his Jacobin past.[64] Montlosier found him an entertaining companion, 'a man of *beaucoup d'esprit*, amiable manners, and distinguished education', but felt ill-used by him, and by 1808 Regnier had fallen out with Peltier and the exiled princes too.[65] George Hammond, under-secretary of state at the Foreign Office, disliked what he wrote, whilst Peltier accused him of professional jealousy.[66]

Gérard, whose precise identity and Christian name are unknown, was, in contrast, mild-mannered and diligent. His dossier in the French foreign ministry describes him as 'a wise man who feels no hatred towards his fellow journalists'.[67] His journalism, and the only known document in his hand, a firm but moderate response to an abusive letter, seem to bear out this judgement.[68] Gérard's employers also had a high opinion of him, and the Foreign

---

in the abridged penguin edition translated by Robert Baldick (first publ. Hamish Hamilton, London 1961), and the six-volume translation by Alexander Texeira de Mattos (London 1902) is rather loose, I have used my own translations.

61 Ibid. i. 416.

62 Roger Portalis (ed.), *H. P. Danloux: peintre des portraits et son journal durant l'émigration*, Paris 1910, 159. Antoine Rivarol (1753–1801) was a celebrated author and royalist journalist. He emigrated in 1791.

63 See PRO, FO 27/90, R. A. [?] Routledge to [C. C.] Smith, Warwick Court, Grays Inn, 20 Jan. 1812; Méhée de la Touche, *Alliance des Jacobins*, 68; AAE, CPA 602, fos 196–209, [Du Bouchet] 'Détails et observations sur mon voyage'.

64 PRO, FO 27/90, R. A. [?]Routledge to [C. C.] Smith, Warwick Court, Grays Inn, 20 Jan. 1812; AN, F^7 6330, dos. 6959, 'Notice sur M. Peltier'.

65 See Montlosier, *Mémoires*, ii. 307–9, and ch. 3 below.

66 Canning papers, bundle 59a, d'Antraigues to Canning, 7 Feb. 1808 (three letters from d'Antraigues in this collection bear this date); *Ambigu* 201 (30 Oct. 1808); 305 (20 Sept. 1811).

67 AAE, mem./docs France 620, 'Gérard'.

68 AAE, mem./docs France 615, fos 203–4, Gérard to Lafitte, 17 Oct. 1810.

Office appears to have valued his sagacity, loyalty and moderation. Routledge gave him this striking testimonial in a letter to the Foreign Office:

> He is a man of abilities and character, and the steady course he has pursued in the conduct of the paper, has added to its character, and we are happy to find he has given satisfaction to the government as well as to ourselves. We have found Mr. Gérard on all occasions punctual and diligent, which was not the case with Mr. Regnier.[69]

Mallet Du Pan was similarly reliable and conscientious, whether working for himself or others. Austere in his private life, he was scrupulously independent in his journalism. Commentators as diverse as Thomas Carlyle and Frances Acomb have considered him the most acute and penetrating contemporary observer of the Revolution. Mallet's good friend Montlosier shared many of his virtues but had an altogether different temperament. He was a man of great enthusiasms and energies whose voracious but idiosyncratic intellect eagerly embraced scientific and pseudo-scientific fads, and occasionally expounded fantastical ideas. His life-long interests included both geology and Mesmerism.[70] Although he possessed great imagination, he lacked a sense of realism and proportion, but he had an independent mind and great intellectual integrity. As a result, from a political and ideological perspective Montlosier was a maverick 'who belonged to no-one but himself'.[71] He was not a natural journalist. His writing is often verbose, tortuous and long-winded, but is interesting nevertheless for both the originality of some of his ideas, and as an example, albeit highly idiosyncratic, of *monarchien* journalism.

Jean-Baptiste Couchery appears to have been a loner. He remained aloof from the rank-and-file of the emigration, some of whom despised him as a former 'patriot' revolutionary, but he impressed the Bourbons with his ability and the British with his honesty.[72] Robert Heron was an accomplished scholar and devout Christian, but also vain, ambitious and extravagant. Temperamentally unbalanced and over-sensitive, he was ill-suited to the precarious demands, rigours and unreliable income of literary life. Confident of his genius, capable of earning a solid living, he was unable to live within

---

[69] PRO, FO 27/90, R. A. [?] Routledge to [C. C. Smith], Warwick Court, Grays Inn, 20 Jan. 1812.

[70] His only significant geological treatise was *Essai sur la théorie des volcans d'Auvergne*, n.p. 1788. On Montlosier and mesmerism see Robert Darnton, *Mesmerism and the end of enlightenment in France*, Cambridge, Mass. 1968, ch. ii; Montlosier, *Mémoires*, i. 132–40, and *Souvenirs*, 207–11, 240–2.

[71] P. H. Beik, *The French revolution seen from the right: social theories in motion*, Philadelphia 1956, 33.

[72] On his relations with the Bourbons see below. On the British ministry's high opinion of Couchery see Canning's pencil note on the reverse of PRO, FO 27/91, Couchery to Street, 21 Dec. 1812. Louis Fauche-Borel's judgement of Couchery as 'un bon diable' in AAE, mem./docs France 620, 'Couchery', seems the product of jealousy, suspicion and recrimination and deserves little faith.

his means and despite a vast and varied publishing output, never saved enough to achieve his ambition of buying the proprietorship of a newspaper. He was emaciated and weary from a life of toil when he became editor of the *Courier de Londres* in 1805. At forty-one he had not long to live.[73]

The abbé Calonne's personality demonstrated numerous contradictions. Under the old regime he seems to have been the epitome of the worldly abbé. His bishop complained of his 'léger esprit', his brother noted his rebelliousness, and his father employed a spy to monitor his dissolute behaviour.[74] Although the abbé's hagiographer imagines he 'dreamt of poverty as his brother dreamt of wealth' as early as 1776, it is doubtful that his spiritual conversion occurred until well after the revolution.[75] However, Montlosier records finding him kneeling before an altar praying for the conversion of a former 'colleague in debauchery' in 1797.[76] In late 1799 the abbé went to Canada as a missionary where his piety, austerity and a handful of conversions earned him his place in Catholic hagiography. However, there are also hints of less virtuous behaviour and motives. The abbé participated in counterfeiting revolutionary currency in 1791–2 and 1794, was involved in personal and counter-revolutionary intrigues until at least 1795, and left clamouring creditors behind when he sailed for Canada.[77] He also seems to have had a personality clash with Verduisant, the editor who preceded him on the *Courier de Londres*. For although Calonne considered Verduisant 'a man of wit, of talents, and of good principles' and admired his work, the abbé complained that due to his excessive 'amour-propre', dissolute lifestyle, laziness and ignorance of the English language, he was having to edit the paper himself.[78] Finally, he sacked Verduisant at the end of October 1793 and took over as editor intending to appoint a replacement when one could be found.[79] The abbé Calonne, in far off Italy, could only accept the *fait accompli*.

---

[73] The only source dealing with Heron's character, R. Chambers, *A biographical dictionary of eminent Scotsmen*, new edn, London 1855, cited in *British biographical archive*, fiche 545, is harsh on his faults but seems fair-minded. The general outline of his life and personality accords with Heron's obituary notices in the *Gentleman's Magazine* and *Annual Register*.
[74] Sr Marguerite-Marie, *Abbé Calonne*, 13.
[75] Ibid. 14.
[76] Montlosier, *Souvenirs*, 248.
[77] On his counterfeiting see R. Lacour-Gayet, *Calonne, financier, réformateur, contre-révolutionnaire, 1734–1802*, Paris 1963, 390; Maurice Hutt, *Chouannerie and counter-revolution: Puisaye, the princes and the British government in the 1790s*, Cambridge 1983, i. 167; AAE, CPA 589, fo. 146, 'Mémoire sur Angleterre', 15 Feb. 1796. On his intrigues see BL, MS Add. 37,859, fos 291–2, J.-L.-J. de Calonne to Windham, 21 July 1795. On his debts see CL xlv/36 (3 May 1799); Sr Marguerite-Marie, *Abbé Calonne*, 27–8.
[78] PRO, PC 1/125, piece 12, Calonne to the prince of Wales, Madrid, 29 Mar. 1793 [minute]; PC 1/130, piece 235, fos 39, 64, Calonne to J.-L.-J. de Calonne, [?Vicenza], 29 Sept. 1793 [minute]; Calonne to J.-L.-J. de Calonne, Vicenza, 6 Oct. 1793 [minute]; PC 1/126, piece 677, J.-L.-J. de Calonne to Calonne, London, 28 Oct. [1793].
[79] PRO, PC 1/126, piece 677, J.-L.-J. de Calonne to Calonne, London, 28 Oct. [1793]. The abbé reported that he had already written to Mallet Du Pan offering him the job and would approach the abbé de Fontenai or abbé Barruel if he refused.

Intriguingly, several of the 'major journalists' were acquainted prior to emigrating. Jean-Gabriel Peltier and Jacques Regnier were old schoolmates, who, together with Montlosier, launched their journalistic careers in October 1789.[80] According to popular tradition, after Regnier had introduced his comrades, they had dinner in a café in the Palais Royale, hotbed of revolutionary excitement. The jottings they made there on the tablecloth formed the basis for the first number of the *Actes des apôtres*.[81] The other émigré journalists also knew Mallet Du Pan and the abbé Calonne, sometimes personally, sometimes by repute.

Most of the major exile journalists were experienced men of letters and at least five had considerable journalistic experience prior to working on the exile press. Mallet Du Pan was a career journalist specialising in political publications. He began his journalistic career writing for Samuel-Frédéric Osterwald's *Journal hélvetique* between 1774 and 1776, and assisted the arch-anti-philosophe Simon-Nicolas-Henri Linguet in the publication of his *Annales politiques, civiles et littéraires du dix-huitième siècle* from 1777 to 1780.[82] In 1782 Mallet was appointed editor of the political part of the *Mercure de France*, and continued in that role for ten years.[83] Robert Heron was both polymath and career journalist, serving briefly on a string of British papers including the *Historical Magazine*, *Agricultural Magazine*, *Oracle*, *Porcupine*, *Morning Chronicle*, *British Press*, *Globe* and *Lloyds Evening Post* before being appointed to the editorship of the *Courier de Londres*. He published books on an impressive range of subjects including chemistry, Scottish and universal history, geography, natural history, his travels in Scotland, political issues and a memoir on the life of Robert Burns.[84] Montlosier, too, was more a man of letters than a journalist. He contributed to the *Actes des apôtres* and published a series of political pamphlets in addition to a geological treatise. After his return to France Montlosier continued to write and in later life won celebrity for his opposition to ultramontanism.[85] Peltier edited a string of titles between October 1789 and 10 August 1792,[86] while Regnier was involved with the *Actes des apôtres* and the comte de Proly's *Cosmopolite*.[87] Couchery briefly contributed to *La Vedette*, a moderate Jacobin paper founded in 1791

---

80 Montlosier, *Mémoires*, ii. 307–8.
81 Murray, *Right-wing press*, 53.
82 Acomb, *Mallet Du Pan*, 106–24, 128–33. Among innumerable studies of Linguet see especially Daniel Baruch, *Simon-Nicolas-Henri Linguet ou l'irrécupérable*, Paris 1991; Darlene Gay Levy, *The ideas and careers of Simon-Nicolas-Henri-Linguet: a study in eighteenth-century French politics*, Urbana–Chicago–London 1980; Jean Cruppi, *Un Avocat-journaliste au XVIIIe siècle: Linguet*, Paris 1895.
83 On Mallet's pre-revolutionary journalistic career see Acomb, *Mallet Du Pan*, chs i–v.
84 For summary bibliographies see *Annual register* (1807), 566–7; *Gentleman's Magazine* (June 1807), 595; Chambers, *Eminent Scotsmen*.
85 On his ill-fated career under Napoleon see Miramon-Fitzjames, 'Montlosier'; on his gallicanism see Bardoux, *Montlosier et le gallicanisme*.
86 See Maspero-Clerc, *Peltier*, 29–62.
87 AN, F[7] 6330, dos. 6959, 'Note sur M. Peltier'; *Courier de Londres et de Paris* 21 (5/10 Aug.

FRENCH EXILE JOURNALISM

Table 3
Length of editorial service of major émigré journalists

Name	Titles edited	Dates as editor	Exile press service
J.-G. Peltier	various *Paris* ... *Ambigu*	Oct. 1792–1795 1795–1802 1802–Nov. 1818	26 yrs 1 month
J. Regnier	*Courier de Londres* *Courier d'Ang.*	June 1802–1805 1805–Mar. 1815	13 yrs 2 months
[?] Gérard	*Courier de Londres*	1806?–9–13–1820+?	from 4 to 20 yrs ?
F. D. de Reynaud, comte de Montlosier	*J. France et d'Ang.* *Courier de Londres*	Jan.–June 1797 1797–June 1802	5 yrs 5 months
J.-L.-J. de Calonne	*Courier de Londres*	Oct. 1793–Dec. 95	5 yrs 2 months
J.-B. Couchery	*Courier de Londres* *Ambigu*	1802?–Apr. 1805? involved 1811–14	from 4–6 yrs probably
J. Mallet Du Pan	*Mercure Britannique*	Sept.1798–Mar.1800	1 yr 6 months
R. Heron	*Courier de Londres*	Apr.1805–1806 ?	1 yr 3 months max.
[?] Verduisant	*Courier de Londres*	Apr.–Oct. 1793	6 months

in his native Besançon, during its early days before it moved to the left. In 1795 he used another Besançon paper, *Le Neuf thermidor*, to publish a denial of allegations of fanaticism levelled against him because he protected priests from persecution, but suggestions that he edited the paper seem unfounded.[88]

Experienced men of letters were less prevalent among our collaborators and minor journalists. Only a handful had prior experience in journalism, but several more were publicists. Serani occasionally filled in for Morande on the *Courier de Londres* prior to being employed on the editorial staff in 1791.[89] Kirwan and his brothers produced a newspaper in Bordeaux from 1797 to 1801, despite official harrassment for their royalist views.[90] Royou probably worked on his brother's celebrated royalist paper, the *Ami du roi*, and Tilly had written for several right-wing papers including the *Actes des apôtres*.[91] One of the Bédées, like his more celebrated cousin Chateaubriand, is

---

1802); Morris Slavin, *The Hébertistes to the guillotine: anatomy of a 'conspiracy' in revolutionary France*, Baton Rouge 1994, 176.

[88] 'Jean-Baptiste Couchery', in *Biographie française*, ix; cf. Gough, *Newspaper press*, 122, and *Nouvelle Biographie générale*. On Couchery's early journalistic career see also Marcel Vogne, *La Presse périodique en Franche-Comté des origines à 1870*, Paris 1977–8, iii. 64–5, 120–4. I would like to thank Professor Gough for this reference.

[89] AAE, CPA 576, fo. 324, [Morande] to Barthelemy, 18 Mar. 1791; PRO, PC 1/127, piece 210, Swinton to Calonne, n.d. [late May or early June 1791].

[90] Gough, *Newspaper press*, 145–6. See also E. Labadie, *La Presse à Bordeaux pendant la révolution*, Bordeaux 1910. My thanks to Professor Gough for confirming that François-David was the unnamed third brother mentioned in his text, and referring me to Labadie's work.

[91] Murray, *Right-wing press*, 35–40, mentions several Royou family members who worked on the *Ami du roi*. For contributors to the *Actes des apôtres* see Maspero-Clerc, *Peltier*, 28n.

Table 4
Social status of journalists and collaborators on the French exile press

	Major journalists	Minor journalists	Known collaborators	Aggregate of whole sample
Nobles	2–3 (22–33%)	2–4 (22–44%)	9 (37.5%)	13–16 (31–38%)
Clergy	1 (11%)	2–4 (22–44%)	none	3–5 (7–12%)
Roturiers	6–7 (67–78%)	3–5 (33–56%)	15 (62.5%)	24–27 (57–64%)

described as a man of letters.[92] D'Antraigues, Tinseau and Calonne were all experienced political polemicists, and Pierre-François Fauche and his brother, Louis Fauche-Borel, had been professional publishers. As legislative deputies Malouet, Henri-Larivière and Pichegru had all published pamphlets and speeches. Although this amounted to substantial experience, none of these men could match the journalistic expertise which Mallet Du Pan, Peltier, Couchery and Regnier brought to London.

The exile pressmen were atypical of the émigrés in several respects. Career journalists, men of letters, professional counter-revolutionaries, their social backgrounds, political activism and financial success marked them out from their exiled compatriots. Among these spokesmen for religion and monarchy, nobles and clergymen were distinctly under-represented. Only two of the major journalists are known to have been nobles, but even between them there was a wide social gulf. The abbé Calonne was a member of the political élite of old regime France and moved in the brightest and most fashionable literary and courtly circles. His father was president of the parlement of Flanders, and his brother, Charles-Alexandre, had a glittering career as a civil servant before being appointed Controller-General of Finances (the equivalent of prime minister) in 1783. The abbé, a clergyman *malgré lui*, was a bibliophile, intellectual, connoisseur of art, *bon viveur* and *conseiller* at the parlement of Flanders. In contrast, Montlosier's family were chevaliers, the lowest rank in the French nobility, and came from the Auvergne. The title 'comte' was only conferred in 1815. Montlosier was, moreover, the youngest of twelve children, and lived in seclusion as a gentleman scholar for most of the 1780s writing a treatise on the extinct volcanoes of his native region. It is possible that Verduisant was also a noble, and may have been related to the marquis de Miran, whose family name, Verdusan, is strikingly similar. The second estate was better represented among the 'minor journalists' and 'collaborators' than among our 'major journalists'. Even so there were disproportionate numbers of *roturiers* (commoners) among the émigré pressmen.

The clergy was even worse represented, numbering only the abbé Calonne among the major journalists and between two and four more including the abbé Châteaugiron amongst the minor journalists. Heron had also had a religious training, but he abandoned the Church to pursue a career in letters.

---

[92] AAE, CPA 582, fo. 271, 'Projet de fabrication des faux assignats' [autumn 1792].

Table 5
Nationalities of journalists and collaborators

Nationalities	Major journalists	Minor journalists	Collaborators	Aggregate
French	6 (67%)	8 (89%)	16 (67%)	30 (71%)
French colonial	1 (11%)	none	none	1 (2%)
Swiss	1 (11%)	none	5 (20%)	6 (14%)
British	1 (11%)	none	2 (8%)	3 (7%)
Naturalised British	1 (11%)	none	1 (4%)	2 (5%)
Franco-Irish	none	1 (11%)	none	1 (2%)
Hungarian	none	none	1 (4%)	1 (2%)

As we have seen, the abbé Calonne's original vocation was little stronger. This lack of clergy among the personnel of the émigré press is remarkable given that about 50 per cent of French émigrés in England were in Roman Catholic holy orders. Moreover, Protestants were over-represented. They included the Mallets and Heron as well, presumably, as Dallas, d'Auerweck, the Fauche brothers (who came from the Prussian canton of Neuchâtel), and possibly some of the other Swiss collaborators. The lack of any women journalists or collaborators is also noteworthy, for there were a handful of notable women journalists and press entrepreneurs in both revolutionary France and Britain at this time. Moreover, many émigré women wrote of their experiences, or worked to support their families while in exile, so it is perhaps remarkable that none turned to professional journalism. In their absence, exile journalism remained an entirely masculine occupation, disproportionately dominated by secular *roturiers* (see table 4), but with surprisingly large contingents of Protestants in its ranks.

Moreover, three of the major journalists, Mallet Du Pan, Heron and Regnier, were not even Frenchmen. The same was true of some minor journalists and collaborators. Nevertheless, several of those born outside France, including both Regnier and Mallet Du Pan can be considered émigrés: Regnier because he was born a French subject and Mallet because he was listed and persecuted as an émigré. For although the law stipulated that only those born or naturalised French could be considered émigrés, Mallet's goods were confiscated and sold.[93] Thus only Heron among the major journalists lacked ties to France and could not be considered a victim of the revolution. The five Swiss collaborators likewise: Jean-Louis Mallet as the son of an émigré; La Corbière and Pradel as members of the French king's élite bodyguard of Swiss Guards; and the Fauche brothers through having become involved in counter-revolutionary conspiracies. François-David Kirwan, although he described himself as an Irishman in his correspondence with the British government, was an émigré of Franco-Irish descent. The case of the

---

93 AN, F^{7*} 105 lists Mallet Du Pan as an émigré. ADS, DQ^{10} c. 614, dos. 1677 inventories his confiscated goods, except books, and the prices they fetched.

Table 6
Social origins and professional backgrounds of major émigré journalists

Name	Birth date	Province/nation of origin	Family status	Previous careers
J. de Calonne	1743	Flanders, France	robe nobles	clergyman, lawyer
J.-B. Couchery	1768	Franche-Comté, France	commoners	teacher, politician, journalist
Gérard	c. 1763	France	commoners	unknown
R. Heron	1764	Scotland, U.K.	commoners	clergyman, writer, journalist
J. Mallet Du Pan	1749	Geneva, Switzerland	patrician commoners	academic, journalist
Montlosier	1755	Auvergne, France	minor nobles	gentleman scholar
J.-G. Peltier	1760	Brittany, France	commoners	financier, merchant, journalist
J. Regnier	c. 1756	Haiti, French colonial	commoners	lawyer, journalist
Verduisant	unknown	French	nobles ?	unknown

Hungarian baron, Louis d'Auerweck de Steillenfels, is perplexing. A former page to Joseph II, it is not clear how and why he became an agent and publicist for Louis XVI during the revolution and collaborated with Peltier in 1793–4. Although he married a noble émigrée who had lost her lands, that was not until 1798.

Family background may have predisposed several of our *roturier* journalists towards counter-revolution, and certainly influenced their writings. The families of both Peltier and Regnier grew rich in the colonial trade with Saint-Domingue and both probably suffered materially from the slave revolt in the colony to which revolutionary turmoil gave rise. Like his father, who dealt in coffee, slaves and sugar, and supplied arms to the American insurgents, the young Jean-Gabriel Peltier became involved in the Caribbean trade, and in 1787 travelled to Saint-Domingue.[94] While he was there his finance house in Paris went bankrupt. According to French police sources he suffered a second bankruptcy at Port-au-Prince and was harried from the island.[95] Regnier, also the son of a merchant, was a Creole born in Saint-Domingue, where he owned land.[96] He was possibly the author of the colonial articles in the *Actes des apôtres*, and in 1798 published three pamphlets on behalf of the dispossessed Saint-Domingue planters, attacking Pierre-Victor Malouet, self-styled mouthpiece of the colonists to the British government.[97]

Mallet Du Pan was the son of a Protestant pastor of French Huguenot

---

[94] Maspero-Clerc, *Peltier*, 1–14.
[95] *Ambigu* 52 (10 Sept. 1804), supplément, 17–18; AN, F⁷ 6330, dos. 6959, 'Note sur M. Peltier'.
[96] *Ambigu* 323 (20 Mar. 1812), 676; PRO, FO 27/44, Charmilly to Grenville, 27 Aug. 1795; *Courrier de Londres et de Paris* 21 (5/10 Aug. 1802).
[97] Copies of Regnier's three *Lettres d'un colon de Saint Domingue à M. Malouet* (all published in 1798) are held respectively in the British Library, the National Library of Scotland and PRO, WO 1/68. For a discussion of their polemical context see Griffiths, 'Malouet', ch. vii, esp. pp. 292–5. Griffiths was unaware that Regnier's second letter survived.

descent.[98] Although a member of Geneva's patrician class, he took the side of the disenfranchised *natifs* in the civil struggles of the 1760s and 1770s. When he defended their cause in print in 1771, his pamphlet was condemned by the city fathers and he had to flee.[99] However, by 1789 he was an affluent journalist and had already developed an anti-revolutionary credo.[100] Nothing is known of the families of Gérard and Verduisant, and biographical sources make no mention of Couchery's background. Although Heron's origins were humble (his father was a weaver), he had affluent relatives and was closely related to a 'celebrated philologist' named Alexander Murray.[101]

All the major émigré journalists were adults at the outbreak of the revolution. The abbé Calonne, the oldest, was born in 1743; Couchery, the youngest, in 1768. Among collaborators and minor journalists only Jean Lewis Mallet, born in 1775, is known to have been under 16 in 1789. Émigré journalism was thus an ageing profession, composed of men who grew up under the old regime. Naturally the major journalists were highly educated, and several had distinguished academic careers. Montlosier was educated at the Jesuit college at Clermont-Ferrand, where he remained even after the order's expulsion from France, but at fourteen entered the town's Sulpiciens' school. He rejected an army career to become a gentleman scholar and study anatomy, chemistry, law, theology and geology.[102] Mallet Du Pan attended the prestigious Auditoire in Geneva where he studied philosophy and law but opted for a career in letters. With Voltaire's patronage he gained a chair at the Academy of Hesse-Cassel, but soon abandoned it.[103] Couchery was a star pupil at the College at Besançon. Although only twenty-one when the revolution broke out, he was already employed as a private tutor. He accompanied his charges into exile, but eventually returned to avoid falling foul of the émigré laws, whereupon he threw himself into Jacobin politics.[104] The abbé Calonne studied classics and law before bowing to family pressure, entering the Church and completing his theological education at the Grand Seminary in Arras and Sulpicien seminary in Paris.[105] Peltier and Regnier both attended the Oratorian college in Nantes, where they were contemporaries of Joseph Fouché; the Oratorians' innovatory syllabus provided a historical and

---

[98] On Mallet Du Pan's ancestry see Charles Edward Mallet, *Family records*, privately printed, London 1917. See also Sayous, *Mémoires et correspondance*, i. 1–2; Acomb, *Mallet Du Pan*, 3–4.
[99] Ibid. 7–8. On his *Compte rendu de la défense des citoyens-bourgeois de Genève, adressé aux commissaires des représentants, par un citoyen natif*, Geneva 1771, see Acomb, *Mallet Du Pan*, 7–20, and Sayous, *Mémoires et correspondance*, i. 14ff.
[100] On the evolution of his political beliefs before 1789 see Acomb, *Mallet Du Pan*, chs i–v.
[101] Chambers, *Eminent Scotsmen*, 64.
[102] Montlosier, *Mémoires*, i. 21–35.
[103] Acomb, *Mallet Du Pan*, 25; Sayous, *Mémoires et correspondance*, i. 18–19.
[104] *Dictionnaire de biographie française*, ix; *Nouvelle Biographie générale*, ix; *Biographie universelle*, ix.
[105] Sr Marguerite-Marie, *Abbé Calonne*, 3–9, 12–15.

literary grounding that served them well in later life.¹⁰⁶ Regnier may have gone on to study law. Heron attended his parish school and Edinburgh University, where he studied for the Church and scraped a living teaching 'young persons at all periods in the course of education from the alphabet to the highest branches of science and literature' as well as writing and translating.¹⁰⁷ None of the émigré journalists seems to have been educated for counter-revolution. Although most of them had studied traditional subjects such as law, theology, philosophy or classics, there is little reason to consider their training conservative. Some had received a very modern education, others developed as autodidacts or were strongly influenced by the *philosophes*. Nothing in their educational backgrounds separates them from the revolutionary élite. Moreover, most either welcomed the revolution initially or supported earlier revolutionary or resistance movements.

By the start of 1789 Mallet Du Pan was a respected professional journalist, editing the political pages of the prestigious *Mercure de France*. The abbé Calonne, though well-known in court and literary circles, had fallen from grace with his brother and joined him in exile in London. Couchery was an obscure private tutor, Regnier a *conseilleur* at the *Cour des aides* in the parlement of Paris. Montlosier had finished his treatise on volcanoes and was looking for new challenges, while Peltier was still suffering from his financial problems and looking for a means to re-establish his fortunes. Heron was still hoping for clerical preferment in Scotland and, unlike the others, had little to hope for from the outbreak of revolution and the opportunities it provided.

The other major journalists seized these opportunities. Several of them became involved in revolutionary politics, and three were elected deputies to various revolutionary assemblies. Montlosier and the abbé Calonne were members of the Estates-General; Couchery was elected to the Conseil de Cinq-cents in 1795. The abbé Calonne stood for election hoping that his brother would be recalled from exile and re-habilitated. He had reason for optimism, for Calonne's recent *Etat de France* had reputedly been well-received at court, and there were rumours that Necker was no longer in favour.¹⁰⁸ Montlosier dreamed of a political career, and aligned himself with Malouet, Mounier, Lally-Tollendal and the moderate *monarchien* faction in the Estates-General.¹⁰⁹ Peltier, too, responded enthusiastically to the revolution. According to police reports he was 'one of the most ardent activists of the Palais Royale' and 'one of the first to hoist the colours of rebellion' and

---

106 *Ambigu* 323 (20 Mar. 1812), 676. On the Oratorian school of Saint-Clément at Nantes see Maspero-Clerc, *Peltier*, 3–4. *Joseph Fouché* (1759–1820) was a *terroriste*, regicide, notorious dechristianiser and Napoleonic police minister. Peltier claimed to have been 'écolier de Fouché' in Peltier, *Trial*, 244, and describes his bullying ways in *Paris* 245 (4 Feb. 1802), 515*. However, Fouché was senior to Peltier by one year only.
107 Chambers, *Eminent Scotsmen*.
108 *Dictionary of Canadian biography*, vi.
109 On the *monarchiens* during the emigration see Griffiths, *Centre perdu*, 9–159.

march on the Bastille on 14 July 1789.[110] Likewise, despite his involvement with the right-wing *Actes des apôtres*, Regnier had a long flirtation with the extreme left, funding and collaborating on the comte de Proly's *Cosmopolite* newspaper.[111] It nearly cost him his life. After four months on the run, Proly was arrested in February 1794 and executed with the Hébertists the following month.[112] It was alleged at his trial that he was an Austrian agent and that the *Cosmopolite* and his extreme patriotism were just means to mislead the people.[113] Although historians have tended to dismiss these allegations, circumstantial evidence hints that they may have been well-founded.[114] Regnier was also imprisoned for fourteen months, probably escaping execution only due to the fall of Robespierre.[115] Couchery too was a revolutionary activist. He threw himself into Jacobin revolutionary politics and was elected *procureur* at Besançon. Although he favoured the execution of Louis XVI, he denounced Parisian Jacobin excesses and the *journées* of 31 May–2 June 1793 and was stripped of his post. However he escaped arrest and retired discreetly to teach. After Thermidor he re-emerged, was elected *procureur-syndic* of Doubs and led the persecution of local Robespierrists. He also protected non-juror priests and émigrés who had returned illegally. Thus by the time he was elected to the Conseil des Cinq-cents in 1795 he was already implicated in conservative politics. It was only natural therefore that he should befriend General Pichegru and support reconciliation with the Bourbons.[116] Several of our 'collaborators' were also members of revolutionary legislatures, namely d'Antraigues, Henri-Larivière, Malouet and Pichegru.

Having seen the light on the road to Damascus and rejected radicalism or revolution, the major émigré journalists wrote with the zeal of apostates. First to turn was Mallet du Pan, who by the 1780s had become convinced of the dangers of demagoguery and the incompatibility of liberty and democracy, a conviction reinforced by the experience of living and writing in revolutionary Paris between 1789 and 1792.[117] The abbé Calonne's involvement in opposition politics under the old regime was probably only ever lukewarm. When Chancellor Maupeou abolished the parlements in 1771, he protested and refused to sit on one of the new *conseils supérieurs* which replaced them,

---

110 AN, F^7 6330, dos. 6959, 'Note sur M. Peltier'.
111 Ibid. and Slavin, *Hébertistes*, 176; *Courier de Londres et de Paris* 21 (5/10 Aug. 1802); *Cosmopolite*.
112 Slavin, *Hébertistes*, 176–7.
113 Ibid. 176n.
114 Among Calonne's papers, PRO, PC 1/124, piece 263, suggestively offers 'information provided by Proly'; Peltier, CP 71 (15 Apr. 1794), indicates that Proly supplied information on left-wing colleagues to the *Actes des apôtres*. Slavin, *Hébertistes*, 176, does not rule out the possibility that Austria helped fund the *Cosmopolite*.
115 PRO, FO 27/44, Charmilly to Grenville, 27 Aug. 1795. It is clear from the details supplied that Charmilly's unnamed friend, recently arrived in England, is Regnier. French police records do not seem to record Regnier's arrest, trial or release.
116 *Biographie française*, xi.
117 Acomb, *Mallet Du Pan*, chs i–vi.

but such protests probably stemmed more from conservatism than a commitment to patriotism. Nor does the abbé's active support for the campaign to stage Beaumarchais's 'not so revolutionary play' *The Marriage of Figaro* indicate a strong commitment to radicalism,[118] and his involvement with revolutionary politics was only momentary.[119] His election for the *bailliage* of Melun was the result of calculation. When Necker was restored after the fall of the Bastille, the abbé had no more to hope for and fled, terrified, no doubt, that the mob would turn on him.[120] Montlosier and Peltier were next to turn against the revolution. Montlosier and the *monarchiens* became increasingly isolated after the rejection of their constitutional programme in the September debates, and were stranded on the right of the Assembly as the revolution lurched to the left. Peltier, after a brief career as an anti-aristocratic and anti-clerical pamphleteer which his enemies never forgot, turned against the revolution after the October days.[121] He began to assert that Mirabeau and the duc d'Orléans were behind a plot to depose the Bourbon dynasty, a conviction he repeated frequently in succeeding years.[122] However, he long remained critical of the emigration and only joined the *pur* camp in 1798. In contrast, Couchery seems to have turned against the revolution for fear of mob-rule only during the Terror. But unless we accept the hypothesis that Proly's *Cosmopolite* was a mere cover for counter-revolutionary espionage, Regnier did not reject the revolution until after his arrest in 1794. His conversion may have been through opportunism or necessity, but probably genuine, for he had suffered more than any émigré journalist at its hands. It had stripped him of his office in the parlement, his lands in Saint-Domingue, his newspaper and his liberty.

The journalists were deeply scarred by their experience during the revolution, and Regnier was not alone in having experienced harrassment or violence. The abbé Calonne was seized and arrested at Nogent-sur-Seine while fleeing France, but was released when the National Assembly told his captors that they had no jurisdiction over him.[123] Mallet Du Pan and Peltier experienced repeated intimidation, including visits from the infamous Zoppi deputation of 15 November 1790, which called on right-wing Parisian jour-

---

[118] Darnton, 'High enlightenment', 15.
[119] On the abbé's campaign for Beaumarchais see Sr Marguerite-Marie, *Abbé Calonne*, 17–19; Proschwitz and Proschwitz, *Beaumarchais*, i. 171; Hervé Biron, 'Un Ami de Beaumarchais aux Trois-Rivières', *Le Nouvelliste* (Trois-Rivières), 12 Dec. 1949. For a copy of this article see AUTR, pièce II–B–6–171.
[120] CL xxvi/10 (5 Aug. 1789).
[121] See Guilhermy's letter to the editor in CL lvi/20 (7 Sept. 1804), which styles Peltier 'author of the *Coup d'equinoxe*, a revolutionary pamphlet that appeared in Paris in 1789'.
[122] Maspero-Clerc, *Peltier*, 15–26; Jean-Gabriel Peltier, *Le Coup d'equinoxe d'octobre 1789: lettre de M. P. . . de Paris à M. M. . . son ami négociant de Nantes*, Paris 1789, and *Domine, salvum fac regem*, Paris 1789; DTP ii. 10–23, 98–9n; CP 7 (16 Nov. 1793); Paris 9 (1 Aug. 1795), 3–10n.
[123] CL xxvi/10 (5 Aug. 1789).

nalists to ask them to stop their insults, lies and attempts to lead the people astray.[124] Mallet's employer, Panckoucke, stood by him when patriots called for his dismissal, but Mallet's daughter never forgot the visitations of angry revolutionary mobs calling her father by the chilling name 'Mallet pendu' (Mallet hanged).[125] Peltier's journal was several times denounced or seized in raids on bookshops, and after the fall of the monarchy the author spent several weeks in hiding before escaping to England.[126] Other counter-revolutionary journalists were not so lucky. One of the most celebrated, François Suleau, died in a fracas after being arrested on 10 August 1792, and another, de Rozoi, was executed a fortnight later. Others were arrested.[127] Likewise Couchery was deprived of his post in the Terror, and was proscribed after the republican *coup d'état* of 18 fructidor of the year V (4 September 1797).[128] In Bordeaux the newspaper edited by Kirwan and his brothers also suffered a succession of seizures and prosecutions, and changed title many times to try to reduce harassment.[129]

The statistical pattern of emigration suggests how atypical the major journalists were as a group when compared with rank-and-file émigrés. The dates of emigration given in table 7 bear little resemblance to the pattern described in the introduction. Only Peltier, who reached England in late September 1792, was among the great wave of refugees who left France between late 1792 and mid-1793. The abbé Calonne left France in the very first wave of emigration, and served his brother and the émigré court at Coblenz by raising loans in Geneva and Genoa before arriving in London in early 1793.[130] Montlosier emigrated after the closure of the Constituent Assembly in 1791, but met with a frosty welcome at Coblenz and returned to France.[131] He returned to Coblenz in April 1792, and although he still encountered hostility, especially from the Calonne brothers, he fought in the émigré cavalry in the campaign of 1792.[132] After the disastrous Valmy campaign he left the princes' service and spent two years wandering on the continent before arriving in England in September 1794.[133] Mallet Du Pan left France permanently in April 1792, charged by Louis XVI with a secret mission to persuade the allied powers to guarantee France's territorial integrity and limit their war aims to the restoration of royal authority. Mallet believed that his

---

124 Murray, *Right-wing press*, 98.
125 Mallet, *Retrospective*, 153–4; Murray, *Right-wing press*, 102. This horrifying pun was apparently coined by Camille Desmoulins.
126 Murray, *Right-wing press*, 90–1; Maspero-Clerc, 'Vicissitudes'; *DTP* ii. 221.
127 Murray, *Right-wing press*, 96–7. On Suleau's death see *DTP* i. 101–5.
128 *Dictionnaire de biographie française*, ix.
129 Gough, *Newspaper press*, 145–6.
130 Lacour-Gayet, *Calonne*, 319. On the Genoese loan see PRO, PC 1/126, pieces 640–52.
131 Montlosier, *Souvenirs*, chs i–iii.
132 Ibid. chs iv–viii; ACC, Z tom. CXXV, fo. 47, is a broadsheet in which Montlosier complains about 'the animosity of certain gentlemen'.
133 Montlosier, *Souvenirs*, chs viii–xiii.

Table 7
Key dates in the emigration of major journalists

Name	Date of emigration	Arrived in England	Definitive return to France
Abbé Calonne	July 1789	1793	did not return
Couchery	Sept. 1797	c. 1800	1814
Gérard	unknown	unknown	unknown
Heron	not applicable	not applicable	not applicable
Mallet Du Pan	Apr. 1792	1798	died in exile 1800
Montlosier	1791/Apr. 1792	Sept. 1794	June 1802
Peltier	Sept. 1792	Sept. 1792	1820
Regnier	1795	1795	naturalised British
Verduisant	unknown	Mar. 1793	unknown

mission had been a success and was bitterly disappointed when Prussia and Austria issued the reactionary Brunswick manifesto.[134] However, although in contact with the British government from 1793, he only arrived in Britain in the summer of 1798, by which time he was convinced no safe havens for political writers remained on continental Europe.[135] In contrast Regnier fled to England immediately after his release from prison in 1795,[136] and in 1804 took the unusual step of naturalising.[137] Couchery lived in Germany from 1797 to 1800 with his friend Pichegru. Although invited to return to France after Brumaire, he returned only briefly to put his affairs in order, before travelling on to London where he rejoined Pichegru.

Since careers and ideology set some of the journalists apart from the rank-and-file of the émigrés, several were treated as outsiders in French refugee circles. Mallet Du Pan and Montlosier found themselves vilified for their moderation and constitutional monarchic views. Their sense of alienation from émigré society is described by Montlosier, Jean-Louis Mallet and Malouet in their memoirs, although there is reason to think that, with hindsight, they exaggerated (see chapter 3). Calonne and his brother were also attacked in 1795–6 for daring to suggest that old regime France had lacked a constitution, and that discontent inside France should not be taken as evidence of support for royalism.[138] Likewise Couchery seems to have felt alienated from his fellow French refugees. In one French source he is

---

134 Sayous, *Mémoires et correspondance*, i. 280–317; Acomb, *Mallet Du Pan*, 250–3.
135 Sayous, *Mémoires et correspondance*, ii. 358–61; Acomb, *Mallet Du Pan*, 265–7.
136 PRO, FO 27/44, Charmilly to Grenville, 27 Aug. 1795.
137 See his letters patent of denization in PRO, HO 1/6.
138 Charles-Alexandre de Calonne, *Le Tableau de l'Europe en novembre 1795; et pensées sur ce qu'on a fait et qu'on n'aurait pas dû faire*, London 1796. The text of this pamphlet first appeared in the CL xxxviii/33–52 (27 Oct. 1795–29 Dec. 1795). In response to émigré attacks, Calonne published an appendix in CL xxxix/2 (5 Jan. 1796). The most significant reply to Calonne was A.-J.-B.-R. Auget de Montyon's *Rapport fait à sa majesté, Louis XVIII (sur le livre intitulé Tableau de l'Europe)*, Constance 1796. The debate between them was

described as a 'revolutionary deputy become editor of the *Courier de Londres* . . . having little regard for the nobles, émigrés and courtiers among whom he is held in low esteem'.[139] Peltier and Regnier seem to have been much more popular with their fellow émigrés, despite their involvement in a succession of personal disputes and vitriolic exchanges. The consideration in which they were held was not entirely political: both were good company, highly gregarious *hommes d'esprit*.

Like other émigrés, some of the journalists struggled desperately when they first arrived. Most tried a number of expedients before resorting to journalism. Peltier, imaginative as ever, made a virtue of necessity, and commissioned a miniature mahogany guillotine with which he both offered a macabre show and slaughtered his dinner. For a crown for a front seat or 1s. for a bench at the rear, a daily audience could watch him behead a goose.[140] Montlosier worked as junior partner with a M. de Leutre in an agency established to handle the legal requirements and correspondence of the émigrés with France.[141] Regnier supplied information to the British government, hoping, no doubt, to be rewarded.[142] A few collaborators were reduced to desperation: for example, the Bédée brothers taught French and sold artificial flowers in the street.[143] However, for the most part the émigré journalists and their collaborators were among the wealthiest and most successful émigrés in London, and many of them made a lucrative living from counter-revolutonary activism.

Many émigré pressmen were married and had families to support (see table 8), but only three of these families are important to this study.[144] Mallet Du Pan was a dutiful husband and father of three, a son Jean-Louis and two daughters. His marriage to Françoise Vallier was a love match of long standing and his children adored him. Peltier married Anne Andoe, who was several years his junior, in 1799. Her family was Irish and had owned a distillery at Bordeaux before emigrating in 1792.[145] Peltier did not share

---

discussed at length in the Parisian press, for example in *Les Nouvelles politiques* (15 Aug. 1796), and by Peltier in *Paris* 64 (23 July 1796), 70 (27 Aug. 1796). See also ch. 4 below.
[139] AAE, mem./docs France 620, 'Couchery'.
[140] Montlosier, *Souvenirs*, 227.
[141] Ibid. 203–5. On de Leutre see Montlosier, *Mémoires*, i. 208. The agency advertised in CL xxxvi/44 (28 Nov. 1794).
[142] PRO, FO 27/44, Charmilly to Grenville, 27 Aug. 1795.
[143] AN, F^7 6480, Mémoire of Prigent to Fouché [early July 1808].
[144] Of the other pressmen, Montlosier was a childless widower; Heron, Couchery and the abbé Calonne never married; d'Antraigues, Béhague, Calonne, Dutheil, Fauche-Borel, Pierre-François Fauche, Henri-Larivière, Kirwan, Malouet, Pichegru, Swinton, Tilly, Tinseau and Tromelin all had families. D'Auerweck, Jean-Louis Mallet and presumably the youngster La Corbière were single. So, it appears, were the Bédée brothers. Information is lacking on Verduisant and Gérard, Velley and the remaining 'collaborators'.
[145] AAE, CPA 601, fo. 96, claim of Catherine Andoe for restitution of property seized during the revolution, 27 ventôse XI (3 Mar. 1803); PRO, FO 27/65, Catherine Andoe to Addington, 20 Apr. 1802.

Table 8
Marital status of journalists and collaborators

	Major journalists	**Minor journalists**	**Collaborators**	**Total**
Married lay	3 (33%)	2 (22%)	13 (54%)	18 (43%)
Unmarried lay	3 (33%)	0	5 (21%)	8 (19%)
Celibate clergy	1 (11%)	3* (33%)	0	4* (9.5%)
Unknown	2 (22%)	4* (44%)	6 (25%)	12* (28.5%)
Sample size	9	9	24	42 (100%)

* These figures assume three clergy and three laymen among *Mercure de France* editors; the 'unmarried' total includes widowers.

Mallet's marital virtues. He had no children and seems to have abused his spouse shamelessly. In 1804 the French spy Méhée de la Touche claimed that Peltier prostituted his wife, sending her to visit wealthy bachelors in search of loans and boasting of her 'secret talents'. However, Méhée's more explicit allegations are probably malicious and are not corroborated elsewhere.[146] Nevertheless, Jean-Gabriel seems to have been habitually unfaithful and to have contracted syphilis.[147] By 1815 the Peltiers were living separately, though apparently without animosity.[148] Regnier cohabited for fourteen years with a woman he called his 'wife', and although the French ambassador doubted that they were legally married, they appear to have been devoted to one another.[149] In 1810, when his 'wife' died, Regnier was inconsolable, and for days afterwards their only daughter accompanied him everywhere.[150] Since most of the wealthier journalists and collaborators were married men, it

---

[146] See Mehée de la Touche, *Alliance des Jacobins*, 69. Maspero-Clerc, who did not know the story's provenance, dismissed it (*Peltier*, 97) on the grounds that Fontanes would not have received a woman of ill-repute, but Méhée's details are usually reliable, if highly coloured.

[147] AAE, mem./docs France 620, 'Peltier' [c. 1813], which describes him as 'covered with ulcers resulting from his misconduct' is roughly contemporaneous with a letter, PRO, FO 27/94, Peltier to [Hamilton or Cooke] 19 Jan. 1813, complaining of ill-health.

[148] On Peltier's marriage see Maspero-Clerc, *Peltier*, esp. pp. 94–9.

[149] See AAE, CPA 600, fo. 137, Andréossi to Talleyrand, 11 nivôse XI (31 Dec. 1802); mem./docs France 644, fo. 133, [Regnier] to D'Antraigues, 1 Oct. 1810. The latter is among several unattributed letters, but the distinctive angular handwriting is undoubtedly Regnier's. It records that 'for fourteen years' his 'amie' had 'only one thought, the well being of me and my child' and describes her as 'the truest, most honest, best heart that ever existed'. Note that Regnier always refers to his 'amie' rather than 'épouse' or 'femme', and never mentions her name.

[150] See AAE, mem./docs France 644, fo. 133, [Regnier] to D'Antraigues, 1 Oct. 1810.

is possible to conclude tentatively that the rewards, risks and rigours of émigré journalism were quite compatible with family life.

When the vast majority of surviving émigrés returned to France after the Napoleonic amnesty of April 1802, Montlosier went with them. Like many of his compatriots he had suffered terribly from homesickness, and never warmed to England and the English.[151] But Montlosier was also drawn ideologically towards Bonapartism, and from May 1800 he was in communication with the French government, although he expressed a desire to avoid becoming 'the slave of Bonaparte'.[152] In March 1801 he visited Paris at the request of the administration, and seems to have obtained permission from Artois to sound out Napoleon on the possibility of a Bourbon restoration.[153] On arrival, Talleyrand's secretary informed Montlosier of plans to recall the émigrés, re-establish the Roman Catholic Church and an honours system, and create a civil code. Montlosier was thus himself seduced by the new regime.[154] On a further visit in March 1802, Montlosier provided information on the émigré community to help Fouché in the preparation of the amnesty.[155] In June he launched a new journal, the *Courrier de Londres et de Paris*, which despite Montlosier's claims to the contrary was clearly produced entirely in France.[156] Montlosier showed too much independence for the regime to tolerate his journal.[157] Nor were his well-meaning attempts to criticise the *Code Civil* welcomed.[158] The paper was suppressed, but in compensation Montlosier received a pension.[159] Montlosier's reaction to Bonapartism was not unique among émigré journalists. In the months before he died Mallet Du

---

[151] See Montlosier, *Souvenirs*, ch. xiii.
[152] See BPUG, MS. Fr. 212, fos 22–4, Montlosier to Fontanes, 20 Aug. 1800. This important letter seems to have escaped the attention of biographers. Montlosier's first communication with Otto, the French agent in London (AAE, CPA 593, fo. 393), was dated 14 May 1800.
[153] For the best discussion of this issue see Miramon-Fitzjames, 'Montlosier', 123–4.
[154] AAE, dossiers de personnel, vol. 52 'Montlosier', fos 263–5, Montlosier to prince de Polignac, 15 Aug. 1829. *Charles-Maurice de Talleyrand-Périgord* (1754–1838), former bishop of Autun, was a diplomat in London 1792–3, in exile 1793–5, French foreign minister 1797–8, Nov. 1799–Jan. 1809, May 1814–15, and chief minister July–Sept 1815.
[155] AN, F⁷ 6286, dos. 5846, report of the Préfet de Police to Fouché, 10 floréal X (30 Apr. 1802).
[156] AAE, dossiers de personnel, vol. 52 'Montlosier', fo. 258, Montlosier to Talleyrand, 3 Aug. 1814, confirms that Montlosier only had an information bureau in London. The prospectus for the *Courrier de Londres et de Paris* is dated London, 26 June 1802. The first number is dated Paris 1 July/London 26 June 1802.
[157] On the paper's relations with the French regime see Miramon Fitzjames, 'Montlosier', 136–43.
[158] For his critique see especially *Courrier de Londres et de Paris* 1 (1 July 1802), 9–12 (17–23 July 1802), 23–4 (14–16 Aug. 1802), 27 (22 Aug. 1802). (Datelines are for Paris; putative London datelines were five days earlier.) See also the articles in CL xlix/44 (2 June 1801); l/5 (16 Sept. 1801).
[159] See AAE, dossiers de personnel, vol. 52 'Montlosier', fo. 260, Montlosier to Talleyrand, 11 July 1815; fos 263–5, Montlosier to Polignac, 15 Aug. 1829.

Pan also offered guarded praise of Napoleon's government. But for each journalist who rallied to Napoleon there were others, including Peltier, Regnier, Couchery and the editors of the *Mercure de France*, who attacked him relentlessly. After the peace of Amiens this torrent of abuse took on a deeper political significance as Napoleon waged a diplomatic campaign to silence Peltier and Regnier which culminated in Peltier standing trial for seditious libel in February 1803 and contributed to the outbreak of war the following May (see chapter 3).

Many of the émigré pressmen were professional activists who participated in both journalism and a range of other profitable and closely related counter-revolutionary activities. Indeed, the list of known collaborators and minor journalists is a virtual *Who's who* of royalist spies and agents operating from England. It includes the celebrated spy-master d'Antraigues who was mysteriously murdered in 1812, and the gullible and frequently inept royalist agent Fauche-Borel, who unwittingly sent his own nephew, Charles-Samuel Vittel, to his death in 1807.[160] However, the émigré princes' main agent in London in the 1790s and early 1800s was Dutheil, who masterminded many of their conspiracies. One of his agents, Alphonse Durfort-Boissières, was his intermediary with Peltier and Regnier. Another, Louis d'Auerweck, a professional conspirator and double-agent, had connections with the *Chouans* and the royalist agent Brottier, undertook several missions to France during the 1790s and was suspected of involvement in the assassination of French negotiators at Rastadt on 28 April 1799.[161] The most famous and unfortunate of all royalist conspirators, however, was the republican general and politician Pichegru who was 'recruited' by Fauche-Borel in 1795, compromised by papers captured on d'Antraigues in Italy in 1797 and deported to Guyana

---

[160] The best studies of d'Antraigues are Colin Duckworth, *The d'Antraigues phenomenon: the making and breaking of a revolutionary royalist espionage agent*, Newcastle-upon-Tyne 1986, and Jacques Godechot, *Le Comte d'Antraigues*, Paris 1986. On Fauche-Borel see G. Lenôtre, *Two royalist spies of the French revolution*, London 1924; Peter de Polnay, *Napoleon's police*, London 1970, 217–33; Philip Mansel, *Louis XVIII*, London 1981, 149–50. In 1806 the French police agent Perlet convinced Fauche-Borel that a 'royalist committee' existed in Paris. When Vittel, sent to meet with them, was arrested and shot, Fauche-Borel accused Puisaye and d'Antraigues of betraying him. Perlet, exposed at the restoration, launched bold printed attacks on Fauche-Borel. After years of litigation against Perlet, Fauche-Borel committed suicide in 1827.

[161] AN, F^7 6415, dos. 8341; F^7 6445, no. 9382 (many pieces in this large and confused dossier are unsigned, undated and lack numbers, making precise references impossible); PRO, FO 27/53, d'Auerweck to Dutheil, 2 June 1798; FO 27/48, Dutheil to Grenville, 27 July 1796. In 1797 d'Auerweck apparently both attempted to recruit the French agent Colleville's spy ring to work for the British, and offered to work for the French. Later he appears to have served the Prussians and the Russians. Napoleon had him incarcerated in the Temple from 1807 until the restoration. On his activities see also PRO, FO 27/51, Dutheil to Canning, 10 Mar. 1797; Dutheil to Hammond, 18 Mar. 1797; Dutheil to Grenville, 29 Mar. 1797; and two notes of d'Auerweck (undated); FO 27/52, 'Suite du compte rendu d'Auerweck', 18 Aug. 1797; AAE, CPA 590, fos 204–5, 287–93, 335, correspondence of Colleville with the French foreign ministry.

after Fructidor. From there he escaped to Germany before moving to London where he became involved in Cadoudal's conspiracies. He was arrested while on a secret mission to Paris in 1804, and died mysteriously in his prison cell before he could be tried.[162] Other counter-revolutionary activists include Tromelin, who was seized with Sidney Smith during a spying mission and escaped death as an émigré *rentré* only by passing himself off as a French Canadian, and Henri-Larivière, who served as an intermediary between the ill-fated Armand de Chateaubriand, Dutheil and the ministry.[163] The Bédée brothers, who were implicated in printing false *assignats* and attacks on a mail coach near Le Havre in 1803; Tinseau, who sent the British government numerous memoranda on military affairs; and Malouet who advised them on the affairs of Saint-Domingue should also perhaps be considered counter-revolutionary activists.[164]

The major journalists were also heavily implicated in counter-revolution, subversion and conspiracy. The abbé Calonne manufactured counterfeit *assignats* for the émigré court at Coblenz and the British, and provided supplies for the British and émigré forces as they prepared for the expedition to Quiberon Bay in 1795.[165] Mallet Du Pan was paid for his political correspondence with the courts of Lisbon (1795–8),[166] Berlin (1794–9)[167] and Vienna (1794–8),[168] and with Lord Elgin, the British minister in The Hague (1793–4).[169] His bulletins provided a mix of intelligence and penetrating

---

[162] On Pichegru see B. Saugier, *Pichegru: histoire d'un suicide*, n.p. 1992; H. Caudrillier, *La Traihison de Pichegru*, Paris 1908; Lenôtre, *Two royalist spies*.

[163] Michael Durey, 'The British secret service and the escape of Sir Sidney Smith from Paris in 1798', *History* lxxxiv (1999), 437–57; AAE, mem./docs France 620, 'Henri-Larivière'; AN, AF^{IV*} 1710, fos 230–1; PRO, FO 27/107, Henri-Larivière to Castlereagh [memoir], 25 July 1814; FO 27/91, Billaud de Veaux to Lord Keats, Plymouth, 27 July 1812.

[164] On the Bédées see AAE, CPA 582, fo. 271, 'Projet de fabrication des faux assignats' [unsigned, 1792]; AN, F^7 3703, minute of police bulletin, 19 ventôse XI (7 Mar. 1803). For some of Tinseau's numerous memoirs see PRO, FO 27/69; Canning papers, bundle 58a. On Malouet's advices see Griffiths, 'Malouet', chs vi–vii.

[165] Lacour-Gayet, *Calonne*, 390; Hutt, *Chouannerie*, i. 167; BL, MS Add. 37,859, J.-L.-J. de Calonne to Windham, n.d. [c. 28 July 1795].

[166] Sayous, *Mémoires et correspondance*, ii. 111–12, gives the dates as 1795–7, but BPUG, MS. Fr. 1269/1, fos 35–6, Da Souza to Mallet Du Pan, 10 Apr. 1798, and Mallet papers, Balliol College, Oxford, #14, Da Souza to Mallet Du Pan, 12 Oct., 3 Nov. 1798, show that the paid correspondence continued into 1798. For published selections of this correspondence see J. de Pins (ed.), 'La Correspondance de Mallet Du Pan avec la cour de Lisbonne', *AHRF* xxxvi (1964), 469–77; xxxvii (1965), 468–84; xxxviii (1966), 84–94.

[167] Copies of this correspondence are in the Mallet papers, #5.

[168] Published as Michel André (ed.), *Correspondance inédite de Mallet du Pan avec la cour de Vienne*, Paris 1884.

[169] These reports may be consulted in Oscar Browning (ed.), *The despatches of Lord Gower*, Cambridge 1885, 314–71, and HMC, *Report on the manuscripts of J. B. Fortescue, esq., preserved at Dropmore*, London 1892–1927, iii. 491–508.

analysis: effectively Mallet was practising both espionage and political consultancy.[170]

In 1794 Mallet acted as the intermediary of Théodore de Lameth, offering the British government a proposal to topple the Committee of Public Safety. The plan came to nothing, but led to a lifelong friendship with the British agent William Wickham.[171]

Peltier's activities were less ambitious. Soon after his arrival in London he began domiciliary visits to discover imposters, spies and those of suspect loyalty among the émigrés.[172] In 1793 he and d'Auerweck were involved in an abortive conspiracy to rescue Marie-Antoinette from prison. Historians have seen the plot as nothing more than a means to extort money from Charlotte Atkins, the rich and romantic former actress who bankrolled the rescue attempt, but Peltier's biographer argues boldly that surviving evidence suggests he was acting in good faith. However, she doubts the intentions of his co-conspirators.[173] Peltier also supplied the British government with news from his sources in Brittany and the Vendée.

Regnier, too, supplied intelligence to the British government in 1795 and 1798, and in 1804 he was duped into recommending a French double agent, the chevalier Sandillaud Du Bouchet, to the British government.[174] From 1806 d'Antraigues, who was sent to London with orders from the tsar to subscribe for a bulk order of the *Courier d'Angleterre*, became Regnier's patron and close friend. French spy reports allege Regnier was involved in 'all the conspiracies of d'Antraigues, Fauche-Borel, Puisaye and Danican with the British ministers Canning and Castlereagh'.[175] In 1808 he acted as a contact for Armand de Chateaubriand and gave him the orders for his fatal

---

[170] For analysis see Sayous, *Mémoires et correspondance*, ii. 92, 111–12; Acomb, *Mallet Du Pan*, 255–9.

[171] Sayous, *Mémoires et correspondance*, ii, ch. iv; Acomb, *Mallet Du Pan*, 264. On Wickham's mission see Harvey Mitchell, *The underground war against revolutionary France: the missions of William Wickham, 1794–1800*, Oxford 1965, esp. pp. 40ff. on Mallet Du Pan's role; W. R. Fryer, *Republic or restoration in France? 1794–1797*, Manchester 1965. Comte Théodore de Lameth (1756–1854), eldest of the Lameth brothers, was a right-wing deputy in the Legislative Assembly. He fled to Switzerland in 1793.

[172] AAE, CPA 582, fo. 356, Noël to Lebrun, 12 Oct. 1792.

[173] Maspero-Clerc, *Peltier*, 100–17; cf. J. B. Morton, *Camille Desmoulins and other studies of the French revolution*, London 1950, 173.

[174] PRO, FO 95/2/4, fo. 410, Regnier to Grenville, 26 June 1798; FO 27/70, fos 554–7, Regnier to [?Hammond], 23 Sept. 1804, enclosing Du Bouchet's plan; fos 580–2, Regnier to Hammond, 23 Oct. 1804, enclosing Du B. (Bouchet) to Regnier, 23 Oct. 1804. AAE, CPA 602, fos 196–209, 'Details et observations sur mon voyage' is Du Bouchet's anonymous account of his trip. On Sandillaud Du Bouchet see also Olivier Blanc, *Les Espions de la révolution et de l'empire*, Paris 1995, 257–61.

[175] E. d'Hauterive (ed.), *La Police secrète du premier empire*, Paris 1908–68, iv, para. 524, bulletin of 29 June 1808. Comte Joseph-Geneviève de Puisaye (1754–1827), Norman soldier, Chouan leader and organiser of the Quiberon expedition, emigrated to London in 1794. General Auguste Danican, commander of insurgent forces of Paris sections in Vendémiaire rising, fled to Britain thereafter. George Canning (1770–1827), was British foreign secretary

mission;[176] and he was also, apparently, d'Auerweck's intermediary with Dutheil.[177] In 1809 Regnier introduced a merchant named Le Roy to the British ministry to supply commercial intelligence and smuggle grain from France.[178] The captured royalist agent Prigent also confessed to links with Regnier in 1808.[179] Thus, in Regnier's case, the fine distinction between the roles of journalist and spy disappeared altogether. The same may have been true, briefly, of Couchery, who was Pichegru's right-hand man, and whose brother Victor was among those arrested with Pichegru in 1804. Thereafter Couchery fell out with the leading émigré conspirators. Henri-Larivière accused him of betraying Pichegru, and Fauche-Borel enviously alleged he had embezzled funds belonging to the general's estate.[180]

Journalism and counter-revolutionary activism could prove lucrative. Mallet Du Pan, Peltier and Regnier lived as gentlemen on the products of their pens, and Calonne proudly boasted that his brother was among those émigrés who 'earned their living' from wages rather than subsisting on the 1s. per day provided by the British government. The same was true of the other editors of the *Courier de Londres*, although Montlosier's *Journal de France et d'Angleterre* left him out of pocket. In addition, émigré journalists supplemented their income with payments from patrons, government pensions and official translation work, especially after 1803. Yet although émigré journalists often enjoyed substantial incomes, financial disaster was never far away. Interruptions in their journals through illness or chance of war, unfortunate speculations or dishonest employees or agents could all spell disaster. Peltier persistently lived beyond his means due to habitual womanising, gambling, incautious speculation and a lavish lifestyle. He went bankrupt five times between 1794 and 1813.[181] Even in old age he spent heavily on jewellery, flowers, millinery and dresses for his mistress, financed by credit. When he died, forgotten and indebted, in Paris on 29 March 1825, his cherished 'Cross of the Polar Star', an award from the king of Sweden conferring knighthood, was on deposit with a pawnbroker.[182] Likewise, both Couchery and Regnier spent time in debtors' prison. In 1802 Regnier was languishing in prison for debts contracted before the revolution, when the proprietors of the *Courier de Londres* hired him to replace Montlosier, and Couchery was gaoled in

---

1807–9 and 1822–7, and thereafter prime minister. *Robert Stewart, Lord Castlereagh* (1769–1822) was war minister 1805–6 and 1807–9, and foreign secretary 1812–22.
[176] See AN, F^7 3762, and Hauterive, *Police*, iv, para. 1029, bulletin of 28 Jan. 1809.
[177] See AN, F^7 4336^A, dos. 3.
[178] See Canning papers, bundle 56a, letters of Regnier to [?Canning], 7, 30 Aug. 1809.
[179] See Hauterive, *Police*, iv, paras 478, 548, bulletins of 16 June, 6 July 1808. See also AAE, mem./docs France 642, Regnier to d'Antraigues, 8 Sept. 1809.
[180] AAE, mem./docs France 604, fo. 139, Fauche-Borel to Artois, 28 Feb. 1807 (copy).
[181] The bankruptcies occurred in 1794, 1795, 1803, 1811 and 1813. See Peltier to Drouin, London, 17 Sept. 1794, ACC, Z tom. CXXV, fos 135–6; *Avis du rédacteur du Tableau de l'Europe*; AAE, mem./docs France 620, 'Peltier'; PRO, B3.3894; Maspero-Clerc, *Peltier*, Annexe IX, p. 319.
[182] ADS, DQ^{10} 1429, dos. 1918.

1812.[183] It is probable that Regnier was bankrupted again soon after he abandoned the *Courier d'Angleterre* and bought the *National Register* newspaper from Eugenius Roche.[184] His promisory notes for £400–500 were not honoured and Roche struggled to pay off a stationer who had accepted them. Regnier, too, probably lost money in the affair, for by 1819 he was working as a French teacher in Manchester, and fruitlessly soliciting rewards from his adopted government.[185] The abbé Calonne also had financial difficulties. Among his unpaid debts when he left for Canada were 500 *louis* borrowed from his brother-in-law, the comte de Saint-Morys, in 1794 to buy out his brother's stake in the *Courier de Londres*.[186] By 1799 St-Morys was dead, but his son took out an injunction to stop the abbé leaving. He was allowed to depart only after he won a court case by arguing that the debt was contracted on the understanding that he would be restored to his property in France.[187] In 1804 the abbé was obliged to return to England to appease clamouring creditors including his nephew, to whom he transferred his share in the *Courier de Londres* in 1806 in lieu of repayment.[188]

Thus the émigré journalists inhabited a financially and politically precarious world on the margins of émigré society, alternately courted and hounded by politicians, spies, creditors, their fellow émigrés and their *confrères*. Themselves intriguers, speculators, professional writers or failed politicians, they embraced journalism through necessity or taste, to exert influence or further their intrigues, but above all because journalism was probably the only way professional writers could hope to earn a reasonable living in emigration. Thus, as the next chapter shows, émigré journalism was a surprisingly extensive business.

---

[183] PRO, FO 27/70, fos 624–5, note of Regnier, n.d. [c. 1804]; AN F^7 3418; AN, F^7 6330, dos. 6959, 'rapport de M. Lamb^e', dated nivôse an XI (Dec. 1802/Jan. 1803); AAE, CPA 597, fo. 473, Otto to Fouché, 5 thermidor X (23 July 1802); CPA 600, fo. 64, Otto to Talleyrand, 7 brumaire XI (28 Oct. 1802); mem./docs France 620, 'Couchery'.
[184] 'Memoir of the author', in Eugenius Roche, *London in one thousand years, with other poems*, London 1830, pp. xiii–xiv.
[185] PRO, FO 27/219, Regnier to Castlereagh, Manchester, 15 June 1819.
[186] See AN, 297AP/2, pièce 85, 'Contrat relative au *Courier de l'Europe*, 1806' [draft]; pièce 89, J.-L.-J. de Calonne to Blondel, Trois-Rivières, 2 Sept. 1816.
[187] See *CL* xlv/36 (3 May 1799).
[188] Sr Marguerite-Marie, *Abbé Calonne*, ch. vi; AN, 297AP/2, pièce 85, 'Contrat relative au *Courier de l'Europe*, 1806' [draft].

2

The Business of Counter-Revolution

Emigré journals were first and foremost commercial ventures and their editors entrepreneurs trying to sell a product. Profit was the bottom line. Conveniently, however, economic self-interest and political belief usually coincided. Thus Regnier asserted that if he did not attack Napoleon from 'conviction' and 'sentiment', he would do so 'from speculation'.[1] He wished to imply both that Napoleon was widely reviled and that there was a large market for anti-Napoleonic literature. In reality, however, the market for émigré journals was fiercely competitive, and those who refused to accept this harsh fact placed themselves at a considerable disadvantage. The two journals that placed other motives before profit failed commercially and hence politically. Both Montlosier's *Journal de France et d'Angleterre*, launched as the party organ of the *monarchiens*, and the non-profit-making *Mercure de France* collapsed within a year.[2]

The competitive environment in which the émigré press operated was a half-way house between the rigorous system of publishing privileges of old regime France and the open capitalist free-for-all of the revolutionary French publishing industry.[3] While England boasted a free press, there were none the less significant rewards available from patrons, especially the British government. The practices and priorities of journalists, distributors and publishers thus resembled the behaviour of their French counterparts in the last decades of the *ancien régime*, when the privilege system was slowly breaking down. This cut-throat publishing world has been described in considerable detail and human colour by Robert Darnton in *The business of enlightenment*, his seminal study of the publishing history of the *Encyclopédie*. Darnton describes how old regime publishers, facing continual problems from delayed subscriptions, dishonest collaborators, self-interested distributors and pirate printings, in turn resorted to underhand means to sell stock, raise extra revenues on their products, gain exclusive privileges, thwart their competitors and protect their interests.[4] The publishing history of the émigré press is also

---

[1] CL liii/48 (17 June 1803).
[2] See Montlosier, *Souvenirs*, 247; MF 1 (10 Apr. 1800), 4–5.
[3] On the transformation of old regime publishing under the impact of revolution see Carla Hesse, *Publishing and cultural politics in revolutionary Paris, 1789–1810*, Berkeley 1991; Popkin, 'Business of political enlightenment'; Robert Darnton and Daniel Roche (eds), *Revolution in print: the press in France, 1775–1800*, Berkeley 1989.
[4] Robert Darnton, *The business of enlightenment: a publishing history of the Encyclopédie*, Cambridge, Mass. 1979.

marked by piracy, malevolent schemes to suppress or ruin rivals and bitter disputes and personal altercations that probably stemmed as much from patronage disputes and circulation wars as ideological differences. Nevertheless, the émigré journalists were in general conspicuously successful in financial terms, and in reaching a wide audience and maintaining independent editorial lines.

The success of émigré journals was due largely to the journalistic skill of individual writers. However, the émigré press industry extended well beyond the journalists. Printers, binders, booksellers and hawkers all depended to a greater or lesser degree on the product of émigré journalism, so that perhaps fifty persons were involved in the industry at any one time. The structure of the London publishing industry, which allowed responsibilities to be subcontracted, was also a significant factor in the success of the émigré press. London-based exile journalists enjoyed many advantages over their continental rivals, including press freedom, protected by the rule of law. Moreover, despite invasion scares, England was probably the safest place in Europe from which to write against the revolution.

Moreover, London was the largest port in the world, and capital of a large empire. Its geographical position facilitated information-gathering from the French coast and Europe, and distribution to Germany, Scandinavia, Russia, Holland, the Americas and the Iberian peninsula. When revolutionary and Napoleonic armies finally closed down many European ports, British naval strength ensured that émigré journals enjoyed a secure passage by sea, wherever friendly ports were open. These factors, combined with the British government's decision to recruit émigré journals to fight its propaganda war after 1803, contributed to the considerable and prolonged success enjoyed by the émigré press.

However, there were difficulties in operating from an English base, especially in the 1790s. The audience in England was more limited by linguistic, political and economic factors than elsewhere in Europe. Fewer people read French than in Germany, where most other émigré papers were based. English readers were generally unfamiliar with both continental writers and the French language, and in general had little taste, and still less need, for journals written in French.[5] The potentially extensive émigré market was hamstrung by poverty, and close-knit enough for single copies to circulate widely. If a larger audience were to be sought, it was necessary to expand distribution abroad, but British prices were uncompetitive. British paper costs, inflated by duties, were higher than elsewhere in Europe, even before the addition of the stamp tax which was payable on the *Courier de Londres*, *Courier d'Angleterre*, *Journal de France et d'Angleterre* and some of Peltier's journals. Within the British market these duties probably favoured the émigré press as they reduced the cost advantage of their English-language

---

5   See Mallet, *Retrospective*, 210.

competitors as a proportion of total price and made any mark-up in the price of émigré products look more reasonable. This made large profits possible on relatively small circulations. Abroad, London-based émigré journals suffered from a competitive disadvantage. Moreover, the parochialism of the English was matched throughout the 1790s by the parsimony of the government. The opportunities for financial and practical support and patronage that existed in the old regime states on the continent were lacking in England. The scale of these difficulties is amply illustrated in the following case study of the launch of Mallet Du Pan's *Mercure britannique*.

Establishing a journal: the *Mercure britannique*

The *Mercure britannique* was a carefully planned venture. Mr Mackintosh, a 'Scotch gentleman' and correspondent of Wickham, living in Berne, suggested that Mallet should establish a journal in 1797, and Wickham promised the idea his support.[6] Mallet considered establishing his journal in Paris, where the right-wing press had enjoyed considerable freedom since the fall of Robespierre, and in early 1797 sent his son to investigate the possibility. Jean-Louis correctly judged the political situation in France inauspicious,[7] for in June the government of Berne, bowing to French pressure, expelled Mallet Du Pan after he published a series of letters in Michaud's *Quotidienne* in which he attacked French territorial ambitions.[8] By early 1798, as revolutionary armies advanced once more, Mallet chose London as a base for the journal, informing a friend:

> As for the public . . . one must leave the continent in order to speak to it; for there is no longer anywhere where anyone can print a line against the Directory and its manoeuvres. I have only been tolerated [to remain] here under the promise of remaining silent. . . . Your continent horrifies me with its slaves and its executioners, its baseness and cowardice. Only in England can one write, think, speak or act.[9]

Meanwhile, Wickham cautioned Mallet that he thought the journal would need support from the British government, clandestinely if necessary, and suggested that he should write to the British loyalist campaigner John Reeves for his opinion and advice.[10]

---

[6] Ibid. 191; Sayous, *Mémoires et correspondance*, ii. 358. A footnote (pp. 358–9) contains an extract of Wickham's letter to Mallet Du Pan, Berne, 10 Oct. [1797].
[7] See Mallet, *Retrospective*, 170–7. Strangely, Sayous does not mention this incident, possibly because it was a rare example of his hero's political prescience failing.
[8] Ibid. 177–9; Sayous, *Mémoires et correspondance*, ii. 293–4; Acomb, *Mallet Du Pan*, 265–6. See also Wickham papers, Hampshire Record Office, Winchester, 38M49/1/79/21, Mallet Du Pan to Michaud [copy], 'probably written from Geneva in June 1797'.
[9] Mallet Du Pan to abbé de Pradt, n.d., cited in Sayous, *Mémoires et correspondance*, ii. 358.
[10] See Wickham to Mallet Du Pan, Berne, 10 Oct. 1797, published ibid. ii. 358–9n. John

Mallet sent Reeves a letter outlining his aims at the end of November and Jean-Louis carried it to England in person.[11] His summary was well calculated to appeal to the sentiments of the English anti-Jacobin:

> [The governors of France] have attempted and to a great extent succeeded in subjugating the liberty of the press abroad as they have in the interior. However, the scope for revealing the ruses and crimes, the character and the motives, the goal and the means of these enemies of the human race has never been greater. Such is the task I will set myself periodically in a work that will break the mould of conventional journals, and, being designed to strike a chord everywhere, offer a new rallying point to wavering opinion.[12]

He stressed that these aims could only be achieved through 'a large circulation'.

Mallet felt that with the burden of a family to support, he was not in a position to make 'the advances, the business arrangements, and the initial sacrifices required for extensive advertising'. He concluded: 'It will thus be necessary that the government or a society of private individuals . . . support this enterprise . . . [it] would be made to appear every week [?] . . . it will be distributed in France and on the continent.'[13] Mallet therefore asked Reeves to discuss the plan with friends and his 'patron', Lord Liverpool.[14]

Reeves responded enthusiastically.[15] He approached Liverpool and 'other persons of consequence', including Windham, the Secretary at War.[16] All gave the idea their 'entire approval'.[17] He also gave the Mallet family use of his house and £100 to cover the costs of their journey.[18] However, the response of the government was less helpful. Liverpool was optimistic of success, but offered little. He doubted that it would serve the journal if the government were to be publicly associated with it, but expressed confidence that it would reach Paris regardless. He predicted a large sale in England, especially if the journal was translated into English, but regretted that Mallet's information sources in France were probably better than the government's own. He also suggested that the émigrés could provide useful information,

---

Reeves, founder of the loyalist Crown and Anchor Association, was a leader of the British anti-Jacobin movement. His activities not always approved by government, he was impeached in 1795.
11 See Mallet papers, #26, Reeves to Mallet Du Pan, 1 Jan. 1798.
12 Ibid. #8, Mallet to Reeves, dated Freybourg-en-Brisgau [sic], 27 Nov. 1797.
13 Ibid. This part of the document is torn and several words are missing from the text.
14 *Charles Jenkinson* (1727–1808), president of the Board of Trade 1786–1804; father of the future prime minister.
15 Mallet papers, #26, Reeves to Mallet, 1 Jan. 1798.
16 Ibid. #3, Windham to Reeves, Fulham, 25 Dec. 1797.
17 Ibid. #26, Reeves to Mallet Du Pan, 1 Jan. 1798.
18 Mallet, *Retrospective*, 192; Reeves to Mallet Du Pan, Cecil Street, London, 15 Jan. 1798 (this letter was among thirty Mallet letters sold at Sotheby's on 8 Nov. 1977 [lot 158] and dispersed). In lieu of the originals, I have consulted the typescript list in the NRA, ref. NRA 18,862. Sayous, *Mémoires et correspondance*, ii. 360, refers to Reeves's generosity.

although their judgement was unreliable. Finally he recommended that Reeves approach Windham, Portland and the Lord Chancellor.[19] Two further letters show his goodwill, and that he had mediated Reeve's request. He thought the government might help by supplying information,[20] and proposed an ambitious but bizarre plan of collaboration between Mallet, Peltier and the conspiracy theorist abbé Augustin Barruel.[21] He suggested that in partnership the three might produce 'an excellent journal', noting that Barruel 'appears evidently disposed to treat religious subjects on the idea of supporting Christianity generally, without any distinctions of sects . . . and therefore he might well act in conjunction with a professed Calvinist'.[22] Mallet had also to fend off offers of collaboration from his old friends, including Malouet, and Montlosier, who, as usual, dreamed up grandiose schemes involving the journal.[23] He also resisted approaches from the comte d'Artois who invited him to Edinburgh with expressions of confidence in an unsubtle attempt to woo him towards the *pur* camp.[24]

Windham's response to Mallet's proposal was more positive than Liverpool's: 'my own opinion is that government ought not to hesitate in giving it the necessary aid; secretly, if the secret can be kept; but otherwise without disguise. – whether others will be of the same opinion I do not know. – I will talk with those whom I think most likely to be so'.[25] Such professions of support resulted in little tangible assistance and Jean-Louis hints that because Pitt was cool towards the project, the rest of the ministry showed little interest.[26] By December 1798 Mallet Du Pan was complaining that he was not even receiving French newspapers from the government, and would have to bear the enormous expense of the subscriptions himself.[27] His complaints apparently resulted in the renewal of a sporadic and unreliable supply of French papers from the government, despatched by Charles Flint,[28] but it

---

[19] Mallet papers, #3, Liverpool to Reeves, Hertford Street, 21 Dec. 1797. *William Henry Cavendish-Bentinck*, 3rd duke of Portland (1738–1809), prime minister 1783, 1807–9; home secretary 1794–1801. *Alexander Wedderburn*, 1st earl of Rosslyn (1733–1805), Lord Chancellor 1793–1801.

[20] Ibid. #3, Liverpool to Reeves, Addiscombe Place, 24 Dec. 1797.

[21] *Augustin de Barruel* (1742–1820). At that moment Barruel had just published the third volume of his *Mémoires pour servir à l'histoire du jacobinisme françois*, which blamed the revolution on a conspiracy of *philosophes* and freemasons.

[22] Mallet papers, #3, Liverpool to Reeves, 5 Jan. 1798.

[23] See ibid. #10, Malouet to Mallet Du Pan, 15 Spring Street, 18 Jan. 1798; Malouet to Mallet Du Pan, 3 Mar. 1798.

[24] Sayous, *Mémoires et correspondance*, ii. 361. See also Mallet, *Retrospective*, 192.

[25] Mallet papers, #3, Windham to Reeves, Fulham, 25 Dec. 1797.

[26] Mallet, *Retrospective*, 202.

[27] See PRO, FO 27/53, Mallet Du Pan to Wickham, 11 Dec. 1798.

[28] See PRO, FO 27/56, Mallet Du Pan to Wickham, 20 Jan. 1800. *Charles Flint* was superintendent of aliens at the Home Office, responsible for correspondence with the émigrés. He was well placed to serve Mallet Du Pan, having been assistant gazette writer at the Foreign Office, *c*. 1793–8. He accompanied Wickham on his mission to Switzerland in 1795: C. R. Middleton, *The administration of British foreign policy, 1782–1856*, Durham, NC 1977, 277.

seems that the administration valued him more for the intelligence he provided in a series of memoranda, letters and communications than for his journalistic endeavours.[29] Mallet later claimed that had he foreseen how little help he would receive, he would never have adopted a plan so similar to that of the Mercure de France, 'for which I had the support of the government, of the [official] correspondence and newspapers of every country'.[30]

Mallet Du Pan arrived in England in May 1798, and immediately began drafting a preliminary plan and negotiating with booksellers.[31] Jean-Louis Mallet says there were only three specialist French booksellers in London, Dulau, Boosey and De Boffe.[32] Of these only De Boffe seemed remotely adequate as a potential publisher, although all had some acquaintance with the émigré journalists. Dulau was 'honest and intelligent', but an émigré, new to business and 'not in circumstances to offer us sufficient security as a publisher'.[33] Boosey was a 'mere retailer', whereas De Boffe, a Swiss who 'spoke wretched English (like most of his class)' was:

> an ignorant drudge, and incapable as well as unwilling to take upon himself the risks of a new publication ... his knowledge of books was, as someone said, *by the square foot*. He nevertheless possessed that sort of common sense and *tact de métier* which is sufficient for all practical purposes, and connived by thrift and prudence, and a sort of monopoly of his trade to accumulate a handsome fortune.[34]

Jean-Louis Mallet's opinion of De Boffe's hard-nosed business sense is confirmed by Chateaubriand, but Chateaubriand also notes that he had an excellent reputation and was widely respected.[35] Although Mallet Du Pan had some reservations,[36] by the end of May a draft agreement was thrashed out between them. De Boffe would bear all the costs of printing, publication, distribution and marketing, and pay Mallet Du Pan a basic £50 per month, plus a further 1s. 6d. for every subscription in excess of 700. Mallet would surrender his rights to the manuscript, give De Boffe preferential rights over the translation, pay for journals and the expenses of his foreign correspondence, and attempt to procure free foreign postage from the government.[37] This draft was submitted to the ministry but the arrangement fell through.

---

[29] These communications can be found in PRO, FO 27/54, pt i, fos 84–5, 96–7; pt ii, fos 335–7.
[30] PRO, FO 27/53, Mallet Du Pan to Wickham, 11 Dec. 1798.
[31] Copies of his 'idée générale', 12 May 1798, are in the Mallet papers, #3; PRO, FO 95/8/13, fos 782–3.
[32] This is clearly wrong. He presumably meant bookseller-publishers.
[33] Mallet, *Retrospective*, 209.
[34] Ibid.
[35] See Chateaubriand, *Mémoires*, i. 416, 422.
[36] PRO, FO 95/8/13 fo. 781, Mallet Du Pan to ?, Cecil Street, 16 May 1798.
[37] Ibid. fo. 791, draft proposal for arrangement between Mallet Du Pan and De Boffe, enclosed in letter of Mallet Du Pan to Foreign Office, 28 May 1798.

Jean-Louis Mallet says that De Boffe was charged only with the London circulation, whereas the Mallets arranged 'the cares of printing, and correspondence with the country and continent, the keeping of accounts, Post Office arrangements, and other details generally managed by a publishing bookseller'.[38]

Meanwhile Mallet opened negotiations for the English translation with the renowned English bookseller Elmsley, publisher of Gibbon's *Decline and fall of the Roman empire*. However, a translator had yet to be found, and Elmsley's prolonged absence in Brighthelmstone (Brighton) caused so many delays that eventually the translation was entrusted to Cadell and Davies. The translator appointed was a novelist called Robert Charles Dallas.[39]

Finally, a continental distributor was necessary. Mallet chose the House of Fauche and Lamaisonfort, based at Hamburg and Brunswick, which undertook distribution through the imperial post. There were good reasons for this choice. Hamburg, the largest centre for the emigration in Germany, enjoyed excellent and regular communications with London, had a vast German hinterland and was the *entrepôt* for the Baltic. Moreover, Fauche and Lamaisonfort already had an established relationship with Mallet, having published his *Correspondance politique pour servir à l'histoire du républicanisme française* in 1796. Moreover, Pierre-François Fauche was a dedicated counter-revolutionary, and experienced bookseller from Neuchâtel in Switzerland, where his father Samuel Fauche was a leading member of the *Société typographique*. Mallet probably met him while living in Neuchâtel in the early 1770s and working for the printer-publisher Osterwald.[40] In the 1790s they may have met again through their mutual involvement with Wickham's mission to Switzerland. Fauche's partner, Lamaisonfort, who was primarily responsible for dealing with Mallet, was a French émigré and royalist agent.[41]

Unfortunately for Mallet, Lamaisonfort proved lazy, truculent and unreliable. He showed no great interest in the success of the *Mercure britannique*, and Mallet suspected, probably correctly, that his main aim was to protect his own in-house journal the *Spectateur du nord*, rather than to promote the *Mercure*.[42] However, there is another possibility. Lamaisonfort expressed indignation at the strength of some of the statements in Mallet's prospectus[43] and asked for his name to be removed from the document, because at Bruns-

---

[38] Mallet, *Retrospective*, 209.
[39] Ibid. 210.
[40] On Mallet's stay at Neuchâtel see Acomb, *Mallet Du Pan*, 29–33.
[41] On Lamaisonfort's activities see PRO, FO 27/54, pt i, 'rescript of Paul I', 14/25 May 1799; FO 27/56, Lamaisonfort to ?, 10 Aug. 1800; AAE, mem./docs France 620, 'Lamaisonfort'; AN, AF^{IV*} 1710, 'Statistique des Bourbons et des Consorts' (1810), p. 177, no. 345. After the restoration he became French minister at Florence.
[42] See Mallet papers, #7, Mallet Du Pan to Gallatin, 25 Oct. 1798; #30, Gallatin to Mallet Du Pan, Berlin, 10 Nov. 1798. On the *Spectateur du nord* see Paul Hazard, 'Le Spectateur du nord', *RHLF* (1906), 26–50.
[43] See Mallet papers, #30, Gallatin to Mallet Du Pan, Berlin, 12 Aug. 1798.

wick he was under the watchful eye of the abbé Siéyès, who was then serving as French ambassador to Berlin.[44] While it is possible, then, that Lamaisonfort's obstructive tactics stemmed from fear, this was probably just a useful pretext. As early as July 1798 Lamaisonfort was claiming that Mallet's letters had gone astray. This destroyed hopes of printing Mallet's *Essai* on Switzerland cheaply on the continent by the agreed deadline, but Lamaisonfort offered to reprint it and split the profits.[45] Lamaisonfort was also disparaging about the journal's chances of success, doubting that it would find the 300 subscribers required to justify reprinting it.[46] Nevertheless, he promised to print Mallet's prospectus as soon as he received it, and to advertise the journal in the German gazettes,[47] in particular the *Correspondant d'Hambourg* (*Correspondenten*), the *Journal de Francfort*, and the *Spectateur du nord*.[48] However, the advertisements never materialised, and at the end of October Mallet Du Pan catalogued an assortment of 'dirty tricks':

> Would you believe that they [the house of Fauche et Lamaisonfort] have not even acknowledged the receipt of my missives, that they have not announced [the appearance of] the work in any gazette, that they turn away subscribers, disparage me, [and] sell, or rather offer, at 11 gold Louis that which is delivered ... [illegible] at Cuxhaven for two guineas? Several people have alerted me [to this] from Hamburg.[49]

Such duplicity, although typical of the cut-throat world of eighteenth-century publishing, was a serious setback for Mallet as he had counted on 1,500–2,000 subscribers on the continent.[50] However, all was not lost. Although Lamaisonfort continued to complain of delays in receiving Mallet's letters and the journal, some pressure seems to have been brought to bear, and Fauche and Lamaisonfort remained the journal's continental distributors. Nevertheless, delays in receiving the paper appear to have remained common: in October 1799, for example, the German counter-revolutionary publicist Frederich von Gentz complained that he had not received a copy for two months and wondered whether Fauche was to blame.[51]

---

[44] Ibid. #26, Lamaisonfort to Mallet Du Pan, Hamburg, 7 Aug. 1798. *Emmanuel-Joseph Siéyès* (1748–1836) was author of the celebrated pamphlet *Qu'est-ce que le tiers état* and an active revolutionary politician and regicide. Ambassador to Berlin in 1798, Director in 1799, he helped to plot the coup of Brumaire.
[45] Mallet papers, #26, Lamaisonfort to Mallet Du Pan, Hamburg, 20 July [1798].
[46] Ibid. 7 Aug. 1798.
[47] Ibid. 20 July [1798].
[48] Ibid. 7 Aug. 1798.
[49] Ibid. #7, Mallet Du Pan to Gallatin, 25 Oct. 1798.
[50] Ibid. #3 and PRO, FO 95/8/13, fos 782–3, 'Idée générale', 12 May 1798. Mallet papers, #7, Mallet Du Pan to Gallatin, 17 July 1798, is more pessimistic, and suggests 5–600 subscriptions would be an achievement.
[51] BPUG, MS. Suppl. 976, fo. 170, Gentz to Francis d'Ivernois, Berlin, 18 Oct. 1799. Mallet papers, #30, Gallatin to Mallet Du Pan, Berlin, 29 Jan. 1799, also complains of inexplicable delays. *Frederich von Gentz* (1764–1832), German publicist and civil servant, was in

Luckily Mallet had another agent in Germany, the chevalier de Gallatin,[52] who circulated Mallet's prospectus and brought a handful of important subscribers including the duke of Brunswick and Tsar Paul I.[53] In November Gallatin assured Mallet that although his suspicions of Fauche seemed justified, his own subscribers were 'exactly served'.[54] Moreover, Mallet does seem to have won the concession of free postage, for the two guineas Lamaisonfort paid was the same as the British subscription.

Business did not run altogether smoothly in London either. The appearance of the prospectus was delayed and problems with the English translation held up the first number.[55] The proposed launch date for Mallet's *Essai* on Switzerland, which made up the first three numbers, was 1 September, but the French edition was not ready until the 24th, and none went on general sale until the 26th, when the English translation was finally ready and had been advertised.[56] To avoid future problems, Mallet undertook that Dallas would receive the last 'demi-feuille' (sixteen pages of text) four days before the English edition was due, allowing three days for the printer to cut and sew them.[57] Such production difficulties were symptomatic of the problems Mallet was to face. He had over-stretched his physical resources in undertaking to provide his reflections on a twice-monthly basis. By the time the *Mercure britannique* finally appeared subscribers had been pressing him for a month, and he was convinced that if production waned, or he fell several numbers behind, his subscribers would abandon him.[58] This fear was both to haunt him and drive him until his death in May 1800.

---

the service of Prussia and from 1802 Austria, where he became one of Metternich's closest advisors.
[52] Gallatin, an old friend from Geneva, married one of Mallet's relatives. He fled Geneva in 1794 and, on Mallet's recommendation, became counsellor to the duke of Brunswick before entering Bavarian service.
[53] Mallet papers, #26, Lamaisonfort to Mallet Du Pan, Brunswick, 4 Sept. [1798], and Lamaisonfort to Mallet Du Pan, 1 Oct. 1798; #30, Gallatin to Mallet Du Pan, Berlin, 12 Aug. 1798. *Charles William Ferdinand*, duke of Brunswick (r. 1780–1806), was Prussian commander-in-chief in the invasion of France in 1792. The reactionary Brunswick manifesto was released in his name.
[54] Ibid. #30, Gallatin to Mallet Du Pan, Berlin, 10 Nov. 1798.
[55] Ibid. #7, Mallet Du Pan to Gallatin, 17 July 1798; BPUG, 1947/19, Mallet Du Pan to Cadell and Davies, Woodstock Street, 13 Sept. 1798. I have not found a copy of the prospectus.
[56] Ibid. #26, Portalis, Jr, to J.-L.Mallet, 26 Aug. 1798; BPUG, 1956/27 D. O., Mallet Du Pan to Cadell and Davies, Woodstock Street, 23 Sept. 1798.
[57] BPUG, 1956/27 D. O., Mallet Du Pan to Cadell and Davies, Woodstock Street, 23 Sept. 1798.
[58] Ibid. and PRO, FO 27/56, Mallet Du Pan to Wickham, 20 Jan. 1800.

Business administration

The tardy publication of the Mercure britannique was atypical. Much of the delay was due to the author's caution: Mallet Du Pan wished to evade financial risk yet negotiate an advantageous contract. He sought similar security and income to that he had enjoyed as Panckoucke's employee on the Mercure de France, but with a much smaller audience. Ultimately he was unable to arrange such terms, because he could not find an entrepreneur willing to place such a premium on his reputation. However, most of the problems that delayed the launch affected all émigré journals. Raising capital or finding a financial backer, employing a reliable printer, advertising the journal and arranging regular distribution were universal difficulties.

Like the early revolutionary journals, the émigré papers only needed a small staff. Mallet Du Pan and his son undertook the entire editorial and office administration of the Mercure britannique. Likewise, Montlosier ran his Journal de France et d'Angleterre almost single-handedly, with a little assistance from Jean-Louis Mallet. Peltier only occasionally resorted to collaborators. The Courier de Londres had a larger editorial staff, but the weekly wage bill was contractually limited to a maximum of seven guineas.[59] This appears to have risen briefly to eight guineas in 1793, but included one guinea for the print foreman.[60] The leading editor from Verduisant to Regnier was paid three guineas per week.[61]

As few personnel were required and printing and distribution tended to be contracted out, a journal might be launched with relatively little financial backing. The main initial expenses were advertising, subscriptions to other journals, paper and writing equipment and advances. Montlosier started the Journal de France et d'Angleterre with just twenty-five guineas lent to him by the princesse d'Hénin, but the inadequacy of that sum may have contributed to the journal's failure. For, as Montlosier admits, 'it was very little with which to start a periodical paper'.[62] The anonymous editors of the Mercure de France appear to have raised their capital by pooling resources and forming a 'society of men of letters'.[63] Regnier, by contrast, raised £1,000 from an

---

[59] See AN, 297AP/2, pièce 85, 'Contrat relative au Courier de l'Europe, 1806' [draft]. PRO, PC 1/127, piece 210, Swinton to Calonne [late May/early June 1791], indicates that Morande's four successors shared six guineas per week.

[60] See PRO, PC 1/130, piece 236, Calonne to J.-L.-J. de Calonne, [?Vicenza], 5 Nov. 1793 [minute].

[61] On Verduisant's wage see ibid. Montlosier made repeated reference to receiving about £150 per year from the paper; AN, F⁷ 6330, dos. 6959, 'extrait du rapport de M. Lamb^e', dated nivôse an XI (Dec. 1802/Jan. 1803), says Regnier received £160 per annum.

[62] Montlosier, Souvenirs, 247. The princesse d'Hénin, monarchien supporter, was Lally-Tollendal's mistress.

[63] See MF 1 (10 Apr. 1800), title page. The wording of their statement imitated the old regime Mercure de France which also claimed to be produced by a 'société de gens de lettres'.

unknown backer, possibly an agent of Louis XVIII,[64] within three weeks of being sacked from the *Courier de Londres*. This was enough to establish the *Courier d'Angleterre*, and a print shop for his partner Thomas Harper.[65] Booksellers also helped to found journals. De Boffe speculated on Peltier's reputation, redeeming him from debtors' prison and paying him a small salary, in return for the profits on the first six months of *Paris pendant l'année*. Peltier complained of his 'miserable remuneration', but after thirty-two numbers he bought out De Boffe's interest,[66] although the latter remained the main distributor. Such arrangements between booksellers and journalists were quite common.[67]

Production of the journals was entrusted to a small group of specialist French printers who developed considerable expertise: as a result, typesetting errors are surprisingly rare in the émigré papers. The printers were also responsible for folding and binding prior to distribution, and it was not unknown for them to insert articles without permission.[68] The most notable French printers in London were Edward Cox and Son, of 75 Great Queen Street, Spilsbury of Snow Hill and Thomas Baylis of Greville Street, whose print shop was, according to Peltier, justly famous for its accuracy and the beauty of its products.[69] Peltier used Glindon for his earliest journals, but was dissatisfied with the quality of his work. He switched to Baylis for *Paris pendant l'année*, and after Baylis merged with Cox and Son in 1802 he retained the merged company as the *Ambigu*'s printers until 1805. Thereafter the journal was printed by Paolo da Ponte (1805–9), and then George Schulze and Company, who bought da Ponte's print shop in 1809. Cox and Son, the original printers of the *Courier de Londres*, remained so after merging with Baylis.[70] From August 1804 to 1806 the printers claimed to be joint proprietors of the *Courier de Londres*, together with Swinton's widow Félicité. Possibly they were the abbé Calonne's agents, or were ceded temporary control of his stake to clear his debts.[71] Regnier's *Courier d'Angleterre* was produced in the print shop of his partner Thomas Harper, which had been established for the purpose. Montlosier's *Journal de France et d'Angleterre*, the *Mercure de France* and the *Mercure britannique* were all printed by Spilsbury.[72]

Distribution in London was generally undertaken through booksellers,

---

[64] See Canning papers, bundle 54, d'Avaray to La Châtre, Gothenburg, 20 Oct. 1807.
[65] See PRO, FO 27/124, Regnier to Castlereagh [memoir], 10 Mar. 1815, enclosed with letter of 23/27 Mar. 1815.
[66] PRO, PRO 30/8/165, fos 216–17, Peltier to Pitt, 4 Jan. 1796; letters of Peltier and De Boffe to subscribers to *Paris*, dated 9 Jan. 1796 (bound with vol. iv in CUL collection).
[67] De Boffe also published Serres de La Tour's short-lived *Journal de l'Europe* in 1789, and Heron made several similar arrangements: *Annual Register* xlix (1807), 566–7.
[68] See PRO, FO 27/71, Regnier to De Boffe, 29 June 1805.
[69] *Paris* 23 (31 Oct. 1795), 448.
[70] The merger was not mentioned in the publishing details until March 1803.
[71] See CL lvi/15 (21 Aug. 1804).
[72] See respective title pages.

some of whom also took readers' subscriptions. Although De Boffe and Dulau were the most important of the French booksellers, several others were involved in the foreign book trade between 1789 and 1814, notably l'Homme, Conchy, Boosey, Debrett and Peltier himself.[73] A number of other London booksellers and merchants of printed ephemera also served as retail outlets. These included Elmsley, Prosper, Owen, Cadell and Davies, Wright and the ubiquitous M. Axtell. They were based around the publishing, bookselling and business heart of the City: Fleet Street, the Strand, Piccadilly, Paternoster Row and the Royal Exchange. Retail trade in the émigré journals was thus circumscribed within a tiny but fashionable area, and restricted to a small élite.

De Boffe and Dulau eventually merged, but their business and invaluable archives were destroyed during the blitz.[74] Both their shops were centres for the émigré community, and it is probable that much more advertising was conducted through their shops than through the émigré press.[75] De Boffe was first and foremost an entrepreneur and lacked both ideological commitment to the *la bonne cause* and moral courage. When the French government began proceedings against him as publisher of Peltier's journal in 1802 he thought only of saving his neck and wrote to Talleyrand stating:

> You know, citizen, of my position as a bookseller.[76] I can assure you from the depths of my soul . . . that I have always been the enemy of any works that might offend any government whatsoever, [and that] as I am nearly blind,[77] and my work prevents me from reading, making me dependent on the good offices of others, I published *L'Ambigu* as I would have published a work of the opposite persuasion, without suspecting the least ill.[78]

He immediately ceased publication of the *Ambigu*,[79] returned all unsold copies and co-operated fully with the attorney-general. The charge against him was dropped and he testified against Peltier at his trial.[80]

Thomas Boosey, probably the third biggest retailer of émigré journals, dealt in all the French periodicals appearing in London between 1795 and 1801, although apparently none of the newspapers. The Boosey family busi-

---

[73] London's French book trade remains largely unexplored. There is nothing on these individuals or on De Boffe or Dulau in the standard reference work, I. Maxted, *The London book trades, 1775–1800: a preliminary checklist of members*, Woking 1977.
[74] Weiner, *French exiles*, 114.
[75] Advertisers in émigré papers and private letters often use their shops as contact addresses: BL, MS Add. 33978, fo. 275, [Serres] de La Tour to Sir Joseph Banks, 7 Dec. 1789; PRO, FO 27/58, Fauche-Borel to Grenville, 11 Mar. 1801.
[76] Talleyrand used De Boffe's store during his stay in London as ambassador and exile.
[77] His handwriting suggests this to be true.
[78] AAE, CPA 596, fo. 491, De Boffe to Talleyrand, London, 7 Sept. 1802.
[79] From *Ambigu* 5 (n.d./?1802), De Boffe's name no longer appears as publisher or distributor.
[80] See PRO, TS 11/429, file 1357; Peltier, *Trial*, 63–8.

ness was founded by his father, John Boosey, probably in the late 1760s, and comprised a bookshop specialising in French, Spanish, Italian, Danish, German, Dutch and Russian titles, and a lending library.[81] By 1816 the company had also established a music business, which still survives as the worldwide music publisher and musical instrument manufacturer Boosey and Hawkes. Little is known about Thomas Boosey besides Jean-Louis Mallet's brief description and that he had a life-long passion for angling.[82] However, it is possible to speculate on the scale of his involvement in émigré publishing. Since De Boffe received fifty copies of Mallet's *Essai . . . sur la ligue hélvetique*, and 200 copies of each of the first four numbers of the *Ambigu*,[83] we may assume that Boosey took considerably fewer, and the lesser retailers only a few dozen each at most.

Delivery in London was organised by the main booksellers or deliverymen employed by the proprietors.[84] Speed was vital and *colporteurs* (hawkers) often worked for English papers as well, frequently selling them directly to the public in the streets. The *Courier de Londres* also announced that it was available from hawkers of English newspapers.[85] At least one *colporteur*, Thomas Brandon, was employed by both Peltier and Regnier, and became caught up in their disputes. When Peltier gave him an ultimatum to choose between employers, the unfortunate man chose Regnier.[86] Outside London distribution was undertaken via the Post Office, which sent newspapers and periodicals free of charge, and on the continent through the house of Fauche and Lamaisonfort, advertised booksellers, or the Foreign Post Office. During the peace of Amiens the *Courier de Londres* even claimed to be available by subscription in Calais and Paris.[87] Besides clandestine distribution by government, there are also documented instances of individuals sending copies to friends and contacts abroad.[88] Moreover, Peltier used a system of agents who sought subscribers in the colonies, and recruited numerous friends and contacts to find new readers for him abroad. Amongst them were Peltier's

---

[81] GGB 132 (18 July 1806); Jeremy Boosey, 'Beethoven, Bellini, ballads and bands', in *Boosey and Hawkes 150th anniversary*, London 1966, 2–4 at p. 4. My thanks to Paula Rainborough of Boosey and Hawkes for providing a copy of this brief publication and attempting, unsuccessfully, to find useful material in company archives.

[82] Thomas Boosey, *Piscatorial reminiscences and gleanings by an old angler and bibliopolist, to which is added a catalogue of books on angling*, London 1835. Sadly this does not contain autobiographical material.

[83] BPUG, 1956/27 D.O., Mallet Du Pan to Cadell and Davies, 23 Sept. 1798; PRO, TS 11/429, file 1357, De Boffe's account with Peltier. De Boffe returned 228 out of the 800 copies unsold.

[84] See PRO, TS 11/429, file 1357, Joseph White to De Boffe, n.d., and De Boffe's account with Peltier.

[85] CL xlii/10 (4 Aug. 1797); lxvii/37 (7 May 1810).

[86] See CA 368 (4 Nov. 1808).

[87] CL li/51 (26 June 1802).

[88] D'Antraigues sent four copies of the *Ambigu* to St Petersburg in October 1806: AAE, mem./docs France 641, fo. 160, Peltier to d'Antraigues, 2 Oct. 1806.

former advocate, James Mackintosh, who agreed to find subscribers in India, where he became solicitor-general in 1803, and an agent called Verguin in Guadeloupe, who appears to have absconded with about 6,000 *livres* of subscriptions in 1818–19.[89] Even Sir Arthur Paget, the former British ambassador to Austria, was pestered for the names of prospective clients on the continent.[90]

Although the business of the press was largely farmed out to printers and booksellers, the journalists' own contribution was heavy and relentless. Merely compiling the necessary information from printed ephemera and oral sources required hours of study daily, and writing and translation for regular deadlines could take a heavy toll. Mallet Du Pan spent eight hours every day in his study, while Regnier claimed he had to spend two nights a week in his printshop to translate and print the *London Gazette*.[91] Regular issues allowed no time for rest or ill-health. In 1795–6 the first pages of Peltier's *Paris pendant l'année* had to be with the printer a whole week before publication, and he excused any confusion of materials by noting he had just four days to compile sixty-four pages.[92] The finishing touches to the *Courier de Londres* were often added only an hour before publication if the date and time given at the top of the 'Postscriptum' is to be believed. Facing similar pressures, Mallet Du Pan's health deteriorated rapidly, as tuberculosis took its toll, while Regnier blamed the loss of his eyesight on long hours working by candlelight in 1813–14.[93] Peltier managed to take four-and-a- half-months' rest in early 1798, during which time he seems to have undertaken his celebrated journey to Stowe, Blenheim, Hampton Court and Oxford with Chateaubriand, but this was his only voluntary prolonged break during his entire exile.[94]

Compiling the news: information sources

In the eighteenth century newspaper reporting was in its infancy. The concept of staff correspondents was almost unknown and there were no regular agencies accumulating news. Instead there developed what Jeremy Black has called 'a far from enclosed system of information' in which newspapers, books and other printed ephemera, together with newsletters, mercan-

---

[89] BL, MS Add. 52451^B, fos 56–7, Peltier to Mackintosh, London, 15 June 1804; ADS, DQ^{10} 1429, dos. 1918.
[90] BL, MS Add. 48413, fo. 39, Peltier to Sir Arthur Paget, 7 Oct. 1803.
[91] PRO, FO 27/56, Mallet Du Pan to Wickham, 20 Jan. 1800 (reproduced in full in Sayous, *Mémoires et correspondance*, ii. 445–7, with extracts in Mallet, *Retrospective*, 242–4); FO 27/219, Regnier to Castlereagh, 15 June 1819.
[92] *Paris* 25 (21 Nov. 1795), 11; 38 (20 Feb. 1796), 339n.
[93] See PRO, FO 27/219, Regnier to Castlereagh, 15 June 1819. Regnier cited Rolleston, chief translator at the Foreign Office, as witness.
[94] See Chateaubriand, *Mémoires*, i. 485–7. Maspero-Clerc, *Peltier*, 188, mistakenly places the journey at the end of 1798, by which time Peltier was working again.

tile correspondence, coffee-house gossip and other oral reports served as mutual and common sources.[95] As a result many eighteenth-century newspaper reports are prefaced by the phrase 'on dit', or its English equivalent 'we hear'.[96] Readers had to make sense of this diverse source material for themselves. Although the émigré newspapers did indicate sources such as private letters, French papers, a 'traveller recently arrived from the continent' or an anonymous 'person worthy of confidence', most foreign news was presented in short reports without context or explanation. Generally, news from abroad was taken from letters or foreign newspapers wherever a dateline and place were indicated. Occasionally the editor commented on the reliability of an item: more often they resorted to the ubiquitous 'on dit'. The modern reader must therefore bear in mind that much was covered by tacit understandings between the journalist and his public, and much more was cryptic or impenetrable.[97]

The émigré press formed part of this system of information. However, much of its value to contemporaries, government and historians, lay in its ability to exploit particular sources. The emigration had dispersed friends, relatives and correspondents of the émigré journalists throughout Europe. Furthermore, for much of the period it was difficult to obtain reliable and fresh information from France, her allies and dependencies. The British government itself at times lacked the means to acquire French newspapers. Charles Jenkinson, when President of the Board of Trade, received his copies of the French papers through De Boffe, but they could not always be obtained, even at great cost.[98] Thus Peltier boasted to Pitt that he received regular communications concerning the *Chouans* from his brother in Nantes and that he regularly received 'the gazette of that town'. For good measure he added that his news from the war-torn Vendée was often only ten days old.[99] Nor was Peltier's brother his only correspondent in France. He also spoke enigmatically of 'the friends that I left in France who are obliged to send me all the information imaginable on the state of affairs in that unfortunate country'.[100] One of these contacts was almost certainly the Parisian publisher J.-F. Michaud, who also had connections with Montlosier and Mallet Du Pan.[101]

---

95 Black, *English press*, 87.
96 On the usage of this term see Jean Sgard, 'On dit', in Harvey Chisick (ed.), *The press in the French revolution*, Oxford 1991, 25–32.
97 For a discussion of eighteenth-century newspaper reporting style see Censer, *French press*, ch. i. On the skill of newspaper reading see Las Cases's account of teaching Napoleon how to read an English newspaper: *Memorial of Saint-Helena*, London 1823, i/2, 124.
98 BL, MS Add. 38229, fo. 1, De Boffe to Jenkinson, Gerard Street, 1 Apr. 1793; PRO, FO 95/3/3, fo. 343, Duroveray to Nepean, 27 July 1793. FO 27/81, Regnier to Culling Charles Smith, 29 Dec. 1810, offers to communicate a means to acquire French newspapers regularly once or twice weekly.
99 PRO, PRO 30/8/165, fos 216–17, Peltier to Pitt, 4 Jan. 1796.
100 Ibid.
101 AN, F^7 7849, Mengaud to Fouché, Calais, 1 germinal IX (21 Mar. 1801); F^7 6286, dos. 5846, Mengaud to Fouché, 19 germinal IX (8 Apr. 1801). There is a possibility of confusion

Peltier also refers to having two friends who ran correspondence networks for the British ministry in 1798.[102] As we have seen, Montlosier's *Courier de Londres* had several paid correspondents: Tromelin accompanied the British army in Egypt and Syria; André de Montluel wrote from Paris; Butet was the paper's established correspondent in Constantinople, and Montlosier hints that there were others.[103] The use of such agents was innovative. The *Courier de Londres* used semi-professional foreign correspondents on a wider scale than most late eighteenth-century newspapers. However, their remuneration was small, for Montlosier paid them advances from his own salary for which he was never reimbursed.[104]

The émigré journalists also enjoyed privileged access to other sources. Mallet Du Pan continued to use the pan-European network of contacts he had developed while in Brussels and Berne and remained in contact with ministers such as Hardenburg in Berlin, Da Souza in Lisbon and Castries in Blanckenbourg.[105] He also had informative correspondence with Germany through the duke of Brunswick, Gentz, the abbé Delille, Gallatin, Portalis, the abbé de Pradt, Dessarts and Quatremère de Quincy.[106] Salis wrote from Zurich of the invasion of the Grisons, and Sumeraw sent intelligence on

---

here because Peltier had a brother-in-law also called Michaud, but Mengaud appears clear in his facts.

[102] See *Paris* 170 (17 Dec. 1798), introduction, p. ix.

[103] Montlosier *Souvenirs*, 251. A second correspondent in Constantinople was indicated in CL xlix/48 (16 June 1801); a correspondent with British forces in Portugal in l/2 (7 July 1801).

[104] Montlosier, *Souvenirs*, 251.

[105] Mallet papers, #14, letters of Da Souza to Mallet Du Pan, dated Lisbon, 12 Oct., 3 Nov. 1798. For Castries's letters to Mallet Du Pan see Mallet papers, #25; for Mallet's correspondence with Castries see BPUG, MS Supp. 866; AN, 306AP/33 bis; E. Chapuisat (ed.), *La Correspondance de Mallet Du Pan et le maréchal de Castries*, Geneva 1948. For Hardenburg's correspondence with Mallet see Mallet papers, #26. *Karl Auguste von Hardenburg* (1750–1822), Prussian diplomat, a close associate of Haugwitz, was appointed Chancellor in 1810. *Charles Eugène-Gabriel*, marquis de Castries (1727–1801) was a former naval minister and adviser to the princes. *Don Roderigo Da Souza-Coutinho* was Portuguese representative at Turin, uncle of the Portuguese foreign minister, brother of the ambassador to London and cousin of the ambassador to Paris.

[106] *Jacques Delille* (1738–1813), was probably the most celebrated French poet of his day. In 1799 Mallet Du Pan asked Gallatin to appraise him of events on the continent, especially of what passed between Berlin and St Petersburg: Mallet papers, #7, Mallet du Pan to Gallatin, West Horsley, 16 Sept. 1799. *Jean-Etienne-Marie Portalis* (1746–1809), member of the Conseil des Anciens, fled France after Fructidor, returned after Brumaire and became Napoleon's minister of religion. The Mallet and Portalis families and Delille spent the winter of 1797–8 in Freiburg-en-Brisgau where they became close friends. The *abbé Dufour de Pradt*, (1759–1837), an old friend, was later almoner to Napoleon and bishop of Poitiers. Dessarts, former syndic at Geneva, sent Mallet Du Pan a memorandum on the means to restore Geneva: Mallet papers, #26, supplement. *Quatremère de Quincy*, architect, *Encyclopédiste* and moderate right-wing publicist, fled France after Fructidor.

Switzerland from Freiburg.[107] The abbé Calonne received bulletins from his brother from Spain and Italy,[108] and from 1806 to 1812 Regnier worked closely with d'Antraigues, who possessed an extensive intelligence network, especially in the north of Europe. Moreover, Regnier and Peltier seem to have had privileged access to the councils of Artois's agents.[109]

Peltier and Regnier also had mercantile and family contacts with the former French colonies, and moved in *colon* circles in London. In the 1790s Peltier's journals included articles by Charmilly and Frouillé, giving up-to-date information on Saint-Domingue, extensive favourable reviews of Charmilly's work and *colon* propaganda (see chapter 4). Furthermore, after 1806, Peltier's diplomatic relations with Haiti often gave him privileged access to news from the Caribbean. Peltier's source for some of the material he published on Napoleon's family and childhood in 1801–3 was probably the Corsican patriot leader Pasquale Paoli, who had been a friend of Bonaparte's parents and lived in exile in London from 1795 until his death in 1807.[110] In 1805 Peltier asserted that Paoli and his clique could confirm the accuracy of hitherto unpublished documents he reproduced concerning Napoleon's condemnation by the *département* of Corsica on 27 May 1793.[111]

Newspapers and periodicals were an expensive but indispensible source of information for the émigré journalists. Peltier boasted that he received more than thirty foreign papers, presumably costing at least £100 *per annum*, and claimed that he compiled his reports on the French legislative councils from more than a dozen French journals, as these were less biased than the *Moniteur*.[112] Mallet Du Pan complained at having to finance foreign papers himself, but there were ways in which such costs could be offset. Mutual exchanges with friendly foreign papers appear to have been quite usual: in 1809 Broval, Louis-Philippe's representative in London, recommended that Regnier make such an arrangement with the editors of the Spanish *Semanario*

---

[107] See Mallet papers, #26 supplement, Salis to Mallet Du Pan, 22 June 1799; Sumeraw to Mallet Du Pan, 31 May 1798.
[108] See PRO, PC 1/130, piece 235, fo. 39, Calonne to J.-L.-J. de Calonne [?Vicenza], 29 Sept. 1793 [minute].
[109] See, for example, Hauterive, *Police* iv, para. 524; AN, F^7 3703.
[110] *Pasquale Paoli*, hero of Corsica's independence struggle in the 1760s, returned to Corsica in 1790 after 20 years in exile. In the ensuing power struggles he and the Bonapartes took opposite sides. In 1793 he encouraged and welcomed British intervention, hoping to establish an independent Corsican kingdom. See Peter Adam Thrasher, *Pasquale Paoli: an enlightened hero, 1725–1807*, London 1970.
[111] *Ambigu* 92 (20 Oct. 1805), 153–4n. The documents were published in *Ambigu* 93 (30 Oct. 1805).
[112] *Paris* 98 (11 Feb. 1797), 382; 36 (6 Feb. 1796), 272.

patriotico.¹¹³ Likewise Gentz sent Mallet Du Pan copies of his journal which was inspired by the *Mercure britannique*.¹¹⁴

It is not clear how newspapers from France and Holland avoided the Napoleonic blockade, but those from Germany tended to arrive by the Hamburg, Heligoland or Gothenburg mails, depending on the diplomatic exigencies of the moment. The Bertin brothers and other smugglers operating out of the Channel Islands kept communications with Brittany and Normandy alive, but there is little evidence of contact with Flanders, Holland or the Pas-de-Calais.¹¹⁵ Moreover, fresh French newspapers were acquired frequently but haphazardly, suggesting a lack of system, and that the French blockade was having a partial effect. They probably arrived *via* clandestine traders, captured shipping, French and Dutch fishermen communicating with the Royal Navy and agents arriving from the continent.

Revenue sources

The émigré journals earned money in a number of ways, not all of them direct. The direct means were subscriptions and advertising revenues. However, advertising was surprisingly light and almost exclusively confined to the *Courier de Londres*, and, after 1805, the *Courier d'Angleterre*. Whereas it was common for British papers to fill the entire front page, equivalent to 25 per cent of available space, with advertising, the *Courier de Londres* never exceeded an annual average of two brief advertising announcements per number, and these were placed on the two back pages. Moreover, from 1789 to 1813 the volume of advertising carried by the paper fell consistently, save for a brief respite during the peace of Amiens (1802–3). In the course of 1789 there were 126 advertisements, but by 1813 only thirty-two. With the coming of peace in 1814 there were 198 advertisements, but this level was shortlived. By contrast, the 163 numbers of the *Courier d'Angleterre* dating from 1807 to 1809 in Lund University Library contain only thirty-one items that appear to be advertisements or paid insertions. The *Courier de Londres*'s most persistent advertisers were the French booksellers, the East India Company, which regularly announced forthcoming sales of coffees, teas and fabrics, and purveyors of quack remedies and medicines. The most frequently advertised medicine was de La Mottes's 'Magnésie du Sieur Glass', which

---

113 PRO, FO 95/636, Broval to D'Antraigues, Seville, 20 May 1809. These editors were Quintana and José Maria Blanco (Blanco White). On Blanco White see Martin Murphy, *Blanco White: self-banished Spaniard*, New Haven, Conn. 1989. See also B. R. Hammett, 'Spanish constitutionalism and the impact of the French revolution, 1808–1814', in W. Doyle and H. T. Mason (eds), *The impact of the French revolution on European consciousness*, Gloucester 1989, 64–80.
114 See BPUG, 1968/28 D.O., Gentz to Mallet Du Pan, 15/19 Jan. 1799; MS Suppl. 976, fos 167–70, Gentz to d'Ivernois, Berlin, 18 Oct. 1799.
115 On the Bertin brothers see their dossier in AAE, mem./docs France 620.

boasted retail outlets from St Petersburg to Bordeaux.[116] In 1800 it was advertised eleven times, contributing 33 per cent of the annual total by number of advertisements. In 1802 the East India Company placed fifteen out of seventy-seven announcements (19.5%), but as their advertisements often exceeded ten lines in length, and therefore paid a surcharge of 1s. a line, they contributed perhaps 40 per cent of advertising revenue. Thus the papers' advertising revenues were heavily dependent on a handful of advertisers. Nevertheless, these revenues were marginal to the financial health of even the *Courier de Londres*. After stamp duty of 3s. 6d. per advertisement, the paper only received 7s. for most advertisements. Thus even in the best years advertising revenues were only a little over £70: in the worst they were about £11 4s. There is also evidence that some articles were inserted for payment. Certainly the anti-slavery lobby paid Swinton to insert William Wilberforce's speeches and abolitionist literature in the *Courier de Londres* in 1789, much to Morande's chagrin, and after the restoration in 1814 the abolitionists courted Peltier assiduously and placed articles in the *Ambigu*.[117]

Given the paucity of advertising in the émigré journals, it is clear that subscriptions provided the vast bulk of their direct revenues. Although no subscription lists survive, we can nevertheless derive fairly accurate estimates of circulation figures (see table 9) and speculate about the composition of the audience. Surviving evidence indicates that it had a political and social preeminence that gave the journals a potential importance that far outweighed their relatively limited circulation. The audience can be broken down into distinct groups.

First there was an émigré audience in England. There is little direct evidence to show how that audience perceived and related to the press, especially outside the journals themselves. However, there are indications that while only the most affluent émigrés could hope to subscribe individually, the journals played an important part in émigré social and cultural life. Certainly the majority of émigrés, who subsisted on British government relief of 1s. per day, could not afford annual subscriptions which after 1810 stood at £4 for the *Courier de Londres* and *Courier d'Angleterre*, or five guineas for the *Ambigu*. However, even some of these impoverished *ci-devants* made considerable sacrifices to obtain the journals. In 1798 the comte de Luillacs wrote thus to Mallet Du Pan, pleading to be allowed to subscribe to the *Mercure britannique* on a six-monthly (rather than an annual) basis:

> I have been an émigré for more than eight years, Monsieur, and am in consequence very poor, my age and infirmity preventing me from adding to the shil-

---

[116] This was apparently milk of magnesia, and thus certainly not a 'quack remedy'.
[117] AAE, CPA 569, fos 262–3, [Morande] to Montmorin, 19 May 1789; fos 332–3 [Morande] to Montmorin, 8 June 1789; BL, MS Add. 51820, fos 61–4, letters of Zachary Macaulay to Lord Holland, 5, 7 Oct. 1814; DUL, Wilberforce papers, file 1814–15, letters of Wilberforce to J. S. Harford, Jr, 12, 24 Oct. 1814.

ling that I receive from the government. Despite that, I cannot refuse myself the pleasure of owning your excellent work and so I attempt to sacrifice from my physical needs something to nourish my spiritual [needs]. . . . Given the small size of the place, I think you will have many subscribers here: I could [get to] read you, but I want to have your precious work to reread over and over again.[118]

If Luillacs really had no other means than the meagre charity of the British government, he was ready to sacrifice two guineas per year from a total income of under eighteen merely to receive a twice-monthly periodical. Clearly, then, some of the émigré community believed that newspapers and periodicals had been and remained an integral part of their lifestyle. Many, faced with newspaper and periodical prices inflated by stamp duty and paper taxes, clubbed together or shared works. For example, Madame Danloux records that the *Courier de Londres* was read aloud at a *soirée* at the home of her husband's friend Brice.[119] A letter from Le François, a priest at Reading, where there was a large community of émigré clergymen, is even more revealing. It implies that the demand for a shared copy of *Paris pendant l'année* was so great that he only got to see it twenty-five days after its publication.[120] Clubbing together to share the expense of subscriptions was normal practice in the late eighteenth century. Jeremy Black cites contemporary references suggesting average readerships of between 10 and 20 per copy for English newspapers.[121] During the revolution a right-wing journalist, the abbé de Fontanai, suggested that he had an aristocratic audience of least seven readers per copy, while in the early 1780s Brissot postulated that there were twenty (and even on one occasion 200) readers per copy of the *Courier de l'Europe*.[122] Another example of the significance of the journals is a three-page poem sent to Peltier's journal, which describes its importance to the émigré community and offers a regular contribution. It opened:

>Monsieur,
>Tous les dix jours, dans vos écrits
>Vous transportez en Angleterre
>La grande ville de Paris,
>Cité qui fut bonne jadis
>Et qui certes n'est plus guere.

---

118 Mallet papers, #26, Luillacs to Mallet Du Pan, St Peter Port, Guernsey, 11 Sept. 1798.
119 Portalis, *H. P. Danloux*, 307. This entry is dated 18 Mar. 1796.
120 See Mallet papers, #26, Lefrançois, curé de Mutrecy to Mallet Du Pan, Reading, 30 Mar. 1800. On the community of 240 Norman priests at Reading see Bellenger, *French exiled clergy*, 78.
121 Black, *English press*, 105.
122 PRO, PC 1/131, piece 56, Fontenai to Conzie, Aix-La-Chapelle, 20 Feb. 1792, claims that Fontenai's *Journal général* had 7,000 subscribers and therefore 50,000 readers. AN, 446AP/3, 'Mémoire pour J. P. Brissot', fos 28, 165, 168. Brissot's larger figure is clearly a mathematical error.

> Vous savez que tous les esprits
> Sont variés par la nature,
> Et vous donnez avec mesure
> Tous les dix jours, par vos récits,
> A chaque esprit sa nourriture.[123]

More intriguing still is a nine-volume set of manuscript notebooks filled with hand-written extracts from the *Courier de Londres* of 1795–8 in the British Library's department of manuscripts entitled *Table des faits les plus marquants arrivés & rapportés dans le Courier de Londres*.[124] Concentrating on news rather than editorial comment, they betray little of their owner's opinions but reveal some of his priorities. The volume covering July to September 1797 contains a note on the flysheet reading: 'This volume is uninteresting concerning the war, because it reports little, but is of great interest for politics and unforeseen events.'[125] The desire for military news was so great that it supported a specialist émigré publication, *Précis des événemens militaires*, edited by General Mathieu Dumas. It was published in Hamburg, and apparently imported to Britain in large numbers. It served as an important source for Peltier and Mallet Du Pan and was translated for English readers.[126] There are also sprinklings of references to the journals in many émigré memoir sources: Danloux's journal, for example, speaks of Peltier's journal three times in the summer of 1797.[127] There was also a small market for secondhand back issues of the journals. In 1813 De Boffe had for sale complete collections of *Paris pendant l'année*, the *Tableau de l'Europe* and the *Journal de France et d'Angleterre*, four volumes of the *Mercure brittanique* and the first thirty-nine volumes of the *Courier de l'Europe* (1776–95).[128] In the same year Dulau advertised the *Mercure britannique*, the *Spectateur du nord* and, less surprisingly, the *Dernier*

---

[123] *Paris* 182 (15 June 1799), 284: 'Sir / Every ten days, in your writings / You transport the city of Paris / To England / A city which was formerly good / But is hardly so any more. / You know that nature makes / Every person different / And you give a good measure / Of nourishment to every person / Each ten days, through your narratives.' According to *Paris* 186 (15 Aug. 1799), 155, the poet lived 400 leagues (1,200 miles) from London. Since his next contribution was entitled 'L'Arbre de Cracovie' it seems probable that he was living in Russian Poland, and was perhaps a member of Louis XVIII's court at Mittau.

[124] BL, MSS Add. 27473–81, manuscript notebooks attributed [erroneously] to the abbé Calonne.

[125] BL, MS Add. 27476, fo. 1.

[126] A copy of the translation, *An epitome of military events*, London 1798–9, exists in the British Library. *Gabriel-Mathieu Dumas* (1753–1837), *aide de camp* to Lafayette, member of the Legislative Assembly, emigrated in 1792 but returned to France. Elected to the Conseil des Anciens, he was expelled after Fructidor. Dumas produced 12 numbers of the journal whilst in exile and continued to publish it in complete volumes after his return to France.

[127] Portalis, *H. P. Danloux*, 376, 388, 392. The diary speaks of Peltier on six other occasions between 1792 and 1800.

[128] *Catalogue alphabétique d'une partie des livres français qui se trouvent chez J. C. De Boffe, No. 10, Nassau Street, Soho, à Londres*, London 1813.

Tableau de Paris.[129] There were also occasional advertisements in the émigré journals from individuals wishing to buy or sell such collections.[130] Moreover, Peltier, De Boffe and several other booksellers imported French-language papers produced in both France and Germany.[131] Thus there is clear, if scanty, evidence to suggest that at least part of the émigré readership regarded newspapers as a basic pre-requisite of their lifestyle. For the comte de Luillacs, possessing a journal not only consoled, it transported him mentally into a world he had lost.

The availability of individual copies catered for a second category of readers. This was the international merchant community which needed a commercial news sheet but knew little or no English. For members of this group French exile journals were the only regular printed source of news and commercial information in London. The *Courier de Londres* was much the most useful paper for this purpose. Shipping news, commercial news, the price of public funds, rates of exchange on metallic coinage and the appearance of Lloyd's shipping list at regular intervals, all imply a considerable foreign merchant and commercial community, avid to be informed in the *lingua franca* of the period. Indeed, the commercial section of the paper gradually expanded over time. By 1813 its 'commerce, navigation, etc.' column not only carried exchange levels, stock market prices and lists of shipwrecks and captured shipping in every number, but also commodity prices and, frequently, news items. Moreover, each number of the paper advised its readers that it was available for sale 'under the columns of the stock exchange' and at the Royal Exchange, fortifying the impression that it was valued commercially.

There was also an English audience for the papers. It is difficult to judge its extent, but English readers' letters and advertisements appear from time to time. The abbé Calonne recommended his paper to the English for educational or recreational purposes,[132] and British statesmen used the journals for information, and perhaps to monitor the émigré journalists. Jean Louis Mallet lists 'the Ministers'' among the *Mercure britannique*'s subscribers, and Pitt subscribed to Peltier's *Paris pendant l'année*.[133] William Eden, Lord Auckland, subscribed to both *Paris pendant l'année*, and *Ambigu*. Copies in Cambridge University Library, annotated in his hand, indicate that he read some informational reports attentively.

Finally there was a Francophone audience abroad, much of it specially

---

[129] *Catalogue général, methodique et raisonné des livres françois, italiens, espagnols, portugais &c. &c. qui se trouvent chez A. B. Dulau & Co. Soho Square*. London Jan. 1813.
[130] For example, an advertiser in CA 352 (8 Sept. 1808) wished to purchase the first 223 issues of the paper.
[131] See the announcements in *Paris* 123 (25 July 1797), 172; *CL* xxxvi/53 (30 Dec. 1794); xxxix/20 (8 Mar. 1796); xlii/44 (1 Dec. 1797).
[132] Ibid. 1 (4 July 1797).
[133] Mallet, *Retrospective*, 210; PRO, PRO 30/8/165, enclosure dated 5 Jan. in Peltier to Pitt, 4 Jan. 1796.

targeted, which conferred much of the émigré press's political importance. The journals were received regularly by an international, cosmopolitan, Francophone élite world-wide. It included men in or close to positions of executive power, the very people taking or advising on diplomatic decisions, in Germany, Russia, Sweden, Haiti, Portugal, Brazil and Spain. This gave the émigré leadership and from 1803 the British government a ready influence through the French journals.

The size of the audience for émigré journals was substantial by the standards of the day. Table 9 gives conservative estimates of circulation figures for the most important of the émigré journals, erring always on the side of caution. The discussion that follows explains the significance of these figures and how they were reached.

Jean-Louis Mallet provides some of the best statistical evidence of circulation. As secretary to his father and office boy to Montlosier, his information is first-hand, although only written down long afterwards.[134] According to Jean-Louis's memoirs, Montlosier's *Journal de France et d'Angleterre* never had more than 300 subscribers, barely enough to break even.[135] After less than three months it was clear that subscriptions would fall for the paper's second quarter, and Montlosier was forced to make a new deal with his printer. On 23 March 1797 Jean Louis Mallet wrote to his father:

> In my next letter I will speak of M. de Montlosier's journal, which progresses so so ['cahin caha'], whose collapse I strongly fear. He has reached an accord with his printer, and by this agreement, necessitated by expenses and lost subscribers ['non-rentrés'], he will earn nothing until he has over 180 subscribers.[136]

Just a week later he wrote again, saying that if Montlosier continued to follow his current plan he would have only 160 subscribers within a year.[137] His forebodings were justified: Montlosier records that when he abandoned the enterprise: 'I found myself owing thirty Louis to Mr. Spilsbury, my printer.'[138] In the absence of documentary evidence, it seems fair to argue that the circulation of the London *Mercure de France* was in a similar range, selling perhaps 200–300 copies, despite the large number of reader contributions it inspired.

Mallet Du Pan's *Mercure britannique* was a much healthier enterprise. According to Jean-Louis Mallet's memoirs its circulation: 'Soon exceeded 500 copies, and in the course of a few months reached 750: a large circulation considering the nature of a publication so little attractive to most English

---

[134] See Mallet, *Retrospective*, 164, 209. Several letters in the appendix to Malouet, *Mémoires*, notably nos L–LIV, relate details of Jean-Louis's collaboration with Montlosier.
[135] Mallet, *Retrospective*, 164.
[136] Malouet, *Mémoires*, ii. 503–4, J.-L. Mallet to Mallet Du Pan, London, 23 Mar. 1797.
[137] Ibid. ii. 508–9, J.-L. Mallet to Mallet Du Pan, London, 31 Mar. 1797.
[138] Montlosier, *Souvenirs*, 147.

Table 9
Minimum, approximate or estimated circulation figures for émigré papers

Title	Approximate circulation	Notes on source
Ambigu	800+ (large fluctuations?)	various surviving figures
Correspondance politique	675 minimum.	Peltier's figures on losses
Courier d'Angleterre	490 approx. in 1808	Stamp Office figures
Courier de Londres	500–900 estimate	based on known costs
Dernier Tableau de Paris	5,000 estimate	based on known editions
Journal de France etc.	160–280 approx.	J.-L. Mallet's letters
Mercure britannique	2,000–2,500 + pirate edns*	all edns, financial info.
Mercure de France	200–300 estimate	educated guess
Paris pendant l'année	1,000 estimate	derived from *Ambigu*'s circulation figures.

* This total is not intended to include editions of Mallet's opening *Essai* on Switzerland, which appeared separately and sold even more widely.

readers.'[139] In fact, Jean-Louis was probably either mistaken in his recollection, or only thinking of the sales of the French edition, as his emphasis on foreign papers suggests. Elsewhere he records that net receipts from the first year of the *Mercure britannique* were over £1,000, which allowed the Mallet family a comfortable lifestyle.[140] Such profits are irreconcilable with 500–750 subscribers paying two guineas subscription each.[141] Moreover, after Mallet Du Pan's death his family retrieved about £1,200 in outstanding debts from his various booksellers, 'although that class of persons are among the worst of debtors'.[142]

Mallet Du Pan's correspondence also indicates a much higher level of public interest. In a letter to the comte de Gallatin, Mallet Du Pan refers to 500 subscriptions for the French edition in England, and says that the English edition would run to a further 1,200. By the end of October 1798 a second print run of the English edition was also nearly exhausted.[143] Indeed, a separate edition was being prepared for America.[144] These figures are not entirely unambiguous, however, as they relate to the circulation of the first three numbers which were published together as the *Essai historique sur la destruction de la ligue et de la liberté helvétique* and were sold separately. Nevertheless, Jean Louis's statement of the profits taken from the journal implies a total circulation, of the combined official English, American, French and Italian

---

[139] Mallet, *Retrospective*, 210. Sayous, *Mémoires et correspondance*, i. 375, Malouet to Mallet Du Pan, London, 26 Aug. [1793], also remarks that the British public was uninterested in foreign productions.
[140] Mallet, *Retrospective*, 240.
[141] Sayous, *Mémoires et correspondance*, ii. 368, cites 500 readers soon rising to 800, but these figures appear to be based on those of Jean-Louis Mallet.
[142] Mallet, *Retrospective*, 252.
[143] Mallet papers, #7, Mallet Du Pan to Gallatin, 25 Oct. 1798.
[144] Ibid. Mallet Du Pan to Gallatin, 28 Sept. 1798.

editions, of at least 2,000–2,500, especially as the English version ran to at least two editions.[145]

To this 'official' circulation we can add a number of known pirated editions, and postulate that there may have been more. These may even have doubled the circulation. The *Essai historique* was pirated both in the United States and at Paris. In Paris the police seized 2,000 copies of a clandestine edition of the work,[146] and in Boston, Massachusetts, Joseph Nancrède printed 1,500 copies that promptly sold out, and by May 1799 had already published a second edition.[147] There was also an officially authorised Portuguese translation of the *Essai historique*.[148] Moreover, in November 1799 Mallet Du Pan warned his readers to beware of counterfeit productions published in Paris and Venice, which, he claimed, had suppressed parts of his text and added to others.[149] The French police also recorded a regular clandestine reprinting of 500 copies inside France (see chapter 3). Thus, although the *Mercure britannique*'s circulation did not compare with that of the old *Mercure de France*, it made Mallet more money, and had a readership comparable with the figures Heron gave for the leading British periodicals of the day (see table 10). It was undoubtedly one of the publishing successes of the late 1790s, and given the social and political complexion of its subscribers, one of the most influential papers in Europe.

The circulation of the *Courier de Londres* was healthy, if unspectacular. In November 1778 the London edition was printing 700 copies[150] and it seems fair to suggest that its British audience was relatively constant, unlike the continental readership which was primarily interested in war and politics.[151] Nevertheless, although the British audience bought the paper for a variety of motives, sales there rose during the pre-revolution, and may have continued to do so with the arrival of the émigrés.[152] Analysis of the paper's finances supports these assumptions. Assuming a net profit, prior to the editorial wage bill, of 2d. per copy sold, the paper required more than 500 subscribers to break even.[153] A further crude indicator of circulation is provided by the

---

145 My own copy of BM ii, is part of 'The second edition, corrected'. There is no mention of this edition in published sources concerning Mallet Du Pan.
146 See APP, Aa 202, pièces 255–63.
147 Mallet papers, #26, Joseph Nancrède to Mallet Du Pan, Boston, 17 May 1799. *Joseph Nancrède was a Boston bookseller and first teacher of French at Harvard University.*
148 Ibid. #14, Da Souza to Mallet Du Pan, Lisbon, 3 Nov. 1798.
149 BM 29 (30 Nov. 1799), 255. This notice is not found in some editions of the journal.
150 Maspero-Clerc, 'Gazette anglo-française', 590.
151 Continental subscriptions peaked at 5–6,000 in 1783 and fell to 1,100 in 1787, before rising to more than 1,500 in the pre-revolutionary crisis: Maspero-Clerc, 'Gazette anglo-française'; Proschwitz and Proschwitz, *Beaumarchais*, ii. 1004, document 513, Morande to Beaumarchais, 17 Jan. 1787.
152 Ibid. document 513, Morande to Beaumarchais, 17 Jan. 1787, records a rise of 100 in English subscriptions.
153 The figures are tentative. Two issues per week at 6d. per copy = 1s. per week revenue per subscriber: deduct 4d. per subscriber per week stamp duty plus 4d. for operating expenses

value of the 50 per cent stake in the paper bought by Calonne. While Calonne paid £2,100 for it in 1789, he sold it to his brother for just '500 Louis' (probably actually 500 guineas or £525) in May 1794, and in 1806 the hardnosed Saint-Morys agitated to be given the shares at a similar value.[154] Thus the entire paper could be valued at £4,200 in 1789 and £1,050 in 1794 and 1806. The circulation in early 1789 was in the region of 2,240, or a little over one subscriber for every £2 of share value.[155] At the same ratio this would indicate approximately 580 subscribers in 1794 and 1806. However, since many costs, including editorial wages, were relatively fixed, the total number of subscribers in both years is likely to have been a little higher. A similar figure can be reached from another angle on the assumption that the paper's owners would expect a dividend of about 10 per cent on share value (marginally less than dividends on the English *Gazeteer* in the mid-1780s).[156] Using the existing assumptions about profits and break-even point, the paper would have had about 620 subscribers in 1795 and 1806. Thus most of the subscribers lost between 1789 and 1795 were almost certainly continental readers, especially as the paper was banned from entering France in the winter of 1792–3.[157] Under Montlosier's editorship, it seems that the paper's subscriptions fell further, and its survival may have been in doubt. However, by 1802 Regnier claimed that he had restored the 200 subscribers he alleged Montlosier had cost the paper,[158] and in 1803, the British government subscribed for a further 200 copies.[159] This mass subscription appears to have continued until the end of 1814.[160] By 1805 the paper was strong enough to survive Regnier's departure to launch the *Courier d'Angleterre*. Although there may have been some overlap in readership, the two papers took very different lines, appealing to different tastes and audiences. Heron's gazette

---

(assumed): = 4*d*. income per week per subscriber net of all costs except editorial wage bill. 504 x 4*d*. = 8 guineas. QED. As a comparison, British daily newspapers generally charged 4½*d*. in 1789–97. Their daily sales, and far higher advertising revenue, allowed a much lower cover price.

154 AN, 297AP/2, pièce 85, 'Contrat relative au *Courier de l'Europe*, 1806' [draft]; pièce 89, J.-L.-J. de Calonne to Blondel d'Aubers, 2 Sept. 1816.

155 This figure includes our postulated 700 British subscribers and assumes that the continental audience remained at its Jan. 1788 level of 1,540. In fact, subscription levels seem to have risen rapidly in both markets in early 1788.

156 According to Robert L. Haig, *The Gazeteer: 1735–1797: a study in the eighteenth-century English newspaper*, Carbondale, Ill. 1960, 210–11, average dividends for *The Gazeteer* for the period 1783–90 were 11.2% *per annum*.

157 The paper was still circulating in France in late December but had been banned by 11 Feb. 1793: PRO, HO 42/23, fo. 507, Swinton to [?Evan Nepean], 24 Dec. 1792; HO 42/24, fo. 438, Swinton to [?Nepean], 11 Feb. 1793.

158 CL lii/14 (17 Aug. 1802).

159 PRO, FO 27/71, Regnier to Mulgrave, 25 Apr. 1805; BL, MS Add. 48413, Peltier to Paget, 12 Oct. 1803.

160 See PRO, FO 27/90, Routledge to [C. C. Smith], 20 Jan. 1812; FO 27/124, instruction of Hamilton to Cooke on reverse of Regnier to Hamilton, 31 Mar. 1815.

became anglocentric in much of its news coverage, whilst Regnier bid for that hard-core émigré audience which found his journalism so 'consoling'.[161]

Regnier's *Courier d'Angleterre* was more reliant on British government subsidies than any other major émigré journal. It is also, due to a peculiar set of circumstances, the only paper for which we have an exact circulation figure in our period. From January 1807 until December 1814 the Foreign Office consistently subscribed for 350 copies of the *Courier d'Angleterre*, except for a brief suspension between September 1807 and March 1808.[162] During this hiatus d'Antraigues took out a subscription for 100 copies to send to Russia.[163] At the end of 1808 Canning received an anonymous denunciation alleging that Regnier was only producing and distributing 100 of the 350 government-subsidised copies.[164] Regnier and d'Antraigues were thus embezzling about £800 *per annum*. Canning at once wrote to the Stamp Office to verify this information. The Stamp Office commissioner replied that the paper had bought 25,000 newspaper stamps in the course of 1808.[165] Since we know that d'Antraigues had taken out a bulk subscription for 100 copies for Russia and Sweden to cover the interval in the government subscription, we can account for at least 10,500 of the 25,000 papers produced.[166] The maximum number of independent subscribers in 1808 is therefore only about 140 (14,500 copies divided by 105 numbers). Thus, when Canning responded by ordering that in future the papers be sent via the British consul in Gothenburg, Mr Freeling, the total circulation would have risen to about 490.[167] Between 1805 and 1815, on this level of circulation and the product of scams and job-printing, Regnier repaid the costs of his print shop (£1,000), losses of £800 in the bankruptcy of Harper, his printer, in 1812, and a further £275 loss on a stolen letter of credit in October 1814.[168]

Circulation figures for Peltier's journals are problematic. Less is known about his production costs, but he certainly made substantial profits. His notoriety, popularity and ceaseless energy probably secured higher sales for his periodicals than the leading émigré newspapers were able to attract. Sales of the *Dernier Tableau de Paris* certainly bordered on the spectacular. It went through at least five French editions, two reprintings, English translations and a pirated edition seized at Paris in 1795 (see chapter 1). Total sales must have been at least 5,000. His other works surely sold less well, but their circu-

---

161 See AAE, CPA 600, fos 136–7, Andréossi to Talleyrand, 11 nivôse XI (31 Dec. 1802).
162 See PRO, FO 27/106, Regnier to Fauche-Borel, 24 Sept. 1807; FO 27/105, P.-F. Fauche to Hamilton, 27 Jan. 1814.
163 AAE, mem./docs France 642, fo. 3, Regnier to d'Antraigues, 16 Dec. 1807.
164 See Canning papers, bundle 56a, anonymous letter to Canning, 20 Dec. [1808].
165 Ibid. L. Booth to Canning, Stamp Office, 11 Jan. 1809.
166 This may seem improbable in the light of the previous sentences, but the distribution did actually occur.
167 PRO, FO 73/69, Regnier to [?Hamilton], 21/23 Aug. 1811.
168 PRO, FO 27/219, 'The humble memorial of James Regnier' [to Castlereagh], Manchester, 15 June 1819.

lations were nevertheless impressive. Peltier revealed that two-thirds of the subscriptions for his *Correspondance politique* came from the continent, and that he lost 900 *louis* in payments from foreign subscribers when Belgium was invaded and funds seized at the Brussels Post Office. This would indicate at least 450 continental subscribers, and a further 225 in England.[169] However, it is probable that the money lost in the post offices at Brussels and Ostend was only a fraction of the total due from continental subscribers, in which case the total subscriptions could have been considerably higher. *Paris pendant l'année* certainly enjoyed, in Calonne's words, 'a very extensive sale', but we can only speculate on the meaning and accuracy of this phrase.[170] Dare we hazard 1,000 copies? The figure is not inconceivable in the light of evidence concerning Peltier's next journal, the *Ambigu*.

In 1802 De Boffe sold 459 copies of the first four numbers of the *Ambigu* and delivered a further 113 to subscribers in London on his behalf.[171] If Peltier's other bookseller, Dulau, disposed of a similar quantity, total sales in the metropolis were a little over 1,100 for the four numbers, or 275 of each issue. Moreover, Peltier had perhaps as many readers in the provinces and more still abroad. In 1811 when Peltier went spectacularly bankrupt, as a result of failed commercial ventures, £800 was still due on subscriptions to the *Ambigu* for the first six months of the year.[172] This sum was presumably due from overseas subscribers and agents in the colonies. It represents about 300 subscribers in arrears, and even if this was the sum total of foreign subscriptions, indicates a massive demand abroad. If such elements of demand were relatively constant, Peltier enjoyed at least 800 subscribers even before the government began to take out bulk subscriptions. However, these figures consistently err on the side of extreme caution. But even this level of support comfortably exceeded the minimum profitable level, and contradicts Peltier's self-serving claims that the *Ambigu* could only survive with government aid.[173] Moreover there are hints that the true circulation figures for both *Paris pendant l'année* and the *Ambigu* were significantly higher than my estimates. For example, in 1802 Otto informed Talleyrand that Dutheil subscribed for 300 copies of *Paris pendant l'année* for Saint-Domingue, a figure that is just conceivable, and Chateaubriand refers to an occasion when Peltier received the proceeds of 100 subscriptions from the West Indies.[174] Even after the Bourbon restoration, according to abolitionist Zachary Macaulay, the *Ambigu* still enjoyed 'a considerable circulation not

---

[169] ACC, Z tom. CXXV, fos 135–6, Peltier to Drouin, London, 17 Sept. 1794. This letter indicates that the continental subscription rate was two guineas per quarter.
[170] Mallet papers, #3, Liverpool to Reeves, 24 Dec. 1797.
[171] See the figures sent to the Treasury solicitor by De Boffe in PRO, TS 11/429, file 1357.
[172] PRO, B3.3894.
[173] See PRO, FO 27/69, Peltier to Hammond, 23 July 1803.
[174] AAE, CPA 597, fo. 271, Otto to Talleyrand, 1 germinal X (23 Mar. 1802); Chateaubriand, *Mémoires*, i. 421.

only in this country [Britain] but in France' and 'on the continent'.[175] Moreover, government spending on the *Ambigu* rose continuously. In 1804 the government spent £254 on the journal, but by late 1807 it was subscribing for 100 copies, at a cost of £420 *per annum*. In 1816 it spent £787 on copies of the *Ambigu*. From an average of fifty copies of each number in 1804, it was taking 160 copies by 1816.[176]

How do these figures compare with mainstream British and French journals? Although at first glance the circulation figures seem low, in historical context they were far from insignificant. In 1802 the twelve Parisian daily papers had a combined sale of 35,580 (averaging 2,965 each). Their individual circulations ranged from 670 to 10,150. The leading literary periodicals, the *Mercure de France*, the *Décade philosophique* and the *Journal des dames et des modes* sold between 666 and 830 copies each in the provinces, and presumably several hundred in Paris.[177] Although total daily newspaper sales had been perhaps eight times higher at the height of the revolutionary decade, sales per title, with one or two notable exceptions, were much the same.[178] In Britain, the growth in total newspaper sales over the eighteenth century steadily outstripped population growth. According to one recent estimate, 340,000 newspapers were sold each week by 1780.[179] The figures for 1792–1814 would be considerably higher. Since Britain's population was only about one-third that of France, these figures indicate that except during the revolutionary decade, there was a far wider market for newspapers in Britain than in France. Nevertheless, sales of leading titles were broadly similar in both countries, primarily because there were more titles in Britain. In 1772 the *Gazeteer* newspaper had a daily circulation of about 5,300, but although this figure had fallen to 1,740 by 1789, it still claimed to be the second most widely disseminated London morning paper.[180] Certainly, figures of 5,000 were considered spectacular at this period, and it is doubtful that any daily regularly sold more copies until the mid-Napoleonic period, when the *Courier*'s normal circulation hit 12,000. The Victorian newspaper historian James Grant was probably correct to believe that this was twice the level reached by any previous daily.[181] Although the most successful London-based weeklies and tri-weeklies apparently had print runs of up to 10,000 as early as the 1720s,[182] by the 1790s, faced with competition from local papers

---

[175] BL, MS Add. 5820, fos 61–4, letters of Macaulay to Lord Holland, London, 5, 7 Oct. 1814.
[176] See Hansard, *Journals of the House of Commons*, xxxiv. 101–2 (1816); Canning papers, bundle 58a, account for 1 July–31 Dec. 1807.
[177] AN, 29 AP/91, fos 52, 118–19. The figures at fo. 52 are dated 'germinal an XI' (Mar./Apr. 1803).
[178] Popkin, *Revolutionary news*, 90, estimates daily sales peaked at around 300,000.
[179] Harris, *Politics and the press*, 60.
[180] Haig, *The Gazeteer*, 211.
[181] James Grant, *The newspaper press, its origin – progress – and present position*, London 1871, i. 355.
[182] Harris, *Politics and the press*, 10.

Table 10
Robert Heron's circulation figures
for leading English periodicals, 1805–6

Title	1805 circulation	1806 circulation
Monthly Magazine	4,500	5,000
Monthly Review	4,000	4,250
Gentleman's Magazine	3,250	3,500
European Magazine	3,000	3,500
Ladies Magazine	not listed	3,000
Medical and Physical Journal	2,500	2,500
British Critic	1,500	2,000
Journal of Voyages and Travels	not listed	1,500
Universal Magazine	not listed	1,500
Critical Review	1,250	1,250
Anti-Jacobin Review	1,250	1,250
Philosophical Review	not listed	1,250
Nicholson's Journal	1,000	not listed
Monthly Mirror	not listed	1,000
Imperial Review	750	not listed

and dailies, their popularity had waned. In 1802 the proprietor of *Bell's Weekly Messenger* claimed that his journal was the most widely read in Britain and regularly sold over 6,000 copies.[183] However, the best standard for comparison for émigré newspaper circulations is probably moderately successful British local weeklies such as the *Salopian Journal*, which printed an average of 680 copies per week in 1794–5, or the *Hampshire Chronicle*, which sold 1,050–1,100 copies per week in the early 1780s.[184] British periodical sales were much higher than their French counterparts. Nevertheless, when Robert Heron, who had worked for a wide variety of titles, estimated sales for the dozen best selling British reviews in 1805 only four sold 3,000 or more (see table 10).[185] Thus, although in Germany cheap news sheets could sell up to 20,000 copies, in a British or French context, the circulation of émigré newspapers and periodicals, with their relatively specialist audiences, is respectable, and perhaps even impressive.[186]

The direct revenues from subscriptions and advertising could be supplemented by funds from patrons and pressure groups, paid 'puffs' (endorse-

---

[183] PRO, FO 27/65, John Bell to Hawkesbury, *Weekly Messenger* Office, 3 Nov. 1802; AAE, CPA 597, fos 472–3, Otto to Fouché, 5 thermidor X (23 July 1802).
[184] Barker, *Press, politics and public opinion*, ch. i; Harris, *Politics and the press*, 11. Reliable figures for other local papers are lacking; however, according to Christine Ferdinand, 'Selling it to the provinces: news and commerce around eighteenth-century Salisbury', in Brewer and Porter, *Consumption and the world of goods*, 393–411 at p. 398, the *Salisbury Journal* claimed to have over 4,000 'readers' in 1780.
[185] GGB 9 (14 May 1805); 114 (16 May 1806).
[186] On German sales see AN, F[18] 12, no. 43, 'Journal de Hambourg dit le *Correspondant*'.

ments) for products, pensions, embezzlement, bribery or even the proceeds of blackmail or extortion. Although there is no evidence that London-based émigré journalists were involved in blackmail, the possibility should not be dismissed out-of-hand. Many eighteenth-century British journalists sold their silence and from 1784 to 1791 the editor of the *Courier de l'Europe* was Théveneau de Morande, the most notorious blackmailer of all. Moreover, Napoleonic police sources allege that early in the revolution Peltier demanded subsidies from right-wing deputies to prevent him joining the Jacobins and even stole a compromising correspondence between the queen and a former minister in order to blackmail them both.[187] Peltier's description of Regnier as a 'Gazetier cuirassé', may also have hinted at Morande-style corruption as well as tone.

However, government pensions offered a more reliable and permanent source of revenue than blackmail. Sometimes, as in Mallet Du Pan's case, British munificence came rather late. Only after Mallet's death did the British government take care of his family's needs. Mallet's widow, apparently on Pitt's own initiative, was granted a £200 pension,[188] a public subscription brought the family a further £1,000 and Jean-Louis Mallet was employed in the civil service.[189] He took British nationality in 1806.[190] The Foreign Office employed Peltier for translation work from 1796 and occasionally commissioned him to write or publish miscellaneous tracts.[191] By 1806 he was receiving a £300 pension from the British government.[192] Couchery also received a £300 pension, but it probably predated his involvement with émigré journalism;[193] so, too, it was alleged, did Gérard, but the evidence is ambiguous.[194] The journalists' collaborators Henri-Larivière, Fauche-Borel, d'Antraigues, Béhague, Pichegru and Tinseau all received British pensions, but not as a result of their journalistic services. Moreover, Regnier and Peltier

---

[187] AN, F⁷ 6330, dos. 6959, 'Note sur M. Peltier'.
[188] See Mallet, *Retrospective*, 250–1.
[189] Ibid. 251.
[190] PRO, HO 1/6, contains Mallet's letters patent of denization, dated 6 May 1806.
[191] Peltier's commissions included an edition of Louis-Marie Turreau's *Memoirs for the history of the war in the Vendée* (London 1796) translated by Mr Sketchley, and his own acclaimed *Les Campagnes de Portugal, 1810–1811* (London 1811). See BL, MS Add. 38769, fo. 204, Peltier to Huskisson, 19 May 1796 [receipt]; fo. 206, Baylis to Peltier, 8 Apr. [1796], [account]; PRO, FO 27/91, Peltier to Castlereagh, 2 June 1812.
[192] PRO, FO 27/91, Peltier to Castlereagh, 2 June 1812, dates his recruitment to 1795, but PRO 30/8/165, Peltier to Pitt, 4 Jan. 1796, seems to pre-date his employment by the Foreign Office. Secret service accounts in BL, MS Add. 51463 show that he was receiving a pension by 1806.
[193] PRO, FO 27/69, Henri-Larivière to Hammond, London, 7 Feb. 1803, implies that he and Couchery both received similar sums as pensions as *fructidorisés*.
[194] The only reference to Gérard's alleged pension of £300, AAE, mem./docs France 620, 'Gérard', looks suspiciously similar to the total editorial emoluments from the paper.

were also paid to translate government documents and the *London Gazette*.[195] In addition, the *Courier de Londres*, the *Ambigu* and Regnier's *Courier d'Angleterre* all received lucrative mass subscriptions from the British government during the Napoleonic wars. For Peltier there were other patrons, too. The self-styled 'agent of all kings' was variously in the pay of several monarchies. He received payments from the French civil list in 1790–2, the Portuguese legation in London in 1811, and sought employment from the Swedish embassy in 1814.[196] From 1806 he was unofficial minister plenipotentiary in London of Henri Christophe, the emperor and thereafter king of Haiti, and so simultaneously denigrated one revolutionary emperor and served another. In 1816 Peltier gained knightly status when he was awarded the Swedish 'Order of the Polar Star'.[197] He was also the agent of the exiled princes. From 1798 he served the comte d'Artois, who, he says, treated him with the affection of a fond father.[198] Regnier too was on the princes' payroll for several years and, as we shall see, Mallet Du Pan and Montlosier also served them.

The influence of patrons and proprietors

Given the importance of patronage to the émigré press, it is natural to ask how autonomous the exile journals actually were. How far did patrons and newspaper proprietors interfere in the day-to-day production and content of émigré journals? Who really controlled this press? Whose views did it propagate? Whose interests did it serve? And what does the example of the émigré press reveal about the role of patronage and political control in the British press and society at large?

Since most émigré editors owned their journals, few had to worry about the opinions of their proprietors. The exceptions were those who worked for the *Courier de Londres*, and Peltier during the early issues of *Paris pendant l'année*, when he worked for De Boffe. The motives of Samuel Swinton, his widow Félicité and De Boffe were primarily, perhaps exclusively, commercial. Thus De Boffe co-operated in Peltier's prosecution and in 1789 Samuel Swinton over-ruled his editor in order to print abolitionist propaganda, for

---

[195] For example, PRO, FO 27/219, Regnier to Castlereagh, Manchester, 15 June 1819, reveals that Regnier produced a French edition of the Vienna treaty papers.
[196] Maspero-Clerc, *Peltier*, 41; AN, F^7 3703, police bulletin of 11 ventôse XI (1 Mar. 1803); PRO, FO 27/87, Peltier to C. C. Smith, 12 May 1811; FO 63/118, Da Souza to Hamilton, 20 May 1811; De La Gardie MSS, Universitetsbibliotek, Lund, 'Journal under en resa till England, Frankrike, Spanien, åren 1813–1815', entries for 22 Jan., 25 Apr. 1814. De La Gardie, who often used Peltier's services, wrote to Bernadotte concerning the journalist on 25 Apr. 1814. PRO, PRO 30/8/165, Peltier to Pitt, 4 Jan. 1796, claims that Louis XVI promised to reward him in happier times.
[197] See De La Gardie MSS, Peltier to De La Gardie, 31 July 1816.
[198] See BL, MS Egerton 3716, fo. 108, Peltier to the duchesse d'Angoulême, 15 Dec. 1818.

which he was paid.[199] In 1805 Regnier was dismissed by Felicité Swinton and her partner R. A. Routledge. Generally, however, the widow Swinton was prepared to act as a 'sleeping partner' and the abbé Calonne was too far away to exert any influence at all from 1799 to 1804. Thus, of all the proprietors of the *Courier de Londres*, only Charles-Alexandre de Calonne repeatedly found himself in conflict with editorial policy.

Calonne's involvement with the newspaper stemmed from his relations with the comtesse de la Motte, the theatrical genius behind the diamond necklace affair who was gaoled for life after a showpiece trial in which she accused the queen of adultery and artifice. In August 1787 the comtesse arrived in London after a sensational escape from the notorious Saltpetrière, and threatened to publish a collection of (fabricated) love letters that would further compromise Marie-Antoinette. Calonne, desperate to win royal favour, was readily duped into attempting to purchase, or edit, the content of these memoirs on the queen's behalf.[200] Morande, informed of the affair from the beginning, published a series of personal attacks on him in the *Courier de Londres*, though whether he was trying to force Calonne to buy his silence, or working for a rival court faction is unclear.[201] Morande's gambit failed, for Calonne secretly bought a 50 per cent stake in the paper[202] and Morande was banned from attacking him in print. Morande never suspected the whole truth and assumed that Calonne had merely bribed Swinton.[203] In fact, the contract allowed Calonne's agent, the banker John Irving, to nominate the paper's editor and insert paragraphs into the paper at will. Swinton was to be indemnified if any such paragraph led to the paper being banned in France.[204]

Calonne's attempts to exercise control over the *Courier de Londres* were not always successful, despite his contractual rights. His insistence on secrecy sometimes limited his freedom of action, as in November 1793 when he

---

[199] See AAE, FPA 569, fos 262–3, [Morande] to Montmorin, 19 May 1789.

[200] On Calonne's relations with Morande and the de La Mottes see Lacour-Gayet, *Calonne*, 248–74; Iain McCalman, 'Queen and courtesan: gender, scandal and public sphere in pre-revolutionary London and Paris', in Martin Fitzpatrick and Iain McCalman (eds), *Enlightenment, Religion and Science*, special issue of *Enlightenment and Dissent*, forthcoming. Mossiker, *Queen's necklace*, makes no mention of Morande's role. The tortuous web of lies, accusations and counter-accusations concerning the incident can be pieced together in Jeanne de La Motte, *An address to the public explaining the motives which have hitherto delayed the publication of the memoirs of the countess de Valois de La Motte . . .*, London 1789; A. de Serres de La Tour, *Appel au bon sens . . .*, London 1788; Calonne's version of events in PRO, FO 95/631, pieces 247, 'Exposé des faits', and piece 248, 'brouillon de l'exposé des faits'. Piece 245 is a copy of Jeanne de La Motte's manuscript, corrected in Calonne's hand.

[201] On this subject see Morande's correspondence with Montmorin in AAE, CPA 567–9; PRO, FO 95/631, piece 247, 'Exposé des faits'; piece 248, 'brouillon de l'exposé des faits'. See also Lacour-Gayet, *Calonne*, 248–74.

[202] AN, 297AP/2, pièce 85, 'Contrat relative au *Courier de l'Europe*, 1806' [draft].

[203] Morande alleged that Calonne bribed Swinton even before the paper had changed hands: AAE, CPA 568, fo. 348, [Morande] to Montmorin, 17 Mar. 1789; CPA 569, fos 6–7, 37, 199–20, letters of [Morande] to Montmorin, 24, 31 Mar., 14 Apr. 1789.

[204] AN, 297AP/2, pièce 85, 'Contrat relative au *Courier de l'Europe*, 1806' [draft].

feared Verduisant might reveal his connection with the paper.[205] Moreover, Calonne found that events often moved too quickly for him, especially after he joined Artois in Turin in the autumn of 1790, and Swinton could prove truculent. In 1791 Swinton appointed new editors without consulting Calonne.[206] Likewise, in June 1792, when Ferdinand Christin, Calonne's accredited agent, tried to place a notice answering calumnies in *The Times* against the Bourbon princes, Swinton refused to oblige without specific instructions and new financial guarantees from Coblenz, on the pretext that the paper might be banned in Brabant. His temporising may have been for economic rather than political motives, for Calonne's banker, Charles Herries, refused to provide guarantees himself and advised Calonne against doing so lest Swinton intrigue to have the paper banned in France.[207] Moreover, Irving was terrified he would be found personally liable if the paper was banned due to materials placed by Calonne's agents. In May 1792 he wrote to Herries expressing his fears that the latest submission from Christin might be taken as a libel against Talleyrand or Chauvelin, the French ambassador, and demanded written authorisation from Calonne for all future submissions and a personal guarantee of protection against legal proceedings.[208] Nevertheless, Calonne's private papers suggest that articles and documents were despatched regularly from Coblenz, Spain and Italy for inclusion in the paper.[209] While Calonne was away from London, he hoped to maintain control by employing trusted editors, such as Verduisant and his brother the abbé Calonne. Yet even the abbé defied him when he sacked Verduisant in October 1793. Thus Calonne frequently found his rights over the *Courier de Londres* severely circumscribed.

If independent proprietors had relatively little impact on the content of émigré journals, can the same be said of patrons? Historians are divided about the role and importance of patronage in the British press in the period 1790–1815. The traditional view of contemporaries and historians ranging from nineteenth century Whigs to Arthur Aspinall, has been that late eighteenth- and early nineteenth-century British newspapers were corrupt party organs dependent on political subsidy.[210] More recently, Karl Sweizer and

---

[205] See PRO, PC 1/130, piece 236, Calonne to J.-L-.J. de Calonne, Vicenza, 5 Nov. 1793 [minute].
[206] PRO, PC 1/127, piece 210, Swinton to Calonne, n.d. [late May/early June 1789].
[207] Ibid. piece 34, Christin to Calonne, 26 June 1792.
[208] PRO, PC 1/126, piece 391, Irving to Calonne (undated copy), inserted in [Herries] to Calonne 22 May 1792. His worries probably stemmed from the *Bulletin de Londres* column in CL xxxi/39 (15 May 1792). Foreign diplomats in London enjoyed special protection from press comments. Even mild remarks risked severe punishment.
[209] See, for example, PRO, PC 1/128, piece 85 (ii). See also PC 1/126, piece 677, J.-L-.J. de Calonne to Calonne, London, 28 Oct. [1793]; PC 1/130, piece 235, fo. 39, Calonne to J.-L-.J. de Calonne, [?Vicenza], 29 Sept. 1793 [minute].
[210] See, for example, Aspinall, *Politics and the press*; Grant, *Newspaper press*; more recently, G. A Cranfield, *The press and society from Caxton to Northcliffe*, London 1978, ch. iii.

Rebecca Klein have shown that by the early 1790s most papers no longer depended on subsidies, and Hannah Barker has argued that even in the 1780s newspapers were self-supporting commercial ventures with many backers, capable of generating substantial profits from subscriptions and advertising. Hence they were autonomous of their political backers, who paid for support on specific issues. Patronage was peripheral to the functioning of a press which stood to increase profit more by raising circulation and advertising revenue than from treasury or opposition bribes.[211] Indeed, given the sums involved, it is debatable whether political subsidy was an important consideration for editors and proprietors even in the Walpole era.

The émigré press offers a valuable litmus test of these assumptions about British press patronage systems for three reasons. First, because in theory at least, the émigré journalists were more vulnerable to political manipulation and control than any other group of scribblers. Their relatively small circulations and negligible advertising revenues, made the them particularly dependent on patronage subsidies, especially from government. Moreover, under the potentially draconian provisions of the Alien Act the journalists were also potentially more vulnerable to government pressure. Whilst no émigré journalist was ever expelled under the provisions of the act, the republican journalist Delatouche was deported in 1793 and the Bonapartist Carl-Francis Badini suffered a similar fate in 1803.[212] Finally, from 1803 the importance of the political objectives entrusted to the papers ought to have ensured close government control over what was written, and other aspects of the papers' management. Thus the émigré press provides a case study of the practical limits of patronage control.

Determining the degree of British government interference in the business and editorial affairs of the émigré papers is difficult, since the government often dealt with the journalists verbally or through intermediaries, and several potentially useful government sources have not survived, most

---

[211] Barker, *Press, politics and public opinion*, ch. i; Karl Schweizer and Rebecca Klein, 'The French revolution and developments in the London daily press to 1793', in Karl Schweizer and Jeremy Black (eds), *Politics and the press in Hanoverian Britain*, Lewiston 1989; Hannah Barker 'Politicians and the press', unpubl. seminar paper, Lincoln College, Oxford, 15 Oct. 1991, and 'The freedom of the press: political manipulation and the role of subsidy in late eighteenth-century newspapers', unpubl. paper, Colloquium on British History, London, 2 Jan. 1992. See also Harris, *Politics and the press*, 45–6.

[212] On Delatouche's expulsion see PRO, FO 27/41, fo. 150, Audibert to Audibert, London, 28 Jan. 1793; *Le Décade philosophique*, 10 fructidor X (27 Aug. 1802), cited in the *Ambigu* 6 (n.d.). *Carl Francis Badini* was a Piedmontese journalist, expelled from England after 40 years in c. Jan. 1803, allegedly for writing too virulently while in the pay of Napoleon in *Bell's Weekly Messenger*. From February to March 1803 he edited the *Argus*, published in Paris in English. On Badini see Louis Goldsmith, *Secret history of the cabinet of Bonaparte*, London 1810, pp. viii, 263–4; PRO, FO 27/67, Whitworth to Hawkesbury, Paris, 3 Mar. 1803; AN, F^7 3703, bulletin of 19 pluviôse XI (7 Feb. 1803); AAE, CPA 597, fo. 435, Otto to Talleyrand, 3 messidor X (21 June 1802). See also W. Hindle, *The Morning Post*, London 1937, 48.

notably the Foreign Post Office and Stamp Office records. Thus we only have one side of the dialogue between émigré journalists and government, and it is often necessary to surmise government attitudes and decisions. Policy seems to have been determined at ministerial level, rather than through cabinet or parliament.

Even after 1803 the government rarely took a direct interest in the administration of the émigré journals, or in the details of what they published. Despite the importance of the British propaganda objectives, government supervision of the émigré publicists appears in general to have been very loose. The Foreign Office lacked the human resources to establish close control, for Canning complained that to deal properly with the voluminous correspondence of d'Antraigues alone would take up his entire staff's time and more.[213] It was generally left to Canning's secretary, Ross, or the undersecretaries of state, to deal with the émigré publicists, and issue vague noises of approbation or disapproval. But there were also other considerations behind the government's loose control. It appears to have wished its links with the émigré papers to remain undetected, and so allowed the journalists a certain leeway. This also reduced the opportunity for direct contact with them: Regnier, for example, usually used d'Antraigues as an intermediary. In addition, there were few ways in which leverage could be applied to the writers. The British government could only offer a limp carrot or wave a very oversized stick: hope of pensions, fear of total loss of government support. Regnier suffered the latter fate thrice: in 1805 when he was sacked; in late 1807 after the peace of Tilsit when government subscriptions were temporarily cancelled; and finally in 1815. In better times he was brushed off with hopes of substantial rewards and reassurances that he was on the right tracks.[214] Yet even these devices were problematic if the government wished their contact with the papers to remain genuinely clandestine. Thus it is only on very rare occasions that there is any evidence of the government supervising what the journalists wrote.

In general it was the journalists who approached the government. In August 1811 Regnier obviously wanted guidance when he informed the Foreign Office that he had for some time spoken of the affairs of Russia only with caution, and that d'Antraigues had refused several requests for articles, saying that he disagreed with certain of the new ministry's ideas concerning Russia.[215] Equally, on one occasion d'Antraigues sent a piece on General Castanos to Canning, asking him whether it would be useful to publish it.[216]

---

[213] Canning papers, bundle 42, Canning to Granville Leveson Gower, 16 May 1807.
[214] See PRO, FO 95/636, Regnier's notes on his conversations with Ross on 9 July 1808 and 14 Jan. 1809.
[215] PRO, FO 73/69, Regnier to [?Hamilton], 21/23 Aug. 1811.
[216] Canning papers, bundle 59a, d'Antraigues to Canning, dated 'Mercredi' [?12 Oct. 1808]. (Pencilled note: 'sent to Mr. Canning, 14 October'.) *Francisco Xavier de Castanos* (1756–1852), Spanish commander, was the victor at Baylen (1808) and a national hero.

When Peltier became minister plenipotentiary for Haiti in 1806 he gave the British government advance warning of materials he intended to publish on behalf of the Haitian administration.[217] However, other than this diplomatic courtesy, the only documented example of Peltier's taking orders from officials on individual issues was in 1810 when he received instructions not to speak ill of Bernadotte. This was a major policy imperative, and Regnier received similar instructions.[218] Nothing else in his many surviving letters suggests that Peltier was under close supervision.

On only one occasion is there clear evidence of a journalist on the French papers having written under direct, specific, instructions.[219] In August 1809 Regnier wrote to d'Antraigues that he had not yet printed anything on the pyrrhic victory of Talavera, not having received any 'order' from Under-Secretary Bagot.[220] The same letter suggests that Canning and d'Antraigues had discussed the reporting of Talavera several days previously. The battle was awkward to report: after an apparent victory, Wellington retreated, and some acrimony developed between the British and the Spanish. It seems therefore that this was a particularly sensitive issue, and that far from demonstrating tight official control, it appears to have been a special case. Since Regnier's paper had become, as it were, an economical extra arm of British diplomacy, his caution was all the more necessary.

Nor did the British government provide the journalists with much copy. Although Swinton invited the government to submit state papers and articles to his paper as early as 1792 and Mallet Du Pan made similar requests later in the decade, little such aid was forthcoming. Although émigré journalists occasionally wrote to ministers to request the texts of official documents, they usually had to copy them from the *London Gazette*. Nowhere do they acknowledge receipt of communicated articles, and although Heron claimed in his first issue that all state papers and acts of the British government in the *Gazette de la Grande-Bretagne* were official, he dropped this claim from his masthead after five numbers, presumably after official pressure. While Heron may have had an official brief, the government was not keen to be publicly associated with his paper. Such secrecy was also required of the *Courier d'Angleterre*, for in 1810 Regnier was reprimanded after Peltier revealed his links with the ministry.[221]

Government was nevertheless keen to prevent the émigré journalists squabbling publicly. When their printed feuds got out of hand in 1811, Culling Smith interviewed Regnier and instructed him not to attack Peltier

---

[217] BL, MS Add. 37870, fo. 248, Peltier to Windham, 30 Dec. 1806.
[218] PRO, FO 27/81, Regnier to C. C. Smith, 29 Dec. 1810.
[219] It is possible, however, that Regnier, Peltier and d'Antraigues were instructed to maintain silence on Russian affairs in 1811. See also chs 3, 5 below.
[220] See Canning papers, bundle 59a, d'Antraigues to Canning, 24 Aug. 1809.
[221] PRO, FO 27/81, Regnier to C. C. Smith, 29 Dec. 1810.

or others who opposed the enemy.[222] However, the former associates' feuding extended beyond print, and each attempted to ruin the other. In 1809, for example, Regnier claimed that Peltier intended to print a stolen manuscript by Gentz, who would be endangered by its publication. He therefore proposed that Peltier be expelled from England if he refused to surrender it and insisted that he should not be reimbursed for his printing costs.[223] Likewise, Peltier was almost certainly privy to the anonymous letter denouncing Regnier in December 1808, which says it is merely confirming what Peltier has published.[224]

On occasion, too, the émigré journalists risked the wrath of government and nation by expounding disagreeable creeds. Among these was the doctrine of assassination, which resulted in a complaint in parliament in June 1811 when Lord Grey drew the attention of the House of Lords to a passage in the *Courier d'Angleterre*, copied from Lewis Goldsmith's *Anti-Gallican Monitor*, inciting the assassination of Bonaparte.[225] Such suggestions were felt by the Lords to be inexpedient upon grounds of reciprocity, taste and morality, but no action could be taken. Indeed, Grey protected Regnier, whom he had previously hired, by suggesting that the insertion had been made inadvertently.[226] This was improbable, for Regnier had long urged Napoleon's assassination: in 1804 he published a translation of the anti-Cromwellian tract *Killing noe murder* under the title *Tuer n'est pas assassiner*, adding notes comparing Bonaparte and Cromwell,[227] and in 1810 he advised the Spanish rebels to place a price on Napoleon's head.[228]

Thus, it appears that by the early 1800s even the émigré press was secure enough to maintain a distance from its government patrons. British government control was surprisingly loose, even in essential matters of political expediency. How far this leeway was due to institutional limitations in the case of the Foreign Office is uncertain. However, it is clear that the independent-minded émigré journalists enjoyed considerable moral and financial freedom from their patrons. After the shock of 1814–15, when it simultaneously lost its remaining émigré readership and government support, the *Courier d'Angleterre* went to the wall, but the *Courier de Londres* and the

---

[222] AAE, mem./docs France 642, fo. 11, Regnier to d'Antraigues, 9 Oct. 1811. *Culling Charles Smith* (1775–1853) was under-secretary at the Foreign Office 1809–12.
[223] AAE, mem./docs France 642, fo. 6, Regnier to d'Antraigues, dated samedi matin 4.
[224] In *Ambigu* 201 (10 Nov. 1808), 223–4, Peltier says his own journal is in order vis-à-vis the Stamp Office but Regnier's newspaper might not be. (The *Ambigu* was not liable for duty.)
[225] The article appeared in CA 642 (precise date unknown). No copies of this number have been found. *Charles Grey*, Lord Howick (1764–1845) was foreign secretary 1806–7 and prime minister 1830–4.
[226] See CL lxix/52 (28 June 1811).
[227] I have not found any copies of Regnier's tract in pamphlet form, but it appears in CL lv/2–5 (6–17 Jan. 1804). *Killing noe murder* appeared in 1657, and was republished more than once in the next century in times of political unrest.
[228] CA 502 (16 Feb. 1810).

Ambigu survived until 1826 and 1818 respectively. The British government's approach seems to have been determined by inclination, policy and realism. If the client was not financially dependent, his relationship with the patron was contingent, not absolute, and depended on goodwill from both sides. Nor did the patron have the resources to monitor the client's every act. Besides, flexibility could guard the anonymity of the patron and help maintain the illusion of the writer's independence. It would help to stimulate his spontaneity and might play upon the credulity of the reader. The relationships of other important patrons with the émigré journalists appear to have been similarly constrained by distance, journalistic independence and the limited nature of the support they offered. Thus at the limits of press patronage there seem to have been unstated barriers which might not be crossed, but within such latitudes even the marginalised and vulnerable émigré journalist might roam free. The existence of such latitude, and the factors that lay behind it, cannot be ignored in any study of patronage and political relations during the French revolutionary era.

Between 1792 and 1814, therefore, London's émigré press was a successful and buoyant, though fiercely competitive, industry. Subscription revenues alone made many émigré journals profitable: advertising and political subsidies merely added to their prosperity. Their audiences were substantial by the standards of the day, but their political influence was enhanced by the social composition of their readership, especially in foreign countries. In consequence, émigré journalists enjoyed significant editorial autonomy, and boasted considerable influence. The remainder of this book examines how they exercised this independence, the messages they spread, and how, and with what consequences, successive French governments struggled to contain their influence.

3

The Propaganda War

From its origins, as the French émigré press attempted to contradict revolutionary propaganda, successive French regimes struggled to suppress, silence, contain or control it. As a result, the émigré press was prominent in the Anglo-French diplomacy and propaganda struggles of its era, as well as being effectively the only French opposition press during the Terror, consulate and empire and to a lesser extent in the aftermath of the Fructidor coup (4 September 1797). The efforts of the émigré journalists, exiled Bourbons and British governments to disseminate émigré journals were thus part of a wider diplomatic, literary and military struggle to gain control over the news media serving the francophone European public sphere.

There were three distinct phases in the propaganda struggle, coinciding broadly with the British government's relations with the émigré press. In the initial phase, prior to 1800, the propaganda struggle was fought at low intensity and government involvement was slight. In the second phase, from 1800 to 1803, Napoleon waged a diplomatic campaign to silence the émigré press and elements of the British press, embarrassing the British ministry and accelerating the descent into war. Finally, from 1803, the British government took out mass subscriptions to the émigré journals to fight a pan-European propaganda war.

The émigré court at Coblenz was the first to use émigré journals for political ends, goaded by Edmund Burke. Burke's criticism of the émigrés' failure to exploit printed propaganda is well known: the galvanising effect his opinions had when repeated to Calonne is not.[1] Calonne at once set about exploiting his stakes in the *Courier de Londres* and *The Times*, and journals were recruited in Paris and Germany, including Fontenai's *Journal général*, Royou's *Ami du roi*, the *Gazette de Paris*, the *Gazette de Cologne* and Jean Manzon's *Courier du Bas-Rhin*.[2] Suleau was summoned from Paris to establish

---

[1] Edmund Burke, *The correspondence of Edmund Burke*, Chicago–Cambridge 1958–70, vi. 241–3, Burke to chevalier de la Bintinaye, Mar. 1791; PRO, PC 1/124, pieces 165–6, letters of Richard Burke to Calonne, dated 4, 10 Oct. 1791. Conor Cruise O'Brien's introduction to Burke's *Reflections on the revolution in France*, London 1968, asserts (p. 52) that 'Burke was disgusted at the lack of interest among French aristocratic refugees in propaganda.'
[2] See PRO, PC 1/127, piece 34, Christin to Calonne, London, 26 June 1792; PC 1/128, piece 85 (ii), Calonne's notes; PC 1/129, piece 413, Sabatier de Castres to Calonne, Vienna, (n.d.); PC 1/130, piece 61 (ii), anon note; piece 85, Hamelin to Calonne, Cleves, 22 Feb. 1792; piece 130, 'adhésion des émigrés' inserted in *Gazette de Paris*; PC 1/131, piece 55, Conzie to Calonne, Aix-la-Chapelle, 21 Feb. 1792; piece 56, Fontenai to Conzie, Aix-la-

his ill-fated *Journal des princes*, and the Revd Charles Este approached to establish a new English paper in London.³ From October 1791 newspaper propaganda was discussed regularly in the princes' councils at Coblenz, and weekly bulletins, drawn up by the princes' secretary, Courvoisier, were sent to designated newspapers.⁴ Thus, by the time Peltier published his first journals in London, the princes and their advisors had already recognised the importance of journalistic propaganda and established connections with London's French press.

In the 1790s diplomats and successive French governments made sporadic attempts to control the distribution of the émigré papers. Peltier was watched from the moment of his arrival in London. As soon as it appeared, the prospectus for the *Dernier Tableau de Paris* was sent to the foreign minister in Paris.⁵ French agents sought to learn who wrote the articles in 'this collection of abominations against France',⁶ and the French envoy, François Noël, suggested that the French establish their own paper in London.⁷ A month later Noël's spy, the comte de Cardo, had won Peltier's confidence and reported with misplaced optimism that there were less than 100 subscribers, all French aristocrats.⁸ In fact, Peltier's English translation appeared just as British opinions were hardening against the revolution and no doubt helped to hasten the metamorphosis in public opinion.⁹ Thus, on 30 October, an alarmed Noël suggested paying the bookseller Rieder, an informer for the French embassy who was charged with distribution of Peltier's journal throughout the United Kingdom, to suppress the circulation.¹⁰ The foreign minister, Lebrun, agreed to the suppression, and it seems it was executed, for Peltier's subsequent editions do not name Rieder as a distributor.¹¹

From outbreak of war in February 1793 until the arrival of Louis Otto as commissioner for the exchange of prisoners in late December 1799 there were no French diplomatic agents in London, and apparently no further

---

Chapelle, 20 Feb. 1792; piece 119, Calonne to Hamelin, Coblenz, 8 June 1792; piece 168, R. Burke to Calonne, London, 6 Dec. 1791; piece 302, letter dated from Coblentz, 9 Feb. 1792; FO 95/630 piece 21A, anon. note.

3   See PRO, PC 1/127, piece 267, Calonne to R. Burke, n.d. [Dec. 1791]. Este wrote for the *Public Advertiser* and co-founded *The World*. I wish to thank Dr Hannah Barker for helping with this identification.

4   See PRO, PC 1/128, piece 85 (ii), Calonne's notes; PC 1/130, piece 61 (ii), anon note; piece 85, Hamelin to Calonne, Cleves, 22 Feb. 1792. PC 1/130, piece 114 (i), agenda for the princes' council meeting, 18 Jan. 1792, item 7, is entitled 'Gazettes-articles à mis en-écrits à faire-etc'.

5   See AAE, CPA supplément 29, fo. 274, Scipion Mourgue to Lebrun, 6 Oct. 1792.

6   Ibid. supplément 30, fo. 57, Dumas to Lebrun, 7 Mar. 1793. See also CPA 583, fo. 12, Noël to Lebrun, 18 Oct. 1792.

7   AAE, CPA 582, fo. 217, Noël to Lebrun, 16 Sept. 1792.

8   Ibid. fo. 356, Noël to Lebrun, 12 Oct. 1792.

9   Maspero-Clerc, *Peltier*, 77.

10 See AAE, CPA 583, fo. 48, Noël to Lebrun, 30 Oct. 1792.

11 Ibid. fo. 275, Lebrun to Noël, 21 Nov. 1792.

attempts to suppress London-based émigré journals. Until 1800 French strategies to restrict the circulation of the émigré press must therefore be seen in the context of sporadic attempts to control the internal dissemination of right-wing materials and banned books. Thus the *Courier de Londres* was banned from France in the winter of 1792–3 and from occupied Switzerland in May 1798.[12] The following January the Minister of Police was concerned at the use of extracts from foreign papers as an indirect means of publishing royalist sentiments in the French right-wing press. He therefore wrote to the departmental administration in Isère, and doubtless other departments, ordering copies of eight foreign journals, including the *Courier de Londres*, to be intercepted in the post.[13] The *Mercure britannique* was also banned by the Directory.[14]

Possession of right-wing and émigré journals could be dangerous. An early biographer claimed that possession of Peltier's *Actes des apôtres* 'was the cause of many persons being sent to the guillotine in 1793 and 1794'.[15] Likewise, a receipt for a subscription to the *Dernier Tableau de Paris* was among evidence listed against Madame Du Barry in November 1793, although no copies were found among 'innumerable counter-revolutionary writings' at her house.[16] However, the few surviving Parisian police records from the 1790s make no mention of émigré papers circulating in Paris prior to the appearance of the *Mercure britannique*. Nevertheless, according to Peltier, an entire edition of the *Dernier Tableau de Paris* was seized at Paris in 1795, and shortened versions were produced at Paris and Lyon in 1797.[17] He also asserted that a few copies of *Paris pendant l'année* circulated in France in early 1797, and the *Mercure de France* claimed to have distributed prospectuses there,[18] but the scale of these operations was probably insignificant. Only the *Mercure britannique* appears to have merited and attracted systematic pursuit by the authorities. It especially worried the Directorial and Consular police both because of its content and because clandestine editions were printed in France and allegedly circulated widely, even in the corridors of power in Paris.[19] Police raids uncovered a number of caches of the journal. The first seizure came in

---

[12] CL xliii/44 (1 June 1798).
[13] See ADI, L 120, fo. 186, Directory's commisioner to Isère to the departmental commissioners, 3 pluviôse VII (22 Jan. 1799). The other banned titles were the *Journal de Hambourg*, *Journal de Francfort* (both French and German editions), *Mercure universel ou Journal de Ratisbonne*, *Gazette de Leyde*, *Spectateur du nord*, *Provinciale Zeytung* (formerly the *Courier du Bas-Rhin*) and *Gazette prussienne*.
[14] BM 24 (15 Aug. 1799), 468–9n. I have been unable to find the decree in question.
[15] See J. Watkins and F. Shoberl, *A biographical dictionary of authors*, n.p. 1816, reproduced in *British biographical archives*, fiche 863, p. 173.
[16] P. Laski, *The trial and execution of Madame Du Barry*, London 1969, 120.
[17] PRO, PRO 30/8/165, Peltier to Pitt, 4 Jan. 1796; *Tableau des massacres des ministres et des martyrs de l'honneur exécutés dans le couvent des Carmes et à l'abbaye de St Germain*, Paris–Lyon 1797.
[18] *Paris* 104 (30 Mar. 1797), 237n.; MF 8 (20 June 1800), 93–4.
[19] BM 24 (15 Aug. 1799), 468–9n.

January 1799, when 2,000 copies of the *Essai historique sur la destruction de la ligue et de la liberté hélvetique* were found at the Clousier brothers' printshop in Paris.[20] However, although found guilty of publishing works which 'tended to incite the re-establishment of royalty', they were cleared of malicious intent and released.[21] A year later, on 10 February 1800, presumably acting on a tip-off, the Paris police raided the print shop and home of citizen Julien in search of the *Mercure britannique*, but found nothing.[22] However, on 27 March, Marguerite Suzanne Gourie was arrested in possession of 33 copies of the journal. Gourie, a habitual hawker of royalist literature, had been arrested twice before, once for peddling the *Mercure britannique*, so could not plead ignorance. As she obstinately denied knowing the name of her supplier she was imprisoned for two months and kept under surveillance thereafter.[23] Poverty and hunger were rejected as mitigating factors.

By early 1800 the police had discovered that the clandestine edition of the *Mercure britannique* was printed at Rouen. The print run, though only 500, exceeded those of several right-wing journals published inside France.[24] The former *Chouan* leader in the Rouen area, General François Mallet-Butigny, was a nephew of Mallet du Pan, so it seems probable that copies of the London edition were smuggled to Rouen via Jersey by his agents.[25] In February police at Rouen seized two sets of proofs, but the printer escaped and transferred production to Paris, where he received the journal via Calais. Placed under police surveillance, he escaped arrest, for by April 1800 the police had concluded that the journal, now generally sympathetic to Bonaparte, was no longer a risk.[26] Nevertheless, in October 1800 several copies were among a consignment of pornographic, counterfeit and anti-government literature seized in Paris at Lambert's bookshop on the Boulevard de la Porte Martin.[27]

Thus available evidence suggests that apart from the *Mercure britannique* and, briefly, the *Supplément au Rédacteur*, penetration into France between 1792 and 1800 was slight. The émigré journals' main continental distribution was elsewhere. Peltier's *Correspondance politique* had at least 450 subscribers in

---

[20] APP, Aa 202, pièce 255.
[21] Ibid. pièce 263.
[22] APP, Aa 165, pièces 80, 81.
[23] See AN, F^7 6240 plaq. 3, pièces 221–30, 232–4. F^7 3701, police bulletin of 8 germinal VIII (28 Mar. 1800), gives her name as Gourlier.
[24] For circulations of royalist journals see Popkin, *Right-wing press*, 177–9.
[25] On François Mallet-Butigny, known in French sources as Mallet dit Crecy and British sources as 'the Rouen chieftain', see AN, F^7 6286, dos. 5841; F^7 3703, minute of police bulletin of 21 vendémiaire XI (21 Sept. 1802); PRO, FO 27/69, François Mallet to Hawkesbury, 14 Mar. 1803. As Acomb and Griffiths have noted, documents on this Mallet in FO 27/53–4, led Jacques Godechot to conclude, mistakenly, that Mallet Du Pan was a British spy. I thank Mike Durey for helping to confirm Mallet dit Crecy's identity.
[26] See AN, F^7 3701, police bulletins of 18–29 germinal VII (7–18 Apr. 1800).
[27] APP, Aa 169, pièces 128, 129.

Brabant, Germany and Italy, served by the imperial posts (see chapter 2). The *Tableau de l'Europe* had so many subscribers in Holland that the French invasion in early 1795 precipitated its collapse.[28] Thereafter, Hamburg became the new entrepôt between the imperial posts and England. The *Journal de France et d'Angleterre* and *Paris pendant l'année* almost certainly took this route to the continent, as did the *Mercure de France* and *Mercure britannique*, both of which were distributed by Fauche and Lamaisonfort.

Although Peltier sought influential patrons and readers in England, counting Pitt and Windham among his subscribers,[29] Mallet Du Pan appears to have been the first émigré writer to attempt deliberately to target a Europe-wide élite audience. Jean-Louis Mallet tells us that in England his subscribers included 'the ministers', George III's sons the dukes of York, Kent and Gloucester, 'many other persons of rank and of parliamentary and literary distinction', and most foreign ambassadors.[30] Abroad they included the diplomats Hardenburg, Da Souza and Reventlow; the prince of Brazil, regent of Portugal, who ordered the *Essai historique* translated into Portuguese 'for the better enlightenment of political opinion here';[31] the duke of Brunswick, who spoke enthusiastically of Mallet; and Tsar Paul I of Russia.[32] Moreover, Mallet Du Pan was assured that Paul, the key figure to be won over if a new anti-French coalition was to be established, would actually read the work, and so Gallatin exhorted him: 'Crush the brigands! Praise their declared enemies! Encourage the timid! As you compose the article on Russia imagine that Paul himself will be reading you. All my hopes rest on him.'[33] At length Gallatin's hopes were fulfilled. On 23 December 1798 Russia declared war on France. Such an audience conferred influence and prestige, but Mallet found the complaints of foreign ambassadors demoralising and debilitating, alleging in particular that the Austrian ambassador had paid Peltier to abuse him for criticising Austria's surrender of Mainz and annexation of Venetia.[34]

The British government was slow to utilise émigré propagandists. In December 1792, after it was stated in parliament that the *Morning Chronicle* and the *Moniteur* were the only means of communication with France, Swinton approached the ministry, informed them about the *Courier de Londres* and invited them 'to insert anything therein . . . provided it contains nothing so very obnoxious to France as to cause my paper to be turned out of

---

[28] Peltier, *Avis du rédacteur du Tableau de l'Europe*.
[29] See PRO, PRO 30/8/165, Peltier to Pitt, 4 Jan. 1796; BL, MS Add. 37855, fo. 174, Peltier to Windham, 23 Mar. 1794.
[30] Mallet, *Retrospective*, 210.
[31] Mallet papers, #14, Da Souza to Mallet Du Pan, Lisbon, 3 Nov. 1798.
[32] Ibid. #26, letters of Lamaisonfort to Mallet Du Pan, 4 Sept. 1798, and Brunswick, 1 Oct. 1798; #30, Gallatin to Mallet Du Pan, Berlin, 12 Aug. 1798.
[33] Ibid. #30, Gallatin to Mallet Du Pan, Brunswick, 9 Sept. 1798.
[34] PRO, FO 27/56, Mallet Du Pan to Windham, 20 Jan. 1800 (J. L. Mallet and Sayous both published this letter); Sayous, *Mémoires et correspondance*, ii. 445n., Mallet Du Pan to St Aldegonde, 23 Apr. 1799.

that country'.³⁵ He repeated his offer on 11 February 1793, arguing that 'if Ministry [sic] should think proper to employ an able writer to furnish me with occasional paragraphs . . . this paper might be converted to great use to the government in serving to influence foreign powers'.³⁶ By then the paper was no longer circulating in France, and the suggestion was again ignored.

However, the ministry did enjoy a limited relationship with the paper in the 1790s. On émigré matters the government's advice was eagerly sought. On hearing the first news of the debacle at Quiberon, the abbé Calonne requested instructions from Windham on how to report the event, and asked whether it was necessary to abandon all hope. But this was probably not part of a regular correspondence, as the request was appended to a letter concerning supplies the abbé had procured for the expedition.³⁷

While Swinton seems to have abandoned hopes of government patronage after his initial approaches, Peltier, Dutheil and Mallet Du Pan did not. The government did not subscribe to Peltier's journals until after 1803, but he was employed as a translator in January 1796 after writing to Pitt and complaining of his destitution, the pittance De Boffe paid him, and his inability to send money to his family and correspondents in France.³⁸ Such work was lucrative and much sought after. Just days later Peltier informed his readers that he had bought out De Boffe's stake.³⁹

Encouraged by Reeves, Liverpool and Windham, Mallet Du Pan pursued relations with the government rather more systematically. When he discovered a gap between words and deeds, and that ministerial support was lacking, Mallet accused the government of indifference. The accusation was repeated by Jean-Louis Mallet, and has been accepted by historians with significant historiographical consequences. Jean-Louis never overcame his grief at the death of his father. He adored and admired Mallet Du Pan with a reverence bordering on fanaticism, and indirectly blamed the government's lack of support, which he considered wilful, for his death. He subsequently generalised this complaint into an accusation that Mallet Du Pan's *monarchien* friends had been treated similarly. Jean-Louis was instrumental in the preparation of the influential memoirs of the *monarchien* circle, and in the preparation of Sayous's biography of his father, which further propagated the myth.⁴⁰

---

35 PRO, HO 42/23, fo. 507, Swinton to [?Nepean], 24 Dec. 1792 (this document is reproduced in Aspinall, *Politics and the press*, appendix X).
36 PRO, HO 42/24, fo. 438, Swinton to [?Nepean], 11 Feb. 1793.
37 BL, MS Add. 37859, fos 327–8, J.-L.-J. de Calonne to Windham, n.d. [c. 29 July 1795].
38 PRO, PRO 30/8/165, Peltier to Pitt, 4 Jan. 1796. Peltier's claim to have worked for the Foreign Office since 1795, PRO, FO 27/91, Peltier to Castlereagh, 2 June 1812, seems to be a mistake.
39 Notice dated 9 Jan. 1796 bound with CUL's collection of *Paris*, vol. iv.
40 BPUG, MS Fr. 1269/2, fos 13–14, Montlosier to J.-L. Mallet, 10 Apr. 1830, requests materials, on 'les malheureuses disputes des émigrés en 1794' for his *Mémoires* (i.e. *Souvenirs d'un émigré*). Sayous's account rests primarily on John Lewis Mallet's annotations to the Mallet papers and his then unpublished *Retrospective*.

Thus the government was accused of indifference to the *monarchiens*, and a short-sighted preference for *purs*, intransigents and intriguers. This was a convenient myth for the *monarchiens*, as it helped conceal the extent of Malouet's relations with the War Office and Foreign Office in the 1790s, knowledge of which could have proved an embarrassment after his return to France and the resumption of his civil service career.[41]

In fact, the British government did not disfavour the *monarchien* journalists. Mallet Du Pan did not receive translation work, but he had no time, no energy and no need for it. Instead, the government showed its favour by employing Jean-Louis as a translator at the Treasury, an almost unheard of favour for a foreigner, and by granting Mallet Du Pan's widow a pension.[42] Moreover, the 'Ministers' (Jean-Louis is not specific) subscribed personally to Mallet's work, and bought twenty-five copies for distribution in captured French West Indian colonies.[43] This was the first government bulk subscription to the émigré journals. For Jean-Louis, however, this was insufficient proof of favour. He compared it with the support given to the *Courier d'Angleterre*, as documented in Fauche-Borel's *Mémoires*.[44] He did not realise that the difference arose from the contrasting imperatives of the 1790s war effort and the propaganda war after 1803. In fact, the only other émigré paper to receive direct financial support from government in the 1790s was Dutheil's short-lived *Supplément au Rédacteur*.

Jean-Louis Mallet claimed moreover that London was the only European capital where a 'public writer' of his father's reputation 'would not have met with some personal attentions from the individuals at the head of government' – but even this allegation was only partially justified.[45] The direct aid that Mallet Du Pan received was certainly marginal. Britain was not an *ancien régime* state like those Jean-Louis had in mind: ministers were accountable, and under Pitt parsimony was the order of the day. Ministers and civil servants could not be expected to occupy themselves with sending memoranda, notices and newspapers to a journalist on a regular basis, especially as the Foreign Office seems to have been particularly overworked (see chapter 2). Clearly it was going to take a major shock to make the government take a more systematic approach to the émigré press.

In contrast, the Bourbons showed considerable interest in the émigré press throughout the revolutionary decade. Condé's secretary, Drouin, seems to have been in semi-regular contact with Peltier in 1794 and many years later may have supplied him with information for his obituary of the duc d'Enghien.[46] But although Peltier published an article communicated to him

---

41 Malouet's *Mémoires* hardly mention his involvement in Saint-Domingue's affairs.
42 Mallet, *Retrospective*, 247–8, 251.
43 Ibid. 202, 210.
44 Ibid. 201–2; Louis Fauche-Borel, *Mémoires*, Paris 1829, iii. 325–9.
45 Mallet, *Retrospective*, 202.
46 ACC, Z tom. CXXV, fos 135–6, Peltier to Drouin, 17 Nov. 1794; Z tom. CXV, fo. 344,

by Bourbon agents in 1796,[47] he seems only to have been recruited onto the princes' payroll in 1797 or 1798. Maspero-Clerc dates the event to May 1798, attributing the resumption of *Paris pendant l'année* to funding from d'Artois.[48] Certainly the introduction to Peltier's new volume hints that he had new patrons: 'The reasons which obliged me to suspend this journal no longer exist, and the interest that people appear to take in my continuing having persuaded me. . . . I decided to take it up again.'[49] However, Dutheil's correspondence with the Foreign Office shows that the princes' interest dates from an earlier period.[50] On 31 January 1798 Dutheil suggested that the government subsidise Louis de Fontanes, newly arrived in London, to collaborate with Peltier in the production of a 'very useful journal' to answer the Directory's 'imputations' against England.[51] The suggestion probably originated with Peltier himself, and Fontanes indeed contributed to *Paris pendant l'année* on its resumption.[52] Montlosier suggests that Peltier was recruited earlier still, at the end of 1796, in response to Montlosier's intention to found the *Journal de France et d'Angleterre*.[53] However, his description of Peltier's moral and ideological conversion sacrifices chronological consistency to poetic cadence.[54] Moreover, despite Montlosier's complaint that his journal and his *monarchien* associates were attacked in Peltier's paper, Lally-Tollendal's *Défense des émigrés* and its author are highly praised therein, as was Mallet Du Pan as late as 1796.[55] Despite a slur against the literary style of a 'journal suisse' in January 1799, Peltier's explicit attacks on Mallet Du Pan and Malouet only began the following August.[56]

By the late 1790s, the *monarchien* journalists too had close relationships with both d'Artois in Edinburgh and Louis XVIII in Mittau. Despite their differences, the Bourbons courted Mallet assiduously from the moment he

---

anonymous note, n.d., citing Peltier as a precedent, requests similar information. The obituary is in *Ambigu* 38 (20 Apr. 1804), 148–52. On d'Enghien see ch. 5 below.

[47] See *Paris* 64 (23 July 1796), 112–20. The article summarised attacks on Calonne in Auget de Montyon's *Rapport à Louis XVIII*.

[48] Maspero-Clerc, *Peltier*, 91.

[49] *Paris* 155 (15 May 1798), *avertissement*, 3.

[50] See Dutheil's letters in PRO, FO 27/53, especially those of 31 Jan., 15 Mar. 1798.

[51] PRO, FO 27/53, Dutheil to [?Grenville], 31 Jan. 1798. *Louis de Fontanes* (1757–1821), didactic poet and journalist, was a future president of the Napoleonic legislature and grand master of the imperial university.

[52] Fontanes wrote a review for *Paris* 156 (15 June 1798), 227–32. He may, as Regnier alleged, have written an anti-Napoleonic epigram in *Paris* 118 (24 June 1797), 518, reproduced in CA 248 (11 Sept. 1807), but this predates his exile.

[53] Montlosier, *Souvenirs*, 246–7.

[54] Ibid. 227–8. Montlosier's account treats Peltier's conversion and abjuration of *monarchien* doctrines (which certainly did not appear in print between December 1796 and June 1799); his marriage in 1799; and Peltier's performances with his model guillotine (1792/3) as virtually contemporaneous.

[55] *Paris* 103 (20 Mar. 1797), 109–15; 36 (6 Feb. 1796), 218–19.

[56] *Paris* 171 (dated 31 Dec. 1798/publ. 3 Jan. 1799), 151; 186 (15 Aug. 1799), 241–66.

announced his intention to found a journal. D'Artois wrote to him to express his admiration in July 1798, and in March 1799 Castries offered him an article refuting the arguments of those favouring a change of dynasty in France.[57] Moreover, when Louis XVIII's entourage wished to issue a moderate manifesto for a Bourbon restoration they chose Malouet to write it and Mallet Du Pan to publish it. The choice was largely pragmatic: the *Mercure britannique* was valuable for Bourbon propaganda because of its wide distribution in France. It is uncertain whether the commission originated with Louis XVIII or with members of his court, but Mallet Du Pan believed it came from the king. Several historians have written about this episode, but none has realised the full significance of the timing and context of Malouet's letter to Mallet Du Pan (published in the *Mercure britannique* on 25 July 1799).[58]

Malouet's article was commissioned by Castries from far-off Wolfenbuttel, but its publication provoked bitter controversy in London émigré circles.[59] Peltier savaged Mallet Du Pan and Malouet for claiming to speak in Louis XVIII's name, and Mallet retaliated by labelling Peltier's paper the '*Père Duchesne*' of the emigration.[60] According to Mallet Du Pan, Peltier's replies were approved in advance by a committee of Bourbon agents including Barentin, Dutheil and the duc d'Harcourt.[61] However, d'Artois's chief advisor, the bishop of Arras, was concerned lest the princes be associated with the attacks, and persuaded d'Artois to silence them. Malouet and Mallet were summoned to a private interview at which d'Artois praised Mallet and blamed the vituperation on a clique headed by the comte de Vaudreuil. Although Mallet doubted d'Artois's sincerity, he acknowledged the 'good effect' of their conversation, that they agreed on all points and that the storm was silenced thereafter.[62]

The younger Mallet, citing a letter from St-Aldegonde, implies that d'Artois's approbation was forced and cynical, and that Mallet Du Pan would have been abandoned at the first sign of an allied victory.[63] But was this true? And

---

[57] Mallet papers, #26, d'Artois to Mallet Du Pan, Edinburgh, 25 July 1798 (published in Sayous, *Mémoires et correspondance*, ii. 502–8); AN, 306AP/33 bis, Castries to Mallet Du Pan, 17 Mar. 1799.
[58] See notably Sayous, *Mémoires et correspondance*, ii. 400–6; Maspero-Clerc, *Peltier*, 120–4; Griffiths, *Centre perdu*, 190–2. Acomb and Mattcuchi ignore the issue.
[59] See Mallet papers, #10, Malouet's transcription and summary of Castries's letter of instructions, dated 'Jeudy'; Sayous, *Mémoires et correspondance*, ii. 392–405; Mallet, *Retrospective*, 229–33.
[60] *Paris* 186 (15 Aug. 1799), 241–66; *BM* 24 (15 Aug. 1799), 468. *Père Duchesne* was Hébert's *enragé* journal.
[61] See Mallet papers, #25, Mallet Du Pan to Castries, 27 Aug. 1799 (reproduced in Mallet, *Retrospective*, 232n.). Barentin was a former magistrate and *Garde des sceaux*.
[62] Sayous, *Mémoires et correspondance*, ii. 403–4; Mallet papers #6, Mallet Du Pan to Castries, 27 Aug. 1799 (reproduced partially in Mallet, *Retrospective*, 232). *Comte Joseph de Vaudreuil* (1749–1817), was a courtier, close friend of d'Artois and lover of Marie-Antoinette's favourite Mme de Polignac. He emigrated on 16 July 1789.
[63] Mallet, *Retrospective*, 232–3, St Aldegonde to Mallet Du Pan, Bremen, 24 Sept. 1799.

was Peltier more favoured than the *monarchien* publicists? Certainly Peltier's *pur* sentiments were more to d'Artois's taste, but Malouet's manifesto was given preference through political expediency. There were good reasons for this, which stemmed from an apparent duality in Bourbon policy at this time. For, while the tsar and Louis XVIII intended to issue an uncompromising statement favouring the re-establishment of king, religion and liberty if and when the Russian army under Suvarov entered French territory,[64] they also wished to present a moderate face in the hope of bringing constitutional change inside France.

In the summer of 1799 the Bourbons hoped that the re-establishment of monarchy was imminent. The annual elections to a third of the seats in the councils had returned a moderate majority and renewed hopes of a Bourbon restoration through constitutional means. Moreover, the Bourbons believed they had a powerful agent inside France, the Director Barras, who admits in his *Mémoires* to treating with Bourbon emissaries. In the spring of 1799 Barras's agent, Guérin, met Stampfort, Pichegru and Fauche-Borel in Berlin to discuss the restoration of Louis XVIII.[65] Fauche-Borel then travelled to Mittau to treat with Louis XVIII, bearing draft powers valid for six months for the restoration of the Bourbons from Barras. These were approved and signed with minor alterations on 10 May 1799, and thus by a curious irony expired at the very moment Napoleon Bonaparte seized power.[66] Fauche-Borel left Mittau on 2 May, and on 25 May (New Style), Tsar Paul I instructed his ambassador in London to inform the British government of his tentative approval of the plan.[67] In his memoirs Barras claims he was deliberately duping the Bourbons from the start, with the full knowledge of his fellow Directors. This is probably true, although as *agent-provocateur* he would have had ample opportunity to play a double game. But the Bourbons, oblivious to duplicity, believed that their greatest obstacle was the risk that an Orléanist or foreign prince would be offered the throne.

The timing of Castries's approach to Malouet coincided with the apparently successful conclusion of the negotiation with Barras. The most politically sensitive and potentially important role entrusted to any of the émigré journalists in the 1790s was thus given not to the *purs*, but to Mallet Du Pan. Nor was this unduly cynical: if Louis was indeed responsible for the approach, it can be seen as part of his progressive retreat from the disastrously reactionary rhetoric and principles of the Brunswick Manifesto.[68] Malouet's article was, however, ahead of the thinking of many in the circle around

---

64 See F. Baldensperger, *Le Mouvement des idées pendant l'émigration*, Paris 1914, ii. 128–9.
65 See J.-N.-P.-F. Barras, *Mémoires*, Paris 1829, iii. 629–42; Fauche-Borel, *Mémoires*, ii. 218ff.; PRO, FO 27/94, Fauche-Borel to Wickham, 16 Feb. 1806.
66 For *pleins pouvoirs* and related correspondence see AAE, mem./docs 607, fos 153–70; Barras, *Mémoires*, iii. 634–7.
67 PRO, FO 27/94, Fauche-Borel to Wickham, 16 Feb. 1806; FO 27/54, pt i, fo. 210, trans. of the 'Rescript of Paul', 14/25 May 1799.
68 On the softening of Louis XVIII's attitude see Mansel, *Louis XVIII*, ch. vi.

d'Artois, and risked the alienation of many Bourbon supporters. The refusal of d'Artois and Louis XVIII to give more open support to Mallet caused the initiative to backfire, and illustrated the divisions in the London emigration. On 27 August 1799 Mallet Du Pan wrote to Castries to insist that in future the king must speak in his own name,[69] and on 23 February 1800 Louis XVIII informed his agents of the abandonment of his attachment to the *ancienne constitution*, expressing his desire for a total amnesty. He continued, however, to refuse any compromise on the *biens nationaux*, and would not concede ministerial responsibility to a permanent, unicameral legislature.[70]

Despite this fiasco, relations between Bourbons and *monarchiens* remained close even after Brumaire. In 1798 and 1800 Montlosier offered d'Artois the right to nominate a new editor to the *Courier de Londres*, if he would support, or win British support for, an absurd scheme to establish a self-financing legion of counter-revolutionary crusaders.[71] He also played a triple game, approaching British government, Bourbons and Bonaparte simultaneously with plans both contradictory and complementary. As late as March 1801, on his trip to France, he still hoped to arrange a compromise between Bonaparte and the Bourbons. His mission seems to have had the forlorn approval of d'Artois, but he certainly did not have written powers for a formal negotiation.[72] When he arrived at Calais he was searched, and since his papers indicated that he was a publicist, he was taken for Peltier and briefly placed under arrest.[73]

The accession of Napoleon in November 1799 was an important watershed for the émigré press, especially as France's new ruler was a master propagandist who controlled information and opinion more systematically than any previous government.[74] His talent as a self-publicist is evident even in his earliest military *bulletins* from Italy. From the moment of his accession the press, literature, history, art, architecture, monuments, *fêtes*, coins and medals were all expected to serve propaganda purposes.[75] Nevertheless, as Martyn Lyons points out, Napoleonic France had no ministry of information or

---

[69] Mallet papers, #6, Mallet Du Pan to Castries, 27 Aug. 1799.
[70] AAE, mem./docs France 607, fo. 84, 'Instructions secrètes pour mon conseil royal', cited in Mansel, *Louis XVIII*, 118.
[71] See BL, MS Add. 38734, fos 330–3, Montlosier to Huskisson, n.d. [Nov./Dec. 1797]; MS Add. 38375, fos 200–13, Montlosier to Huskisson (memoir), Dec. 1798; MS Add. 38764, fos 120–76, Montlosier to Huskisson (memoir), n.d.; PRO, FO 27/53, Dutheil to Grenville, 28 Aug. 1798; FO 27/56, Dutheil to Grenville, 28 Aug. 1800.
[72] See Miramon Fitz-James, 'Montlosier', 123–6. Fitz-James's discussion of Montlosier's mission draws heavily on a memoir in his own possession of Montlosier to the duc de Maillé dated 7 Aug. 1823. I have not been able to see this.
[73] See AN, F⁷ 7849, dos. 7608; F⁷ 6286, dos. 5846.
[74] Martyn Lyons, *Napoleon Bonaparte and the legacy of the French revolution*, London 1994, 178, even claims that Bonaparte was 'perhaps the first ruler to elevate propaganda into a weapon of war'. On earlier propaganda regimes see Oliver Thomson, *Mass persuasion in history: an historical analysis of the development of propaganda techniques*, Edinburgh 1977.
[75] On the Napoleonic propaganda state see Holtman, *Napoleonic propaganda*.

propaganda.[76] Instead, Napoleon personally supervised the propaganda campaign, writing many newspaper articles himself.[77] This was both a strength and a weakness of the Napoleonic propaganda system, allowing close control, but placing limits on available resources. Moreover, contemporaries quickly perceived Napoleon's hand behind his propaganda enterprises.[78] Napoleon's contribution to the art of propaganda consists primarily in his extension and systematisation of previous propaganda strategies rather than the introduction of new techniques. What was new was the extent of his attempt to establish control over a pan-European public information system, especially through control of the press.

The campaign to restrict press criticism throughout Europe began with the muzzling of the French domestic press. One of Napoleon's first significant acts as First Consul, the decree of 17 January 1800, reduced the number of Parisian political journals from about sixty to thirteen. These were further reduced to nine titles by the end of the year. Further censorship regulations followed. Not content with silencing critical comment inside France, Napoleon also aspired to extend his censorship beyond French borders to create an ideological *cordon sanitaire* around mainland Europe, something that had proved beyond the means of the *ancien régime* French state. The spoils of victory in this struggle were potentially enormous: a monopoly over the primary means for communicating information to governments and forming opinion across Europe.

There were three prongs to the French campaign to control the press beyond their frontiers. First, attempts were made to subvert émigré journalists through bribery, coercion and ideological conversion. Montlosier, as we have seen, was won over on his trip to Paris in March 1801. On his return to London he played an important role, proselytising for the new regime among the émigré community, and from January 1802 wrote under French diplomatic supervision.[79] Equally, from July 1800 Baudus, the editor of the influential *Spectateur du nord*, changed his journal's tone in preparation for his return to France.[80] The Bourbons did not let Montlosier desert them without a struggle, however, and in mid-1801 the princes and their courtiers threatened to withdraw their subscriptions over a hostile article.[81] Nor did the French abandon their attempts to control the *Courier de Londres* when, following quarrels with Félicité Swinton, Montlosier was replaced by Regnier. In late 1802 a French agent, probably Joseph Fiévée, who had been sent to London and charged to bribe British editors, approached the Swintons and offered to

---

[76] Lyons, *Napoleon*, 178.
[77] See Périvier, *Napoléon journaliste*.
[78] Ibid.; Holtman, *Napoleonic propaganda*.
[79] AAE, CPA 597, fo. 173, Otto to Talleyrand, 11 pluviôse X (30 Jan. 1802).
[80] See Hazard, '*Spectateur du nord*', esp. pp. 45ff.
[81] See AAE, CPA 595, fo. 157, Otto to Talleyrand, 21 messidor IX (9 July 1801). The princes dropped their protests after learning that the article was solicited by prominent government MP Sir John Macpherson. It appeared in *CL* xlix/50 (23 June 1801).

buy their interest in the paper.[82] However, the agent's hope of associating Jean-Louis Mallet with La Corbière in the editorship probably owed more to optimism than judgement.[83] The French did not give up, however, and according to Regnier another French agent, probably Badini, approached the Swintons early in 1803 and offered to edit the paper unpaid.[84]

Secondly, the content and circulation of hostile journals were closely watched. This police observation may have pre-dated Brumaire but the relevant files have not survived. Certainly the abbé Calonne told his readers that the Directory received his paper even prior to Fructidor (4 September 1797),[85] but the frequency of references to *Paris pendant l'année* and the *Mercure britannique* in 1800 in French police bulletins suggests that observation was stepped up after Brumaire.[86] Thirdly, the French government launched a diplomatic offensive against hostile journalists across Europe. On 18 July 1800, following severe diplomatic pressure, the Hamburg Senate arrested the authors of the *Censeur*, Bertin d'Antilly and the marquis de Mesmont. The French apparently hoped to extradite them, but they were released after the comte d'Artois persuaded the Russians to intervene on their behalf.[87] Thus diplomatic initiatives against the British press and London-based émigré journalists were part of a wider campaign, but from 1801 they gave rise to specific grievances between the two countries which were to contribute to the outbreak of war in May 1803.[88]

The importance of the press issue in the outbreak of war has been under-

---

[82] AN, F^7 6330, dos. 6959 'Rapport de M.Lamb^e', dated nivôse an XI (Dec. 1802/Jan. 1803).
[83] See AAE, CPA 600, fo. 144, Talleyrand to Andréossi, 18 nivôse XI (7 Jan. 1803), (duplicated CPA supplément 29, fo. 9); BL, MS Add. 38245, fos 112–18, Peltier to Liverpool, 26 June 1810.
[84] CL liv/19 (2 Sept. 1803). Regnier says that the man, who was 'foreign' but not 'French', was arrested six months earlier: both details fit Badini.
[85] CL xlii/18 (1 Sept. 1797).
[86] Police bulletins for 1800 (AN, F^7 3701; F^7 3702) refer to the former four times and the latter six times.
[87] PRO, FO 27/56, comtesse de la Chapelle to Grenville, 9 Aug. 1800; BHVP, MS 723, fo. 61 (1); *Paris* 208 (31 July 1800), 506–7; CL xlviii/10 (1 Aug. 1800); xlviii/11 (5 Aug. 1800); xlviii/37 (4 Nov. 1800). *Louis-Auguste Bertin d'Antilly*, previously a Jacobin playwright, became an extremist right-wing journalist under the Directory. Popkin, *Right wing press*, 10, suggests that his conversion was 'speculative' but his exile and opposition to Bonaparte call this judgement into question.
[88] On the press issue see Simon Burrows, 'Culture and misperception: the law and the press in the outbreak of war in 1803', *IHR* xviii (1996), 793–818; T. Ebbinghaus, *England, Napoleon, und die Presse*, Munich–Berlin 1914, 144ff.; Hélène Maspero-Clerc, 'Un Journaliste émigré jugé à Londres pour diffamation du Premier Consul', *Revue d'histoire moderne et contemporaine* xviii (1971), 261–81; Périvier, *Napoléon journaliste*, 200–25. See also Maspero-Clerc, *Peltier*, 139–79, and Conrad Gill, 'The relations between England and France in 1802', *EHR* xxiv (1909), 61–78. I wish to thank the editors of the *IHR* for permission to reuse material which has appeared in their journal.

estimated by historians: many of the men on the spot felt that it, rather than economic and territorial–strategic concerns, was the direct precipitant of the conflict. Bourrienne, Napoleon's secretary during the crisis, later lamented: 'it is sad to think that an excessive sensitivity to the injuries contained in English newspapers and libels contributed certainly as much, and perhaps more, than the great political questions to the renewal of hostilities'.[89] Bourrienne's testimony is corroborated by the French foreign minister, Talleyrand, who opined that 'it will be wounded *amour propre* that decides [between peace and] war',[90] and Whitworth, the British ambassador, who wrote, 'I am persuaded that, if the First Consul has recourse to the desperate alternative of war, it must be attributed more to the irritation kept constantly alive by the public prints than to the nature of the questions at issue, however delicate.'[91]

However, rather than providing the *causa belli*, disputes over the press seem to have hastened the descent into war, and created a climate in which compromise between the two powers was impossible. In 1802 both France and Britain had high hopes of the peace and, as Paul Schroeder has shown, the treaties of Luneville and Amiens established a potentially workable balance of power.[92] Both powers had genuine reasons for seeking peace. Britain was alarmed at the cost of war to industry and trade, had lost all hope of allies on the continent, and had little hope of victory and no prospect of further significant colonial gains. The British prime minister, Henry Addington, wished to buy an exhausted nation time to recover, while hoping, but never expecting, that somehow a stable peace could be established. Thus he was willing to make considerable concessions.[93] This resulted in a treaty with considerable loopholes for France to exploit 'if it chose' whereas Britain was left with little opportunity to take counter-measures without violating the letter of the treaty.[94] The French regime had an urgent need to consolidate its support and power at home. It was not in France's strategic interest to go to war in May 1803. Although Bonaparte certainly contemplated a resumption of hostilities, he did not want war before the end of 1805, by which time his fleet would have been largely rebuilt with timber supplied by Russia.[95] The British ministry's sudden apparent willingness to resume hostilities in the spring of 1803 therefore came as an unpleasant surprise. How, then, did Napoleon's policy goad a reluctant Britain into a declaration

---

[89] L.-A. Fauvalet de Bourrienne, *Mémoires*, 3rd edn, Paris 1830, iv. 307.
[90] A. Sorel, *L'Europe et la révolution française*, Paris 1885–1905, vi. 220; Maspero-Clerc, *Peltier*, 170.
[91] PRO, FO 27/67, Whitworth to Hawkesbury, 3 Mar. 1803.
[92] Paul W. Schroeder, *The transformation of European politics, 1763–1848*, Oxford 1994, 229.
[93] See Philip Ziegler, *Addington: a life of Henry Addington, first Viscount Sidmouth*, London 1965, 116–18ff.; A. B. Rodger, *The war of the second coalition 1798–1801: a strategic commentary*, Oxford 1964, 286.
[94] Schroeder, *European politics*, 227–8.
[95] See Gill, 'England and France', 66.

of war at such an inopportune date? The press issue appears to provide the key to this conundrum.

Differences over the press were intensified by several important cultural differences between the two countries that stemmed from their different legal traditions. Differences between the English common law and the French civil law systems gave rise to a series of misperceptions that can be readily detected in diplomatic documents emanating from the two sides.[96] Firstly, under English law, the letter of the law has to be respected: it is not possible to use *travaux préparatoires* and other documents to interpret the intent of the legislator when interpreting the law. This proved important in discussions concerning the interpretation of the treaty of Amiens, the Alien Act and English libel laws. Secondly, English law requires the plaintiff in a libel case to prove malicious falsehood and damage to reputation; in civil law systems it is possible to bring an action for impairment of dignity (insult). Moreover, in England, parliament's sphere for legislative action was limited by a large body of customary rights that were habitually observed by government. Thus any attempt to seek legislative solutions to morally culpable abuses of the liberty of the subject would appear illegitimate attacks on the rights and liberties of freeborn Englishmen. Finally, the French seem to have been reluctant to accept that the British government lacked the ability to create particular laws at will, because it could not rely on a parliamentary majority in any particular case.[97]

French irritation against the British press and émigré conspirators surfaced even before the treaty was signed. For, in the wake of the *rue Niçaise* bomb plot against Napoleon in December 1800, Louis Otto, the French representative in London, drew Talleyrand's attention to articles in *The Times* and other British papers which expressed hopes that the next assassination attempt would succeed.[98] The French government, in turn, alleged that the bomb plot had been masterminded by Dutheil and demanded his extradition or expulsion.[99] Hawkesbury, the British foreign minister, refused, saying it would be contrary to the laws and usages of the kingdom, but the British government nevertheless broke off all direct contact with Dutheil.[100] Otto also blamed 'a

---

[96] On misperception in international relations see Robert Jervis, *Perception and misperception in international politics*, Princeton 1976; Richard Ned Lebow, *Between peace and war: the nature of international crisis*, Baltimore 1981; James L. Richardson, *Crisis diplomacy: the great powers since the mid-nineteenth century*, Cambridge 1994.
[97] In drawing up this list I found R. C. van Caenegem, *Judges, legislators and professors: chapters in European legal history*, Cambridge 1987, and David M. Walker, *The Oxford companion to law*, Oxford 1980, particularly useful.
[98] AAE, CPA 594, fos 141–2, Otto to Talleyrand, London, 12 nivôse X (1 Jan. 1801).
[99] See ibid. fos 308, 312, Otto to Talleyrand, London, 26 germinal XI (15 Apr. 1801), and 28 germinal IX (17 Apr. 1801); PRO, FO 27/66, Otto to [?Hawkesbury], 16 Apr. 1801. The allegation was probably correct, but the French provided no evidence and the bomb had already served as a pretext to clamp down on Jacobinism.
[100] See ibid., Hawkesbury to Arras, Downing Street, 18 Apr. [1801], (draft copy).

certain class of émigrés' for articles in the English dailies to which Talleyrand had objected.[101] Thus a link was drawn between the princes' party and the British press, a connection which became more apparent in the following months.

On 16 June 1801 Otto complained of émigré insults in the Treasury-subsidised gazettes, which were intended to widen the breach between the two governments,[102] and explained to Hawkesbury 'how the base calumnies of these writers dishonour the government which is sensed to employ them'.[103] A month later several British papers, including William Cobbett's *Porcupine*, accused Otto of spying and promoting rebellion.[104] Otto immediately offered Hawkesbury his resignation.[105] This was, Otto informed Talleyrand, a last attempt to gauge the sincerity of the British government.[106] When Hawkesbury requested him to reconsider, Otto acquiesced,[107] but thereafter he shared his masters' zeal to control the British press.

Soon afterwards Bonaparte began targeting émigré journalists specifically. As his most vociferous critics, they were both natural targets and a useful means of testing British resolve. Their punishment would be a way of chastening the British press and a first step towards the expulsion of the Bourbon agents, even eventually perhaps d'Artois himself. In addition, Bonaparte appears to have been genuinely wounded by the journalists' abuse of his family, regime and person, especially comments on his marriage in *Paris pendant l'année*.[108]

French police sources suggest that the Bourbons' relationship with the *pur* journalists was never closer than during the period 1800–3. They allege that both Peltier and Regnier wrote at Dutheil's command and that Peltier was briefed at 8 a.m. daily by his agent Alphonse Durfort-Boissières.[109] The inaccuracy of Peltier's reports could thus be taken as proof that Dutheil's agents lacked reliable sources in Paris.[110] Copies of Bourbon correspondence intercepted, copied, decoded and resealed by British agents confirm the impres-

---

101 AAE, CPA 594, fo. 308, Otto to Talleyrand, London, 26 germinal IX (15 Apr. 1801). CPA 597, fos 126–7, Otto to Talleyrand, London, 10 nivôse X (30 Dec. 1801), repeats the claim.
102 AAE, CPA 595, fo. 111, Otto to Talleyrand, 28 prairial IX (16 June 1801).
103 Ibid. fo. 147, Otto to Talleyrand, London, 8 messidor IX (26 June 1801).
104 Ibid. fo. 215, Otto to Talleyrand, London, 15 thermidor IX (2 Aug. 1801); PRO, FO 27/66, Otto to Hawkesbury, 3 Aug. 1801. *William Cobbett* (1762–1835), the great English reformer, was then still in his ultra-Tory phase.
105 See ibid., Otto to Hawkesbury, Hereford Street, 1 Aug. 1801.
106 AAE, CPA 595, fo. 230, Otto to Talleyrand, London, 23 thermidor IX (10 Aug. 1801).
107 PRO, FO 27/66, Hawkesbury to Otto, Roehampton, 2 Aug. 1801 (copy); Otto to Hawkesbury, 3 Aug. 1801.
108 *Paris* 243 (30 Dec. 1801), 337–8; 244 (20 Jan. 1802), 444. On Napoleon's sensitivity to journalistic attacks see Bourrienne, *Mémoires*, iv. 305–7.
109 AN, F^7 6415, dos. 8341, 'Emigrés qui ont reçu de l'argent de l'Angleterre', n.d. (c. 1802/3); F^7 6330, dos. 6980, pièces 2243, 2248, 2251; F^7 4336^A, dos 3, 4.
110 AN, F^7 3703, minute du bulletin de police, 30 frimaire XI (20 Dec. 1802).

sion of a close relationship.[111] Regnier and Peltier were even given numerical codes in royalist cipher.[112] Nevertheless, Peltier's vitriolic prose was considered indecent, and at times detrimental to the cause. On 8 January 1802 d'Artois complained: 'I know it is impossible to contain the brave and rash [Mr] Peltier, but I wish it to be known that we censure his diatribes.'[113] Three days later he wished himself further distanced from Peltier's more outrageous statements:

> Since Peltier is incorrigible, there is nothing which can be done about him, but I think it vital that the conversation of p12 [the duc de Serent], the baron [de Roll?], and especially p49 [the bishop of Arras] prove to the public that our band censures diatribes which are so damaging to our interests.[114]

Nevertheless, Peltier was simultaneously receiving encouragement from both d'Artois and Louis XVIII. For on 20 February 1802 d'Artois wrote to thank Louis for what he had done for 'M. de Pelletier' [sic],[115] and when Peltier abandoned *Paris pendant l'année* in June, Arras instructed Dutheil:

> 201 [Dutheil] can tell 288 [Peltier] that 112 [d'Artois] was perfectly satisfied with the conclusion of his last issue and the good sentiments he displayed in taking leave of the public. 288 [Peltier] is a brave [man] who deserves the full protection of 112 [d'Artois], who is well disposed to accord it to him, as well as whatever [pecuniary] support that 201 [Dutheil] judges appropriate to propose for him.[116]

Peltier's farewell address was dictated by Dutheil in accordance with the princes' wishes, and Arras encouraged Peltier to submit paragraphs to English newspapers.[117] Nevertheless, the princes' party had no say in Regnier's appointment to the *Courier de Londres*. On 6 July 1802 Arras was still ignorant of Regnier's identity, but in October Dutheil sought to employ Regnier and Peltier to prepare a propagandist edition of Delille's *Le Malheur et la pitié*.[118] In January 1803 Arras noted approvingly that '286 [Regnier] in his

---

[111] PRO, FO 95/637–8; Canning papers, bundles 54–6.
[112] Peltier's code was '288': PRO, FO 95/637, Arras to Dutheil, Edinburgh, 1 Mar. 1802. The writer referred to as '286' in FO 95/638, Dutheil to Arras, 30 Oct. 1802, can only be Regnier.
[113] PRO, FO 95/637, d'Artois to Arras, Edinburgh, 8 Jan. 1802.
[114] PRO, FO 95/638, d'Artois to Arras, Edinburgh, 11 Jan. 1802. Code numbers for persons and places have been collated from annotations of British agents on various documents.
[115] Ibid. d'Artois to Louis XVIII, Edinburgh, 20 Feb. 1802.
[116] Ibid. Arras to Dutheil, Edinburgh, 26 June 1802.
[117] Ibid. Dutheil to Arras, London, 30 June 1802; Arras to Dutheil, Edinburgh, 6 July 1802.
[118] Ibid. and FO 95/638, Dutheil to Arras, London, 30 Oct. 1802. Since *Le Malheur et la pitié* treated the revolution and emigration, the Parisian edition was highly censored. The propaganda edition was the initiative of the émigré bookseller, Mervé, who sought British or Bourbon patronage for an edition taken from the original manuscript. See also on this subject FO 27/70, fo. 221, [Mervé] to Hawkesbury, n.d. [copy]; fos 236–7, Mervé to Hawkesbury, London, 9 Jan. 1804.

journal does 836 [Napoleon] sufficient justice in displaying him naked before the public. It is the sarcasm of 286 [Regnier] which sends 836 [Napoleon] into a rage, and make him exhale his fury in his *Moniteur*'.[119]

Napoleon launched his personal crusade against Peltier on 1 February 1802, ordering Talleyrand to commence his instructions to Otto: 'how can a government that portrays itself as the natural defender of civilisation tolerate such horrors? Whatever the liberty of the press in England, the government always has means at its disposal to prevent or punish such disgusting abuses'. Otto was thus to protest, stressing the principle of reciprocity: 'Why', asked Talleyrand, 'when there is such respect and delicacy on one side is there so little on the other? Is it necessary to establish reciprocity of injuries and libels?' Talleyrand had high expectations: 'the government hopes that . . . sufficient measures will be taken by the Court of St James [Londres] to avoid any new subject for discontent'.[120]

Otto dutifully presented several 'indecent' paragraphs from Peltier's recent numbers to Addington. Addington deplored the libels, and promised to communicate them to the cabinet, while regretting that English laws could not accord the reciprocity the French sought. Otto replied that while this might be true, up to a point, for English libellers, provisions existed under the 1793 Alien Act for the deportation of foreign writers. Addington's response was significant. He refuted Otto's interpretation of the Alien Act, which only gave provisions to deport those who were a threat to the security of the realm. Nevertheless, he promised that 'the cabinet will do everything in its power to give us satisfaction', and assured Otto that once the definitive peace was signed, the courts would offer a means of redress.[121] This assurance became the basis of Britain's diplomatic position. The government would strive to meet French demands within the letter of their interpretation of the existing laws. Unfortunately, this did not equate with the powers attributed to the British government by the French, or to their interpretation of the Alien Act. The French were therefore disappointed by genuine British attempts to redress their grievances.

Meanwhile, Joseph Bonaparte, the French negotiator at Amiens, was instructed to draft the first article of the treaty so as to cover libellers and obscure conspirators in the clause whereby both parties agreed not to harbour traitors and rebels.[122] Cornwallis, representing the British, said that this was impossible, as he did not think English law could afford a foreign government a protection unavailable to the ministry itself.[123] In consequence, on 22 February 1802, Talleyrand instructed Otto to hint that if Peltier were not

---

119 PRO, FO 95/638, Arras to Dutheil, Edinburgh, 18 Jan. 1803.
120 AAE, CPA 597, fos 177–8, Talleyrand to Otto, 13 pluviôse X (1 Feb. 1802).
121 Ibid. fo. 195, Otto to Talleyrand, 24 pluviôse X (12 Feb. 1802).
122 AAE, CPA 599, fo. 31, instructions to Joseph Bonaparte, 13 pluviôse X (1 Feb. 1802).
123 Ibid. fo. 76, Joseph Bonaparte to Talleyrand, Amiens, 27 pluviôse X (15 Feb. 1802).

silenced the negotiations might be jeopardised.¹²⁴ Clearly, the French were prepared to pursue the matter beyond a mere complaint, but their failure to insert an explicit clause in the treaty was to prove significant: after the treaty was signed they could only invoke 'the spirit of article one' against the journalists.¹²⁵

Nevertheless, French protests had some immediate results. In mid-February Otto reported that the ministry would not afford interviews to any émigré, and that the Prince Regent had warned Pelham, the home secretary, that he would be held personally responsible for any impact the libels had on the talks.¹²⁶ Otto also reported rumours that Peltier intended to abandon his paper after Vansittart had threatened him with expulsion.¹²⁷ However, Otto advised Talleyrand that expelling Peltier, though undoubtedly within the government's power, might prove counter-productive, by turning the press against the government, arousing public interest and encouraging other journalists to revive Peltier's title for profit. The courts therefore seemed the best method to silence him, despite the danger of an acquittal.¹²⁸

Peltier's next number, a sterile digest of Parisian papers, did not give Otto any pretext for complaint.¹²⁹ Although Otto suspected that Peltier wrote an 'indecent' paragraph in *The Times*,¹³⁰ for three months he had no cause to complain about his paper. Nevertheless, the British press, especially the *Morning Chronicle*, continued to trouble him, and he requested permission to demand the extradition or punishment of 'gazetteers' who attacked the French government.¹³¹ Meanwhile, articles on Britain and her press in Napoleon's 'official' paper, the *Moniteur*, provoked angry retorts in the British papers.

On 21 March 1802 Otto reported, on supposedly good authority, that Dutheil and his associates were threatening to publish a compromising ministerial correspondence.¹³² Perhaps the suggestion that mere blackmail was motivating British reticence encouraged the French to step up diplomatic pressure, for on 28 May Otto delivered a list of demands to the British government. The list demanded the removal of the Bourbon princes, the

---

124 See AAE, CPA 597, fo. 215, Talleyrand to Otto, Paris, 4 ventôse IX (22 Feb. 1802).
125 See ibid. fo. 450, Otto to Talleyrand, London, 13 messidor X (1 July 1802).
126 Ibid. fos 198, 202, Otto to Talleyrand, London, 25 pluviôse X (13 Feb. 1802); 28 pluviôse X (16 Feb. 1802).
127 Ibid. fos 218–19, Otto to Talleyrand, London, 11 ventôse X (1 Mar. 1802). Nicholas Vansittart (1766–1851) was joint-secretary to the Treasury 1801–4 and 1806–7.
128 Ibid. fos 202–5, Otto to Talleyrand, London, 28 pluviôse X (16 Feb. 1802); fos 207–8, J. M. P. to Otto, Brompton, 13 Feb. 1802.
129 Ibid. fos 260–1, Otto to Talleyrand, London, 28 ventôse X (18 Mar. 1802). Although *Paris* 246 was dated 15 Mar. 1802, its appearance was only noted in AAE, CPA 597, fo. 285, Otto to Talleyrand, London, 6 germinal X (26 Mar. 1802).
130 See ibid.
131 Ibid. fos 393, 397–8, letters of Otto to Talleyrand, London, 4 floréal X (23 Apr. 1802); 25 floréal X (14 May 1802); 29 floréal X (18 May 1802).
132 Ibid. fo. 271, Otto to Talleyrand, London, 1 germinal X (21 Mar. 1802).

conspirator Georges Cadoudal and the bishops of Arras and St Pol de Léon from England, in accordance with the treaty, and insisted that *ancien régime* decorations should not be worn in Britain. It did not, however, demand the expulsion of émigré journalists.[133]

Then, in early July, after Peltier had published another provocative number, Otto finally wrote to Hawkesbury invoking article one of the treaty against him, and asked Talleyrand for instructions about what punishment to demand. He also gave a new reason for concern, following French intervention in Saint-Domingue, arguing 'that Peltier's paper, as well as the *Courier [de Londres]*, is principally written for distribution in our colonies... to spread false intelligence concerning the state of France and the intentions of her First Magistrate'.[134] Informed that Dutheil was sending 300 copies of *Paris pendant l'année* to Saint-Domingue, the French began distributing their Paris-based English language newspaper, *The Argus*, in the West Indies.[135]

On 11 July Talleyrand replied to Otto's request, having consulted Napoleon, who asked that Otto protest in the strongest terms. Talleyrand thus instructed Otto that 'it is impossible to believe that Mr. Addington will not find the means to silence these libellers, seeing that he has the will to do so, and he must be particularly indignant to see attempts to reduce the advantages of the peace by such reprehensible attacks'.[136] Three days later, the police minister, Fouché, ordered Otto to press the British government to introduce new legislation, remarking that 'liberty of the press does not legitimise calumny any more than the fabrication of arms legitimises murder'.[137] In response Otto informed Fouché that he would strive to make the British government understand that:

> It would be absurd to continue to justify a violation of the law of nations by the non-existence of laws, and to oblige the minister of a foreign power to appear before a court to obtain the punishment of a political misdemeanour. The authority that signed the peace must have the means to conserve it, otherwise it must bear responsibility for the consequences.[138]

The views expressed by Bonaparte, Talleyrand, Fouché and Otto at this juncture encapsulate the French perspective on the press issue. They were convinced that the attacks on the French government were libellous and that existing laws never intended that they should be tolerated. It was therefore inconceivable that laws or abstract 'rights' should prevent them being punished, especially as they could be considered 'political' rather than 'crim-

---

[133] Ibid. fo. 407, Talleyrand to Otto, Paris, 9 prairial X (28 May 1802)
[134] Ibid. fo. 450, Otto to Talleyrand, London, 13 messidor X (1 July 1802).
[135] Ibid. fo. 271, Otto to Talleyrand, London, 1 germinal X (21 Mar. 1802); Gill, 'England and France', 64.
[136] AAE, CPA 597, fo. 455, Talleyrand to Otto, Paris, 23 messidor X (11 July 1802).
[137] Ibid. fos 468–9, Fouché to Otto, Paris, 26 messidor X (14 July 1802).
[138] Ibid. fos 470–3, Otto to Fouché, 5 thermidor X (23 July 1802), (copy).

inal' offences. The British government thus had a clear obligation to act, and ought to possess the power to do so. These themes recur frequently in subsequent French complaints and diplomatic correspondence.

On 25 July Otto informed Hawkesbury that his government had authorised him to demand the punishment of Peltier. He noted the 'unfavourable impact' Peltier, Regnier, Cobbett 'and other writers who resemble them' were having 'on the cordial relations subsisting between the two countries', and objected to the protection given to men 'whose writings are in open contradiction of the principles of the peace', observing that:

> even if article one of the treaty of Amiens had not provided for the conservation of the respect which two independent states mutually owe one another, the general principles of the law of nations would formally condemn so revolting an abuse of the liberty of the press. It is impossible to believe that the laws can give more latitude to a libeller than any other individual, who without a declaration of war, allows himself to offend against neighbourly obligations.[139]

Hawkesbury responded as positively as possible, although from a French perspective his answer seemed barely satisfactory. He referred the Peltier affair to the attorney-general, informed Otto of the difficulties attendant upon a trial, and reiterated that the government would try to ensure a conviction.[140] Otto therefore informed Paris that in England only false and calumnious facts could be punished under the law and warned of the danger of an unsympathetic jury, adding that defeat would necessitate his own recall and result in a rupture.[141]

The French attributed the British failure to meet their demands to pusillanimity. Otto asserted that 'if, despite my numerous complaints, the King's Council has still not used the [full] power of the law, it can only be attributed to the extreme feebleness of Lord Pelham, the minister of the interior' and Talleyrand noted 'from here everything appears to bear a character of feebleness'.[142] This misperception encouraged the French to increase diplomatic pressure.

Thus, on 11 August, Talleyrand told Otto to insist on British compliance with the demands of 28 May, the silencing of 'diatribes' in émigré and English journals and the removal of France's enemies from Jersey.[143] Six days later Otto delivered Hawkesbury a note concentrating on the press issue which

---

[139] PRO, FO 27/66, Otto to Hawkesbury, 25 July 1802; a copy in AAE, CPA 597, fos 474–5 is dated 26 July 1802.
[140] See AAE, CPA 597, fo. 482, Hawkesbury to Otto, Downing Street, 29 July [1802].
[141] Ibid. fo. 477, Otto to Talleyrand, London, 8 thermidor X (26 July 1802); fo. 480, Otto to Talleyrand, London, 12 thermidor X (30 July 1802); fo. 470, Otto to Talleyrand, London, 5 thermidor X (23 July 1802).
[142] Ibid. fo. 502, Otto to Talleyrand, London, 28 thermidor X (15 Aug. 1802); fos 494–5, Talleyrand to Otto, Paris, 24 thermidor X (11 Aug. 1802), at fo. 494.
[143] Ibid. fos 494–5, Talleyrand to Otto, Paris, 24 thermidor X (11 Aug. 1802), at fo. 495.

stated that a government which failed to suppress press attacks on foreign powers provided a few libellers with power to compromise 'the public peace'. While the British constitution might allow that 'the rights of the state be silenced by the rights of the people', this consideration should not over-rule the 'public law of nations'. He asserted that article one of the treaty of Amiens forbade either power to harbour persons whose activities were prejudicial to the other, directly or indirectly, and added:

> the greatest of prejudices is undoubtedly that which tends to degrade a foreign government or to excite civil or religious disturbances on her soil, and the most striking protection is that which shields men who seek not only to disturb the political tranquillity of Europe but to dissolve the bonds of society itself.

Otto alleged that the entire French nation was the victim of a deliberate scheme of defamation by French and English writers, both journalists and authors of tracts attacking Napoleon's concordat with the pope. He insisted again on the fulfilment of the demands of 28 May, referring explicitly to article one of the Alien Act, which allowed for the deportation of aliens following an Order in Council.[144] Hawkesbury was surprised by this French ultimatum, and concluded that since war was against French interests, 'temper' rather than 'policy' was to blame. He therefore instructed Anthony Merry, the British *chargé d'affaires* in Paris, to give 'a frank explanation' of the British government's line to remove the 'irritation' between the two governments. Merry was to provide assurances that Cadoudal and any *Chouans* remaining in Jersey would be removed. However, Hawkesbury reiterated that 'his majesty cannot and never will in consequence of any representation from a foreign power make any concession which can be in the smallest degree dangerous to the liberty of the press as secured by the constitution of this country'.[145]

On 19 August the attorney-general confirmed that the first number of Peltier's *Ambigu* was indeed criminally libellous. However, he also expressed concern that an article published in the *Moniteur* of 9 August could prejudice the jury.[146] The article in question was almost certainly written by Napoleon himself. It accused the British government of pusillanimity or bad faith. Either the British government lacked sufficient authority to make its will felt, and therefore could not be considered a sovereign power at all, or it was deliberately shielding the journalists and promoting attacks on a sovereign state with which it was at peace. The publication of this article was a grave

---

[144] Ibid. fos 504–8, Otto to Hawkesbury, 28 thermidor X (15 Aug. 1802), (copy). A copy in PRO, FO 27/66 is dated 17 Aug. 1802.
[145] PRO, FO 27/63, Hawkesbury to Merry, confidential instructions, Downing Street, 28 Aug. 1802. There was a delay between complaint and response while Hawkesbury consulted with several cabinet members who were away in the country.
[146] AAE, CPA 597, fo. 517, Otto to Talleyrand, London, 2 fructidor X (19 Aug. 1802).

miscalculation. According to Otto, several cabinet members felt that Hawkesbury should reply to his complaints by listing grievances against the *Moniteur*, especially its absurd and distasteful suggestion that Cadoudal would have been awarded the Order of the Garter had the *machine infernale* killed Napoleon. The proposal was overturned, but it was suggested that the French government should publish a retraction to help ensure Peltier's conviction.[147]

The French, mistaking Hawkesbury's conciliatory gestures for weakness, pushed for more positive action, and in an interview on 4 September Talleyrand refuted Merry's claims that the British constitution was inviolate by referring to the suspension of *Habeas corpus* during the revolutionary wars. He insisted that it was incumbent upon the British to regulate their laws and constitution in accordance with the paramount principles of the 'general law of nations' and have the libellers punished. Merry replied courageously that such a principle would 'subvert the independence of a state' and subject it to 'the arbitrary opinion of another'. The constitutional remedy to the complaint had already been indicated to the French government, and it had already prevented the circulation of the libels in France by banning English journals.[148] Two days later Otto informed Talleyrand that proceedings had been started against Peltier.[149]

The events of August and early September hardened British resolve. The *Moniteur* of 9 August provoked angry retorts from the British press and hardened the ministry's attitude. Previously it was broadly accepted that the French had a legitimate grievance against the press, and the government seems to have made genuine attempts at conciliation, but this article was deemed more outrageous than the original offence. Hawkesbury thought it 'inexcusable'.[150] After consultations with the cabinet he wrote to Merry explaining the government's position:

> The French government would have been warranted in expecting every redress that the laws of this country could afford them – but as instead ... they have thought fit to resort to recrimination themselves ... they could have no right to complain if subsequent appeals to H. M. had failed to produce the effect that otherwise would have attended it. Whatever may have been the nature of the prior injury, they have in fact taken the law into their own hands.

Moreover, whereas the British government disapproved of the English newspaper articles:

---

[147] See ibid. fo. 530, Otto to Talleyrand, London, 16 fructidor X (2 Sept. 1802); PRO, FO 27/64, Merry to Hawkesbury, Paris, 5 Sept. 1802.
[148] Ibid.
[149] AAE, CPA 597, fo. 530, Otto to Talleyrand, London, 20 fructidor X (6 Sept. 1802).
[150] PRO, FO 27/63, Hawkesbury to Merry, 13 Aug. 1802.

the paragraph in the *Moniteur* appeared in a paper avowedly official, for which the government are therefore considered ... responsible ... and this retort is not confined to the unauthorised English newspapers, or to the other publications of which complaint is made, but is converted into, and made a pretence for a direct attack upon the government of His Majesty.

Hawkesbury reaffirmed that the government would neither compromise the liberty of the press by introducing prior constraints, nor change the constitution to gratify the wishes of a foreign power. The French government had every right to ban any publication on their own soil, but they should refrain from interfering in English internal affairs, save through due process of law. If they could prove that the bishops of St Pol de Léon and Arras had distributed seditious papers along the French coast, the government would feel obliged to expel them. In the interim the last *Chouans* were being removed from Jersey and Cadoudal's fate was being considered. However, although they did not desire their presence, it would not be lawful or honourable for the government to expel the Bourbon princes provided that they lived quietly and peaceably.[151]

Moreover, in late August, the British ignored a flagrant violation of treaty obligations when Bonaparte ordered his customs service to disregard three articles of the agreement signed between the English and French post offices after the conclusion of the peace. These violations, trivial in themselves, were brought to the government's attention on 21 August,[152] the very day Otto delivered an ultimatum insisting that the British evacuate Malta in accordance with treaty stipulations, and illustrate the importance Napoleon attached to the press issue. For the British soon discovered that Napoleon was apparently motivated by 'a personal indisposition to Mr Freeling, the secretary of the Post Office' because he owned shares in the offending *True Briton* and *Sun* newspapers.[153] The British government's silence on the issue, which was never reported in the press, suggests that they sensed that war could be imminent, and a vociferous protest was unwise if they sought peace. They considered the issue insignificant and hoped French measures would be tacitly revoked.[154]

Thus, although unyielding on the press issue, the British government was prepared to make other concessions. However, Otto's note, the postal violations and the *Moniteur* article had made it realise just how seriously Napoleon took the press issue. His concern was not mere political posturing to extort diplomatic concessions: he was in deadly earnest in his attempts to silence critical opposition throughout Europe. It was in these circumstances that Pelham wrote to his predecessor, Portland, on 1 September 1802, expressing the seriousness of the crisis:

---

[151] Ibid. Hawkesbury to Merry, confidential instructions, Downing Street, 28 Aug. 1802.
[152] PRO, FO 27/65, Freeling to Lord Harvey, 21 Aug. 1802.
[153] PRO, FO 323/4, Hawkesbury to Whitworth, Addiscombe Place, 27 Sept. 1802.
[154] Ibid.

I shall be very glad to have some conversation with you . . . upon Otto's last note which involves many very serious considerations, much more serious than many of our colleagues seem to attribute to them; we have got over the difficulty for the moment, without doing any mischief, but I am sure that the First Consul will not give up the point and we shall have more complaints and more unpleasant discussions.

He also indicated his attitude to Peltier, stressing his concern to maintain press freedom as a buttress of English liberty:

I am determined not to remove Peltier or any other Alien for libels against France, under any authority which by a forced construction, I may be supposed to have under the Alien Bill: and I confess that I am unwilling to check the freest discussion of the demerits of the French government and Constitution, as I consider such discussions very useful in satisfying the people of this country, that they can not improve their situation by any attempts to follow the example of France.[155]

Pelham's pragmatic fear of the power of the press was probably genuine. However, the British government was reluctant to be deliberately obstructive, and so editors of pro-government papers were informally notified that the government disapproved of attacks on Napoleon. Consequently in August 1802 Heriot, proprietor of the *True Briton*, dismissed his editor, Henry Redhead Yorke, after the government complained about a paragraph attacking Bonaparte's character.[156] However, Addington assured Otto that Yorke's dismissal was a private favour: the government had no direct influence over the paper, or any other so-called 'ministerial' papers.[157] Any attempt to claim such a power, he said, would certainly drive that paper into opposition. This was probably true enough. By 1802 the major ministerial papers were financially independent and would rather lose political subsidies than risk taking an unpopular editorial line.[158] Yet it was also common knowledge that the prime minister's brother, Hiley Addington, frequently placed articles in pro-government journals.[159] French confusion over the extent to which the government controlled the 'ministerial' press was therefore understandable, and it was natural that they should equate the British 'ministerial' papers with the French 'official' journals. This could only increase their perception of British duplicity.

---

155 BL, MS Add. 33109, fos 406–7, Pelham to Portland, Wimbledon, 1 Sept. 1802 (copy).
156 Ziegler, *Addington*, 165. See also Aspinall, *Politics and the press*, 204–5.
157 AAE, CPA 597, fos 513–15, Addington to Otto, Langford Court, 15 Aug. 1802. Addington's reference to the *Sun* in this letter was a natural mistake: Heriot owned both papers.
158 Aspinall, *Politics and the press*, 204–5.
159 On Hiley's role see ibid. 205–6; Ziegler, *Addington*, 130–1.

Meanwhile, Peltier continued to distribute the *Ambigu* clandestinely,[160] and the French government received reports that Peltier and Regnier had sent their wives to Paris and ordered a thorough police search.[161] It proved fruitless, for the women were almost certainly not in Paris, but at Bordeaux gathering facts to support Peltier's mother-in-law's claims for compensation for her husband's distillery.[162] Simultaneously, Otto continued to complain against the English press and the *Courier de Londres*, and the new French ambassador to London, Andréossi, became convinced that Regnier served several masters, and probably had links to members of Pitt's ministry, who were opposed to peace.[163] Talleyrand protested against the *Gazette de Jersey*, alleging that it was distributed on the French coast with British collusion.[164] He repeated his belief that the British government quite possibly subsidised 'libels directed against the present administration of France', and complained against the British press, in particular the *Morning Post*.[165] He demanded action, musing 'what faith can we place in the assurances of the ministers that they are powerless to act when we see that the papers do not indulge in attacks against the English ministers, nor the royal family, nor the public credit?' and 'if its [i.e. the British government's] power is so limited, what confidence can it inspire?'[166]

Against this background of continuing recrimination and agitation, more fundamental issues began to emerge. The French annexation of Piedmont on 21 September and Act of Mediation in Switzerland nine days later aroused British disquiet. However, a more important issue was the future of the strategic island of Malta. Under article 10 of the treaty Britain was to return Malta to the Knights of St John after the election of a new grand master by the pope. The independence of the order was to be guaranteed by the major European powers, but the order was now based in St Petersburg, and although

---

[160] See AAE, CPA 597, fos 533–6, Otto to Talleyrand, London, 20 fructidor X (6 Sept. 1802); CPA 600, fos 10–13, Otto to Talleyrand, 11 vendémiaire XI (2 Oct. 1802).

[161] See AAE, CPA 600, fo. 137, Andréossi to Talleyrand, 11 nivôse XI (31 Dec. 1802) (duplicated CPA supp. 21, fo. 256); AN, F^7 6330, dos. 6959, Talleyrand to Grand Justice Regnier, 20 nivôse XI (9 Jan. 1803) and subsequent correspondence of Regnier with the Prefect of Police.

[162] AAE, CPA 601, fos 96ff., list of British subjects claiming compensation for property seized in the revolution, 27 ventôse XI (17 Mar. 1803). The factual detail of the claim suggests it was researched at source.

[163] AAE, CPA 600, fos 5–6, Talleyrand to Otto, Paris, 3 vendémiaire XI (24 Sept. 1802); fo. 136, Andréossi to Talleyrand, 11 nîvose XI (31 Dec. 1802). Andréossi's assertion seems probable. Windham's letters to Cobbett in BL, MS Add. 37853, show that Windham and Cobbett were in regular contact during 1802–3.

[164] AAE, CPA 600, fo. 43, Talleyrand to Otto, Paris, 1 brumaire XI (22 Oct. 1802). CPA 601, fos 76–7, Joseph Chépy to Talleyrand, St Helier, 18 pluviôse XI (6 Feb. 1803), confirms the distribution.

[165] AAE, CPA 600, fo. 111, Talleyrand to Andréossi, Paris, 11 frimaire XI (1 Dec. 1802); PRO, FO 27/67, Talleyrand to Whitworth, Paris, 11 Feb. 1803; Whitworth to Talleyrand, Paris, 11 Feb. 1803; Whitworth to Hawkesbury, Paris, 11 Feb. 1803.

[166] AAE, CPA 600, fos 5–6, Talleyrand to Otto, Paris, 3 vendémiaire XI (23 Sept. 1802).

the election was meant to take place on Malta, candidates had already been nominated. This provided an excuse for Russia to withhold its guarantee, and in the event only Austria supplied one. None the less, the British appear to have still been intent on withdrawal in early August when Hawkesbury requested a guarantee from Prussia.[167] However, by the end of the year they were prevaricating: the instructions to the new British ambassador, Whitworth, dated 14 November 1802, advised him against making any commitment on Malta even if arrangements were made to carry out the rest of article 10.[168]

What made the British government change its mind? The initial motive appears to have been fears that France and Russia were planning to dismember the Ottoman empire. In late June the British ambassador in Vienna reported that Napoleon had declared that he envisaged a further war with Britain, and in August Russia's refusal to guarantee Malta gave serious cause for alarm. News of Colonel Sébastiani's departure on a mission to Egypt on 25 September seemed to confirm renewed French interest in the region. By November the British ambassador to Russia was stressing the importance of retaining Malta to show that the British intended to restrain French and Russian advances in the region. Nevertheless, deprived of hope of Russian support, and advised that their forces were insufficient, on 16 November the government ordered the evacuation of British forces from Egypt, rather than risk war over failure to meet the terms of Amiens. The British government also continued, unsuccessfully, to renegotiate the treaty of Amiens to establish a lasting settlement through a revised balance.[169]

The British decision to keep Malta was forced by publication of Sébastiani's memorandum, which questioned the capacity of the British troops remaining in Egypt and suggested that 10,000 Frenchmen could easily retake the country, in the *Moniteur* on 30 January 1803. Presumably the French hoped to intimidate the British. If so, Napoleon's hopes backfired. The memorandum convinced the British that the French intended to partition the Ottoman empire. This possibility also alarmed the Russians, who had been approached about a partition but feared a French presence on their southern border.[170] Thus on 9 February 1803, bolstered by assurances that the tsar 'wished the English to keep Malta', Hawkesbury instructed Whitworth to inform the French that the British would withdraw from Malta only when satisfied that the French had no plans to return to Egypt.[171]

Twelve days later Peltier's case finally reached court. The trial attracted a

---

[167] Gill, 'England and France', 71.
[168] PRO, FO 27/67, Hawkesbury to Whitworth, Downing Street (draft), 14 Nov. 1802.
[169] Schroeder, *European politics*, 243.
[170] Norman E. Saul, *Russia and the Mediterranean, 1797–1807*, Chicago 1970, 175–7.
[171] Edward Ingram, 'The geo-politics of the first British expedition to Egypt, IV: Occupation and withdrawal, 1801–1803', *Middle Eastern Studies* xxxi (1995), 317–46 at pp. 336–7.

large crowd, and Peltier and his counsel could scarcely force their way into the courtroom.[172] Peltier claimed that stock-jobbers had sent runners to bring news of the verdict, for the City of London believed an acquittal would result in war.[173]

The case against Peltier was based upon five satirical pieces from the early numbers of the *Ambigu*. The key passages cited in the indictment were two long poems from the first number, an *Ode attribuée à Chénier, le 18 brumaire an VIII*, and the *Voeu d'un bon patriote hollandois*. Both made allegorical parallels between France and imperial Rome, and appeared to urge Napoleon's assassination. The key passage in the official translation of the *Ode attribuée à Chénier* read:

> Oh eternal disgrace of France!
> Caesar on the banks of the Rubicon,
> Has against him, in his quarrel,
> The Senate, Pompey and Cato,
> And in the plains of Pharsalia,
> If fortune is unequal
> If you must yield to the destinies,
> Rome, in this sad reverse,
> At least there remains to avenge you
> A poniard among the last Romans.[174]

Incitement to assassination in the *Voeu d'un bon patriote hollandois* was less explicit:

> Kings are at his feet begging his favour.
> He is desired to secure the supreme authority in his hands.
> The French, nay, kings themselves,
> Hasten to congratulate him,
> And would take the oath to him like subjects.
> As for me, far from envying his lot,
> Let him name, I consent to it, his successor.
> Carried on the shield, let him be elected emperor!
> Finally (and Romulus recalls the thing to mind)
> I wish that on the morrow he may have his apotheosis.
> AMEN.[175]

Three other prose passages taken from the third number, which urged rebellion and poured scorn on Napoleon and his government, were also cited in the indictment. They were epitomised in the following address to the French people, contained in a parody of a harangue of Lepidus against Sulla:

---

172 Peltier, *Trial*, introduction, pp. vi–viii.
173 Ibid. p. xviii.
174 Ibid. 5; *Annual Register* xlv (1803), 605.
175 Peltier, *Trial*, 10; *Annual Register* xlv (1803), 606.

Plate 3. Vignette of Bonaparte as a sphinx from the *Ambigu* 1 (n.d. 1802). This print appeared as part of the masthead of the first volume of the journal, but when Napoleon authorised legal proceedings against Peltier for criminal libel, Peltier retaliated by decapitating the sphinx. A headless sphinx can be found on the front-page of the *Ambigu* 5–9 (n.d. 1802–3).

And now this tiger, who dares to call himself the founder, or the regenerator of France, enjoys the fruit of your labours as spoil taken from an enemy. . . . His wickedness increases every day: in spite of the security he enjoys, he enters into new passions. . . . You must act, citizens, you must march, you must oppose what is passing . . . reckon only upon yourselves, unless indeed you have the stupidity to suppose, that he will wantonly expose himself to danger by abdicating through weariness, or shame of tyranny, that which he holds by force of crimes.[176]

In addition, the vignette of a sphinx with Napoleon's head which adorned the early numbers of the *Ambigu* was cited against Peltier, although not on the indictment. In *The trial of John Peltier*, its author explains its meaning in detail. The sphinx's lion-like body 'symbolises [Napoleon's] power', the tail between his legs 'dissimulation'. His extended paws symbolise 'ambition, ready to pounce on all that is within his reach'. The crown on his 'Brutus-like head' represents 'the anti-republican intrigues at his court to have him named king or emperor, consul for a term or for life, hereditarily or electing his successor'. An Egyptian spirit, with one wing pointing to the sphinx's

---

[176] Peltier, *Trial*, 30; *Annual Register* xlv (1803), 603.

head, the other to his tail, symbolises the vigilance with which 'every pen' should reveal his open and secret designs and his methods. The hieroglyphs of a crown between two eyes at the centre on the sphinx's pedestal indicate the object of his gaze; two sparrow hawks or *Chouans* on the right and left of the crown are 'its imperturbable guardians'. A ladder and axe 'indicate the punishments awaiting regicides, rebels and thieves'. Finally a dog and a cat, at the two outer extremes, 'indicate the concord and unity that reign far from the crown'.[177] When Napoleon began proceedings against him Peltier retaliated by symbolically decapitating the sphinx.

Peltier was defended by the celebrated Whig orator, James Mackintosh, one of the most respected lawyers of his day, famed for his defence of the French revolution, *Vindiciae gallicae*.[178] Mackintosh accepted the case as a five-guinea brief, as an opportunity to build his reputation.[179] His defence served his own interests better than his client, for he began with a virtual admission of Peltier's guilt.[180] He acknowledged that the courts had a general duty to punish libellers, but appealed to the jury's compassion and generosity: since the work was intended for Peltier's companions in misfortune, could not be understood by the English, and was unable to enter France, it could hardly have a malicious effect. He also put Peltier's case into a broader perspective by veiled references to French encroachments upon press freedoms throughout Europe, stating: 'I consider it [Peltier's case] as the first of a long series of conflicts between the greatest power in the world and the only free press remaining in Europe.'[181] Mackintosh went on to contend that libel was relative, differing according to context, and was never closely defined by England's 'wise ancestors' who had deliberately left it to juries to distinguish malicious libels while protecting legitimate inquiry. He argued that while rigorous enforcement of most laws only frightens the guilty, severe execution of libel laws frightens the innocent and deters men from meritorious acts.

Brilliantly, but without much hope of success, Mackintosh then answered the individual charges against Peltier. He suggested that Peltier might not be the author of the *Ode, attribuée à Chénier*, and that it could be a piece of republican satire circulating in Paris. But even were this not the case, the piece had to be considered a satire on Marie-Joseph Chénier's views rather than an incitement for royalists to assassinate Bonaparte. In a similar argument in defence of the *Voeu d'un bon patriote Hollandois*, Mackintosh advanced

---

[177] Peltier, *Trial*, 286 (my translation).
[178] J. Mackintosh, *Vindiciae gallicae: a defence of the French revolution and its English admirers against the accusations of the Right Hon. Edmund Burke*, London 1791. Mackintosh had a family interest in the press issue: his brother-in-law, Daniel Stuart, was proprietor and editor of the *Morning Post* (1795–1801) and later joint-owner of the *Courier*.
[179] See P. O'Leary, *Sir James Mackintosh: the Whig Cicero*, Aberdeen 1989, 66.
[180] See Peltier, *Trial*, 76–83. See also O'Leary, *Mackintosh*, 66–7. BL, MS Add. 37853, fo. 68, Cobbett to Windham, Duke Street, 'Tuesday morning' [i.e. 22 Feb. 1803], suggests that Mackintosh betrayed Peltier. However, Peltier and Mackintosh remained friends.
[181] Peltier, *Trial*, 83.

the technically correct but contextually absurd argument that in looking forward to Napoleon's imminent 'apotheosis', the Dutch patriot was not necessarily wishing Napoleon dead. More plausibly, he quoted from some of the despatches Fouché wrote during the Terror to answer suggestions that Peltier had rendered Fouché odious in his parody of the harangue of Lepidus. He also denied that Peltier's subtitle *Variétés atroces et amusantes* could be taken as an admission of guilt. For who would designate their own works as abominable?[182] Such casuistry convinced no-one. Mackintosh's oratory was applauded,[183] but Peltier's malicious intent was beyond doubt. The judge, Lord Ellenborough, directed the jury to find Peltier guilty of criminal libel, and it took less than a minute to agree on this verdict.[184]

It proved a pyrrhic victory for Bonaparte, for Peltier published a bi-lingual account of the trial which he sold by subscription, with the backing of d'Artois.[185] In the process he circulated his libels to a wider audience and made his fortune. Meanwhile, the *Courier de Londres* kept the case in the public eye by fomenting a debate about the faithfulness of the translations used in court. In Jersey, Philip Mourant appeared before the *Cour royale* following complaints against an article in his *Gazette de Jersey*, but escaped with a warning after it was found to be copied from the *Courier de Londres*. Another proprietor was similarly warned.[186]

Diplomatic pressure continued as the trial approached. On 7 January 1803 Talleyrand reminded Andréossi to agitate frequently against the press. On 18 February a dispatch clearly timed to arrive just after the trial, instructed him to press for the evacuation of Malta and Alexandria, the expulsion of Cadoudal and his followers, the suppression and punishment of the émigré papers, and the prevention of further press outrages against Napoleon.[187] On the same day Napoleon held a public interview with Whitworth, in which he asserted 'I'd rather have a British army in the Faubourg Saint-Antoine than in Malta.' Napoleon also alleged that the *Courier de Londres* was financed by Pelham and asserted that the peace could be kept if the British government adhered to the treaty of Amiens, contained press abuse, and withdrew support from France's enemies.[188] This public humiliation of the ambassador

---

[182] See ibid. 76–180. The pieces used at the trial all appeared in *Ambigu* 1–5 (n.d.); extracts are given in Maspero-Clerc, *Peltier*, 315–17.
[183] See, for example, BL, MS Add. 52451B, fo. 42, Erskine to Mackintosh, Monday evening [21 Feb. 1803]; MS Add. 51653, fos 5–6, Lord Holland to Mackintosh, Valencia, 14 Mar. 1803. Erskine conducted the prosecution case against Peltier.
[184] Peltier, *Trial*, 206–7.
[185] AAE, CPA 600, fo. 191, unknown agent to Andréossi, Edinburgh, 9 ventôse X (28 Feb. 1803).
[186] See AAE, CPA 601, fos 76–7, Chépy to Talleyrand, St Helier, 18 pluviôse XI (6 Feb. 1803). G. R. Balleine's, *A biographical dictionary of Jersey*, London n.d., contains an informative entry on Philip Mourant.
[187] AAE, CPA 600, fos 182ff., Talleyrand to Andréossi, Paris, 30 pluviôse XI (7 Jan. 1803) (duplicated in CPA supplément 31, fo. 17ff.).
[188] See PRO, FO 27/67, Whitworth to Hawkesbury, Paris, 21 Feb. 1803.

soon became notorious. Although it is unlikely that Napoleon would have made the press issue the *causa belli* had his other demands been met, this outburst proves that the press and émigré issues had now become central concerns, and fundamental to his perception that the British acted in bad faith.

Following the trial the French continued to demand the evacuation of Malta and complain of press outrages.[189] The flames were fanned further by British diplomatic and press complaints against Sébastiani's memorandum, and Talleyrand's response that 'by her tolerance of outrages ... against all that is great and respectable on the continent, the British ministry has lost the right to complain of any offence of the same nature'.[190] With the crisis now spinning out of control, the British government made efforts to reassure the French that it would do its utmost to prosecute all libellous use of the press if French papers kept a moderate tone.[191] Andréossi misperceived this initiative for pacific intent, and assured Paris that England [sic] strongly desired peace and could see no advantage in the resumption of hostilities. This misperception seems to have been fatal, for Bonaparte and his advisers now assumed that the decision for war or peace lay with them alone. In fact Whitworth's despatches not only described Napoleon's vacillations over Malta, but also urged his government to bring matters to a head swiftly.[192]

After much agonising, Addington determined that if necessary he would go to war for Malta. Whitworth was therefore instructed to present an ultimatum: the British were to keep Malta, and the French to withdraw from Holland. If these or similar terms were not agreed, war would follow.[193] The French were caught unprepared by the British ultimatum and Whitworth's demand for passports on 2 May. Despite all Talleyrand's subsequent efforts to stall for time, French attempts to evade war were in vain. As for Peltier, it seems that sentence was never passed following the outbreak of hostilities on 18 May.

The explanation of the timing of the outbreak of war thus seems to lie in a combination of serious misperceptions. The decisive misperception was the British conviction that Bonaparte intended to send a second expedition to Egypt.[194] However, the deterioration in relations which preceded the

---

[189] See AAE, CPA 600, fos 240–3, Talleyrand to Andréossi, Paris, 27 ventôse XI (17 Mar. 1803); fos 257–8, Andréossi to Talleyrand, London, 30 ventôse XI (20 Mar. 1803); fo. 259, Andréossi to Hawkesbury, 28 ventôse XI (18 Mar. 1803).
[190] Ibid. fos 240–3, Talleyrand to Andréossi, Paris, 27 ventôse XI (17 Mar. 1803). Talleyrand alludes here to Robert T. Wilson, *History of the British expedition to Egypt*, London 1802, which first told of alleged atrocities committed under Bonaparte's orders. The French apparently considered publication of Sébastiani's work an act of reciprocity.
[191] AAE, CPA 600, fos 268–9, Andréossi to Talleyrand, London, 7 germinal XI (27 Mar. 1803).
[192] See PRO, FO 27/67, Whitworth's despatches to Hawkesbury, 5, 10, 21 Mar. 1803.
[193] Ziegler, *Addington*, 182–4.
[194] See Ingram, 'Geo-politics, IV'.

outbreak of war was the result of more fundamental misperceptions arising from press and émigré issues that stemmed from divergent cultural traditions concerning law and the nature of government noted earlier. Clearly the French considered Addington insincere when he explained to Otto:

> In this country, as you well know, a Minister must act according to existing laws: some of these may possibly be thought by foreigners too weak. If so, the fault to be found should be with the laws, and not with the government. That degree of power in this respect, which may be perfectly well suited to France, would not be tolerated here; and though the liberty of the press is so grossly abused, a minister would undertake a bold and fruitless task, who should attempt to introduce a bill to contract that, which Englishmen certainly prize next to the Trial by Jury.[195]

Napoleon's contrary views, expressed in the *Moniteur* article of 9 August, stemmed from conviction. Since the libellers' actions were evidently culpable, the government that claimed to be unable to prevent them, especially as they appeared to breach solemn treaty obligations, clearly lacked authority to govern, or acted in bad faith. British protestations of impotence and regret were therefore perceived as provocative hypocrisy rather than conciliatory acts. Whatever Napoleon's hidden agenda may have been, he did not think his demands unrealistic or unreasonable, for the seventh secret article in the draft treaty between the two countries proposed by the French in August 1806 reads:

> The two contracting parties will take all the measures that the constitutions of their country will allow, sincerely and in good faith, to put an end henceforth to all personal invective and excesses that persons may wish to insert whether into the public prints or any other publication in their respective states.
> They shall apply themselves principally to prevent the publication and circulation of any periodical paper or public writing containing such personal invectives and excesses which are published in any language other than that which is used habitually in the country submitted to their authority.[196]

Clearly then, in 1802–3 British and French statesmen were speaking two mutually incomprehensible languages, and as a result both became convinced of the other's malevolence and bad faith. These misperceptions coloured each side's interpretation of the other's actions, and it appears that Napoleon's anger at the British refusal to act increased his determination to subjugate the 'nation of shopkeepers'. Moreover, they had already soured relations considerably before territorial and strategic issues became prominent. Thus mutual hostility conditioned the negotiating stance and perceptions of both parties. While perhaps insufficient to provide a *causa belli*, misperceptions and quarrels over the press and émigré conspirators engendered an atmosphere of

---

[195] AAE, CPA 597, fos 513–15, Addington to Otto, Langford Court, 15 Aug. 1802.
[196] AAE, CPA 603, fo. 204, draft treaty of peace between France and England, Aug. 1806.

suspicion and recrimination in which both sides were drawn into a conflict which neither wanted, and for which both were unprepared.

The resumption of hostilities opened new vistas for the émigré press. British sponsorship of émigré journals throughout Europe also gave the French regime a new imperative and renewed urgency to suppress hostile criticism. More important, it raised the stakes in Napoleon's campaign to control the press. The French now threatened to monopolise the complex inputs of fact, notion and suggestion that form the agenda and basis for intricate executive policy decisions. It was to counter this attempt, when faced with the progressive loss of alternative informational sources, and to promote a rival, British-orientated agenda, that the émigré press was recruited. The British had little intention of creating a mass-movement against Bonapartism, although there were attempts to promote European nationalisms and harness them against Napoleon in the émigré journals. Their purpose was rather to contact and influence persons in cabinets, councils and élite circles close to executive power. Thus as late as 1816 Castlereagh justified continuing government support for the *Ambigu* to parliament by saying it was for: 'Conveying instruction to the continent when no other mode could be found.'[197] Reflecting these aims, the distribution patterns for the journals show a sophisticated and targeted propaganda campaign according to the changing exigencies of a pan-European war.

Throughout the Napoleonic era the French government kept records on writers outside its jurisdiction. A list drawn up between 1810 and 1813 for the foreign ministry provides a checklist of French and Swiss émigré writers then in British pay.[198] It names ten writers, five of them editors of journals or major collaborators. Four of these were London-based: Peltier, Regnier, Couchery and Henri-Larivière. The fifth was comte Paoli de Chagny, a Burgundian émigré recruited by British agents and paid to edit a series of periodicals in Germany between 1803 and 1805.[199] To this list we can add several other journalists identified by the French police at various times: the celebrated writer Sabatier de Castres; Gérard; the barons d'Angely who edited the *Abeille* at Altona;[200] and Hyde de Neuville, who edited the *Journal des dames* in New York.[201]

---

[197] Hansard, *Commons journals*, xxxiv. 101 (30 Apr. 1816).
[198] AAE, mém./docs France 620, 'Statistique, 1810'. A similar document, 'Statistique des Bourbons et des consorts', in AN, AF^{IV*} 1710, was apparently started simultaneously but maintained separately.
[199] See PRO, FO 27/71, Paoli de Chagny to [?Hammond], London, 24 Mar. 1805; FO 27/144, Paoli de Chagny to Foreign Office, Hamburg, 6 July 1816; *Nouvelle Biographie générale*, xxxix. 154, gives his dates as c. 1750–1830. His journals were *Le Mercure universel*, *Le Pour et le contre* and *Les Annales politiques du dix-neuvième siècle*.
[200] No hard evidence proves that the barons d'Angely were British-funded. The seized papers of George Rumbold, British minister at Hamburg, who was responsible for liaising with émigré journalists in north Germany, in AAE, CPA supplément 15, which presumably contained evidence for French assertions, no longer survive.
[201] Again we must rely on French assertions of British sponsorship. Hauterive, *Police*, v,

Although the Foreign Office was also supporting a haphazard pamphleteering campaign, their main propaganda drive, both in terms of funding and regularity, revolved around the sponsorship of émigré newspaper and periodical publications.[202] Apart from the brief small-scale experiments with the *Mercure britannique* and *Supplément au Rédacteur* in the late 1790s, the British had only used newspaper propaganda previously in a domestic context. Yet after 1803, the Foreign Office was willing to spend considerable sums from its secret service funds on hiring foreign writers to produce works in an alien tongue as an auxiliary arm of foreign policy. The total annual commitment to émigré journalism seems to have amounted to about £5,000 *per annum*, or 10 per cent of official secret service funds.[203] This was considerably more than the government had spent on the entire British press during the alarming years at the start of the 1790s.[204]

The newspaper medium was ideally suited to British aims, not only as the best means for disseminating a wide range of information, but also because it allowed for subtle insinuation, especially through the use of continuous suggestion. Short, punchy articles offered a varied diet of fresh information, polemic, satire, entertainment and invective that avoided the staleness, monotony and tortuous arguments of pamphlet literature. Moreover newspapers offered a regular point of contact, immediacy, and a mix of opinion interspersed with the factual informational pieces on which the government set most value.

Almost immediately after the opening of hostilities in May 1803 the government subscribed for 200 copies of Regnier's *Courier de Londres*. It began to make occasional bulk purchases of Peltier's *Ambigu* soon afterwards, and by mid-1807 had taken out 100 subscriptions. It subscribed to the *Courier d'Angleterre* at the end of 1806. Support for all three London-based francophone journals continued through to the end of 1814, and in Peltier's case beyond.

As we have seen (chapter 2), the control exercised by the ministry was vague, amorphous and prone to changes in direction, and there is little

---

para. 713, bulletin of 16 May 1810, affirms Neuville's 'close links' with Jackson, who dealt with émigré publicists in Germany. Neuville, a former *Chouan* and conspirator, later became Bourbon ambassador to the USA. However, according to Marino's account in 'Frenchrefugee newspapers', 163–72, Neuville published the journal from January to December 1810 to raise money for a school attended by the children of exiles from Saint-Domingue.

[202] On the pamphlet campaign see Simon Burrows, 'The struggle for European opinion in the Napoleonic wars: British francophone propaganda, 1803–1814', *French History* xi (1997), 29–53. I thank the journal's editors for allowing me to reproduce material from *French History* here.

[203] This total includes £1,950 for 550 newspaper subscriptions (rising to £2,200 after the 1809 stamp duty increases); £500 on average to support Peltier's *Ambigu*; the costs of occasional tracts, reprints of journal articles, translations of the *London Gazette*; funding for continental journals; and journalists' pensions. About £600 would be recouped in stamp office receipts.

[204] See Aspinall, *Politics and the press*, 69.

evidence to suggest that precise instructions were the norm. Instead, vague noises of approbation intermingled with harsher warnings or positive action whenever the bounds of policy, politic good sense or standards of decency were transgressed. The most extreme example of government heavy-handedness was Regnier's removal from the *Courier de Londres* by Mulgrave. His replacement, Heron, possibly acting on positive instructions from the government, changed the whole emphasis of the paper, and purged it of much of its vitriolic and declamatory style. However, Regnier's strident tone was probably not the sole reason for his removal, and it certainly did not prevent the British from employing him again from November 1806. It is probable, however, that the new foreign secretary desired to 'clear the decks' of potential obstacles to peace with Napoleon, prior to commencing negotiations. This was precisely how the French police agent monitoring the paper's content interpreted the change of editorial policy.[205] Moreover, as we have seen, the émigré press was not forgotten by the imperial regime when peace was discussed in 1806.

However, if Mulgrave intended to silence Regnier, he did not succeed. Regnier founded a rival organ almost immediately, with borrowed funds, and even wrote to the Foreign Office making known his intentions. He would write in the same spirit as before and attack Heron's paper at every opportunity, lest its claims to be 'official' should damage the British cause and mislead opinion on the continent as to British intentions.[206] Significantly, only a few weeks after the breakdown of preliminary peace negotiations at the end of August 1806, the British Foreign Office showed a renewed interest in Regnier's writing,[207] taking its first few copies of the *Courier d'Angleterre* on 13 November, and the first mass subscriptions on 21 November.[208] However, Regnier's style continued to displease some in government circles, including Hammond, who was possibly the prime mover behind Regnier's dismissal in 1805.[209]

The émigré journalists' relationship with the princes weakened progressively after 1803. From 1805 to 1807 Louis XVIII helped to finance Regnier's *Courier d'Angleterre*, but by October his minister d'Avaray was complaining to the comte de La Châtre of the journal's tone:

> the king [i.e. Louis XVIII] very strongly condemns the virulence of the articles on the Emperor Alexander in the *Courier d'Angleterre*. You [must] therefore have no influence over this journal: and the expenses that the king has made

---

[205] See Hauterive, *Police*, i, para. 1402, police bulletin of 8 prairial XIII (28 May 1805).
[206] PRO, FO 27/71, Regnier to [Mulgrave], 25 Apr. 1805.
[207] See AAE, mem./docs France 635, fos 141–2, [Fauche-Borel] to d'Antraigues, dated Sept. 1806.
[208] See the secret service receipts in BL, MS Add. 51464, fos 70, 73.
[209] See Canning papers, bundle 59a, d'Antraigues to Canning, 7 Feb. 1808 (three letters in this bundle share this date). Heron's obituary, *Annual Register* (1807), 566–7, states that one of the under-secretaries brought Heron to Mulgrave's attention.

to support it have been useless, otherwise it would surely not have printed the paragraph included in the edition of 13 October.... Make sure Mr. Alopeus knows that this is the king's opinion.[210]

Regnier's rupture with the Bourbons was soon complete, for on 7 February 1808 d'Antraigues remarked on the princes' hatred of Regnier in a letter to Canning.[211] By then, however, Regnier had established alternative sources of patronage through d'Antraigues and the Foreign Office. The break was permanent: in 1814 the restored regime would not even admit the *Courier d'Angleterre* to France.[212]

The umbilical cord linking Peltier to the Bourbons was never entirely cut. In 1810, when he and his wife paid their respects to Louis XVIII and the duchesse d'Angoulême, after the death of the queen of France, Louis expressed his pleasure with the *Ambigu* in front of 200 witnesses.[213] Nevertheless, Peltier also risked royal displeasure on several occasions. In the very first number of the *Ambigu*, he equated Louis-Philippe d'Orléans with Damiens, would-be assassin of Louis XV, provoking a serious complaint.[214] In 1810 Broval, Louis-Philippe's representative, sought to prevent Peltier circulating a letter purporting to be from his master to the Spanish council of regency. Broval demanded to know Peltier's intentions, his sponsor, why it was printed in Spanish and asked Louis XVIII to suppress it if he deemed it necessary.[215] Peltier replied imperiously that he needed no authorisation to print anything. As he received the work in printed form, he considered it public property and assumed that the prince's agents would be communicating it to other journalists: he published it in Spanish for speed and accuracy. Moreover, the document's contents seemed wholly honourable to Louis-Philippe.[216] The incident is curious, and can perhaps be explained by an excess of zeal on Broval's part, influenced by Peltier's known distaste for the Orléanist branch of the royal family. However, in 1807 Peltier was also reprimanded by d'Artois for a tirade against Fauche-Borel concerning Pichegru's legacy, a matter of dispute between Couchery and Fauche-Borel.[217]

Peltier's service of Christophe also led to friction with the Bourbons, especially after he espoused the abolitionist cause. Courted by Wilberforce and

---

[210] Canning papers, bundle 54, D'Avaray to La Châtre, Gothenburg, 20 Oct. 1807. *Maximilien Alopeus* (1748–1821) was the Russian ambassador to London in 1806.
[211] Ibid. 59a, d'Antraigues to Canning, 7 Feb. 1808.
[212] See PRO, FO 27/109, Regnier to FO, 24 Dec. 1814.
[213] BL, MS Egerton 3716, fo. 109, Peltier to the duchesse d'Angoulême, London, 15 Dec. 1818; *Ambigu* 323 (20 Mar. 1812), 680.
[214] See BL, MS Add. 33109, fo. 325, Louis-Philippe to Pelham, Twickenham, 1 Aug. 1802.
[215] See AAE, mem./docs France 615, fo. 234, Broval to La Châtre, n.d. [?Dec. 1810]. The piece was published as a supplement to *Ambigu* 276 (30 Nov. 1810).
[216] See AAE, mem./docs France 615, fo. 236, La Châtre to Broval, 11 Dec. 1810.
[217] See AAE, mem./docs France 604, fos 139–42, Fauche-Borel to d'Artois, 28 Feb. 1807 (copy); Fauche-Borel to d'Avaray, 6 Mar. 1807. The offending article is in *Ambigu* 140 (20 Feb. 1807), 363–4.

his associates,[218] his support of the abolitionists may have been the motive for British subsidies after the restoration. Certainly Peltier blamed his disfavour with the Bourbons on his service with the Haitian emperor.[219] By contrast, Bourbon ministers were reluctant to reward his services after 1815 due to the 'libellous' nature of his journal.[220] However, by 1825 he had redeemed himself sufficiently to enjoy pensions of 3,000 francs *per annum* from the French Foreign Ministry, and 6,000 from the Ministry of the Interior.[221]

Peltier was perhaps too valuable to leave in disfavour. In addition to his journalism, he was a useful source of information on Haiti, and addressed a series of memoranda, as well as diplomatic messages on this and colonial subjects to the Bourbons and the British.[222] Furthermore, by 1809 he and Couchery acted as the princes' liaisons with the British press, especially through their relations with Street, editor of the influential ministerial *Courier*.[223] The Bourbons' efforts to have Peltier attached to the Portuguese legation in London in 1811 so he could avoid debtors' prison show how much they valued him. The move was initially rejected by Culling Smith, but apparently approved after the intervention of Arthur Wellesley.[224] Similar moves may have been behind his approaches to the Swedish legation in 1813.[225]

The relationship of the Bourbons with the *Courier de Londres* after Regnier's departure remains mysterious. In 1807 d'Avaray noted an article 'written in an excellent sense' in the paper, on the subject of Louis XVIII's arrival at Carlscrone *en route* for England, and commented that as it was impossible to keep Louis's advent a secret 'it will be necessary to take measures to monitor the language of the press'.[226] The implication is that the

---

[218] See Wilberforce papers, file 1814–15, Wilberforce to J. S. Harford, Jr, 12 Oct. 1814; Wilberforce to T. Harrison, 24 Oct. 1814; BL, MS Add. 51,820, fos 61–4, letters of Zachary Macaulay to Lord Holland, 5, 7 Oct. 1814.
[219] DUL, J. W. Croker papers, Peltier to J. W. Croker, 3 Apr. 1819.
[220] See AN, O^3 777, 'Etat des personnes rentrées'; F^7 6888, no. 6333, minister of police to Rochefort, 24 Nov. 1818.
[221] See Peltier's accounts in ADS, DQ^{10} 1429, dos. 1918.
[222] See, for example, AAE, mem./docs France 605, fo. 212, Peltier to Blancas, 28 Feb. 1811; AN, O^3 614, Peltier to Blancas, 16 Sept. 1814; PRO, FO 27/87, letters of Peltier to C. C. Smith, 30 May, 1, 6 July 1811; FO 27/91, Peltier to Castlereagh, 2 June 1812; FO 27/106, Limonade to Peltier, 10 June 1814; FO 27/144, Peltier to Hamilton, 6 Jan. 1816; BL, MS Add. 37,870, fo. 248, Peltier to Windham; MS Add. 38,245, fos 108–18, Peltier to Liverpool, 24/26 June 1810; BL, loan 57/4, piece 369, Peltier to Bathurst, 21 June 1808.
[223] See Canning papers, bundle 59a, d'Antraigues to Canning, dated July 1809.
[224] See PRO, FO 27/87, Peltier to C. C. Smith, 12 May 1811. On the reverse Smith wrote 'cannot be recommended by the foreign office'; FO 63/118, fos 87–8, Da Souza to Hamilton, 20 May 1811. *Arthur Wellesley* (1769–1852), British soldier and statesman, became duke of Wellington in 1814.
[225] See De La Gardie MSS, De la Gardie journal.
[226] Canning papers, bundle 54, d'Avaray to La Châtre, Gothenburg, 12 Oct. 1807.

THE PROPAGANDA WAR

Courier de Londres had at least a tenuous connection with the Bourbon court, and was being eyed as a potential Bourbon organ. Nevertheless, even the French secret police did not attempt to establish a direct connection between Gérard and the Bourbons. Indeed, the presence in the Fonds Bourbons of a correspondence in which Gérard defends himself against allegations that he calumniated French officers who had served the British flag, suggests that he was held in some suspicion by the princes.[227]

Although evidence in British and French archives is far from complete, a clear pattern can be discerned in the distribution of the émigré journals, evidence of a sophisticated propaganda campaign targeted according to the changing exigencies of a pan-European war.[228] In a first phase, from 1803 to 1806, the main propaganda battlefield was Germany, where it was essential to maintain a functional public sphere to counteract growing French political leadership. Prior to 1806 the *Courier de Londres*, the *Ambigu* and Paoli de Chagny's journals were disseminated widely in northern Germany, where French and pro-French newspapers would otherwise have circulated without contradiction. Otto reported as early as July 1802 that the majority of Peltier's journals were sent to Hamburg, and in 1804 French agents discovered that the princesse de Monaco was distributing free copies of the *Ambigu* in Hamburg.[229] In 1805 she was reported to be circulating the *Courier de Londres* in Swabia, and the French suspected similar distributions were taking place elsewhere.[230]

In response to British propaganda, the French government intensified its counter-campaign. The counter-revolutionary journalist Sabatier de Castres was won over for a while with bribes, but soon recanted.[231] Nevertheless, where bribery failed, diplomatic channels often proved sufficient. On 5 December 1803 Paoli de Chagny's *Mercure universel*, edited at Ratisbon, was suppressed at the request of France, on an order direct from Napoleon.[232] According to Regnier, the French tried to suppress his *Courier de Londres* wherever they had influence.[233] It was banned in the Batavian Republic on 27 August 1804, at Hamburg the following October, and in Saxony in March

---

[227] See AAE, mem./docs France 615, fo. 203, Lafite to Gérard, 13, 17 Oct. 1810 [copy]; fo. 204, Gérard to Lafite, 17 Oct. 1810. See also CL lxviii/29 (9 Oct. 1810); *The Observer* (7 Oct. 1810).

[228] The loss of the Foreign Post Office records is particularly regrettable, as it was responsible for distributing both CL and *Ambigu*.

[229] AAE, CPA 597, fo. 481, Otto to Talleyrand, London, 12 thermidor X (30 July 1802); Hauterive, *Police*, i, paras 93, 97, bulletins of 14, 15 thermidor XII (2, 3 Aug. 1804).

[230] Ibid. i, para. 1073, bulletin of 2 germinal XIII (23 Mar. 1805).

[231] Ibid. i, paras 211, 727, 819, 887; ii, para. 533: police bulletins of 10 fructidor XII (28 Aug. 1804), 10 nivôse XIII (31 Dec. 1804), 2, 18 pluviôse XIII (22 Jan., 7 Feb. 1805), 2 frimaire XIV (23 Nov. 1805). See also AAE, mem./docs France 620, 'Sabatier de Castres'; AN, AF^{IV*} 1710, p. 233.

[232] Hauterive, Police, i, para. 1061, bulletin of 30 ventôse XIII (21 Mar. 1805); AAE, mem./docs France 1774, fo. 94, Napoleon to Talleyrand, 1 Nov. 1803.

[233] PRO, FO 27/71, Regnier to Mulgrave, 25 Apr. 1805.

1805.[234] Moreover, in November 1805 the Hamburg Senate agreed to discover and punish the printer of a new journal, the *Annales politiques du dix-neuvième siècle*. Again the author proved to be Paoli de Chagny.[235] The collaboration of the Hamburg government was of particular significance for the French campaign to control the German public sphere, for the city was still the main *entrepôt* by which British publications arrived on the continent, and home to extensive publishing interests and a large émigré community. Finally, in 1806, the French campaign to suppress the *Courier d'Angleterre* in Saxony apparently brought the paper to the tsar's attention.[236] The production and circulation of émigré papers in Germany appears to have come to an end soon afterwards, following the summary execution of the Nuremberg bookseller Palm in June 1806 for refusing to identify the authors of *Deutschland in siener tiefen Erniedrigung*, and French victories at Jena and Auerstadt (14 October 1806), which assured French domination of Germany.

By early 1807 the focus of the propaganda struggle had switched to the north and entered a second phase. In the autumn of 1806 the comte d'Antraigues approached Spencer Perceval on the tsar's behalf, with a request to subscribe for 250 copies of the *Courier d'Angleterre*.[237] The prime minister, Grenville, was receptive to the idea, but was apparently reluctant to let the paper pass into foreign control, having perhaps been alarmed by an article directed against Arch-Chancellor Dalberg, prince-primate of the Napoleonic Confederation of the Rhine, which d'Antraigues had already published, ostensibly at the tsar's request.[238] Whatever his reasons, Grenville directed d'Antraigues to approach the Foreign Office.[239]

---

[234] See CL lvi/22 (14 Sept. 1804); lvii/25 (26 Mar. 1805); Hauterive, *Police*, i, para. 441, bulletin of 27 vendémiaire XIII (18 Oct. 1804).

[235] CL lvii/25 (26 Mar. 1805); Hauterive, *Police*, ii, paras 533, 605, bulletins of 2, 26 frimaire XIV (23 Nov./17 Dec. 1805).

[236] PRO, FO 27/86, d'Antraigues to Smith, 10 Mar. 1811; BL, MS Add. 37290, fo. 62, d'Antraigues to Arthur Wellesley, 4 Jan. 1810.

[237] See AAE, mem./docs France 635, fos 141–2, [Fauche-Borel] to d'Antraigues, Sept. 1806. The correspondence of Regnier with d'Antraigues attests the tsar's interest in the paper. However, verification from other sources including d'Antraigues's correspondence with Czartoryski (AAE, mem./docs France 633), Grenville (BL, MS Add. 59035), or Howick (Durham University Library Archives) proved impossible. Nevertheless, certain references seem to dispel any doubt, for example BL, MS Add. 37290, fos 64–5, Regnier to d'Antraigues, 4 Jan. 1810, and d'Antraigues to R. C. Wellesley, 4 Jan. 1810. See also PRO, FO 27/86, d'Antraigues to [?C. C. Smith], 10 Mar. 1811; note of d'Antraigues to Fauche-Borel, dated 1806, in Louis Fauche-Borel, *Exposition of the persecutions which Louis Fauche-Borel has experienced from MM. d'Antraigues et de Puisaye* . . ., London 1812, 42. Spencer Perceval (1762–1812) was attorney-general 1802–6, chancellor of the exchequer 1807–9, and prime minister 1809–12.

[238] See BL, MS Add. 59035, fo. 20, d'Antraigues to Grenville, 1 Oct. 1806. D'Antraigues gives Dalberg's name and title as 'archi-chancellier d'Albery', but his identity is clear. The article appeared in CA, 30 Sept. 1806. No surviving copies of this issue are known.

[239] BL, MS Add. 59035, fo. 20, d'Antraigues to Grenville, 1 Oct. 1806. See also PRO, FO

The Foreign Office agreed to take out 350 subscriptions to the *Courier d'Angleterre*.[240] Not all were sent to Russia: fifty were kept by the Foreign Office, and 150 were sent to Sweden, where Pierre-François Fauche was granted permission to circulate the paper and given a list of notables to whom the Swedish government wished it to be delivered.[241] Originally the papers were sent by mail twice a week, via the British consuls in Sweden.[242] However, Mr Holland, the packet-boat agent in Gothenburg, was soon charged with receiving and passing them to Fauche for distribution.[243] In October 1807 the British government cancelled its subscriptions, but the distribution of the paper in the north did not cease altogether, as d'Antraigues took out 100 subscriptions on his own account for the interim period.[244] The government reconsidered their decision within months after complaints from the Swedes, and when the distribution resumed at the beginning of March 1808 d'Antraigues seems to have taken the opportunity to compensate himself.[245] When, in early 1809, Canning discovered that d'Antraigues and Regnier were only delivering 100 of the government's papers and pocketing the difference, he did not cancel the subscriptions or reprimand the journalists.[246] Instead, he ordered that the British consuls again be charged with receiving the papers.[247] This would make it impossible to continue the fraud. The incident appears to prove the importance Canning attributed to propaganda warfare, although it is also possible he wished to conceal the fact that he had been duped.[248] In addition, Canning had no desire to antagonise d'Antraigues, whom he valued as a source of information, especially after he

27/105, 'Declaration of Fauche-Borel', 4 Feb. 1814, enclosed in P.-F. Fauche to Hamilton, 2 Apr. 1814.
240 Secret service receipts in BL, MS Add. 51464, fos 70, 73, show that the first few copies were taken on 13 Nov. 1806, and mass subscriptions from 21 Nov. 1806.
241 See PRO, FO 27/105, 'Exposé de P.-F. Fauche', dated both 1 June 1812 and 23 Dec. 1813, and endorsed by J. Smith, British consul to Gothenburg, 16 July 1812; P.-F. Fauche to De La Gardie, 20 Jan. 1814, (copy); FO 27/90, P.-F. Fauche to [?Hamilton], 28 Feb. 1812. Fauche-Borel, *Mémoires*, iii. 329, says that the list had 50 names. Dr P. G. Ottosson, archivist at the Riksarkivet in Stockholm, was not able to discover the list in the indices of the Hovkanslerns Arkiv (Records of the court chancellor).
242 Canning papers, bundle 59a, d'Antraigues to Canning, 7 Feb. 1807.
243 See AAE, mems/docs France 635, fo. 183, 'Extract of a letter from P.-F. Fauche', 11 Sept. 1807 in Fauche-Borel to d'Antraigues, 14 Sept. 1807; fo. 187, P.-F. Fauche to Fauche-Borel, Gothenburg, 28 Sept. 1807 (extract).
244 AAE, mems/docs France 642, fo. 3, Regnier to d'Antraigues, 16 Dec. 1807.
245 See PRO, FO 27/105, P.-F. Fauche to Hamilton, 27 Jan. 1814.
246 Canning papers, bundle 56a, anonymous letter, dated 20 Dec. [1808]; L. Booth, Stamp Office registrar, to Canning, Stamp Office, 11 Jan. 1809.
247 PRO, FO 73/69, Regnier to [?Hamilton], 21/23 Aug. 1811. PRO, FO 27/105, 'Exposé of P. F. Fauche' attests that Fauche only distributed the paper until 1809.
248 This may explain why all papers concerning the incident are in an obscure dossier in Canning's private papers. Certainly Regnier did not realise that he had been caught red-handed.

provided details of the secret articles of the Tilsit in 1807.[249] Thus, several days later, Ross, Canning's secretary, expressed the minister's approbation of the newspaper to Regnier.[250]

The Swedish *coup d'état* of 13 March 1809, in which Gustave IV was replaced by his uncle Charles XIII, led to the interruption of the paper's distribution in Sweden. However, by the end of the year it was circulating again, perhaps clandestinely.[251] In November 1810 Sweden half-heartedly declared war on Britain, and although it is not clear whether this again interrupted distribution, by August 1811, as Franco-Swedish relations deteriorated, the *Courier d'Angleterre* was again being circulated openly by Freeling, the British consul in Gothenburg, despite the theoretical state of war.[252]

There were three distinct phases in the circulation of the *Courier d'Angleterre* in Russia.[253] At first Fontassy, the Russian consul in Gothenburg forwarded copies to Russia, with the approval of his foreign minister, Budberg.[254] After the peace of Tilsit, in July 1807, Fontassy was ordered to prevent the paper's distribution, and following the *coup* of 13 March 1809 he collaborated with the French to have Fauche, who was also supervising the correspondence of Louis XVIII's agents in the north, expelled from Sweden.[255] However, Tilsit did not end the paper's circulation in Russia for Prince Adam Czartoryski and Count Nikita Panin, each of whom had served Alexander I as *de facto* foreign minister, helped d'Antraigues to continue circulating it among opponents of the French alliance.[256] In 1808 the paper was being sent to Russia via Prague, whence Gentz forwarded it to Grodno, on the frontier between Russia and the grand duchy of Warsaw. The newspapers were then circulated with the connivance of the Russian director of posts, Radzivllow [sic, possibly Radzivill].[257]

This new clandestine distribution was accompanied by a new, more subversive policy. D'Antraigues later claimed it aimed to forge a Russian national consciousness to promote a 'national' revolution to topple Alexander and save Russia and Europe.[258] However, while the paper certainly

---

[249] See Duckworth, *D'Antraigues phenomenon*, 292 and passim.
[250] See PRO, FO 95/636, 'compte rendu par Regnier de sa conversation avec Ross', 14 Jan. 1809.
[251] See BL, MS Add. 37290, fo. 62, d'Antraigues to Arthur Wellesley, 4 Jan. 1810.
[252] PRO, FO 73/69, Regnier to [?Hamilton], 21/23 Aug. 1811.
[253] See also Burrows, 'Propaganda for Russia'.
[254] PRO, FO 27/105, 'Exposé of P.-F. Fauche'; AAE, mem./docs France 635, fo. 187, P.-F. Fauche to Fauche-Borel, Gothenburg, 28 Sept. 1807 (extract).
[255] PRO, FO 27/105, 'Exposé of P.-F. Fauche'; Riksarkivet, Stockholm, Hovkanslerns Arkiv, vol. 60, letters of P.-F. Fauche to M. le baron [?de Wetterstedt] 16, 17 Aug. 1809.
[256] See AN, 419AP/1, 'Etat de Russie, 1 janvier 1810', fo. 26. *Nikita Panin*, was *de facto* foreign minister for six months in 1801. He was a nephew of Catherine II's minister of the same name.
[257] See Canning papers, bundle 59b, d'Antraigues to Canning, 6 May 1808. See also bundle 59a, d'Antraigues to Canning, 16 Dec. 1809.
[258] AN 419AP/1, 'Etat de Russie, 1 Janvier 1810', fo. 26.

attacked Alexander's policy and made attempts to separate his cause from that of Russia and her people, it would be erroneous to accept d'Antraigues's claims at face value and to view its distribution as part of an anti-Alexandrine plot. For while Panin had a history of conspiracy and had been involved in the *coup* of 1801 against Paul I, Czartoryski was a man of honour, devoted to Alexander on a personal level, who enjoyed direct access to the tsar even when in opposition.[259] He may have been aware of Alexander's ambiguous attitude to the Napoleonic alliance and his secret diplomacy with France's enemies, conducted behind the back of his pro-French foreign minister Rumyantsev.[260] On the other hand, the promotion of nationalism by the *Courier d'Angleterre* no doubt appealed to both Panin and Czartoryski. Panin was a Russian nationalist by instinct, while Czartoryski, the architect of the third coalition, was, like Gentz, a great advocate of the power of opinion and had long believed that European nationalism was the only force capable of defeating France. The paper may thus be seen as a tool for promoting Czartoryski's ideas on the subject among the Russian political élite. Clearly the paper served both men's agenda.

The third stage of the *Courier d'Angleterre's* distribution in Russia began with the recall of d'Antraigues's friends to positions of influence. Czartoryski's gradual return to favour began in December 1809, and when Armfeldt was recalled to St Petersburg in September 1811 it was clear that the Francophobes were gaining control of Russian policy.[261] Armfeldt therefore wrote at once to d'Antraigues to order the rehabilitation of the tsar in the *Courier d'Angleterre*. It must continue to praise the Russian nation, cease attacking Alexander, and turn all its fire against Rumyantsev.[262] By this time the paper was circulating in very influential circles. Its distributors included Czartoryski, the diplomat David Alopeus,[263] Count Panin, Prince Paul Volkonski, councillor Priedonski and the historian Nicholas Karamzin,[264] who was charged with drawing up 'manuscript bulletins' for further distribution in

---

[259] See M. Kukiel, *Czartoryski and European unity, 1770–1861*, Princeton 1955, 98–9 and passim; A. Zawadzki, *A man of honour: Adam Czartoryski, minister of Russia and Poland*, Oxford 1993.
[260] See P. K. Grimsted, *The foreign ministers of Alexander I: political attitudes and the conduct of foreign policy, 1801–1825*, Berkeley 1969, 181–3.
[261] *Gustave Maurice Armfeldt* (1757–1814), Finnish baron, transferred from Swedish to Russian service in 1810 after the Russian conquest of Sweden. He was a correspondent of d'Antraigues and reader of the CA from as early as 1806. See AAE, mem./docs France 630, fos 36–40, Armfeldt to D'Antraigues, Stralsund, 10 Oct. 1806.
[262] See ibid. fos 63–7, Armfeldt to d'Antraigues, Arminium, dated 21 Aug. [1811] Old Style/27 Sept. New Style [*sic*].
[263] *David Alopeus* (1769–1831), Russian ambassador to Stockholm, was brother to Maximilien Alopeus.
[264] *Nicholas Mikhailovich Karamzin* (1765–1826), journalist and celebrated Russian historian.

Moscow.[265] This list is impressive by any standards: the *Courier d'Angleterre* was now circulating among the leading Francophobes and advisers to the tsar.

The *Ambigu* also circulated in the north of Europe, partly at British expense. D'Antraigues was sending a handful of copies to St Petersburg in 1806, and in 1807 a portion of the Foreign Office's 100 subscriptions were destined for St Petersburg and Gothenburg.[266] In 1810 the Foreign Post Office was regularly sending twenty-five copies of the journal to Mr Foster at Gothenburg on the orders of the Foreign Office.[267] Likewise the *Courier de Londres* circulated in the north, where Armfeldt read it regularly. His efforts to comment on its content imply that it, too, was distributed in some numbers.[268]

The invasion of the Iberian peninsula in 1807–8 opened a new chapter in the propaganda struggle. Even prior to the French invasion of Portugal in November 1807 the British government was circulating the *Ambigu* in Madrid and Lisbon.[269] The *Courier d'Angleterre* had a separate subscription rate for Lisbon and in September 1808 extended this rate to 'Spain and Portugal', and quoted another rate for Brazil, where the Portuguese court had taken refuge.[270] The *Courier de Londres* also offered subscription rates for Spain, Brazil and Portugal,[271] and Peltier habitually published Spanish documents in the original language in detachable supplements. These were copied as far away as Mexico City, where the first Spanish translation of the papal bull of 9 June 1809, the explosive document which excommunicated Napoleon and was thus censored across the French empire, was taken from Peltier's French version of the text in the *Ambigu*.[272] Moreover, extracts of the *Courier d'Angleterre* were translated and distributed in Spain in a series of four-side octavo propaganda leaflets, presumably at British expense.[273] The *Courier de Londres* went one better, and gained royal permission to publish a Portuguese edition at Lisbon which appeared throughout 1809, and possibly longer.[274] In addition, the British government paid to distribute newspaper propaganda in the peninsula and Spanish colonies. By December 1808 100 of the govern-

---

265 PRO, FO 73/69, Regnier to [?Hamilton], 21/23 Aug. 1811.
266 AAE, mem./docs France 641, fo. 160, Peltier to d'Antraigues, 2 Oct. 1806; Canning papers, bundle 58a, account dated '1 July to 30 Dec. 1807'.
267 PRO, FO 27/73, Stanhope to C. C. Smith, 17 May 1810.
268 See AAE, mem./docs France 630, fos 68–9, Armfeldt to abbé Pierrard, St Petersburg, 8 Jan. 1812.
269 Canning papers, bundle 58a, account dated '1 July to 30 Dec. 1807'.
270 CA 351 (6 Sept. 1808).
271 A rate for Brazil was first offered in CL lxiii/2 (5 Jan. 1808), following the court's flight from Portugal.
272 *Traduccion del número 237 del Ambigu, en que se incertan las letras Apostolicas . . . en 10 de Junio de 1809*, Mexico City 1810. There is a copy in the British Library.
273 The Bodleian library possesses no. 9 in the series, *Concluyen las noticias del exercito Ingles*.
274 The Bodleian library possesses the *Tradducão do Correio de Londres* for 1809. It is a translation without additions or deletions.

ment's subscription to the *Courier d'Angleterre* were earmarked for Spain,[275] and by mid-1811 the government was also sending copies to Mexico via Jamaica.[276]

All three London émigré journals enjoyed a symbiotic relationship with the nascent Spanish patriotic free press that arose in the chaos following the invasion. They cited a vast range of Spanish papers as information sources, and developed a system of exchanging subscriptions with the Spanish editors, via the Spanish ambassador in London.[277] Equally, foreign papers copied the London émigré press. Regnier was extensively copied by Spanish gazettes such as the *Seminario patriotico*, while Peltier claimed his journal was 'regularly translated or copied in more than thirty foreign papers' and 'has great influence on opinion in all parts of America, from Canada to Paraguay . . . but above all among England's allies in the [Iberian] Peninsula'.[278] This claim may not be greatly exaggerated. Spanish journalism was still in its infancy, and any journal with an original news content or analysis was widely copied. In this way the readership of British-sponsored journalistic propaganda was not confined to the readership of the London émigré press, but reached out into the newly emergent Spanish public sphere towards an immeasurable, and potentially almost limitless, audience.

The émigré journals also continued to circulate in the West Indies, the United States and in former French Caribbean colonies, where Peltier had agents as early as 1795.[279] By 1807 the *Ambigu* was being sent to 'the United States and every part of the West Indies' at British government expense. But since their 100 subscriptions were being divided among Russia, Sweden, the Iberian Peninsula, Sicily and the Cape of Good Hope, the government-funded papers can only have been reaching a tiny part of the Caribbean élite.[280] However, Christophe of Haiti also patronised the *Ambigu*, which he used as a semi-official gazette: copies were sent to Haiti with Peltier's diplomatic despatches.[281] It is probable too that the government sponsored occasional distributions of journals in captured West Indian colonies. In 1811, on news of the fall of the French Indian Ocean colony of Mauritius (Ile de France), Peltier immediately wrote to the Foreign Office to ask permission to send three packets of his journal for dissemination there, and it seems fair to assume similar distributions took place in the West Indies.[282] Likewise, Regnier sent copies of the *Courier d'Angleterre* to a friend in Savannah and to

---

[275] Canning papers, bundle 56a, anonymous letter, dated 20 Dec. 1808. At this time d'Antraigues and Regnier were only sending 75 copies, and pocketing the difference.
[276] See PRO, FO 73/69, Regnier to [?Hamilton], 21/23 Aug. 1811.
[277] See PRO, FO 95/636, M. B. [Broval] to d'Antraigues, Seville, 20 May 1809.
[278] Ibid.; PRO, FO 27/91, Peltier to Castlereagh, 2 June 1812. A letter in *Ambigu* 318 (30 Jan. 1811), 233, refers to the paper's wide circulation in Spain.
[279] Peltier, *Avis du rédacteur du Tableau de l'Europe*, refers to the seizure of an agent in the West Indies in 1795.
[280] Canning papers, bundle 58a, account dated '1 July to 30 Dec. 1807'.
[281] See PRO, FO 27/106, Limonade to Peltier, 10 June 1814.
[282] PRO, FO 27/86, Peltier to C. C. Smith, 25 Feb. 1811.

the Spanish Ambassador in Philadelphia.[283] In 1807 he also received a bulk subscription for twenty copies for Martinique.[284]

France was never completely hermetically sealed against British propaganda, but the control of the posts and French domination of Germany presented serious obstacles.[285] In 1812–13 the Foreign Office arranged for copies of the *London Gazette* to be dropped on the Loire, Garonne, Breton and Norman coasts. The papers were translated, and often printed, by Peltier and Regnier, and thrown ashore by fishermen and smugglers operating out of the Channel Islands.[286] However, according to a certain George Davis, the fishermen avoided doing the job properly, and customs officials retrieved most of the bundles of newspapers from the shore. He proposed an alternative method: balloons carrying timing devices could drop twenty papers per minute over France.[287] Both methods testify to the desperation of the British and the success of the French in sealing the coast, but have an enduring significance. They represent a shift in emphasis of British propaganda initiatives away from an attempt to appeal to an élite of policy-makers, as with their émigré newspapers, or to an essentially restricted political public's opinion. Instead they attempted to influence the sentiments of a 'general public', selected at random from the population of France's northern maritime provinces, in belated recognition that lasting counter-revolution might require the conquest of French opinion as well as the application of force.

However, there are indications that some émigré propaganda was also trickling into France. Pocket-sized brochures of eight or twelve sides could be sent clandestinely through the post, a technique d'Antraigues pioneered while at Berlin in 1805.[288] In England, from 1806, d'Antraigues appears to have encouraged Regnier to print extracts of the *Courier d'Angleterre* in the same manner.[289] Nevertheless, the relative absence of police seizures or evidence of British support for widespread pamphlet dissemination, suggest that these pamphlets had a very limited, clandestine circulation.

Likewise, a few copies of émigré journals also reached France and occupied Europe. In 1802 Otto believed that a portion of Peltier's production was sent

---

[283] See PRO, FO 73/69, Regnier to [?Hamilton], 21/23 Aug. 1811.
[284] Canning papers, bundle 56a, Regnier [to Canning], 30 Dec. 1807.
[285] AN, F^{18} 12, plaq. 5, dos. 52, correspondence of the Interior Ministry with prefects of the western *départements* shows French concern at the circulation of British newspapers in Nov. 1813.
[286] See PRO, FO 27/124, Regnier to Castlereagh, [memoir], 10 Mar. 1815, enclosed with letter of 23/27 Mar. 1815; FO 27/219, 'The humble memorial of James Regnier' [to Castlereagh], Manchester, 15 June 1819; FO 27/94, Peltier to Foreign Office, 19 Jan. 1813. On distribution from Jersey see FO 27/92, letters of General Don to Cooke, 25 Aug. 1812–11 July 1813, passim.
[287] PRO, FO 27/91, Davis to Bathurst, 14 Oct. 1812.
[288] See Hauterive, *Police*, ii, paras 533, 605, police bulletins of 23 Nov., 17 Dec. 1805.
[289] For examples of these pamphlets see PRO, FO 95/636; Canning papers, bundles 59, 59a.

THE PROPAGANDA WAR

to Ostend,[290] and in 1805 a hand-copied ode against Bonaparte was seized in Bayonne. In nearby Pau copies of an *Oraison funèbre du duc d'Enghien* and the Blanchardist *Réclamations canoniques* were also confiscated.[291] Although the authorities were unaware of it, all three had been published recently by Peltier, and were probably copied from a single copy or cluster of the *Ambigu* circulating clandestinely. Equally, in April 1804 Regnier claimed his paper circulated in France despite police vigilance, and in 1807 he claimed to have six subscribers in Holland.[292] Moreover, in 1810 Fauche-Borel requested between six and twelve copies of the *Courier de Londres*, and two copies of the *Ambigu*, from the Foreign Office for his secret agent Claude Gilles de Caen to take to France, commenting that these papers were 'always useful to disseminate in the interior'.[293] However, given concern at the highest levels of French government to prevent the circulation of *libelles*, and lack of other recorded examples, the penetration of émigré newspapers and periodicals into France appears to have been haphazard and minimal.

The government-sponsored distribution of the *Courier d'Angleterre* and the *Courier de Londres* ended in December 1814, when Hamilton informed Regnier that the paper could be of no further service to the government 'in the present state of Europe'.[294] When the *Courier d'Angleterre* folded in March 1815, Regnier's requests for a pension were refused by the British government, as were those of Pierre François Fauche, and subsequently his widow.[295] Peltier's journal survived, with British backing, but after his requests for a pension from Louis XVIII were refused, it became an organ of the ultra-royalist opposition. The *Courier de Londres* struggled on until 1826, having bought Regnier's subscription list and merged the two papers. The British government and the Bourbons had dropped the émigré propagandists as quickly as they had hired them.

Nevertheless, for twenty years the French émigré journals played an important, though immeasurable, role in the history and councils of Europe, and the reliance the British government placed upon them after 1803 is evidence of the success of Bonaparte's campaign to control the European public sphere. For, across the continent, the public sphere had proven to be very precariously established – far weaker than Habermasian theory would suggest – and surprisingly susceptible to control and manipulation by a hegemonic power. Thus, the French struggle to suppress the émigré and

---

[290] AAE, CPA 597, fo. 481, Otto to Talleyrand, 12 thermidor X (30 July 1802).
[291] Hauterive, *Police*, i, para. 1258, police bulletin of 29 Apr. 1805.
[292] CL lv/28 (6 Apr. 1804); Canning papers, bundle 56a, Regnier [to Canning], 30 Dec. 1807.
[293] PRO, FO 27/80, Fauche-Borel to Hamilton, 19 Jan. 1810.
[294] PRO, FO 27/124, Regnier to Castlereagh, [memoir], 10 Mar. 1815, enclosed with letter of 23/27 Mar. 1815; FO 27/219, 'The humble memorial of James Regnier' [to Castlereagh], Manchester, 15 June 1819.
[295] PRO, FO 27/219, Regnier to Castlereagh, Manchester, 15 June 1819; FO 27/108, Mme P.-F. Fauche to Hamilton, Oct. 1814.

foreign presses across Europe from 1800 formed an integral part of Napoleonic diplomacy and was at times determinant of French policy rather than subservient to it. The full impact and implications of the Napoleonic system of information control on European diplomacy and politics have yet to be explored and integrated into the historical accounts of the period, but there can be little doubt of their significance.[296] The British propaganda campaign thus marks an important milestone in the development of modern propaganda warfare, because it responded to new problems of communication and dissemination, notably Napoleon's tight control over information inside his empire and his effective destruction of traditional channels of communication. The émigré journals enabled British propaganda to reach many of the leading figures in allied or neutral countries and former French colonies. In a Europe of francophone élites, the Foreign Office had little choice but to farm out the task of fighting an international propaganda war to a small group of French émigré journalists. If the British drew on a limited pool of writers and talent, this reflects constraints on resources, and the limited informational sources on which the government could draw. If they allowed their writers ample latitude in what they wrote, this again was primarily due to limited resources, especially of personnel, and to mask their own involvement. The interplay of British and French propaganda campaigns demonstrates the importance of a limited European élite opinion and of public information in warfare, as well as an emergent 'public opinion'. Propaganda had now evolved beyond crude polemical pamphleteering to a random or sympathetic audience. Instead, a selected audience was targeted repeatedly through the use of newspapers in a common language according to strategic and political imperatives. The objective was to maintain a vital flow of information and to manipulate opinion using both open and subtle methods. If the target of this propaganda remained primarily an élite audience, this fitted the political realities and technological constraints of European power politics in the Napoleonic era.

---

[296] Stuart Woolf, *Napoleon's integration of Europe*, London 1991, for example, does not even list the press among Napoleon's 'tools of conquest'. It has no index references to the press, printing, newspapers, journalism or the *Moniteur*. There are only three references to French propaganda, and despite brief discussions of the use of diplomats as propagandists (p. 68) and of the iconography of the Napoleonic myth (p. 168), there is no recognition of the systematic nature and extent of Napoleonic propaganda.

4

Reactions to Revolution, 1792–1799

Between 1792 and 1814, the émigré press provided its readers with a continuous stream of information on revolutionary governments and European politics and in the process served a vital integrative function. It offered its European élite and émigré audience a sense of regular engagement with political events, bound together in a cohesive counter-revolutionary narrative. Unlike other forms of publication, it gave readers immediate and up-to-date interpretations of events as they unfolded. Where the great tomes of counter-revolutionary theory written by writers like Barruel, Burke, Gentz, de Maistre, de Bonald, d'Ivernois, Calonne and, indeed, Mallet Du Pan and Montlosier, offered broad interpretations, the émigré press offered nuance, reinterpretation in the light of events, repetition and reinforcement. Thus it promoted a continuous narrative discourse which filled the chronological and geographical space between readers, isolated publications and lone counter-revolutionary propagandists, several of whom read the émigré journals avidly. Thus the exile press's role in the evolution of counter-revolutionary ideology and politics was probably just as important as the ideas of the leading counter-revolutionary propagandists who feature in standard treatments of counter-revolutionary thought.[1] Moreover, the journals wove materials on apparently disparate themes into a single textual format, and in the process both implicitly and explicitly suggested important relationships between them. In the 1790s the main themes included the causes of the revolution of 1789–92, the dynamics of continuing revolution and suitable counter-revolutionary responses, the character of the revolutionary leadership, the revolution in the colonies, war and international relations, French finances and British politics. The journals were also involved in a number of publicity campaigns against the revolution. All of these issues are discussed below.

The émigré journalists were conscious of their publicity role. In late 1792, in his *Dernier Tableau de Paris*, still the only avowedly émigré journal published in London, Peltier insisted that his mission was to contradict the revolutionaries' version of events, and to justify the king and his Swiss guards

---

[1] Both Godechot, *Counter-revolution*, and Beik, *French revolution from the right*, ignore periodical publications almost entirely. James Osen, *Royalist political thought during the French revolution*, Westport, Conn. 1995, only deals with writers domiciled in France and, to its detriment, ignores newspapers and periodicals altogether.

in the face of their calumnies.² The impact of Peltier's detailed accounts of the atrocities and horrors perpetrated by the revolutionaries is of course immeasurable. However, with its timely appearance, authentic accounts, relatively wide circulation and chilling empirical proof of the perspicacity of Edmund Burke's predictions, Peltier's work undoubtedly contributed to the hardening of opinion against the revolution in Britain. But the British reaction was primarily a response to political events, especially the imprisonment, trial and execution of Louis XVI, the outbreak of war on 1 February and the beginnings of the Terror. Peltier's work would probably have had a greater impact if he had published the horrific details of the September massacres in the first volume, rather than the second, which only appeared well after Louis's execution.³ The *Dernier Tableau de Paris* also expounded on most of the major themes of later émigré journals. It discussed the causes of the revolution, its nature and the reasons for its success, the personalities of the revolutionary leaders and even the risk to British colonies.

Initially, the main task facing the émigré journalists was to explain why the revolution had occurred. According to Peltier, it was the result of the king's pusillanimity in ruling a people with corrupted morals, who rejected religion. Such a people could only be held down by fear of punishment: 'When you succeed in snuffing out all religious sentiment in a nation; when the spirit of banditry and idleness has been substituted for the spirit of order and work, among a people whose morals are completely depraved, the government can only be maintained *by chastisements*.'⁴ In consequence it was necessary ruthlessly to suppress the slightest manifestations of revolt. Louis XVI's goodwill was thus a weakness, his clemency a crime.⁵ Like Burke, Peltier argued that the revolutionary threat was universal, especially since the king's deposition, 'the moment at which the French revolution began actively to propagate revolutions in [the rest of] Europe'.⁶ Thus it was vital for the powers to make common cause and respond to future disturbances with sufficient force.⁷ Peltier even contended that as the aims and means of popular rebellions were 'error and pillage', 'terror and preservation' should be the instruments and duties of kings.⁸

Peltier insisted that the revolution was inherently unpopular, the work of a few activists. A hundred factious individuals had required several months to summon and organise enough support to accomplish the revolution of 10 August. They had only succeeded by using auxiliaries summoned from Marseilles and members of the urban under-classes enflamed by alcohol and

---

2   DTP i, esp. pp. iv–vi, 66–8, 140–5.
3   Ibid. ii. 235ff.
4   Ibid. i. 178.
5   Ibid. i. 179.
6   Ibid. i. 149.
7   Ibid. i. 179.
8   Ibid. i. 182.

seduced by cash, hope of pillage and an orgy of destruction.[9] These people were the blind instrument of the revolutionary leaders.[10] As further proof that the revolution lacked popular support, Peltier argued that in 1789 the moderate and royalist press had three times as many titles and over seventeen times as many readers as Jacobin papers. This reflected the true state of public opinion.[11] Years later he argued that the Napoleonic plebiscites were unrepresentative of 'French opinion', because there were only 3 million voters among a population of more than 25 million, and they were motivated by terror, intimidation or hopes of advancement.[12] Thus despite ridiculing Siéyès for discovering, in *Qu'est-ce que le tiers etat*, 'that the greatest [number] is the greatest [number]', the émigré publicists were not averse to invoking hazy notions of a general will to legitimise their case.[13]

Peltier also emphasised the role and power of the press in the revolution. He named it as the primary motive force for the coup of 10 August, claiming that the origin of the conflict between the factions of Brissot and [Alexandre] Lameth lay in the jealous rivalry of journalists. Thus, 'One disputed the influence or subscribers of the other and Europe was overthrown to satisfy the printers and the pride of a flat foot [pied plat], who was for a long time employed correcting the proofs of the *Courier de l'Europe* [i.e. Brissot]'.[14] The suppression of the royalist press after 10 August showed the nature of the new regime: 'Like all despotic governments, its first object was to suffer no obstacle in its path, and for that it was necessary to hasten to destroy whatever could contradict it or enlighten public opinion.'[15] Peltier even published a letter which alleged that France declared war on Savoy, Spain and the empire because they had banned Jacobin newspapers, noting that each French army was accompanied by printing presses 'just as it is by the strongest train of artillery'.[16]

Both Peltier and successive editors of the *Courier de Londres* accused the *philosophes* of preparing the revolution by undermining religion and hence morality.[17] The belief that the revolution was a direct consequence of the philosophical movement of the French enlightenment, or even the result of a *philosophe* conspiracy, was of course commonplace in counter-revolutionary

---

[9] Ibid. i. 143-4.
[10] Ibid. i. 81.
[11] Ibid. i. 44. A review of titles contradicts his figures, but subscription information is sketchy for pro-revolutionary titles.
[12] See, for example, *Paris* 218 (31 Dec. 1800), 476; 245 (15 May 1802), 460. Mallet Du Pan in *BM* 35 (15 Mar. 1800), 173, took the opposite view: even if all enfranchised abstainers opposed Napoleon, he still had a 67% mandate.
[13] *DTP* i. 14n.
[14] Ibid. i. 202n.
[15] Ibid. i. 200.
[16] Ibid. i, appendix to no. 6, p. 68.
[17] See, for example, *DTP* i, p. vii; ii. 4, 396n.; *CL* xxxiv/9 (30 July 1793); xxxv/12 (11 Feb. 1794).

thought. Its most extreme manifestations were found in the freemasonic conspiracy theories of abbé Augustin de Barruel's *Mémoires pour servir à l'histoire du Jacobinisme*[18] or Cadet de Gassicourt's anonymous *Tombeau de Jacques Molai*.[19] The idea of Masonic conspiracy was endorsed in the *pur* journals,[20] but disavowed by Mallet Du Pan and Montlosier.[21] Montlosier argued that conspiracies required a group of men who could dispose of followers: 'They speak of conspiracy, and [yet] in the whole course of the revolution I have never known a single man who could say to me . . . "I have another man at my disposal".'[22] Yet although the *monarchien* journalists denied the existence of a conspiracy, they were adamant that enlightenment philosophy had helped to dissolve social bonds and the mechanisms of moral control. Even Mallet Du Pan, although he exonerated Voltaire and Rousseau of culpable intent, accused Diderot and Condorcet of being the real heads of the revolutionary school. He spoke for all émigré journalists when he contended:

> That a class of opinions equally subversive of religion, morality and society, had been systematically propagated in France for sixty years past; that a class of men of letters and men of the world had been the promoters, partisans and protectors of those opinions; and that their school has given birth to a crowd of fanatic pedants, sophists and demoniacs, who from its origin seized upon the revolution as by right of conquest, are historical truths beyond all controversy and no longer stand in need of demonstration.[23]

Likewise, while denying that the spirit of liberty and of irreligion had had a causal role, Montlosier nevertheless admitted that they had had a strong coincidental influence on the nature of the revolution.[24] The less moderate writers continued to see conspiracies everywhere: the second volume of *Dernier Tableau de Paris* continued to allege that the revolution derived from an Orléanist plot, backed by Marat, and the *Courier de Londres* agreed, transmuting Philippe-Egalité into the double headed monster Marat-d'Orléans.[25]

---

18 London 1797–8.
19 Charles-Louis Cadet de Gassicourt (attrib.), *Le Tombeau de Jacques Molai, ou le secret des conspirations à ceux qui veulent tout savoir: oeuvre posthume de C. L. C. G. D. L. S. D. M. B. C. D. V.*, Paris an IV [?1796]. According to the British Library's *Catalogue of printed books* the initials stand for 'C.-L. Cadet de Gassicourt, de la section de Montblanc, condamné de Vendémiaire'. Popkin, *Right-wing press*, 168, claims that Gassicourt's work was much more influential in France in the 1790s than Barruel's, which went unremarked in the domestic right-wing press. An expanded version was printed in 1797 [an V].
20 See *Paris* 169 (30 Nov. 1798), 594–5; 170 (17 Dec. 1798), 114–18; *CL* xli/16 (24 Feb. 1797); MF 4 (10 May 1800), 245ff.
21 See JFA 12 (7 Apr. 1797), 161–84; 14 (22 Apr. 1797), 290; BM 14 (15 Mar. 1799), 335–63.
22 JFA 12 (7 Apr. 1797), 167.
23 BM 14 (15 Mar. 1799), 335.
24 JFA 14 (22 Apr. 1797), 289ff.
25 *DTP* ii. 10–23; *CL* xxxiii/23 (12 Mar. 1793). Peltier repeats allegations of an Orléanist plot in *CP* 7 (16 Nov. 1793); *Paris* 9 (1 Aug. 1795).

The implicit connection between enlightenment literary culture and revolution coloured the émigré journalists' coverage of literary and cultural issues throughout the revolutionary and Napoleonic periods. Although such issues are peripheral to the subject of this study, they are worthy of brief attention here.[26] The cultural content of the exile press was intimately connected with the émigré journalists' attempts to portray the émigrés as the legitimate representatives of the *patrie* they had lost. They defined a quintessential French national character composed of good manners, refined behaviour, honour, loyalty and generosity. Stripped of these characteristics, the inhabitants of revolutionary France were transformed from the most civilised people in the world to the most barbarous.[27] In particular, the émigré journalists defined their 'other France' in exile in terms of high culture, especially literature. They sought to legitimise their opposition to the revolution by appropriating *belles-lettres*, and French *esprit*, *moeurs*, and *sensibilité*. They insinuated that the revolution had rejected these aspects of French culture and the national character and was thus inherently un-French. French literary and cultural traditions were the patrimony of the exile community, which in any case included much of the literary and cultural élite of *ancien régime* France. It was their duty to preserve a purer, alternative France in exile, free from revolutionary corruption. In consequence, as case studies illustrate, the reception of the works of writers such as Madame de Staël, Marie-Joseph Chénier, Chateaubriand, Louis de Fontanes and the abbé Delille in the émigré press depends more on their political stance at the moment of publication than perceptions of literary merit.[28] Cultural agenda were thus subsumed within and subordinate to political imperatives, as Peltier made explicit in his rhetorical assertion that: 'a magnanimous and disinterested act, a romance written in prison, a piece of beautiful and elegant poetry, are not these in a way all motions for the monarchy?'[29] Where de Bonald declared that 'literature is the reflection of society', Peltier added that 'theatre is a portrait of the morals of a people'.[30] 'Revolutionary' authors such as Marie-Joseph Chénier were thus systematically denigrated on the grounds of literary merit, form and moral content in the émigré press, even when, as in Chénier's case, they adopted austere classical models that ought to have appealed to the émigrés' stylistic conservatism. Where the journalists conceded due credit to French literary productions, it was usually accompanied by some explicit contrast with the general run of French products, or an attempt to claim the

---

[26] On the French exile press's coverage of literature, high culture and French émigré identity see Simon Burrows, 'The cultural politics of exile: French émigré literary journalism in London, 1793–1814', *Journal of European Studies* xxix (1999), 157–77

[27] This sentiment is expressed by a Swiss correspondent in MF 4 (10 May 1800), 303.

[28] See Burrows, 'Cultural politics'.

[29] *Paris* 1 (6 June 1795), 38–9. Peltier admitted that though literary and political sections were theoretically equal, political and military subjects sometimes took precedence: *Paris* 165 (29 Sept. 1798), 3; *Ambigu* 341 (20 Sept. 1812), 589.

[30] *Paris* 171 (31 Dec. 1798), 149. De Bonald's dictum is cited in GGB 133 (22 July 1806).

work or its author for the royalist cause. Alternatively, works could be described as a symptom of the change of spirits in the French populace. In the short term the cultural role of the émigré journals merely reinforced their political position and evolutionary direction. However, the literary-cultural discourse of the émigré press, in which revolutionary and Napoleonic literature and high culture were synonymous with moral and cultural decay, outlived its progenitor and has had an enduring and profound impact on the way the revolution has been perceived. For after the restoration, this discourse became hegemonic even inside France, and remained so for 150 years. Its triumph was so complete that, as Carla Hesse has observed, 'historians and literary critics have traditionally treated the literary culture of the French revolution with total disregard if not utter contempt'.[31] This was the most enduring ideological victory of the counter-revolution, and much credit for it surely belongs to the émigré press.

Because the revolution was blamed on irreligion and the corruption of morality, the émigré journalists also saw it as providential justice. They were not alone in this. De Bonald, de Maistre and Barruel, to name but three, shared the same conviction. But if the revolution was the judgement of heaven, it was by implication a temporary phenomenon. Thus, having expressed their grief at the execution of Louis XVI, the editors of the *Courier de Londres* threatened the regicides with divine justice, and Peltier looked forward to witnessing heaven's vengeance for so many heinous crimes.[32] These expectations were soon realised. Verduisant saw the hand of providence behind the quarrels of the Girondins and Montagnards, and Peltier and the abbé Calonne saw it in the guillotining of Philippe-Egalité and Danton.[33] It would be wrong to be too cynical about these statements. After the restoration, the abbé Calonne's letters to his nephew reverberate with providential language and almost millennial expectations.[34] Peltier, too, consistently blamed events in France from 1792 to 1794 on 'heavenly vengeance' and argued that 'eras of corruption occur where great misfortunes are necessary to recall men to the great truths'.[35] If such rhetoric became less common after Thermidor, it was probably because the shock of events had subsided, and the blood letting in France was reduced. Nevertheless, providential explanations of the revolution remained implicit in the émigré journals, and there were clear biblical resonances in the frequent use of the word *fléau* [scourge] to describe revolution, Jacobins or Napoleon. Indeed, in early 1799 even the soberly Calvinistic Mallet Du Pan condemned Bonaparte's

---

[31] Hesse, *Publishing and cultural politics*, 1.
[32] CL xxxiii/8–9 (25–9 Jan. 1793); HR, letter 1 (31 Mar. 1793), 3.
[33] See, for example, CP 7 (16 Nov. 1793); 68 (8 Apr. 1794); CL xxxiv/8 (26 July 1793); xxxiv/40 (15 Nov. 1793).
[34] See AN, 297AP/2, pièces 97–9, letters of J.-L.-J. de Calonne to Blondel d'Aubers, Trois-Rivières 1818, n.d. [?1819] and 19 Jan. 1820.
[35] *DTP* i, appendix to no. 6, p. 72.

irreligion by noting: 'Providence will never permit such shame to triumph long. Buonaparte is dancing over graves; the day will come when men will dance over his.'[36]

Scandalous behaviour was to be expected from France's new leaders. Naturally, a revolution whose causes included a breakdown in public and private morality was likely to be led by scoundrels. According to Peltier, the leaders of the republic shared common personality traits including 'venality, a propensity for intrigue [l'esprit d'intrigue], rapacity, thirst for pillage'.[37] Most were revolutionaries by speculation. Hence he denounced the Director Rewbell's 'sordid avarice' in acquiring annual revenues of 3,000,000 from Alsatian lands purchased with worthless *assignats*,[38] and repeated Mirabeau's *bon mot* concerning Talleyrand's greed: ' "he sells himself to whosoever wants to buy him, and he gets a good deal, for he trades gold against mud" '.[39] Moreover, journalists offered anecdotal evidence to prove that revolutionaries were hypocrites who betrayed their deepest principles in private life. For example, Peltier gave an account of Camille Desmoulin's wedding, noting it was celebrated by a non-juring priest, with Robespierre and Saint-Just as witnesses. Peltier's account is correct in most of its details, naming the priest as Fr Bérardier, who had taught Robespierre and Desmoulins at the Collège Louis-le-Grand. However, the marriage was celebrated on 30 December 1790, three days after the king sanctioned the decree requiring the clerical oath, and four days before Bérardier, as a clerical deputy, was required to take it, so technically he was not yet a non-juror, or at least not culpably so in the eyes of the French state. However, he did become one and, as Peltier noted, survived the Terror unmolested.[40] On a more general level, Peltier alleged that renewed measures against the émigrés in the summer of 1795 were motivated:

> By the personal fear of men who have seized power that they will see themselves dispossessed of their wives and mistresses by the returning [émigrés]. People have no idea of the immorality that has reigned in France since three years ago. A large number of daughters and wives of émigrés have been obliged to throw themselves into the arms of the revolutionaries, both members of the Convention and [revolutionaries] in the *départements*, to escape the guillotine or relieve themselves from hunger. I could name a large number of them, but that would distress their families needlessly.[41]

---

[36] BM 11 (29 Jan. 1799), 160.
[37] *Paris* 156 (30 May 1798), 134.
[38] *Paris* 166 (15 Oct. 1798), 193.
[39] *Paris* 156 (30 May 1798), 134.
[40] *Paris* 4 (27 June 1795), 206–8. The actual witnesses were Robespierre, Pétion, Louis-Sébastien Mercier and the marquis de Sillery. Peltier's allegation that Lucile Duplessis was a bastard daughter of the abbé Terray appears to be a malicious slander.
[41] *Paris* 14 (5 Sept. 1795), 350–1.

As proof of his contention, he observed that the prime movers behind the policy were le Gendre [sic], whose mistress had previously bestowed her favours on an émigré *constitutionnel*, and Tallien, who married Thérèse Cabarrus, ex-wife of another émigré, whom he encountered in the prisons of Bordeaux while *représentant en mission*.[42]

In the eyes of the émigré journalists the faction fights of the Terror offered further proof that the revolutionaries were merely power-hungry rogues, and that in anarchic conditions victory went to the most ruthless. Thus, according to Peltier, the Girondins went to the guillotine for being 'a little less scoundrels' than their accusers, but the *Courier de Londres* suggested that Brissot was silent on the scaffold because he was still plotting.[43] Other revolutionaries took pleasure in bloodletting and crime. Thus the abbé Calonne found a 'perfect description' of the 'real Jacobin innovators' in the logic and morality of the bloodthirsty Jacobin hero of Robert Jephson's satirical novel *Confessions of Jean-Baptiste Couteau*.[44] Peltier suggested that when Bentabole attacked Hébert in the Convention, his audience were surprised he had not condemned him for failing to denounce his brothers, kill his father, poison his mother and rape his sisters.[45] This tendency to represent atrocious deeds satirically perhaps stemmed from a conviction that the reality behind them was too horrific for print. Peltier used morbid humour to reinforce accounts of the September massacres, his comprehensive lists of the victims of the Terror and the personal experience of many émigrés. Moreover, accounts of the dechristianisation campaign, desecration of churches and revolutionary cults, were certain to arouse revulsion:

> Each day sees new pillaging of the Churches. Profanation is mingled with robbery. Men riding the wagons charged with images of saints . . . parodying the ceremonies of the Church, horses draped in pontifical vestments . . . succeed in destroying the last traces of the Christian religion. When they wished to substitute a festival to the new divinities of the French people, REASON and LIBERTY, they fetched two prostitutes from the Opera, and these new idols of a burlesque cult were so astonished . . . that they could not contain their peals of laughter during the ceremony.[46]

---

[42] Ibid. 367. *Louis Legendre* (1752–97), Parisian butcher, founder member of the Cordeliers Club, *conventionnel*, briefly member of the Committee of General Security, and Thermidorian. *Jean-Lambert Tallien* (1767–1820), prominent Thermidorian: a former radical journalist and *communard*, he played a prominent role in the *journée* of 10 August 1792 and the September massacres. Speculation abounded that he forced Cabarrus into a sexual bargain. Peltier discusses their liaison in *TE* ii, pt 1, 60–1n.
[43] *CP* 5 (12 Nov. 1793); *CL* xxxiv/39 (12 Nov. 1793).
[44] *CL* xxxvi/2 (4 July 1794); R. Jephson, *Confessions of Jean-Baptiste Couteau, citizen of France, written by himself and translated by Mr Jephson*, London 1794.
[45] *CP* 23 (24 Dec. 1793). *Pierre-Louis Bentabole* (1756–98), *conventionnel*, violent Jacobin and *représentant en mission* in 1793, he became an active Thermidorian.
[46] *CP* 12 (28 Nov. 1793).

Such descriptions could only reinforce Peltier's claim that the revolution was disputed between '*philosophes* and thieves'.[47] Nor did Robespierre's fall change the way revolutionaries were portrayed in the émigré press. Indeed, after Thermidor the trials and executions of such notorious Terrorists as Jean-Baptiste Carrier, who orchestrated the *noyades* [mass drownings] at Nantes, and Antoine-Quentin Fouquier-Tinville, the public prosecutor on the revolutionary tribunal, served a double purpose. They gave the journalists an excuse and opportunity both to publicise the full extent of blood letting, and to highlight the complicity of Thermidorian leaders like Fouché and Tallien, who had been responsible for killings at Lyon and Bordeaux.[48] Tallien's career, a favourite and particularly vulnerable target for the journalists, was summarised thus by Peltier in a satire of the *Apostles' Creed* for the use of revolutionaries:

> I believe in Marat the all powerful, creator of [Jacobin] clubs and massacre, and in Tallien his bastard son, our lord, who was conceived of the 2nd September [1792], was born of the Commune of Paris, suffered under [Thérèse] Cabarrus, crucified, killed and buried Bordeaux in the underworld [enseleví Bordeaux dans les enfers].... I believe ... in permission to steal, the resurrection of the prisons and licence everlasting. Amen.[49]

In August 1794 the abbé Calonne informed his readers that Tallien 'likes women, food, gambling and every form of pleasure' and asked them: 'to remember that Tallien ... shared in all the crimes of the Jacobins and voted for the king's death'.[50] The other émigré journalists shared the conviction that the Thermidorians were Terrorists by nature, a conviction intensified by their perception that Tallien was their most prominent leader. Hence Montlosier also produced a *Pater républicain* to highlight the continuing irreligion and reign of criminals in France:

> Our father in the Luxembourg [ie. the Directory], hallowed be your name (in spite of almost all the nation and yourself) ... forgive us our little peccadilloes (rape, theft, denunciations, depredations etc., etc.) as we forgive you your acts of despotism, your violations of the constitution...[51]

Peltier also offered a parody of the *Lord's Prayer* for Jacobins to address to the guillotine which included the chilling line 'Give us today our daily blood' and ended 'do not leave us to succumb to the *Chouans*, but deliver us from the people ... and God'.[52] These parodies are all the more notable for being

---

[47] *DTP* i, p. vii.
[48] On Carrier's trial see CL xxxvi/43 (25 Nov. 1794); on the execution of Fouquier-Tinville see *Paris* 1 (6 June 1795), 113–21; *TE* ii, pt vi, 1–72.
[49] *Paris* 120 (10 July 1797), 642–3.
[50] CL xxxvi/16 (22 Aug. 1794).
[51] JFA 8 (25 Feb. 1797), 604.
[52] *Paris* 120 (10 July 1797), 642.

published shortly before Fructidor, during a period of relative toleration and liberalism inside France, when both Montlosier and Peltier briefly softened in their attitude to the regime. Thus the political climate inside France made relatively little difference to the collective image of revolutionary leaders in the émigré journals. Nor did the political outlook or personalities of the journalists. *Monarchiens* as well as *purs* chorused their disdain for the revolutionaries. Montlosier published an account of Barras's early life describing his taste for gambling and brothels, adding, for good measure, that many émigrés had lent him small sums but had never been repaid. He added: 'a wit, an energy, or if you prefer, a great audacity, these are the principal characteristics of his revolutionary life. Moreover, we are assured that his present opinions as well as his morals have lost nothing of their former dissoluteness'.[53] He also noted a bold defamatory paragraph in the *Quotidienne* which remarked that in the reference to a league of five kings in *Genesis* xiv. 2, the 'director' of Sodom was called Barras.[54] Even the rational, cool-headed Mallet Du Pan was venomous towards many revolutionary leaders, denouncing them as 'wicked men'.[55] Among those he most despised was Lazare Carnot, even after his proscription at Fructidor. According to Mallet, Carnot was 'wicked by reflection'. Those who thought he would convert to royalism in exile were gravely mistaken. Even Danton or Desmoulins might have recanted – but never a Carnot nor a Garat, for 'never was a sophist plunged in crime by reasoning redeemed'.[56] Mallet's distaste for calculated cynicism also influenced his treatment of General Bonaparte, especially after the proclamation to the Egyptians of 24 messidor VI (12 July 1798), in which Napoleon claimed that the French were children of the prophet who had made war against the pope:

> He who is the exterminator of Egypt, is the same man who harangues in academies, who bends the knee to Mahomet as he has done to the pope in Italy, and to Atheism at Paris; and he who builds play-houses and concert-rooms over the corpses of the Africans.[57]

Thus Napoleon's 'Mohamadanism', an enduring theme with anti-Napoleonic Black Legend propagandists, was first broached in the émigré journals by a *monarchien* who was later to find much to admire in his regime. Mallet even denigrated Bonaparte's military talents, asserting that the revolution had no need for 'the name or the talents of a Corsican who was placed by chance at

---

53   JFA 3 (20 Jan. 1797), 162.
54   Ibid. 163. The French spelling of the Sodomite king's name is 'Béra', but in the Vulgate it is 'Bara', which sounds almost identical to Barras.
55   BM 23 (30 July 1799), 404n.
56   BM 16 (15 Apr. 1799), 456–7. *Lazare-Nicolas-Marguerite Carnot* (1753–1823), the Committee of Public Safety's 'organiser of victory', moved rightwards politically after being elected Director in 1795.
57   BM 11 (29 Jan. 1799), 160.

the head of a victorious army which would have conquered without him'.[58] Yet if, as Mallet implied, the faces and factions at the head of the revolution were prone to change, the revolution itself proved both resilient and enduring.

As the revolution progressed and began to appear a continuing process rather than a finite series of events, the journalists began to search for its hidden dynamic. Their interest was not mere historical curiosity. On the contrary, it was imperative that they succeed, for if they could discover what drove the revolution, it would be possible to halt and hopefully reverse the process. Thus their comprehension of the revolutionary dynamic is inextricably interwoven with their ideas of how to effect a counter-revolution and their conception of a restored Bourbon regime. As a result the three themes are treated together here.

The only successful London-based French paper in the early revolution, and hence the first to respond to the revolution, was the *Courier de Londres*, then edited by Théveneau de Morande. Between 1789 and 1791 Morande considered himself a *patriote royaliste* and advocated parliamentary government and the end of ministerial despotism, celebrating the reform of abuses while castigating extremists of both left and right.[59] After Morande's departure in May 1791, the *Courier de Londres* was edited by a team of *patriotes*, who may have been joined by Calonne's nominee, Velley, in early 1792, after which it underwent a gradual metamorphosis. It is not clear whether this shift was due to evolving editorial opinions or a change in editorial personnel, but the paper's loyalties certainly became increasingly divided at this time. In part this may reflect the activity of Ferdinand Christin, an agent of Calonne, who joined another agent, the chevalier de La Bintinaye in London in February.[60] As war approached the paper's pro-French editorial position (it branded the military emigration 'desertion', and the allied powers 'enemies of liberty'), dissolved into conflicting loyalties as the king became increasingly isolated and Paris increasingly radical. Reports sent from Coblenz and miscellaneous pieces probably inserted by Calonne's agents increased this ambiguity. These included a review recommending La Bintinaye's *Observations . . . sur un article inséré dans le Morning Chronicle* which, while defending the clergy, magistracy and nobility of France, blamed the revolution on the financial policies of Calonne's old rivals, Brienne and Necker.[61]

---

[58] Ibid. 160–1.
[59] Proschwitz and Proschwitz, *Beaumarchais*, i. 180–96; Burrows, 'Exile press', 271–80, and 'A literary low-life', at pp. 10–14. Robiquet, *Théveneau de Morande*, 240–302, discusses Morande's reaction to the revolution in the *Argus patriote* but not the *Courier de l'Europe*.
[60] PRO, PC 1/129, piece 422, Christin to Calonne, London, 14 Feb. 1792. Christin is mentioned in PC 1/126, piece 391, Irving to Charles Herries (undated copy), inserted in [Herries] to Calonne, 22 May 1792, as the 'gentleman living in Mr. Calonne's house' who instructed Irving to insert articles and comment on the paper's contents.
[61] *CL* xxxi/37 (8 May 1792). La Bintinaye's work was published in London by Debrett in May 1792.

These insertions on Calonne's behalf were in fact censored prior to publication by both Calonne's agent, John Irving, and Swinton. Swinton seems to have wavered between intriguing to have his paper banned in France in order to claim compensation from Calonne and fearing the cost should his guarantees prove insufficient. Thus in June 1792 Charles Herries advised Calonne to refuse Swinton's demands for new guarantees and to sell his share in the paper, since it would become entirely *démocrate* in either case.[62]

However, Calonne ignored his advice and by mid-May the paper foresaw that military defeat would give the Jacobins a pretext to overthrow the monarchy and France would collapse into anarchy.[63] Antagonism towards Jacobinism crystallised into a solid counter-revolutionary position as the gulf between the revolutionary authorities and constitutionalism widened. The *journée* of 20 June, when a mob entered the Tuileries and forced Louis to don the cap of liberty, was strongly denounced,[64] and in July the paper attacked the 'fanatical faction' besieging the throne, and asserted that persons and property were no longer safe. The authorities were unwilling or unable to prevent armed assemblies of ill-disposed persons. Republicanism had thrown off its mask.[65]

Accounts of the overthrow of Louis XVI on 10 August 1792 and the September massacres were provided as simple narrative without editorial comment, but accompanied by documents and lists of arrests, executions and emigrations. This neutrality was probably ordered by Swinton, still worried that the interdiction of his paper in France would cost him £300 *per annum*, yet aware of the potential of an increasing émigré audience in London, whose influx was noted in late September.[66] However, any lingering sympathy for revolution soon disappeared. While the paper was reluctant to launch a full-scale attack on the regime, it became highly critical of individual measures. Rather than denying its libertarian tradition, it argued that the prison massacres throughout France were an affront to liberty.[67] Manifestations of discord and discontent throughout Europe would deserve applause if they were 'the effect of a regulated liberty', but sadly the agitators had different motives.[68] Simultaneously, a series of articles ridiculed the idea of natural equality between men of different estates, races and moral qualities. The most direct piece imagined a poor, malicious, black cut-throat comparing his character and estate with a respectable upright European, ending each point with the statement 'but I am your equal'. To ram the moral home, he summarised his

---

62 PRO, PC 1/127, piece 34, Christin to Calonne, London, 26 June 1792.
63 CL xxxi/42–3 (25–9 May 1792).
64 Ibid. 51 (26 June 1792).
65 See, especially, CL xxxii/4–8 (13–27 July 1792).
66 PRO, HO 42/23, fo. 507, Swinton to [?Nepean], 24 Dec. 1792; CL xxxii/25 (25 Sept. 1792).
67 Ibid. 24 (21 Sept. 1792).
68 Ibid. 35 (30 Oct. 1792).

case: 'in brief, you are superior physically and morally; but I am your equal'.[69] Finally, in December, a letter from 'John Bull' warned of the pan-European threat posed by the revolution, arguing that revolution drew its strength from 'the lowest class of the people' whom it styled the 'nation' though they had nothing.[70] Thus, for the editors of the *Courier de Londres*, the revolution had betrayed liberty to pursue the chimerical and dangerous principle of equality. Thereafter, coverage of the king's imprisonment and trial was unambiguous and portrayed Louis as innocence persecuted.[71] His virtues, especially his piety and devotion to his son's education during his imprisonment, were praised.[72] Nevertheless, the paper was still reluctant to commit itself explicitly, presumably because Swinton still prized the French market. Only on 29 January 1793, when it announced a change in editorial policy and became a solely émigré organ, did the *Courier de Londres* drop its claim to be open to all parties.[73] Even thereafter it kept its ancient motto 'Tros Tyriusue [sic] mihi nullo discrimine agetur [I shall not discriminate between Trojans and Tyrians]'.[74] But with the king's execution, an apparent change of editor and the coming of war (which ended its circulation in France), the paper abandoned all restraint and adopted a new, uncompromising, *pur* rhetoric, far to the right of Peltier.

Reporting the Terror was one of the simpler, if more distressing, tasks for the émigré journalists. Peltier condemned the failure of the English papers to report 'anecdotes which could make the excesses of the Jacobins known in all their horror', lamenting that they gave 'not a single detail . . . on either the massacres committed at Nantes by Carrier or the daily murders committed by Fouquier-Tinville in Paris'.[75] In the *Correspondance politique* he announced that he would report every victim of the revolutionary tribunal, and he kept his promise after Thermidor by concluding a supposedly comprehensive list in the *Tableau de l'Europe*.[76] In the process he provided a valuable service for émigrés desperate for news of family and friends and advertised the scale of the killings to the rest of Europe. In contrast, Verduisant preferred not to

---

[69] Ibid.
[70] Ibid. 47 (11 Dec. 1792).
[71] On the imprisonment, trial and execution of Louis XVI see especially CL xxxii/41 (20 Nov. 1792); 43 (27 Nov. 1792); xxxiii/1 supplément (1 Jan. 1793); 2–3 (4–8 Jan. 1793); 5–9 (15–29 Jan. 1793). The supplement to CL xxxiii/1 was delivered free to subscribers, probably at Bertrand de Molleville's expense.
[72] CL xxxii/41 (20 Nov. 1792); 43 (27 Nov. 1792).
[73] The notice cryptically announces a change in ownership ['propriété'], but seemingly means only that the abbé Calonne had taken control, since documentary evidence shows that neither Calonne nor Swinton had sold their stake in the paper. It implies strongly that the editorship has changed.
[74] The motto, from *Aeniad* i, line 574, was used throughout the paper's existence save during 1805–7.
[75] *Paris* 1 (6 June 1795), 39–40.
[76] CP 87 (22 May 1794); TE i, pt iii, n.d. [1794].

'oppress' his readers and spared their '*sensibilité*' by only reporting the most significant victims.[77]

The Terror helped to clarify certain aspects of the revolution's character for the émigré journalists. In particular it seemed to confirm that the revolution was opposed to all property and hence a universal threat that had to be defeated, with force if necessary. Peltier's prediction that Madame Du Barry would not be forgiven for her wealth rapidly came true.[78] After her conviction, his assertion that she was found guilty of having mourned Louis XVI in London, associated with the British ministry, and worn a pendant bearing Pitt's inscription, seemed to prove his prescience.[79] The Terror also proved that blood was essential to the revolution, an allegation kept alive by the revolutionary wars.[80] Thus when some observers asserted that the purges of Hébertists and Dantonists in March 1794 heralded the advent of a new order, Peltier rightly contradicted them, pointing out that Saint-Just's report on the police offered further insights into the 'cult of Moloch' and its human sacrifice.[81] Likewise, several months later he downplayed the significance of Thermidor, as did the abbé Calonne.

Peltier argued that the Thermidor coup was only the replacement of one faction by another.[82] The Thermidorians behaved 'honestly' as a concession to popular outrage, in order to preserve their own heads.[83] The revolution consisted of an endless procession of factions, each only temporarily in control of the reins of government, because the destruction of legitimacy in turn legitimised successive *coups*. This remained Peltier's view of the revolution's essential dynamic until 1814 and even beyond. His belief was self-fulfilling, allowing no possibility of compromise with the revolution and little scope for substantial reforms of the monarchy.

Events inside France in 1795 appeared to support Peltier's conviction. For although the Constitution of the Year III established a much narrower property-based franchise than previous revolutionary constitutions, it was followed by the notorious Two-Thirds Decree, by which only one third of the members of the new legislature would stand for election each year. Initially, two-thirds of the new legislature would be members of the Convention. Peltier was infuriated by the Two-Thirds Decree. Dismissing the *conventionnels*' justification that it would protect public liberty, he argued that their real motive was their fear that following free elections they would all be arrested.[84] He added that future democrats would be astonished that 'an

---

[77] See CL xxxiv/19 (3 Sept. 1793).
[78] CP 5 (12 Nov. 1793). Madame Du Barry (1743–93) was Louis XV's last mistress.
[79] CP 22 (21 Dec. 1793).
[80] See, for example, CP 44 (11 Feb. 1794).
[81] CP 76 (26 Apr. 1794). *Louis-Antoine-Léon Saint-Just* (1767–94) was Robespierre's closest associate. Moloch was a Canaanite God associated with blood sacrifices.
[82] TE i, pt ii. 34.
[83] Ibid. 50.
[84] Paris 14 (5 Sept. 1795), 333.

assembly which proclaimed the sovereignty of the people with such noise has dared to pass such a law'.[85] Moreover, he reported that the Convention was manipulating electoral lists, by preventing *radiations* from the émigré lists until after the elections, and subsidising friendly publicists.[86] Throughout September both Peltier and the abbé Calonne reproduced propaganda from the Parisian right-wing press, campaigning against the ratification of the constitution and decrees, but when the results were announced on 23 September both constitution and Two-Thirds Decree achieved popular though lukewarm mandates. Peltier suggested the vote reflected fear of further uncertainty and added that none of the Paris *sections* supported the decree.[87] This proved a warning of the events to follow. Some *sections* began to arm and on 5 October (12 vendémiaire), after a tense stand off, republican troops opened fire on the insurgents and eventually dispersed them. Despite the defeat of the insurrection, Peltier took heart from the fact that the Convention 'for the present has no other resource than Terror and revolutionary measures, but we know where Terror has taken it'.[88] The victors would soon be at each others' throats again. Moreover, although the Two-Thirds Decree and establishment of a five-man executive Directory from among their number had perpetuated the power of the Convention, the former *conventionnels* had to steer a treacherous middle course between royalists, whom as regicides they feared, and unforgiving Jacobins, whom they had overthrown at Thermidor. However, *in extremis*, they preferred the Jacobins as fellow regicides, *terroristes* and *criminels*. As the 1795 elections showed a clear preference for moderates and royalists, and France's constitutional arrangements violated the wishes of the political nation, Peltier predicted that the constitution would be abandoned whenever royalist, moderate or Jacobin gains threatened the *conventionnel* hegemony.[89]

In contrast to Peltier, the abbé Calonne gradually moved from an uncompromising *pur* position to a more moderate stance, following his brother's lead. In 1793, although he considered inviting Mallet Du Pan to edit the *Courier de Londres*, the abbé's ideological position was well to the right of Peltier's. In mid-1793 Charles Alexandre de Calonne was still highly critical of the moderates, believing that they had reduced the chances of a restoration. In consequence, he was incensed by a commentary which he attributed to Malouet on the address of General Dumouriez to the French people in the

---

[85] *Paris* 15 (12 Sept. 1795), 435.
[86] Ibid. 437.
[87] *Paris* 18 (3 Oct. 1795), 108. The constitution passed by 1,057,000 votes to 49,000, the Two Thirds Decree by 205,498 to 108,754. Nearly 4,000,000 voters did not participate. Several unanimous Parisian returns were discounted for failing to record exact numbers of voters present. See William Doyle, *The Oxford history of the French revolution*, Oxford 1989, 320.
[88] *Paris* 21 (24 Oct. 1795), 317.
[89] See, for example, *Paris* 132 (9 Sept. 1797), 57ff.

Courier de Londres of 16 April 1793.[90] The article asserted that the powers sensed that it would be impossible to form a government in France without the consent of the people, and argued that opponents of anarchy must therefore lay aside their differences to create a single royalist party.[91] Calonne was infuriated both by the writer's apparent endorsement of the doctrine of popular sovereignty and his solution, which would give undue influence to moderates and other groups he considered culpable for the revolution. Thus when the abbé became editor of the *Courier de Londres* he told Calonne that he would lose no opportunity to attack the *constitutionnels* and *monarchiens*.[92] He was probably responsible for a review attacking Montlosier's 'monarchien' principles on 15 October 1793 and a rather laboured piece of satirical invective in the style of a biblical prophecy published in November.[93] Indeed, between the summer of 1793 and early 1794 the abbé and Verduisant published a succession of articles attacking the moderate position. They included a contributed piece which attacked Lally-Tollendal's promise to swear absolute obedience to any form of monarchic government established in France, opposed all innovation as dangerous, asserted that France already had a fixed constitution and demanded a return to integral absolutism.[94] Moreover, the abbé argued that it was impossible to mix different types of government and hence in the interests and intentions of sovereigns to re-establish absolutism.[95] If any seed of the revolutionary regime survived, new troubles would continue to arise. It was thus essential to restore the nobility and clergy to all their former rights.[96] He insisted that these policies also favoured the third estate, informing them that they had been duped by the revolutionaries and that their true interest lay in the re-establishment of the monarchy.[97]

However, in the spring of 1795 the abbé retreated from this uncompromising *pur* integral absolutist position. He noted that the royalists' allies in France now included some of the very authors whose journals, pamphlets and placards had promoted the revolution by detaching public opinion from royalty.[98] Consequently he called for émigré and royalist unity and castigated the French nobility: 'It is this aristocracy that I denounce to itself as its own

---

90 PRO, PC 1/125, piece 218, Calonne to the duc de Coigny, Madrid, 17 May 1793. Dumouriez's address, an attempt to rally the French people against the government, was issued shortly before he fled to the allies on 5 Apr. 1793.
91 *CL* xxxiii/31 (16 Apr. 1793).
92 PRO, PC 1/126, piece 677, J.-L.-J. de Calonne to Calonne, 28 Oct. 1793.
93 *CL* xxxiv/31 (15 Oct. 1793); 40–1 (15–19 Nov. 1793).
94 The article appeared in *CL* xxxiii/50–1 (21–5 June 1793); xxxiv/3 (9 July 1793); 8 (26 July 1793).
95 See *CL* xxxiv/47 (10 Dec. 1793); xxxv/24–5 (25–8 Mar. 1794).
96 Ibid.
97 Ibid. 31–2 (18–22 Apr. 1794); 37 (9 May 1794).
98 *CL* xxxvii/32 (21 Apr. 1795). Among the most prominent of these were Jean-Charles-Dominique Lacretelle (1766–1855), formerly a Jacobin and then Feuillant journalist; Jean-François La Harpe, formerly Voltaire's secretary, a *philosophe* and revolutionary become

[worst] enemy; that [aristocracy] which doesn't find M. Mallet Du Pan good enough for it, which condemns M. Lally Tollendal, wavers towards M. de Montlausier [sic] and disgusts M. de Cazalès.'[99] In April he went further, advising *sagesse* and *modération*, and advocating the renunciation of a few rights to regain everything else.[100]

The Calonne brothers broke definitively with the *pur* camp when Charles-Alexandre published *Le Tableau de l'Europe en novembre 1795*, an important pamphlet which appeared first on the pages of the *Courier de Londres*. For Calonne now categorically denied that *ancien régime* France had a constitution and alleged that the émigrés misunderstood the nature of discontent in France. Rather than indicating royalist sympathies, the unrest and demands for change stemmed from fear of arbitrary or anarchic government, concern for property, worries about the nation's finances and a desire to conserve religion. The abbé endorsed his brother's position on 5 January 1796, agreeing that although the French monarchy had developed 'usages' sanctioned by time, there was no fixed or agreed *dépôt* for the *ancienne constitution*, and it was therefore not clear which laws should be considered fundamental and immutable. Somewhat undiplomatically, he also contended that all but the most singularly blind servants of *la bonne cause* must realise that the king's interests lay in recognising that:

> monarchic power must be regulated and tempered by fundamental laws which are fixed and established constitutionally, consigned to a solemn code, and preserved by sufficiently efficacious measures from the mutability to which they were subject when they depended entirely on the will of the king to maintain or depart from them.[101]

The Calonne brothers' assertions provoked several hostile replies. The most significant, Auget de Montyon's *Rapport à Louis XVIII*, published in the late spring of 1796, argued that *ancien régime* France had a constitution based on the co-existence of the king and Estates-General and the obedience of both to the laws.[102] This was a classic statement of the moderate *pur* position, arguing that the French constitution accorded approximately with the status the nobility had attained in early 1789.[103]

Thus the reconciliation of the Calonne brothers and Montlosier, and the merger of their journals, was preceded by an ideological convergence.

Catholic royalist in the Terror; and *Jean-Thomas-Elisabeth Richer-Sérizy*, another former Jacobin journalist and friend of Camille Desmoulins.
[99] CL xxxvii/19 (6 Mar. 1795). *Jacques-Antoine-Marie de Cazalès* (1758–1805) was a prominent but maverick right-wing deputy whose efforts to join the émigré forces were initially rejected.
[100] Ibid. 34 (28 Apr. 1795).
[101] CL xxxix/2 (5 Jan. 1796).
[102] Montyon, *Rapport à Louis XVIII*. For a discussion of Montyon's position and career see Beik, *French revolution from the right*, 96–9.
[103] Ibid. 98.

Although the abbé disagreed with Montlosier on several issues in the spring of 1797, above all perhaps with the *Journal de France et d'Angleterre*'s assertion that after Thermidor 'reason regained her rights, humanity her empire',[104] these were generally questions of degree. Indeed, one recent historian of the counter-revolution suggests that Calonne should be considered a *monarchien* after November 1795.[105]

Montlosier meanwhile offered a deeper sociological explanation of the revolution and its progress, which he expounded at length in the *Journal de France et d'Angleterre*. He now defined a revolution as a displacement of power. Thus the first revolution occurred with the decision to summon the Estates General, and was sanctioned by all three orders in their *cahiers de doléances* when they agreed to establish a representative government with rights over taxation, legislation and aspects of state administration. Thereafter, he argued, there were a series of further revolutions. The first occurred on 14 July 1789 when the nobility and clergy found themselves unable to hold on to the power they had snatched during the pre-revolutionary crisis. This was the outcome of a long-term trend in French society, born of the French monarchy's struggle to level French society by raising the poor and reducing the powerful. Between July 1789 and the Terror, France had witnessed three further revolutions: the removal of the monarchy from Versailles to Paris on 6 October 1789; the overthrow of the monarchy on 10 August 1792; and the passage of power from the Gironde to the *sans-culottes* on 31 May 1793. In the process, first the king, then the nobility and clergy, then their replacements, and finally property owners in general had been excluded from the 'nation'. Moreover, the French revolution was unique because these revolutions were not made by leaders or parties, but by a vague entity called 'le peuple'. Thus the revolution changed character as often as the term 'le peuple' changed its meaning. A parallel and consequential movement divested property of its rights. Thus those who believed that the revolution stemmed from a spirit of irreligion or love of liberty were wrong. These factors played an accidental role in the revolution, but they should not be confused with causes. After all, Louis XV was served scrupulously by a court full of *philosophes*, and the Roman republicanism of Corneille's plays had made no stir under Louis XIV. Instead of aiming at liberty, the revolution moved towards equality of the only sort understood by the lower orders: economic equality. Thermidor seemed to give the revolution a new direction: the displacement of power and property was consummated, the revolution was complete. Vendémiaire briefly restored tyranny, but it could not last because *l'esprit public* had changed. Montlosier was therefore optimistic that the revolution would be rolled back, arguing that two great advances had already been made in that

---

[104] The abbé wrongly believed that the article was by Montlosier himself: JFA 7 (17 Feb. 1797), 473–89, 540; CL xli/16 (24 Feb. 1797). Montlosier was also criticised ibid. 33 (25 Apr. 1797) for remarks in JFA 14 (22 Apr. 1794).
[105] Roberts, *The counter-revolution*, 47.

direction. First, independent courts now absolved or condemned 'with no other rule than conscience, with no other law than justice'. Secondly, the acts of government were now placed under the scrutiny of property holders and the legislative councils, whose support the government now needed, and so an independent 'public opinion' was now a force. The two obstacles remaining were the Jacobins, who must never be allowed to regain power, and the Directory, who opposed peace and appeared to hope that the resources of conquered territories would help them to regain their independence.[106]

In the spring and early summer of 1797, Montlosier's optimism was shared, to some extent, by his fellow journalists. As the last remaining *conventionnels* were now standing for re-election and a right-wing victory seemed a foregone conclusion, royalists and émigrés began to hope that a restoration might at last be achieved by constitutional means. By the start of September, after the elections, the abbé Calonne was even encouraging the émigré clergy to return to France after the new legislative councils invited them back.[107] Nevertheless, Montlosier had forebodings of an impending struggle and concluded that peace depended upon the councils' overcoming the Directory, while Peltier argued that the Directory could not follow the impulsion of the councils because it contained four regicides.[108]

The coup of 18 Fructidor, although not a complete surprise, dispelled the hopes of the émigré journalists. It was, however, part of a now familiar pattern of violence. Thus Peltier saw it as the work of a single faction which had usurped all the instruments of power, designed to perpetuate the revolution by suppressing the popular will: 'Yet another revolution; once more the regime of the Terror is substituted for that of the constitution! So put your trust in all these constitutions of 1791, 1793 and 1795!'[109]

Save for a brief moment of optimism in the summer of 1799, the period from Fructidor to Brumaire was generally one of disillusionment for the émigré journalists, during which they attempted to convince Europe and its sovereigns of the same basic set of propositions as in 1793–5. These were expounded most ably by Mallet Du Pan in the *Mercure britannique*. He contended that the powers no longer had any choice between peace and war. Long experience and the fate of Spain, Sardinia and Switzerland had proven that the French were as oppressive in peace as in war.[110] Lasting peace had to be based on balance, but the revolution had destroyed all equilibrium in Europe. Those who believed the powers could negotiate a solid peace with the French republic were deluded.[111] France's attempts to spread revolu-

---

[106] JFA 14 (22 Apr. 1797), 290–305.
[107] See CL xlii/18 (1 Sept. 1797).
[108] See ibid. 14 (18 Aug. 1797); 17 (29 Aug. 1797); Paris 131 (5 Sept. 1797), 4.
[109] Paris 132 (9 Sept. 1797), 61.
[110] BM 4 (15 Oct. 1798), 271–98.
[111] Ibid. 272.

tionary doctrines placed her on a permanent war footing with the rest of the world: her huge population in which every man was a soldier made her a threat to all. Moreover, she would attempt to subvert every state with which she came into contact, because of the paranoid suspicions of her leaders. Peace would only be possible when the Directory renounced tyranny, disorder and rapine, and set about restoring a balance of power: 'when the rights of man shall cease to conspire against the rights of man in society'.[112] Moreover, there was a self-interested economic logic behind Directorial policy:

> She revolutionises Nations that she may plunder them; and she plunders them to enable her to exist. The circle of her philosophy extends no further. She would exchange all the characters of the Rights of Man for a good bag of crown pieces, were not those Republican characters and trappings in her hands what a drowsy potion is in the hands of robbers.[113]

In consequence Mallet proposed a new coalition, with proper co-operation between partners, pitting all Europe and whole nations in arms against the revolution. He blamed the failure of previous coalitions not on providence, or military factors, or corruption, or the other causes commonly suggested, but on allied disunity and the cohesion of French forces.[114] He counselled ruthlessness in the execution of the war, favouring moderation of ends over moderation of means: 'Moderation should be found in the ends we propose, not in our resistance of wicked actions and wicked men'.[115] Mallet Du Pan concurred with his journalistic colleagues that France had become a military oligarchy.[116] Moreover, he agreed with Calonne that Frenchmen did not favour royalism. Their discontent could be assuaged and, if offered liberty, property and the exercise of their religion, they would rally to the Directory.[117] Similarly, he agreed with Montlosier that France had ceased to be a monarchy without becoming a true republic, for she had no fixed laws, religion or institutions, and created a new constitution for every crisis.[118] The revolution had become synonymous with destruction: when it ceased to destroy it would cease to exist.[119]

After Fructidor Montlosier fell into despondency and malaise, until in 1799 he began reworking his scheme for raising a volunteer counter-revolutionary crusading army into a tortuous and opaque article on the means

---

[112] BM 6 (15 Nov. 1798), 449.
[113] BM 11 (29 Jan. 1799), 130.
[114] BM 12 (15 Feb. 1799), 191–208.
[115] BM 23 (30 July 1799), 404n.
[116] BM 6 (10 Nov. 1798), 413. The same view was expressed by the abbé Calonne in CL xlii/22 (15 Sept. 1797), and Montlosier in xlii/52 (29 Dec. 1797). Peltier preferred to define the coup as a return to government by Terror or demi-Terror.
[117] BM 11 (29 Jan. 1799), 166–7.
[118] Ibid. 131; CL xlii/52 (29 Dec. 1797); xliv/16 (24 Aug. 1798).
[119] See, especially, ibid. 25 (25 Sept. 1798).

to oppose a moral force to the revolution.[120] However, as Russian troops advanced on the French border in the summer of 1799, émigré spirits revived and renewed demands were made for recognition of Louis XVIII.[121] Peltier even found consolations in the success of the left in the councils in purging the Directory on 29–30 prairial VII (17–18 June 1799), arguing that 'any revolution, and even a counter-revolution, will henceforth only depend on a very small number of active, energetic men, who strongly desire that what they have plotted is achieved'.[122] It was against this background that Mallet Du Pan published Malouet's letter on the restoration of the Bourbons. Malouet argued that the safety of Europe depended on the overthrow of the revolution and the establishment of 'a monarchy wisely modified'. It would be harder to turn the clock back to 1788 than to adapt the government of China to French purposes, because France had changed enormously in ten years of revolution. He argued for leniency towards the revolutionaries, asking: 'What have the revolutionists, those who were not regicides, to fear, when almost the whole nation have to reproach themselves, if not with guilt, at least with great errors, and which have been sufficiently expiated by ten years of wretchedness.'[123] He therefore argued that compromise, tact and moderation would be vital if the monarchy was to avoid further injustices: 'What other power than that of a coalition of strong and enlightened minds can be of use to the monarch on the subject of setting the taxes, the lot of the state-annuitants, that of the purchasers of national property, of the republican army and of the old and new clergy.'[124] Moreover Louis XVIII was the man for the job, because his 'prudent and mild disposition ... his experience and his understanding, the extent of which no one disputes, guide him from the paths of arbitrary power, and show him its insufficiency and danger in the present state of intelligence'.[125] The king therefore had only to guard against 'pretension, resentment and vengeance' and summon to his aid 'men of virtue and talents, to reframe by them the public mind, and the power of his government, which, in the hands of weak, passionate or corrupt men, would again inevitably perish'.[126] Thus it was not only the moderate tone of Malouet's manifesto, but its slurs upon the characters, abilities and usefulness of the *purs* which so incensed Peltier. The debate which followed (see chapter 3), only exacerbated his anger. For after Peltier attacked Malouet, Mallet Du Pan remarked that the emigration included some 'irascible spirits' who 'if you talk to them of legal government ... will have nothing to do either with legality or government. The whole art of governing men, according to them, consists

---

[120] See *CL* xlv/16 (22 Feb. 1799) and subsequent numbers.
[121] See, for example, *CL* xlvi/6 (19 July 1799).
[122] *Paris* 184 (15 July 1799), 550–1.
[123] *BM* 23 (30 July 1799), 422.
[124] Ibid. 421.
[125] Ibid. 420.
[126] Ibid. 421.

in hanging, breaking on the wheel and subduing all spirit, without submitting themselves to any other rule than that of their caprices'.[127] When Peltier labelled Mallet's allegations 'perverse', Mallet replied by asserting that it was incumbent on the royalists to persuade France that the maxims of Louis XVIII were not those of a 'choleric, absurd and vindictive émigré'.[128] The debate itself was inimical to the achievement of this aim. The result was embarrassment, confusion and, when Peltier continued to pursue Mallet even after his death, distaste. In 1799–1800 the émigré press singularly failed to serve the exile cause. Far from providing a united front, it was still recovering from this bitter polemic which had emphasised all too clearly the political divisions among the émigrés and the moral cowardice of their leaders, when the coup of Brumaire shattered their ideological landscape.

If the reporting of French politics in the émigré press of the 1790s was highly partisan, the reporting of British politics was quite the opposite. This is perhaps surprising, for, as we have seen, Peltier alleged that the *Courier de l'Europe*'s parliamentary reporting had helped cause the revolution, by stimulating a vogue for opposition in France. Moreover, parliamentary reporting continued to be important in the papers throughout the revolutionary and Napoleonic period. However, because they were dependent on British newspapers for their accounts of parliamentary sessions and tried to give impartial summaries of major speeches without comment, they generally avoided partisan statements on British internal policy.[129] Coverage of British parliamentary politics was intended primarily as a means of following British policy and of providing models of the oratory that eighteenth-century Europeans had been educated to admire. Yet even this neutral parliamentary reporting presented readers with an implicit contrast between the conduct of British politics and the stormy sessions of the Convention, unconstitutional proceedings in the legislative councils under the Directory or the elaborately manipulated discussions of the muzzled Napoleonic legislature. Peltier saw Britain as the model of parliamentary government and in 1794 asserted: 'The last two sessions of her parliament are in a way the catechism of the *philosophe* and the statesman. A work which offers a good review of them will be worthy of being a supplement to *Spirit of the laws*.'[130] No reader of the papers' parliamentary coverage could remain ignorant of parliamentary government and procedure, and indeed it is probably fair to say that as a result the émigrés who accompanied Louis XVIII in 1814 had a greater exposure to effective parliamentary government than those who remained inside France. Moreover journalists sought to educate their readers on the concept and practice of a loyal

---

[127] BM 24 (15 Aug. 1799), 467. For Peltier's first attack on Malouet's letter see *Paris* 186 (15 Aug. 1799), 166–7.
[128] BM 26 (15 Oct. 1799), 88.
[129] CP 38 (21 Jan. 1794), states that British newspapers were Peltier's source for parliamentary reports. For Montlosier's comments on his neutrality see *JFA* 8 (25 Feb. 1797), 541–2.
[130] *TE* i. pt. ii, 15.

opposition, which, according to Montlosier should make itself useful to 'the constitution, the people and the crown'.[131] When the émigré papers did comment on British politics it was usually to applaud government actions in times of crisis, or provide constructively critical suggestions. The émigré journalists not unnaturally considered the British government justified in clamping down on radicals in 1793–4, and both the abbé Calonne and Montlosier became alarmed that the country was close to revolution in 1797.[132] However, the émigré journalists commented more freely on the war effort.

Supporting the war posed several problems for the émigré community in general and the émigré press in particular. While the exiled princes had long demanded foreign intervention against the revolution, war forced the journalists to justify the princes' alliance with their country's enemies and promotion of civil war. Moreover, the gulf between émigré demands for the restoration of the *ancien régime*, and the pragmatism of the allies, gave the journalists an invidious choice. They could support the British war effort wholeheartedly and abrogate all patriotic and legitimist sentiment, or they could promote the war while deploring the conduct, fearing the motives and criticising the policy of the allies.[133]

From 1793 to 1795 and again after 1797, the émigré journalists' position on the war was unambiguous. The revolution was a universal and extraordinary threat against all society, all states, all religion and all property and therefore required a universal response, and a more energetic form of warfare.[134] The émigré journalists, though their argument was self-interested, were among the first to grasp the huge military potential unleashed by the revolution in France, whereas allied governments persistently underestimated the military threat facing them. Thus Peltier complained with evident bitterness that his advice, and that of both émigrés and royalist journalists in France, had been ignored.[135]

A more contentious part of the journalists' analysis concerned the means to end the war and the revolutionary threat, which they argued could only be done by destroying revolutionary government, lock, stock, and barrel. This in turn could only be achieved by restoring the Bourbon monarchy. It was impossible to have a just and lasting peace with the revolution. Thus, according to the émigré journalists, war was being made on the revolution, not upon France. This provided both a patriotic rationale for fighting the 'armies of the guillotine',[136] and a coherent moral and intellectual justifica-

---

[131] *CL* xliii/33 (24 Apr. 1798).
[132] *CP* 90 (29 May 1794); *JFA* 8 (25 Feb. 1797), 550–1; *CL* xxxiv/47 (10 Dec. 1793); xxxv/4 (14 Jan. 1794); xli/23 (21 Mar. 1797).
[133] Peltier makes this very point in *Paris* 206 (30 June 1800), 236n.
[134] See *DTP* i. 149, 179; *TE* i, p. iii; *CP* 2 (4 Nov. 1793); *CL* xxxiii/10 (1 Feb. 1793); 12 (8 Feb. 1793).
[135] See *HR* 2 (letter dated 6 Apr. 1793), 38; *CP* 27 (2 Jan. 1794). See also *CL* xl/29 (7 Oct. 1796).
[136] This term was used by Peltier in *CP* 92 (3 June 1794).

tion for arguing that the allies should not impose indemnities or reparations. However, as the other European powers had spent much of the previous century attempting to contain French Bourbon expansionism, a restoration of the Bourbon monarchy not only wholly intact, but possibly regenerated, was improbable. It is therefore not surprising that the journalists' moral arguments were reinforced by practical and pragmatic propositions: the cause of European royalty was, like the revolutionary republic, 'one and indivisible',[137] and hence France would be more easily divided than dismembered;[138] the best way to reorganise France was through France herself.[139]

The émigré journalists campaigned for British assistance to the insurgents in north-west France in 1793–5, especially because such intervention would add a crucial weight to their demands for recognition of the Bourbons. In May 1793 Verduisant proposed a British descent on Brittany, accompanied by the Breton émigrés,[140] and Peltier indicated the advantages of seizing Quiberon and the Gulf of Morbihan as early as February 1794.[141] In the wake of the loss of Noirmoutiers, which cut communications with northern France, the seizure of the Gulf of Morbihan, the best natural harbour on the Breton coast, was an attractive strategic proposition. Possibly Pierre de la Roberie suggested the idea to Peltier, and it is tempting to suppose that the idea of a landing at Quiberon was first mooted by Peltier after la Roberie's description of the actions of Charette and the royalist army in the *Correspondance politique* in January 1794. This is improbable. Many Breton émigrés in London must have remembered the value of the harbour in the 1759 campaign, and Calonne, too, suggested the Quiberon project in a letter to Pitt on 15 April 1794.[142] Nevertheless, Peltier first popularised the idea in print. He also promoted the impression that the insurgent *armée Catholique et royaliste* was a distinct, well-organised unit which would rally to the allies at the first opportunity, serving as an operational, semi-regular force. This misconception of *Chouan* forces, promoted by la Roberie and later Puisaye, and abetted by the émigré press, had serious consequences for British strategic planning.[143] It would be wrong, however, to accuse the journalists of deliberate deception: they had too much at stake. Indeed, the abbé Calonne campaigned vigorously to recruit troops for the émigré units destined for Quiberon, appealing to the honour of émigré youth. He and Peltier were thus the dupes of their own expectations, sending friends and relatives to their deaths.

---

[137] CP 27 (2 Jan. 1794).
[138] CP 105 (3 July 1794).
[139] CP 66 (3 Apr. 1794).
[140] CL xxxiii/39 (14 May 1793); 41 (21 May 1793).
[141] See CP 44 (11 Feb. 1794).
[142] PRO, PC 1/130, piece 108, Calonne to Pitt, 15 Apr. 1794.
[143] On this misconception see Hutt, *Chouannerie*, i. 224ff.; Roberts, *The counter revolution*, 22–43, stresses the gulf between the émigré view of counter-revolution and internal realities. For further examples of émigré press promoting action see CL xxxiii/42 (24 May 1793), which discusses the forces of the mythical Gaston.

Preparations for the Quiberon adventure were accompanied by renewed demands for the recognition of the Bourbons in order to rally Frenchmen loyal to the monarchy.[144] These demands were boosted by the death of Louis XVII and the 'accession' of Louis XVIII, which gave a new legitimacy to the émigré cause and new authority to its leaders. Recognition would serve as a declaration of intent, and make it impossible for the revolutionary government to play on the fears and uncertainty of the populace.[145] This oft-repeated plea was not sufficient to overcome the pragmatic and self-interested opposition of the powers. Louis XVIII was not to be recognised, save by Gustave III of Sweden, until after the Senate deposed Napoleon and proclaimed him king in 1814. Nevertheless, the hope was not entirely chimerical. Following Admiral Hood's declaration of 28 August 1793, which took possession of Toulon in the name of Louis XVII, the London journalists had reason for optimism. When the government, surprised and not entirely pleased by Hood's initiative, clarified the position by releasing a *Royal proclamation on the war*, the *Courier de Londres* praised Britain's generosity and lack of territorial ambition and asserted that the other powers would be similarly reluctant to meddle in French internal affairs.[146] In subsequent editions the paper announced correctly that England was finally ready to take vigorous measures to sustain the royalists in France, and claimed that the powers aimed to restore absolutism, rather than the 1791 constitution.[147] This was a total misreading of British declarations and the intentions of her allies. Moreover, the evacuation of Toulon, and the reluctance of Britain's allies, combined with a pragmatic response to the changing military position, destroyed any hope of a firmer commitment.[148]

The disaster at Quiberon in 1795 did not dash émigré hopes of a major British descent on northern France.[149] In an attempt to explain the *débâcle*, Peltier blamed the failure of the Bretons to rise in numbers on the inadequate size of the British force and its inability to protect the insurgents.[150] This argument was inconsistent and indicates that even the émigrés were beginning to suspect the weakness and limitations of the *Chouan* forces, as the justification for Quiberon had been that a vast *Chouan* army was awaiting support from Britain. The failure of royalist conspiracies and the refusal of the allies to commit themselves to restore the Bourbons led some émigrés to conclude that hopes of a restoration by violent means were misplaced. Thus

---

144 See *Paris* 3 (20 June 1795), 190–2; *CL* xxxvii/50 (23 June 1795).
145 This argument was made specifically in *CL* xxxiii/40 (17 May 1793).
146 See *CL* xxxiv/35 (29 Oct. 1793). As Verduisant was sacked at this time, it is uncertain who wrote this passage.
147 Ibid. 42 (22 Nov. 1793); 47 (10 Dec. 1793).
148 On the British ministry's policy objectives and debates concerning Toulon see Jennifer Mori, 'The British government and the Bourbon restoration: the occupation of Toulon, 1793', *Historical Journal* xl (1997), 699–719.
149 See, for example, *CL* xxxviii/9 (31 July 1795).
150 *Paris* 9 (1 Aug. 1795), 62–4.

in early October 1796 the abbé Calonne redefined the purpose of the war, claiming it was to make the French recognise the desirability of an alternative form of government.[151] On 14 October he went further and suggested that peace was the émigrés' only hope, as the powers had no interest in restoring the Bourbons.[152] Similarly, the *monarchiens*, including Montlosier, had become increasingly disillusioned with the war, and began to argue that peace represented the best opportunity for change.[153] The only obstacles to be overcome were the Jacobins and the Directory. Even Peltier, while apparently not believing that peace with the revolution was possible, saw the possibility of peaceful internal change. This sea-change in the attitudes of the émigré journalists stemmed from the hopes they placed in the elections of the spring of 1797, but did not survive the coup of Fructidor. Thereafter, as we have seen, the papers reverted to promoting an anti-revolutionary crusade, backing their arguments with references to the Directory's imperialism and atrocities in Switzerland and elsewhere.

Emigré attitudes to the war in the Caribbean, the main non-European theatre of war, were more problematic. The brutal and destructive slave revolt and civil strife which erupted in France's immensely rich colony of Saint-Domingue in 1791 deeply divided both émigré *colons* (planters) and journalists, several of whom had a personal commitment in the struggle. The *colon* interest, probably the richest section of the émigré community in London, had an influence out of all proportion to its size. In all they numbered about 110 men, including Regnier and possibly Peltier who may also have had colonial estates. Moreover, Malouet, a close friend of Mallet Du Pan and Montlosier, was elected by the *colons* in 1793 to represent their interests to the British government. The *colons*' motive in selecting him was pragmatic: Malouet's reputation and colonial and diplomatic experience would ensure that he was heard. Unfortunately, however, Malouet's interests diverged fundamentally from those of most *colons*, for he saw himself primarily as a servant of the French state, and was therefore keen to ensure that Saint-Domingue should one day revert to French control. Most *colons*, by contrast, favoured greater colonial autonomy and were desperate for massive British intervention to restore their estates at any price.[154] Thus it is unsurprising that debates over the future of Saint-Domingue and colonial slavery had a high profile in the exile press in the 1790s.

The first references in Peltier's journals to the troubles in Saint-Domingue

---

[151] CL xl/29 (7 Oct. 1796).
[152] Ibid. 32 (18 Oct. 1796).
[153] See, in particular, *JFA* 8 (25 Feb. 1797), 552–6 (the author of this contributed article was probably Lally-Tollendal, but possibly Malouet or another *monarchien*); 14 (22 Apr. 1797), 289–305.
[154] Griffiths, 'Malouet', 234. Geggus, *Slavery, war, and revolution*, 446 n. 19, disputes this interpretation, suggesting that Malouet would have settled for an independent Saint-Domingue, but certainly both émigré perceptions and the journal content suggest that at several crucial junctures Malouet was intent that the island remain French.

used them as propaganda to attack the revolution and promote the British cause in the Caribbean. In his *Dernier Tableau de Paris* Peltier warned property owners that revolution only favoured intriguers and rogues, suggesting that all colonies risked Saint-Domingue's fate.[155] When British troops landed in Saint-Domingue in 1793, he praised the British for respecting the Catholic faith and preferring non-juror and émigré priests.[156]

The *Courier de Londres* was slower to pronounce on affairs in Saint-Domingue, perhaps because Swinton was reluctant to abandon his potentially lucrative links with the slave trade abolitionists. Morande's immediate successors remained true to the abolitionist cause, condemning an advertisement offering a slave couple for sale together or separately, even though they were lovers.[157] Yet within months the paper advised slave owners and colonial merchants to sue abolitionists calling for a boycott of slave-produced goods.[158] Nevertheless, in early 1793 it published a letter from a Jamaican planter which, while defending the institution of slavery, argued that in practice it was vicious and in the long term would have to be reformed.[159] However, when the Convention finally decreed the abolition of slavery in French territories, the abbé Calonne ridiculed Danton's sudden concern with humanitarian issues.[160] Peltier more realistically commented that the slaves had only been freed because the Convention knew they could not hold their colonies and wished to ensure maximum chaos for their subsequent owners.[161] Although his verdict has, to a large extent, been that of subsequent historians, Peltier nevertheless rejoiced at the British capture of Port-au-Prince on 6 June.[162]

Several months later, on 4 November 1794, Vénault de Charmilly, commander of the émigré *Légion britannique* on Saint-Domingue, sent Peltier an important memorandum on the state of the colony which was intended to raise confidence in the economy of the British-occupied zone. The picture he painted was optimistic and highly propagandist, but he swore it was true. He asserted that when he left the island in late August, the British were already in control of 90 per cent of the rich and fertile western province and that only ten out of 112 sugar refineries there were destroyed. The others, although abandoned and pillaged, could be up and running within months. Moreover, coffee plantations in the province had hardly suffered, especially as coffee plants were hardy with deep roots and difficult to burn because always green. He was even bullish about the prospects for the most devastated parts of the province. At Léogane, where only six out of fifty-four refineries had been

[155] *DTP* i, appendices, p. 70.
[156] *CP* 17 (10 Dec. 1793).
[157] *CL* xxix/48 (17 June 1791).
[158] *CL* xxx/33 (21 Oct. 1791).
[159] *CL* xxxiii/22 (15 Mar. 93).
[160] *CL* xxxv/15 (21 Feb. 1794).
[161] *CP* 48 (20 Feb. 1794).
[162] *CP* 113 (22 July 1794).

spared, the cane was looking healthy and would bring good returns. Moreover, the blacks, exhausted by the rebellion, were flocking back to the plantations 'joyfully to resume their work, blessing the protector who assures them once more of the peace of mind and well-being that they used to experience, under masters they naturally cherish'. The rebellion was without effective leadership since the departure of the Convention's *commissaires civils* and only a few areas of insurgency remained. Thus the British should easily conclude mopping-up operations, but should do so quickly to ensure the safety of other colonies. Finally, to emphasise the value of Saint-Domingue he presented a table of its trade in 1788, when it was probably the richest colony in the world.[163] Unfortunately, the capture of Port-au-Prince was to prove the high point of the British invasion of the island.[164]

Charmilly's picture typifies the *colon* propaganda published in émigré journals throughout the 1790s. They emphasised the economic importance of Saint-Domingue prior to the revolution and suggested that it could be retaken with relative ease. In contrast, they were anxious to down-play damage done to the economic and social fabric of the island and suggested that master–slave relations were founded on benevolent paternalism.[165] This idealised image bore little relationship to true conditions for slaves in the French colonies, and contrasted with the propaganda of the pro-slavery lobby in Britain, which hardly dared to justify its cause on any grounds but economic and military pragmatism.[166]

The *colons* also needed to justify British intervention, and their own support for it. Thus Peltier reinforced Charmilly's article with a justification of British invasion. How, he asked, could Britain protect her own colonies if she did not intervene, especially after the freeing of the slaves? How could she refuse the protection the *colons* requested? How could she not secure her growing trade with the islands?

Within months, however, the British position on the island had greatly deteriorated, as the majority of their European troops succumbed to yellow fever, malaria or the enemy. Moreover, the Convention's decision to emancipate the slaves and Victor Hugues's liberation of Guadeloupe, whence he

---

163 TE ii, pt i, 7–14. Internal evidence suggests that this edition was published at the end of November 1794.
164 D. Geggus 'The Anglo-French conflict in the Caribbean in the 1790's', in Colin Jones (ed.), *Britain and revolutionary France: conflict, subversion and propaganda*, Exeter 1983, 27–39 at p. 33.
165 *Paris* 63 (16 July 1796), 64, claimed that freed blacks regretted the end of slavery because of the low wages they now received. In CL xlii/12 (11 Aug. 1797), the abbé Calonne asserted, like Peltier, that the blacks were far happier as slaves under masters who provided them with subsistence, security, care in sickness and old age, and a small plot to cultivate, than under the 'barbaric despotism of the petty tyrants of that country'. They were better off than many European peasants and no worse treated than slaves in British colonies.
166 Christopher Brown, 'Anti-slavery petitions: origins of the anti-slavery movement in the 1780s', unpubl. seminar paper, Lincoln College, Oxford, Feb. 1992.

launched a series of raids and privateering expeditions against other British-held colonies, had 'forced the British on to the defensive' by the end of the year.[167] In 1795 forces backed by Hugues on the previously French island of Grenada rebelled, with devastating consequences. The initial report in the *Courier de Londres*, which is lost, blamed French subjects for the rebellion[168] and provoked a dismayed response from several subscribers in Grenada. They asserted that the rebellion was actually started by three 'gens de couleur' sent from Guadeloupe with 250 rifles, whose leader Noël Foedon summoned the island's 'mulattos'[169] to join him on pain of death. Most obeyed, whether through fear or love of disorder. It also asserted that Foedon had massacred his English prisoners, and that 'of all the insurrections for which the French revolution has served as the motive or pretext, this has had the saddest consequences'. The inhabitants were totally ruined and only a dozen sugar refineries remained. Moreover, whereas the other Caribbean revolts began with divisions among the free population between advocates and opponents of the revolution, in Grenada mulattos, free blacks and slaves had united to dispossess the whites.[170] This was something of a misrepresentation of the other revolts, but the message was clear: the revolutionary contagion threatened all the colonies, even those where the white élite maintained a unified front.

Although large numbers of British reinforcements reached Saint-Domingue in the spring of 1796, they were followed in May by a strong French squadron carrying troops and weapons for their black and mulatto allies.[171] Peltier used this news to reiterate the value of the colony, publishing a letter from Le Havre which noted that the French had finally realised that their colonies and commerce were worth more than 'certain principles'. For good measure, his correspondent claimed that the abolitionist [*Société des*] *Amis des noirs* was 'a collection of scoundrels, imposters or imbeciles' and labelled Brissot, one of the founding fathers of French abolitionism, 'the professor of robbery', and his associate, Condorcet, 'impious' and 'ungrateful'.[172] Peltier blamed renewed struggles among the black leaders on the return of the French *commissaires* Rochambeau and Sonthonax, who as men of party were bound to stir up rivalries.[173] In October he reproduced a letter

---

[167] Geggus, *Slavery, war, and revolution*, 187, and 'Conflict in the Caribbean', 34.
[168] CL xxxvii/45 (4 June 1795). This number is missing from the Bodleian's collection.
[169] The term 'mulatto' is used throughout this discussion for colonial inhabitants of mixed blood as the best rendering of the French term 'mulâtre'. While the term 'gens de couleur' is sometimes also encountered in the émigré texts, it is usually shorthand for 'free men of colour' and thus includes freed slaves and their offspring as well as those of mixed blood. It usually, implicitly, excludes slaves.
[170] CL xxxviii/29 (9 Oct. 1795). The letter was dated 24 July 1795.
[171] Geggus, *Slavery, war, and revolution*, 196; Paris 63 (16 July 1796), 59–71, reports their arrival but underestimates the French force's strength.
[172] Paris 70 (27 Aug. 1796), 515–16.
[173] Paris 76 (8 Oct. 1796), 238–47. *Donatien-Marie-Joseph de Vimeur*, vicomte de Rochambeau (1750–1813) was a career soldier with a reputation for ferocity in handling the slave

to the *Gazette française* which contradicted positive reports coming from the French republican zone, and alleged that black leaders had forced many white women to become their concubines or wet nurses for their children. In the same edition Peltier reported that Sonthonax had embezzled 200,000 *livres* earmarked as pay for French soldiers in order to pay for 'debauches and orgies' to celebrate his marriage 'to a woman from a family descended from Africans'.[174] Peltier's allegations, though they reflected rumours circulating on the island, were almost certainly false.[175] In any case, by late 1796 the republican part of the island had 'achieved a new degree of stability' as power became concentrated in the hands of the black leaders and the fear of British conquest dissolved.[176]

Meanwhile, in the abortive Anglo-French peace talks which took place between October and December 1796, the British government apparently espoused Malouet's advice with regard to Saint-Domingue. Malouet expounded his position in two pamphlets published in January and February 1797. He insisted that Saint-Domingue should remain French and argued for the reversal of emancipation, even while admitting that slavery would be abolished eventually. Moreover, he demanded that the West Indian colonies be subject to an international agreement. They should be considered neutral in wartime, have a common police regime and have trade regulations based on reciprocal arrangements rather than rivalry. These policies would eliminate the contagion of revolution and remove colonial rivalry from international relations.[177] These pamphlets were applauded by Montlosier in the *Journal de France et d'Angleterre*, but drew desperate fire from the *colons* who, in a flurry of addresses to the British government, repudiated Malouet as their spokesman.[178] In particular they resented Malouet's suggestions that the metropolis should exercise greater control over the colonies and opposed returning the colony to France. These attacks culminated in a pamphlet by a M. Bréard, which unfortunately appears not to survive, but which Montlosier and Malouet refuted. Both attacked Bréard for the vulgar style and inaccuracy of his attack and his unworthiness to serve as a spokesman for the *colons*.

---

revolt in 1792–3; Léger-Félicité Sonthonax (1763–1813) took the slaves' part in 1793 and liberated them as an expedient against British and Spanish aggression.
174 *Paris* 79 (15 Oct. 1796), 429–30.
175 Sonthonax was hated and feared by the whites as a zealous republican and as liberator of the slaves, and by mulatto commanders allied to the French because of his investigations into their blatant corruption. The rumours, almost certainly false, were intended to discredit him with the French government and former slaves. Wenda Parkinson, *This gilded African: Toussaint L'Ouverture*, London 1978, which is far from generous to Sonthonax, is insistent (p. 107) that he was not financially corrupt.
176 Geggus, *Slavery, war, and revolution*, 204.
177 On Malouet's arguments and their similarity to British policy see Griffiths, 'Malouet', 263–7; JFA 3 (20 Jan. 1797), 192–3; 6 (10 Feb. 1797), 454–6. This paragraph and the next draw strongly on Griffiths's work.
178 JFA 3 (20 Jan. 1797), 192–3; 6 (10 Feb. 1797), 454–6; Griffiths, 'Malouet', 267.

They also refuted his personal attacks on Malouet, whom Bréard described as a revolutionary. Malouet also justified his relatively pessimistic calculation of the value of Saint-Domingue, based upon its current condition, whereas the *colons* repeatedly invoked its former value. Nevertheless, he felt that the colony was still tremendously valuable and denied having any intention to encourage a British withdrawal from former French colonies. Unfortunately, Malouet's comments did not address the central concern of *colons* in both Saint-Domingue and London: fear that the island would be returned to France.[179] Nor was Malouet's pragmatic position on slavery very reassuring, for while he repeated his view that 'the colonies could not be governed and retained by a strict application of philanthropic principles', he was 'nevertheless convinced of the pure intentions' of those who advocated abolition.[180]

In early 1798 Regnier's three pamphlet *Lettres d'un colon* launched further bitter defamatory attacks on Malouet. Again Malouet's claims to speak for the *colons* were questioned, for according to Regnier he spoke for a party of one. Regnier's pamphlets were part of a campaign to undermine Malouet's sinking credit, in the hope that the government would listen to Charmilly. However, by the late autumn of 1797 the British position was desperate and they ignored Charmilly's calls for a further offensive.[181] On 20 August 1798 hostilities were suspended and the British withdrew.[182] Thus, although Montlosier dutifully took Malouet's part in the *Courier de Londres*, the dispute proved to be mere shadow boxing.[183]

In some respects Malouet was indeed a party of one, for Montlosier was a far keener advocate of slavery than his friend. When the British parliament debated the slave trade, he strongly advocated maintaining slavery on pragmatic, humanitarian, historical and religious grounds. He argued that slavery was a near universal phenomenon, and that since abolitionism was a recent fashion, it could not be divinely ordained. The Bible merely regulated slavery for St Paul instructed that slaves should be treated as equity demands.[184] In addition, those who had discussed the question seriously had proved it was far less humane to destroy slavery in the colonies than to maintain it.[185] He therefore argued that abolitionism was part of a wider politics of jealousy that aimed by stages to strip the ancient first orders of the state of strength, dignity or glory. The agitation for abolition, having begun in England and been transmitted to France then Saint-Domingue, where it had led to massacres of whites by blacks and vice-versa, had brought untold destruction and now

---

[179] JFA 10 (14 Mar. 1797), 82; 11 (25 Mar. 1797), 138–42.
[180] Ibid. 142.
[181] Geggus, *Slavery, war, and revolution*, 374.
[182] Ibid. 381.
[183] CL xliii/30 (13 Apr. 1798); 38 (10 May 1798).
[184] CL xlv/43 (28 May 1799).
[185] CL xlii/25 (26 Sept. 1797).

threatened Jamaica with the same fate.[186] None the less, he admitted that those who had unleashed the destruction on France and her colonies were the same sort of honest, well-meaning men as those now labouring in the British parliament to destroy Jamaica.[187] Abolition would be a generous gift from Britain to her enemies and rapidly regretted.[188]

Moreover, Montlosier repeated the standard claims that the slave trade was more humane than its alternatives, and indeed a moral imperative. If slaves were not sold to European traders, they would either be sold to their fellow Africans, or massacred. Montlosier even asserted that once they learned that the Europeans were not cannibals, the Africans were happy with their fate. For had not the celebrated explorer Mungo Park said that three-quarters of Africans were slaves who faced the same labours as in the Americas? Allegedly most slaves came from areas in the distant African interior, unknown to Europeans, which suffered from terrible famines, where children and free men offered themselves for sale freely.[189] Montlosier admitted that to buy free men in order to deliver them up to harsh labour, starvation and misery would be wrong and ought to be stopped. But if the people purchased were already slaves, on the verge of being massacred, and would enjoy a better life in the colonies, it was a moral duty to purchase as many as possible.[190] There is little reason to believe that Montlosier, a principled and independent thinker, was not sincere in these views, even though they display a profound ignorance of the horrors of the Middle Passage and the brutal economics of the plantation system. His grasp of the situation of the colony remained naïve to the end. When Leclerc's expedition to reassert direct French control and re-establish slavery landed in Saint-Domingue in 1801, he expected them to re-conquer the colony bloodlessly, despite the evidence provided by the long and bloody struggles of the 1790s.[191] When reports from the island made it clear that the black general and *de facto* ruler of the colony, Toussaint L'Ouverture, intended to fight, Montlosier commented that 'fear of slavery makes many heroes' and that the struggle would only end with the wholesale destruction of one side or other. However, he attributed this tragic situation to 'the disastrous principals disseminated in the colonies by the first authors of the French revolution'.[192]

Although his journal remained a mouthpiece for Charmilly and the *colon* interest in the final years of the British occupation, Peltier steered clear of Charmilly's personal dispute with Malouet. Instead he turned his fire on the British abolitionist MP Bryan Edwards whose *Historical survey of the island of*

[186] CL xlv/43 (28 May 1799).
[187] Ibid. 38 (10 May 1799).
[188] Ibid. 50 (21 June 1799).
[189] Ibid.
[190] Ibid. and xlvii/37 (9 May 1800).
[191] CL li/23 (19 Mar. 1802). *Victor-Emmanuel Leclerc* (1772–1802) was Napoleon's brother-in-law.
[192] Ibid. 43 (28 May 1802).

St Domingo, published in March 1797, attacked British policy towards the island and argued that it would prove impossible to conquer. When Charmilly refuted Edwards in print, Peltier published a glowing three-part review. Peltier insisted that Charmilly had disproved Edwards's assertion that the slave trade was a cause of the rebellion, by showing that most recently-imported slaves had been in the south of the colony, the last area to rise. Creole (island-born) blacks, whose passions had been stirred up by the mulattos and *Amis des noirs*, had been most ready to rebel. Brissot and the *Amis des noirs* had willed the destruction of the colonies as a way to revolutionise Europe, since the *colons* were almost all noblemen, émigrés or their sympathisers. Thus, as in France, the mass of the people would never have considered rebellion without the impulsion and pretensions of a small group of men from the middle ranks of society, in this case the mulattos. Charmilly reinforced this point by asserting that the blacks had a child-like simplicity, and went so far as to argue that 'there were few men more generally happy than the negro [nègre] in the colonies'. The climate was ideal for them and they had few worries. They knew their masters would care for them and their children in infancy, ill-health and old age, and would not work them so hard as to wear them out. The blacks accepted that they were born to work: liberty meant nothing to them. Charmilly also argued that the wiser colonists favoured British intervention from the start, as the only way to guarantee their safety. Britain was right to come to their aid, because if Saint-Domingue fell, Jamaica and the other colonies in the region would soon succumb. He ridiculed Edwards's assertion that the mulatto rising was justified by oppression, arguing that the mulattos in British colonies were worse treated, and that the same principle would justify lackeys and white blackguards rising against the law excluding them from sitting in the British parliament. Charmilly also accused Edwards of favouring the ruin of Saint-Domingue, because the revenues of his Jamaican estate had already doubled as a result, and attacked him for his ignorance of the war. For the duration of the French revolution, France could not be allowed any colonies. However, if ever she had an 'equitable' and 'popular' [i.e. Bourbon] government, England should return her colonies, as otherwise France would fight their trading monopoly to the death.[193]

Many of these points were reiterated several weeks later in a letter from the marquis de Frouillé which outlined the value of the colony and called for an attack from the north. He argued that many Britons failed to realise the value of the West Indies due to their predilection for India. However, Malouet and Charmilly had proved the value of the islands, and once they were all secure they would easily be guarded by a minimal naval and military force, and the blacks, left to themselves, were not inclined to rebel.

---

[193] *Paris* 129 (25 Aug. 1797) 543–8; 137 (5 Oct. 1797), 341–8; 138 (10 Oct. 1797), 397–402. Charmilly's tract was entitled *Lettre à M. Bryan Edwards en réfutation de ses vues historiques sur la colonie de St Domingue*.

Compared to India, which required an army of 100,000 men to protect it, the Antilles would be a cheap conquest.[194] Even this strategy was opposed by some *colons*, for one wrote to Peltier accusing Frouillé of self-interest because his own estates were in the north, and instead proposed a blockade to flush the enemy into the coastal plain.[195]

After the British evacuation, Saint-Domingue ceased to be an issue for the émigré journalists. By 1806 Peltier combined the editorship of the *Ambigu* with representing King Henri Christophe, and after the restoration even promoted abolitionism. However, throughout the 1790s disputes in the émigré press over Saint-Domingue revealed tensions between metropolitan émigrés with a nationalist or civil servant ethos, such as Malouet and Montlosier, and a small but vociferous colonial lobby in London, who wished to be reinstated in their estates under stable British rule. At the same time, however, the papers' colonial coverage allowed the émigrés to emphasise the universality of the revolutionary threat and the danger it represented to all property and to spread anti-abolitionist propaganda.

Another means by which the émigré press supported the war effort was by printing financial propaganda and information. The French government feared the power of enemy economic analysts to undermine confidence, and so French and English journalists made mutual allegations of economic instability. A particular *bête noire* of successive French regimes was the Genevan economist François d'Ivernois, whose miscellaneous works and annual analysis of revolutionary finances were regularly dissected in the émigré press.[196] D'Ivernois both influenced the ministry and provided an empirical basis for the counter-revolutionary theory of his friend and compatriot Mallet Du Pan. One French diplomat even alleged that d'Ivernois's writings persuaded Pitt and Grenville to continue the war in 1796 on the grounds that French finances, the sinews of war, were about to collapse.[197] The case was probably over-stated, but Pitt certainly valued indicators of French economic performance, and d'Ivernois's reports had important implications for allied strategy.[198] If France were about to collapse, it was only necessary to fight a defensive holding operation: if not, a more offensive strategy was required. Thus when Calonne answered d'Ivernois in his *Tableau de l'Europe*, more was at stake than the intellectual credibility of two leading experts on French finances.[199] Calonne argued that despite the collapse of the *assignat*, the revo-

---

194 *Paris* 141 (25 Oct. 1797), 602–8.
195 *Paris* 144 (11 Nov. 1797), 103–5.
196 On d'Ivernois see Otto Karmin, *Sir Francis d'Ivernois (1757–1842): sa vie, son oeuvre et son temps*, Geneva 1920.
197 AAE, CPA 589, fo. 331, Nettement to Delacroix, 27 July 1796. D'Ivernois made the case for impending financial collapse in pamphlets entitled *Réflexions sur la guerre*, London 1795, and *Coup d'oeil sur les assignats*, London 1795. Both were translated into English.
198 See Jennifer Mori, 'The impact of the French revolution on the ideas and policies of William Pitt', unpubl. DPhil. diss. Oxford 1992, 100.
199 The pamphlet appeared in *CL* xxxviii/34–52 (27 Oct.–29 Dec. 1795); an appendix

lution, having proved it could survive without regular finances, was certain to find alternative expedients, either through the new paper currency, the *mandats territoriaux*, or some other method. The Calonnes therefore advocated a vigorous offensive campaign for the spring of 1796 and the abbé had good reason for his subsequent complaints that the powers had ignored their advice.[200]

Economic intelligence and the proposition that property was seriously endangered also underpinned the most significant practical campaign of the émigré press during the Terror, for both the *Courier de Londres* and Peltier's *Correspondance politique* were intent on persuading merchants that the revolution threatened them directly. On 28 November 1793 Peltier claimed that the bankers of Paris and merchants of Bordeaux, Lyon and Marseilles had paid with their lives for the crime of being rich. Of all France's great mercantile centres only Nantes had been spared.[201] Three weeks later he entitled accounts of events at Lyon written by refugees *Avis à toutes les villes riches du monde*, and warned all towns affected by the spirit of Jacobinism to rally to their legitimate governments.[202] The *Courier de Londres* also published an *Avis à tous les négociants de l'Europe* which questioned the wisdom of their predilection for revolution and cited a rhetorical question posed by Danton in a speech of 31 August 1793: 'by what right do you wish that your property, very often acquired by unjust and vexatious means, be respected?'[203] Peltier reinforced persuasion by a campaign to shame and boycott those mercantile houses of Europe that supplied France with provisions. In late March 1794, on the authority of letters from Switzerland, he denounced the house of Pourtalès in Neuchâtel, saying it was sending France large quantites of provisions, livestock, leather, fabrics and other goods, and suggested that this was treason in a Prussian subject.[204] Though he later retracted the allegation, Peltier insisted it was a royalist's responsibility to publicise such information, even if it risked premature judgements.[205] Thus on 10 April he denounced the presence of two bankers in Holland to acquire provisions for the republic, and two days later published a list of the forty-two Paris bankers charged with provisioning France. He urged other journalists to publish the list to alert allied and neutral powers to French plans and threatened to denounce traders who 'lent themselves to Robespierre as his supports for a modest commission', claiming to have 'relations' which allowed him to watch their correspon-

---

appeared in xxxix/2 (5 Jan. 1796). According to an advertisement ibid. 3 (8 Jan. 1796), the work was published in pamphlet form by De Boffe on 11 Jan. 1796. A second, corrected edition and English translation were announced ibid. 6 (19 Jan. 1796) for publication on 3 February.
[200] See CL xl/29 (7 Oct. 1796).
[201] CP 12 (28 Nov. 1793).
[202] CP 21 (19 Dec. 1793).
[203] CL xxxiv/25 (24 Sept. 1793).
[204] See CP 61–2 (22–5 Mar. 1794); 65 (1 Apr. 1794).
[205] CP 82 (10 May 1794).

dence with the republic.[206] Thus, however insignificantly, the émigré press played a part in attempts both to establish an embargo against revolutionary France and in the campaign to undermine confidence in the *assignats*.

Although the émigré press was deeply divided, therefore, on a range of political issues, it nevertheless provided a continuous political narrative based around persistent themes. It repeatedly insinuated that all revolutionaries were base, self-serving schemers who were ill-suited to rule and could not be trusted, and although it offered a number of models for the revolutionary dynamic, all suggested that revolution was a continuous and universal threat that had to be reversed. It therefore promoted international intervention against the revolution in Europe and the Caribbean, although in both 1797 and 1799 some journalists briefly hoped for, and promoted, counter-revolution through parliamentary and constitutional means. At the same time it emphasised that the best means to guard against future revolution would be to restore the legitimate monarchy. In the 1790s all the émigré journalists agreed that the *ancien régime* required some measure of reform, but nevertheless differed on a range of important issues. Their differences stemmed from opposing views as to the best way of reversing the revolution and protecting colonial interests, and the policy to be followed after a Bourbon restoration. The moderates believed that the revolution had a genuine constituency of support in France and thus a restored regime would need to take a conciliatory attitude, establish a constitution with representative institutions and recognise the permanency of many revolutionary changes. Ironically, perhaps for careerist reasons, some of them were less willing to compromise on the question of French rule in Saint-Domingue. The *pur* journalists believed that *ancien régime* France already had a constitution and that a restored regime needed only to revive it, cleanse it of abuses and continue to observe it while regularly consulting the Estates-General. They also believed that royalism was genuinely popular in France, that the revolution was the work of a small group of conspirators who had deceived and misled the French people, and that *monarchiens*, *constitutionnels* and other moderates had released the revolutionary genie. Thus while the émigré press had a precarious unity on broad questions of interpretation, on the details of revolutionary history, tactics and strategy there were numerous points of tension, which were to become still more evident after Brumaire.

---

[206] CP 69–70 (10–12 Apr. 1794).

5

The Challenge of Bonaparte, 1799–1814

The coup of 18 brumaire VIII (9 November 1799) was the most significant single event in the history of the émigré press. Its impact and consequences were not merely political and ideological: it also influenced the audience, market, purpose and justification for the journals. The coup and its aftermath shattered the broad anti-revolutionary consensus of the émigré press. The new constitution established government by a single ruler endorsed by plebiscite and presented the émigrés with an ideological dilemma: should they embrace a *de facto* constitutional monarchy with the appearance of popular consent or continue their support for impotent legitimism? The resultant debate, and the related dispute over whether Napoleon continued or terminated the revolution, dominated the émigré press until mid-1802.

The majority of English-based émigrés were happy to be reconciled with the Napoleonic regime. Many returned even before a general amnesty, pardoning all but 1,000 intransigents, was declared on 26 April 1802. By year's end well over two-thirds had returned to France. This background is perhaps as important as the opinions and activities of the journalists themselves in explaining the changing tones of the émigré journals between 1799 and 1802. The premature death, if not still-birth, of the excellent *Mercure de France*, demonstrated that the market was no longer suitable for journals with a literary orientation aimed too narrowly at the émigré community. New strategies were needed to promote a wider appeal, or better target the rump of intransigent émigrés. Couchery, Regnier and Peltier's resort to uncompromising satire and vitriol can be interpreted partly in this light. For, as Andréossi observed, the *pur* community sought something more than information in a newspaper: 'The émigrés read that gazette [the *Courier de Londres*] avidly. – "It consoles us" they say, and they go off gaily to dine with a few shillings provided by what they call "the charity of the English government".'[1] The journalism of Peltier, Couchery and Regnier provided comfort and an intellectually easy view of a world dominated by personalities rather than issues. But the shift was also a response to the concentration of power in the hands of a single ruler, a bid for notoriety and a deliberate attempt to destabilise relations between England and France. In contrast, Montlosier's rallying to the French government, was ultimately self-defeating from a financial perspective, for by praising and publicising the merits of the French government, he helped reconcile his audience to returning to France. Moreover,

---

[1] AAE, CPA 600, fos 136–7, Andréossi to Talleyrand, 11 nivôse XI (31 Dec. 1802).

after Montlosier's own definitive return to France in mid-1802, the London émigré press was dominated by a *pur* consensus.

From 1803 the content of the émigré journals was increasingly influenced by the policy considerations of British and foreign patrons. The aims of the émigré journalists were mostly coincident with allied and especially British positions, but there were on occasion notable divergences, both within the press and between the press and its patrons. The French writers were ahead of British thinking on some points, not being shackled by the political, diplomatic and internal constraints facing the ministry. Thus émigré journalists continued to argue the need to promote nationalist resistance movements against the revolution,[2] to develop an ideology of total war and to advance the Clausewitzian proposition that, for Napoleon, peace was merely a continuation of war by other means.[3]

This background influenced the political and propaganda campaigns and ideological evolution of the émigré journals between 1799 and 1814, including its reactions to Brumaire, the new regime and religious settlement; its political, polemical and informational campaigns; and its use of satire and role in the genesis of the anti-Napoleonic Black Legend. All these issues are treated below.

On Friday 15 November 1799, Montlosier became the first émigré journalist to report the coup of Brumaire, offering a short telegraphic [ie. semaphore] bulletin from France: 'Bonaparte is in command of Paris – Moreau commands the Directorial Guard – the Council of 500 is at Saint-Cloud – Barras has resigned – and Paris is calm.'[4] He broke the story cautiously on minimal information, warning that the news was unreliable, unexpected, unconfirmed and possibly a hoax, especially as the bulletins were written in poor French. However, it was Peltier who turned the story into a 'scoop'. With true journalistic acumen he delayed publication until further details arrived, although sceptical of the story's veracity. By evening on 16 November the news was confirmed,[5] and Peltier remarked with bitter irony: 'Thus expired the sublime constitution of the year III on 19 Brumaire year VIII, after subsisting in name for a little over four years. Thus disappeared this beautiful masterpiece of the human spirit, signed . . . over 3,000 corpses . . . by Barras, and Bonaparte himself. O *Altitudo!*'[6]

Superficially, Peltier was dismissive of Brumaire's ideological impact. It only represented a change of leadership. Napoleon might be a more formi-

---

2 This idea was expounded as early as 1799 in BM 12 (10 Feb. 1799), 208–15. See also CA 312 (22 Apr. 1808); 370 (11 Nov.); *Ambigu* 343 (10 Oct. 1812), 81; CL lxxiii/35 (30 Apr. 1813).
3 See, for example, *Ambigu* 102 (30 Jan. 1806), 145; CA 179 (13 Jan. 1807).
4 CL xlvi/40 (15 Nov. 1799). *General Jean-Victor Moreau* (1763–1813).
5 *Paris* 192 (15 Nov. 1799/publ. 16 Nov.), 361.
6 Ibid. 376. The 3,000 corpses are a reference to the *journée* of Vendémiaire, but the death toll is exaggerated, though not greatly.

dable adversary, but only because he was more cynical and cleverer than previous revolutionary leaders and exercised a more absolute form of despotic power. Napoleon perpetuated the revolution: he was the incarnation of its principles. He accepted compromise reluctantly because, as a result of his power, the rift with his natural allies, the Jacobins, had become unbridgeable. Consequently, his passions and freedom were heavily circumscribed. Peltier elaborated: 'The declaration of his moderation is the basis of his popularity; thus it is politic for him to sacrifice several aspects of his personality to his collaborators, but his actions are forever revealing of his base and hate filled passions.'[7] Far from preferring the establishment of a monarchic form of government, Peltier insisted that legitimacy alone could provide that 'charm' which binds millions to the commands of a single man.[8] Once this was destroyed the French had become slaves to force.[9] Their government did not even guarantee the most fundamental rights, rights which Peltier believed a restored Bourbon monarchy would uphold: the integrity of posts, freedom of thought, liberty of the press and safety of the person.[10] The same men and principles still held sway. 'Des philosophes bouchers' had replaced 'des bouchers philosophes'.[11]

Similarly, the émigré *Mercure de France* pledged allegiance to, and repeatedly stressed the sacred alliance between, throne and altar.[12] Its punchy foreign and political reports reflected an uncompromising position. Napoleon was castigated as a military despot surrounded by republican forms. His supposed clemency was only justice; the French people only rallied to him through necessity after years of oppression; the forms were changed but the same revolutionary men always held power.[13] His moderation was a sham. It only required the two things it could never have to appeal to all loyal French men: solidity and legitimacy.[14] Such pronouncements from the regime's sworn enemies seem to indicate the practical strength of the Napoleonic compromise. The journal's other themes are also familiar. The powers must declare that they do not make war on France or her *ancien régime* liberties and recognise and re-establish Louis XVIII.[15] They must realise Napoleon's duplicity, the revolutionary nature of his administration, and that peace would consecrate the political existence of a state without base, government without regular form, and people without religion and morals.[16] Nevertheless, peace was desirable for the émigré community, but only because of the

---

[7] *Paris* 195 (15 Jan. 1800), 103.
[8] Peltier used this image in *DTP* i. 10.
[9] *Paris* 193 (30 Nov. 1799), 479.
[10] See *DTP* i, avertissement at p. ii.
[11] *Paris* 194 (24 Dec. 1799), 610.
[12] See, for example, MF 5 (20 May 1800), 391.
[13] MF 1 (10 Apr. 1800), 35–65.
[14] MF 2 (20 Apr. 1800), 134.
[15] See MF 4 (10 May 1800), 319; 5 (20 May 1800), 391; 10 (10 July 1800), 260.
[16] Ibid. 253–4.

singular failure of the powers to support Louis XVIII and their own interests.[17] While supporting the allies, the *Mercure de France* was keen not to be accused of a lack of patriotism in advocating internal political interference. Thus France was elevated to a special case over-riding normal principles of non-interference, on the grounds of the continuing revolutionary conditions. These conditions included:

> a people in revolt, without religion, without regular government, drunk on blood and plunged into an anarchy which favours their every revolt [tous ses attentats]; . . . a troupe of factious men, the usurpers of the supreme authority and executioners of their own monarch; . . . an audacious and rebellious subject, ascended from crime to crime even to the throne of his benefactor.[18]

It was a classic call for order. Yet although a common theme in all counter-revolutionary thought, the primacy accorded to the demand for order became a weakness in the ideology of counter-revolution. Order is a precondition for all government, not a positive role or sustaining ideology in a changing world. While moderates like Montlosier hoped to reserve a wider role for government once order was re-established, their more reactionary colleagues made a fetish of the demand for order itself. Moreover, they equated order with legitimism in every sphere: cultural life, social life, economic life and especially political life. Regnier, Peltier, Gérard, Couchery and the editors of the *Mercure de France* were thus all representative of a mentality that in advocating legitimism was advocating sterility. They saw no need to create a positive rationale for Bourbonism because they refused to acknowledge that any other order could be established in France. From July 1802 this was the consensus in the émigré press. Thereafter, the ultimate and explicit aim of all the émigré newspapers was to depose Napoleon and his government. This aim was reinforced by an ideology and world-view based on the proposition that the French regime was still manifestly revolutionary in both nature and deed. Simultaneously the émigré journalists developed a definition of revolution that better embraced Napoleon, so there is some circularity in their argument.

To prove the revolutionary nature of the regime, the journalists attempted to establish a number of subsidiary propositions. They argued that Napoleon was a usurper and a tyrant, and hence that his government was illegitimate, unjust and inherently unstable. It could therefore be neither relied upon nor trusted. Furthermore, it was revolutionary not only in origins but in dynamic, driven by motors of cupidity and egoism. In consequence, Napoleonic France was bound to threaten Europe for as long as it survived, in a perpetual quest for internal stability by external pillage.

To rally support against Napoleon it was necessary to prove both that he

---

[17] Ibid. 260–2.
[18] MF 4 (10 May 1800), 319.

threatened all of Europe and that he was not invincible. It was also desirable to prove that Britain's opposition to Bonaparte was not driven by self-interest and the quest for naval and commercial hegemony. Finally, in order to facilitate the rallying of former revolutionaries to a Bourbon regime, to preserve French national pride and promote the legitimist cause, it was vital to separate his cause from that of the French nation. One way to do this was to portray Napoleon himself as a detestable character, and thus even moderate *pur* journalists promoted some of the more excessive images of the Black Legend cycle.

Monarchien reactions to Brumaire were both more nuanced and more ambiguous. Montlosier initially believed that Siéyès was the guiding force of the new regime, and concluded that Napoleon was just a tool. He expected little positive to emerge from the coup. He doubted both Napoleon's sincerity and, because of his near-fatal failure of nerve before the Conseil des Cinq-Cents on 19 brumaire, his capacity. Thus Montlosier was pessimistic about Napoleon's chances of surviving as a civil magistrate. He doubted that Bonaparte could control revolutionary factions and initially mistook his tactical manoeuvres to outflank Siéyès on the constitutional issue for a fatal rift in the ruling alliance.[19] His hostility towards the new government only evaporated as Bonaparte demonstrated mastery and political abilities to match his military talent. Thus Montlosier reacted to the constitution proclaimed on 13 December 1799 with relief and enthusiasm. He believed it denied influence to demagogues while maintaining sufficient revolutionary integrity to preserve democratic forms, thereby neutralising the threat from the egalitarian forces that he believed to be the essence of the revolution. Napoleon's genius was 'to preserve revolutionary institutions while terminating the revolution'.[20] Montlosier was also impressed by the concentration, centralisation and bureaucratisation of power in the new constitution, for, as Robert Griffiths has demonstrated, the constitution realised many of the aims of the *monarchien* programme.[21] Montlosier believed it recognised the three great truths required for a *monarchie limitée*:

[1] the necessity of an aristocratic intervention as a necessary ingredient for a great state and in consequence the absurdity of an absolute democracy. . . .
[2] the necessity of concentrating authority . . . there is ten times more monarchy in the current republic than in the constitutional monarchy of 1791. . . .
[3] that one does not govern the people by the people.

Moreover, the lessons of the revolution had finally been learned: legislative initiative was to be left with the chief magistrate of the republic. The consti-

---

[19] CL xlvi/45 (3 Dec. 1799).
[20] Ibid. 52 (27 Dec. 1799).
[21] Griffiths, *Centre perdu*, 253–7.

tution was thus 'infinitely superior to everything of its type that we have seen'.[22]

The priorities expressed by Montlosier seem to confirm Robert Griffith's conclusion that it is chimerical to see Malouet's *monarchien* circle as 'anglophiles'. Eschewing mention of English-style checks and balances, Montlosier stresses the importance of strong centralised executive and bureaucratic government. This is a very different model from Britain's minimalist government and localised administrations. Rather than serving as counter-weights to balance the power of the monarchy, Montlosier propounded that parliamentary bodies should fill the role of Montesquieu's 'intermediary power'. If these views had wide currency among the émigrés, it goes far towards explaining both the appeal of the Napoleonic compromise and the style of politics under the restoration.

Mallet Du Pan shared many of Montlosier's responses to Brumaire. He, too, doubted Napoleon's capacity. Writing just prior to learning of Brumaire, he described tales of Napoleon's achievement in Egypt as 'a sufficient harvest of whim, ridicule and romance, jumbled with incontestable proofs of courage and talent, to compose an heroic–comic poem . . . able and powerful in action, he becomes ludicrous when he attempts to speak'.[23] Mallet realised at once that Bonaparte and Siéyès formed a very uneasy partnership. He believed that Siéyès had long hoped to stage a coup, for 'a man so superior to the mob of incendiaries, intriguers, and rulers to whom he saw France abandoned' would naturally seek to dominate and lead them.[24] Like Peltier, Mallet also denounced the revolutionaries' hypocrisy, the instability of their works and the shifting nature of their opinions with regard to the 1795 constitution. 'They who had been its most enthusiastic panegyrists, the Garats, Danous [sic.], Chéniers, now raise their voices against it in a chorus of curses: it is the Priesthood breaking the Ark of the Covenant.'[25] However, he also agreed with Montlosier's favourable impressions of the new regime. It was, he asserted, 'a more tolerable government', and he correctly predicted it would rely on 'moderates', 'mild constitutionalists' and 'mild royalists' as a power base.[26] It provided what the Directory lacked in order to survive: 'discretion and a pliant constitution'. Thus it secured the middle ground that d'Antraigues and the intransigent royalists had failed to seize.[27] On 11 December 1799, Mallet argued that Jacobinism could only re-emerge if royalism again

---

[22] CL xlvi/52 (27 Dec. 1799).
[23] BM 28 (15 Nov. 1799), 248.
[24] BM 29 (30 Nov. 1799), 297; see also 9 (30 Dec. 1798), 28–32.
[25] BM 29 (30 Nov. 1799), 293. *Dominique-Joseph Garat* (1749–1833), lawyer, *littérateur* and member of the Conseil des Anciens; *Pierre-Claude Daunou* (1760–1840), *conventionnel*, helped draft the constitution of year III; *Marie-Joseph Chénier* (1764–1811) *conventionnel*, republican poet and member of the Conseil de Cinq-Cents.
[26] BM 30 (16 Dec. 1799), 340, 346–7.
[27] Ibid. 372.

mounted a serious challenge, but he expected a wise constitution to bury this threat for the foreseeable future.[28]

Montlosier felt that Jacobinism would destroy civilisation if it ever regained power, but asserted that the new constitution would exclude it from the regime, thus depriving the revolution of its greatest support.[29] The destruction of the Jacobins, apparent moderation and a balanced constitution were enough eventually to reconcile him to Bonapartism. Mallet, however, had a different conception of both despotism and constitutional balance. He saw no balance in the constitution because he conceived it in purely institutional terms, whereas Montlosier viewed it in terms of 'intermediary powers', envisaging an active though ill-defined aristocracy. Mallet correctly foresaw that the executive would far outweigh the other arms of the administration and condemned the constitution for giving a single man discretion to invest himself with emergency powers.[30] Mallet was also sceptical about the chances for peace, contending that everything in Bonaparte's character and history provided an 'antidote to confidence', and that it would be against his interests to embrace a pacific policy, because that would be to 'sacrifice his genius to philosophy'.[31] At the risk of enraging the *purs*, he also argued that it would be counter-productive to adopt the Bourbon restoration as a specific war aim. Experience and reflection suggested that Louis XVIII would only be restored when totally forgotten, without the help of foreign armies, civil war or conspirators. Only then would royalism no longer be feared.[32] In his last two numbers, Mallet gave his studied judgement on the regime. He listed the beneficial and unforeseen changes it had effected to restore the Roman Catholic Church, empty the prisons, ameliorate the treatment of émigrés and establish the rule of law, and declared:

> Surely this enumeration renders it unnecessary to prove that, however there may be a continuance of usurpation, there is certainly no continuation of the former system; and that nothing can differ more than the regulations and policies adopted by Bonaparte and those invariably observed by his predecessors.[33]

In his final number he added:

> We feel no prepossession for Bonaparte. Neither his favour nor his anger can reach us; and it is always disgusting to us to see that unnatural alliance of revolutionary men and maxims with reason and justice, which can alone put an end to the revolution. But we do not hesitate to repeat, that all that has passed

---

[28] Ibid. 366–7.
[29] CL xlvi/42 (22 Nov. 1799).
[30] BM 32 (15 Jan. 1800), 463.
[31] BM 34 (15 Feb. 1800), 106; 31 (30 Dec. 1799), 389.
[32] BM 34 (15 Feb. 1800), 113–14.
[33] BM 35 (15 Mar. 1800), 170.

for these four months seems to us altogether more fortunate than unfortunate, for France as well as the rest of Europe.³⁴

Montlosier's approval of the regime also remained contingent. He awaited proof that the constitution would meet his expectations and remained cautious about revealing the successive stages of his realignment into the Bonapartist camp. Whether his motives were fear of alienating his audience, forced obedience to Madame Swinton or a reluctance to burn his bridges is unclear. However, there are time-lags between his overtures to the French government and declarations of support for Napoleonic policies in his paper. Documentary evidence suggests that the main stages in Montlosier's 'conversion' were the opening of communications with Otto in May 1800 and his visit to Paris in March 1801. In his journalism the watersheds, so far as they can be identified, were somewhat different. Montlosier claims that the first turning point was the translation of Turenne's remains to the Invalides, on 1 vendémiaire IX (23 September 1800), which he believed symbolised 'the making of peace between the century of Bonaparte and the century of Louis XIV', and 'brought to an end the unnatural war of the new France against the former France, the war of children against their fathers'.³⁵ This was precisely the way Napoleon had intended the spectacle to be interpreted.³⁶ The second milestone was the signing of the preliminaries of the peace of Amiens in October 1801. Yet, curiously, it was not until 5 January 1802 that he declared that henceforth, as a result of this peace:

> it would be too little on our part to cease all hostile measures; we have decided, as far as we possibly can, to support all measures for internal order which may be taken by the French government. We will do the same with regard to all external measures that aim to cement the peace.

This decision was consistent with Montlosier's principles, as he indeed claimed. He did not deny his support for monarchy in announcing his absolute support for the French administration. His respect for the Bourbons was undiminished, but he claimed to 'have fought not only for a particular form of government, but also for [the cause of] laws, religion, good morals [des bonnes moeurs], of property, of security, of liberty. These are all bonds of family and *patrie* that we have wished to defend'. Tired of attempting the impossible, his mission would be to unite all friends of liberty, religion and morality to restore France to a place among the circle of nations. Unperturbed by the circularity and casuistry of his argument, he noted that men, when questioned about their favourite form of government, all had one desire in common. Whether they replied 'a monarchic state', 'a republican state' or 'a

---

34 BM 36 (31 Mar. 1800), 239–40. Although this final number was completed by Malouet, it is clearly Mallet's editorial voice speaking here.
35 CL li/2 (5 Jan. 1802).
36 Louis Madelin, *Le Consulat et l'empire*, Paris 1937–54, iv. 21.

despotic state', they all wanted 'a state'. Montlosier concluded: 'let's first make sure that there is a state in France. Afterwards we will see what that state can or ought to be'.[37] In Montlosier's opinion the anarchy was over. Order was restored. The revolution was ended. However, it must not be overlooked that when Montlosier wrote this declaration he was hoping to attract French patronage. He sent a copy to Otto with a covering note declaring his invariable desire to serve 'the good and glory of his country' and asking him to mention this to his superiors.[38] Otto suggested to Talleyrand that Montlosier could indeed be useful to France,[39] but there is no evidence that he ever received 'official articles' from the French government as Maspero-Clerc claims.[40] Probably he merely copied and elaborated upon articles in the French newspapers. His paper still bears the stamp of his independence of mind and in the spring of 1802 he was locked in a private battle with the *Citoyen français* and *Clef du cabinet*, which attacked his constructively critical comments on French policy and cast aspersions on his loyalty.[41]

Montlosier's journal remained generally ill-disposed to the new regime throughout 1800 and early 1801, continuing to argue that the revolution was not over, the regime was unstable, and that the powers should use royalism and declare for a Bourbon restoration.[42] Their previous efforts against the revolution having failed, the only untested expedient was to place Louis XVIII in charge of a large army to rally French royalists.[43] Nor was the proposal a pipe dream, for at the start of the 1800 campaign the allies appeared likely to gain a foothold in France. Montlosier continued to insist that peace with France was impossible, because the revolution had overthrown the old cosmopolitan balance of Europe by generalising all its sentiments. Thus opposition to Louis XVI had become hatred of all royalty; hatred of nobles transformed into opposition to all inequality of rank; and priests had been drowned at Nantes not through anti-clericalism, but through hatred of Christianity.[44] Bonaparte had more masks than Harlequin, playing a Catholic in Rome, an atheist in Paris, a Muslim in Egypt.[45] His moderation was merely a means to disarm the counter-revolution. The biggest danger to Europe was that people accepted Napoleon's insistence that the revolution was over.[46]

---

[37] *CL* li/2 (5 Jan. 1802).
[38] BMN, MS 675, pièce 214, Montlosier to Otto, 5 Jan. 1802. This letter appears in Maspero-Clerc, 'Montlosier', at p. 98.
[39] AAE, CPA 597, fo. 173, Otto to Talleyrand, 11 pluviôse X (30 Jan. 1802).
[40] Maspero-Clerc, 'Montlosier', 99.
[41] See *CL* li/19 (5 Mar. 1802); 21 (12 Mar. 1802); 31 (16 Apr. 1802). No. 31 was produced while Montlosier was away in France, probably by La Corbière.
[42] See, for example, *CL* xlvii/4 (14 Jan. 1800); 8 (28 Jan. 1800); 12 (11 Feb. 1800); 20 (11 Mar. 1800); xlviii/11 (5 Aug. 1800); 13 (12 Aug. 1800); xlix/1 (2 Jan. 1801).
[43] *CL* xlvii/12 (11 Feb. 1800).
[44] Ibid. 20 (11 Mar. 1800).
[45] Ibid. 2 (7 Jan. 1800); 20 (11 Mar. 1800); 49 (20 June 1800).
[46] *CL* xlviii/11 (5 Aug. 1800).

More sinister than ever, the revolution began to seduce by its form.[47] The continuous revolutionary cycle of coups and instability was not over. Regardless of whether there was war or peace, France and Europe should expect new revolutions.[48]

Nevertheless, the *fête* of 1 vendémiaire IX was indeed a turning point in Montlosier's journalism. He declared that the speech of the minister of the interior, Lucien Bonaparte, on this occasion was one of 'the most beautiful speeches' of the revolutionary era, not only for its style, images and eloquence, but also for its political content. Although he censured its attacks on monarchy and England, Montlosier believed the speech proved that the French government had sensed that the revolution was a 'fever', but wished to reveal this truth slowly, for fear of new disturbances.[49] In October 1800 Montlosier reacted with enthusiasm to the report which recommended the recall of most of the émigrés.[50] Nevertheless, if the French government's actions demonstrated a new degree of moderation, its motivation remained suspect. It drew its strength from uncertainty about its intentions.[51] Its policy was a combination of liberal and equivocal acts.[52] Even the émigré report was forced on the government by circumstances. Although liberal compared with the previous proscriptive émigré legislation, émigrés still had to 'swear an oath to the [very] laws which rob us'.[53] The revolutionary government, while ameliorated in form, remained revolutionary in essence.[54] Her peace overtures remained suspect, but their outcome would provide the acid test of the government's alleged moderation.[55] Montlosier's misgivings were aggravated by fears that the League of Armed Neutrality would join the French in a grand naval alliance and threaten Britain with invasion.[56] He clearly considered Napoleon's peace tactics a means to isolate and conquer Britain. However, the formation of the Addington ministry in February 1801 gave renewed hopes of a negotiated settlement between Britain and France, and at the end of March an *article communiqué*, probably written by Sir John MacPherson, expounded on the subject.[57] The people of both countries favoured peace, and the new ministry had a fresh outlook, lacking their predecessors' paranoid fear of French Jacobin subversion of the British consti-

---

[47] Ibid. 13 (12 Aug. 1800).
[48] Ibid. 19 (2 Sept. 1800).
[49] Ibid. 29 (7 Oct. 1800).
[50] Ibid. 35 (28 Oct. 1800). No. 33 (21 Oct. 1800) published a piece under the unique rubric 'article particulier' announcing the measure, and that the 'intention of the First Consul is to open the gates of France'. This item was possibly placed by Otto.
[51] Ibid. 34 (24 Oct. 1800).
[52] Ibid. 37 (4 Nov. 1800).
[53] Ibid.
[54] CL xlix/1 (2 Jan. 1801).
[55] Ibid. 4 (13 Jan. 1801).
[56] Montlosier warned of this possibility ibid. 8 (20 Jan. 1801). The League of Armed Neutrality consisted of Russia, Denmark, Sweden and Prussia.
[57] *Sir John MacPherson* (1745–1821), former governor-general of India and opposition MP.

tution.⁵⁸ Several days later, news of the British victory at Copenhagen (2 April) and the murder of Paul I (24 March) removed the fear of invasion.⁵⁹

Despite Montlosier's trip to France in March and early April 1801, he remained sceptical about the continental peace. An article of 15 May noted that the peace provided no relief for countries occupied by French forces, and reported rumours that Holland was to be annexed and that French ambitions against Portugal were certain.⁶⁰ Montlosier was similarly ungenerous in many of his criticisms of the legislative spirit of the projected *code civil*, which were published in both the *Courier de Londres* and separately at Paris.⁶¹ Although he had identified the need for a code as early as January 1798,⁶² he felt that the provisions of the code, which strengthened patriarchal authority, made divorce more difficult and regulated inheritance laws, were still too liberal on these very issues. He accused the authors of the code of believing that society still existed in France, yet if society still existed there would be no need for a code. This mistaken premise led the framers of the code into serious mistakes. They failed to realise that the family was the basic social unit and the building block of the state. Moreover, they took the *moeurs* of the late *ancien régime* period as their guide, rather than France's *moeurs anciennes*. This made their task impossible, as the vital questions of adultery, divorce, property, law, legislation and paternal authority could not be decided in the light of the philosophy of the late eighteenth century.⁶³ This socially conservative critique caused Montlosier problems after he returned to France and repeated his views in the *Courrier de Londres et de Paris*.⁶⁴ However, while critical of the legislative spirit of the codes, Montlosier accepted the opinions of three émigré *jurisconsultes* among his friends who found the proposed code admirable in terms of judicial organisation and execution.⁶⁵

Montlosier was also unhappy with French policy towards the émigré clergy. One of the main obstacles to reconciliation between the Roman Catholic Church and French state was a duplication of prelates wherever the revolution had appointed new bishops to replace the exiles. Consequently, when they signed their concordat in July 1801, the pope and Bonaparte agreed to press for the resignation of all episcopal incumbents. Erskine, the

---

58 *CL* xlix/26 (31 Mar. 1801).
59 Both events were reported ibid. 31 (17 Apr. 1801).
60 Ibid. 39 (15 May 1801).
61 See ibid. 44 (2 June 1801); l/5 (17 July 1801); 19 (4 Sept. 1801). See also Montlosier, *Observations sur le projet du code civil présenté par la commissaire nommé par le gouvernement le 24 thermidor an VIII*, Paris 1801. As Miramon-Fitzjames, Montlosier, 129, points out, Portalis's draft observations on his project (published posthumously in 1844 as *Discours sur le code civil*), attack Montlosier more than any other critic.
62 *CL* xliii/1 (2 Jan. 1798).
63 *CL* xlix/44 (2 June 1801).
64 See *Courrier de Londres et de Paris*, esp. nos 19 (1/6 Aug. 1802), 23 (9/14 Aug. 1802), 24 (11/16 Aug. 1802), 25 (13/18 Aug. 1802). See also Miramon-Fitzjames, 'Montlosier', 136–40
65 See *CL* l/19 (4 Sept. 1801).

papal legate in London, therefore sent a circular letter to the émigré bishops asking them to resign their sees within ten days. These measures outraged Montlosier's Gallican principles and sense of justice and property, and were denounced in an uncompromising 'letter to the editor' of the *Courier de Londres* on 18 September 1801:

> This is how these illustrious prelates, escaped from the furies of the revolution, find themselves attacked in their last asylum by the hand of the chief of Christianity [sic] himself. All other means of oppression are exhausted; it is now the pope himself who ranges himself among their ranks. He is not even a free and voluntary agent in this. He avows that he was constrained by the exigencies of the time . . . the pope appears condemned as much as the bishops to remain a stranger to the new state religion of France.[66]

Montlosier may have been the author of this letter; he certainly endorsed its views in his next number.[67] Freely interpreting his private assurances from Fouché concerning the re-establishment of religion,[68] he also claimed to know that Napoleon had intended to recall the entire Gallican Church, but that political considerations had modified this determination. Montlosier suggested that even if the bishops separated considerations of religious duty from their duty as royalists, there were still strong objections to acquiescence in both spheres. He also confided that conversations with friends among the bishops showed that their deliberations would be divided.[69] He was correct. Of eighteen French bishops in London, thirteen eventually refused to resign.[70] Montlosier reiterated his support for them on a number of occasions, even after returning to France, [71] rejecting the counter-arguments his friend Lally-Tollendal expounded in four anonymous pamphlets addressed *au rédacteur du Courier de Londres*.[72]

Yet in the same number that he defended the *non-démissionnaire* bishops from their critics, Montlosier was also stressing the need to work within the regime. Interminable internal struggle and foreign war had not undermined the revolution: now was the time to begin working with the republic's leader-

---

[66] Ibid. 23 (18 Sept. 1801).
[67] Maspero-Clerc had little doubt that he was the author: 'Montlosier', 92.
[68] These assurances are mentioned in AAE, dossiers de personnel, vol. 52, 'Montlosier', fos 263–5, Montlosier to Polignac, 15 Aug. 1829.
[69] *CL* 1/24 (22 Sept. 1801).
[70] Bellenger, *French exiled clergy*, 114. Montlosier gave the number as fourteen *non-démissionnaires*: *CL* 1/26 (29 Sept. 1801).
[71] *Courier de Londres et de Paris* 2 (28 June/5 July 1802).
[72] T.-G. de Lally-Tollendal, *Première Lettre au rédacteur du Courier de Londres; et au correspondant, auteur de la notice insérée dans le no.* [i.e. vol.] *50 de ce journal sur le bref du pape aux évêques français*, London 1801; *Seconde Lettre au rédacteur du Courier de Londres précédée d'une traduction du bref du S. S. avec l'original à côté*, London 1801; *Troisième Lettre au rédacteur du Courier de Londres sur cette question: la religion catholique est-elle à rétablir en France?*, London 1801; *Quatrième et Dernière Lettre sur les questions relatives aux affaires ecclésiastiques de France*, London 1801. For Montlosier's response see *CL* 1/39 (13 Nov. 1801).

ship.[73] At the end of September 1801 he observed that the peace preliminaries with Britain would probably succeed, since they were the outcome of six months of negotiations, rather than the battlefield and that Britain had achieved her chief objectives: survival, independence and a future equilibrium in Europe. France's career of blood was closed. It was unreasonable to expect Napoleon to act as a revolutionary any longer. The sceptre of counter-revolution seemed to have fallen into his hands.[74] Montlosier's acceptance of Bonaparte was no longer contingent. He was soon arguing that French pretensions to dominate Europe should not be reproached. All powers, including monarchic France, entertained aspirations to hegemony when it seemed within reach.[75]

The other émigré journalists and a host of religious publicists were not as generous as Montlosier towards Napoleon's attempts to secure the resignation of the bishops. The bishops themselves produced a *Mémoire*, 'at heart a rehearsal of traditional Gallican doctrine',[76] which asserted that bishops as well as the pope were called to 'rule and govern' and that their bond with their dioceses was indissoluble. They defined the bishop as 'the doctor of his diocese, the master of religious instruction, the judge of disputes concerning faith'. The bishop's role was divinely appointed and hence not negotiable: 'His rights are as old as the [Christian] religion, as divine as the institution of the episcopate, as immutable as the word of Jesus Christ.'[77] This justification removed the need to admit any dilemma of conscience, and remained the basis for the bishops' refusal to admit the concordat. The Gallican Church of the pre-revolutionary era, loyal to God and king, was the only acceptable 'ecclesiastical polity'. The *Mémoire* was followed by a flurry of anti-concordataire tracts. The most notable was Pierre-Louis Blanchard's *Controverse pacifique*, published in 1802. Blanchard, a former canon of Lisieux cathedral and a professor of theology, argued that the pope's novel pretensions were undermining the constitution of the Roman Catholic Church by despoiling the bishops of rights accorded to them by Christ himself. Thus, according to Blanchard, the concordat and demand for resignations were paradoxically undermining the Church rather than re-establishing order and unity, because they disenfranchised the only source of authority, the bishop. Although none of the *non-démissionaire* bishops would endorse the *Controverse pacifique*, Blanchard gathered a schismatical following among the exiled clergy. If the arguments of this so-called *petite église* were strong intellectually in terms of Gallican theology, the practical implication – that both pope and

---

[73] Ibid. 26 (29 Sept. 1801).
[74] Ibid. 28 (6 Oct. 1801).
[75] Ibid. 46 (8 Dec. 1801).
[76] Bellenger, *French exiled clergy*, 115.
[77] Ibid. My summary of the early stages of the controversy draws heavily on pp. 115–22. Since Bellenger only perused the *Ambigu* for 1804 and 1806–7, he was unaware of its role in the Blanchardist controversy from 1808.

Roman Catholic Church world-wide were schismatics – was absurd, and their political impact was negligible. Nevertheless, the simmerings of their subversive doctrine began to cause concern among British Catholic authorities.

Against this background, the savagery of Peltier's attacks on the concordat becomes comprehensible. Although he excused himself for resorting to his customary arsenal of ridicule because he was ignorant of theology,[78] he rehearsed some of the arguments of the Blanchardists, and reprinted several of their most important tracts.[79] Peltier insisted that Pius VII was as unfree as Louis XVI on 6 October 1789 and a tool of Bonaparte, who intended to form and to direct his own Church.[80] Although the Napoleonic Church appeared less illegitimate than the Constitutional Church, the concordat was in reality a coup against the vestiges of the true French Church, which was scattered across Europe and still lamenting the blood of the martyrs of the revolution.[81] In his clearest theological exposition he argued that although the pope was the father of all believers, a father cannot violate the rights of any of his children, even for the supposed benefit of others. The bishops were sovereignly constituted as the *dépôt* of sacred laws, just as sovereign courts were the *dépôt* of political laws.[82] Peltier also reprinted Napoleon's notorious proclamation to the Egyptians of 24 messidor VI (12 July 1798) in which he claimed that the French were children of the prophet.[83] He savaged and ridiculed Lally-Tollendal's *Lettres au rédacteur du Courier de Londres*,[84] and caricatured the return of the five *démissionnaire* bishops from London to France with characteristic crudity.[85] Peltier also invested Napoleon 'furti defensor [defender of thieves]'[86] and suggested his royal motto should be '*Diable et mon Epée* [the devil and my sword]'.[87] The alleged incompatibility of pure religion and usurpation could not have been encapsulated more succinctly.

Religious controversy continued after 1803. Even after the establishment of the concordat, religious propaganda was considered among the most dangerous by both the regime and its opponents. The religious element of *Chouannerie* no doubt contributed to this belief, and events in Spain from 1808 reinforced it. Thus Blanchardist assumptions continued to underpin the journalists' comments on Napoleon's treatment of the Church and Pope Pius VII. Hence Peltier suggested that Napoleon's '*soi-disant évêques* [self-styled

---

[78] *Paris* 237 (30 Sept. 1801), 145.
[79] See *Paris* 239–43 (31 Oct.–31 Dec. 1801), passim, and references below.
[80] *Paris* 236 (15 Sept. 1801), 102–3; 237 (30 Sept. 1801), 181 passim.
[81] Ibid. 182.
[82] Ibid. 180.
[83] Ibid. 162.
[84] See *Paris* 238–45 (15 Oct. 1801–4 Feb. 1802), passim.
[85] *Paris* 244 (20 Jan. 1802), 436–7.
[86] *Paris* 236 (15 Sept. 1801), 104.
[87] *Paris* 240 (16 Nov. 1801), 565.

bishops]' were 'mitred slaves',[88] and when the pope crowned Napoleon, Regnier alleged he had sold his conscience to keep his throne. Napoleon, he claimed, had overcome his scruples by explaining 'that if the law of God banned robbery and murder, continental law is superior to the law of God, just as a dynasty of six months is superior to a dynasty of seven centuries'.[89] However, until 1808, religious commentary in the émigré journals comprised only reprinted documents, rancorous jibes on the insincerity of Napoleon's faith and the hypocrisy of his bishops, accounts of the supposed blasphemies of Bonaparte and his entourage and occasional *resumés* or reviews of the most significant Blanchardist tracts.[90]

However, in 1808, shortly after the condemnation of Blanchard and his associates by the Synod of Vicars Apostolic,[91] Peltier became personally involved in the Blanchardist debate. Without directly condemning the pope, he published comments on a pro-Bonaparte pastoral letter of the bishop-inquisitor of the Algarve. These comments, which he apparently wrote himself, alleged that the concordat renewed the Civil Constitution of the Clergy, allowed the civil power to appropriate the riches of the Church, impoverished the clergy, placed schismatics in the Church and subjected the Church to civil authority. In short, the article accused the pope of creating a schismatic sect and made the renunciation of the Concordat a central plank in resistance to Bonaparte. The language Peltier adopted must also be seen as part of the attempt to stimulate resistance to Napoleon in Spain and Portugal:

> It is necessary for us to choose: if we condemn the Concordat as destructive of the Church, as contrary to justice and the most sacred of rights, we must condemn its author and denounce him to the Catholic Church; and if we do not dare condemn him . . . we must accept the Concordat and with it the ruin of religion and annihilation of the rights of the legitimate Sovereign. . . . Buonaparté is an impious man. However, he has a lively and constant interest in his new *concordataire* religion . . . he derives great support from it.[92]

Peltier went on to argue that, like Napoleon, the opponents of revolution must learn to use the ministers of the Church.

Such statements, especially the accusation that the pope himself had become schismatic, did not go unnoticed by the vicars-apostolic of the English Roman Catholic community. Bishop Douglass and Bishop Milner, already struggling against the spread of Blanchardism among the French

---

[88] *Ambigu* 152 (20 June 1807), 545; 157 (10 Aug. 1807), 234.
[89] *CL* lvi/45 (4 Dec. 1804). See also on this topic 46–7 (7–11 Dec. 1804).
[90] See, for example, *Ambigu* 14 (n.d.), 101–8; *CL* lv/7 (21 Jan. 1804).
[91] See Bellenger, *French exiled clergy*, 117.
[92] *Ambigu* 185 (20 May 1808), 305–7. These comments also appeared anonymously in pamphlet form, but Milner implies that they appeared after 1 June, and hence were original to Peltier.

clergy in their dioceses, took the danger of anti-papal ideas and insubordination very seriously indeed, not least because émigré priests still outnumbered English ones by at least three to one. In August 1808 Milner published a pastoral letter which claimed that the schism was gaining ground among his own clergy, some of whom had even labelled him a 'concordatist'. Milner's main targets were the latest pamphlets of Blanchard and Gaschet, whose invectives he compared to those of Luther. However, he also added dismissively: 'I shall take no notice whatsoever of . . . the journals of Mr. Peltier because he is a layman, and therefore presumed to be unacquainted with questions of theology.'[93]

Peltier was unchastened. On 10 September 1808 he responded with a blistering counter-attack, advancing eleven propositions, each commencing: 'We are not theologians, but . . .'. They argued that it was well known that ultramontanism was created in the eleventh century by Pope Gregory VII and that the pretensions of the episcopate had driven many princes from the Roman Church. The Gallican Church, being always attached to the teachings of the primitive Church and recognising the independence of sovereigns, had become a leading support of both monarchy and the social order. Pius VII, in exaggerating his pretensions, had become Napoleon's plaything. Peltier asserted, moreover, that 'no-one can persuade us that it is permissible, in the name of God, to place the crown of a legitimate Sovereign on the head of a usurper, and to call for heavenly benediction on a man whose very existence is a continual offence against the justice taught by heaven itself'.[94]

After a further tirade in defence of Blanchard, Peltier let the matter rest temporarily.[95] Perhaps he felt he had got the better of the exchange. Certainly it was a delicate subject for the English bishops, and Peltier was a dangerous opponent. The slur on Milner's patriotism was particularly dangerous for the Catholic community in England, and one wonders whether many English Catholics would have dared to make it. The transfer of the debate to the English forum illustrates how Peltier was prepared to broaden the framework of counter-revolution and establish it as a single, over-riding priority.

The debate did not end there, however. In 1809 the annexation of the papal states, followed by Pius VII's protests and eventual excommunication of Napoleon, resulted in new attacks on Milner, Douglass and the Irish bishops. Peltier, Blanchard and their adherents felt that the excommunication vindicated their position. Commenting on the pope's letters apostolic, Peltier asked what position Milner would now espouse, having maintained that the

---

[93] J. Milner, *A pastoral letter addressed by the Right Rev. J, Milner, bishop of Castabala, vicar apostolic, &c. to the Roman Catholic clergy of his district in England* . . . , Dublin 1808, 7. Milner's text was dated 10 Aug. 1808.
[94] *Ambigu* 195 (10 Sept. 1808), 391.
[95] *Ambigu* 198 (10 Oct. 1808), 613–25.

Catholic religion was perfectly re-established in France?[96] His following number contained an article by Blanchard himself, entitled 'Les Evêques d'Irlande et M. Milner réfutés par le bref . . . de Pie VII', summarising arguments in his recent pamphlets.[97] Shortly afterwards Peltier added insult to injury by defending the proposed British policy on Irish Catholic appointments, on the grounds that a veto was a necessary police regulation against ultramontanism and the risk of a future Bonapartist pope.[98]

Blanchard submitted further articles unique to the *Ambigu* in 1811. The first attacked the 'criminal apostasy' of Cardinal Maury, Louis XVIII's ambitious representative to Rome who had defected to Bonaparte in 1804.[99] The second denounced Napoleon's attempts to transport the pope to France, arguing the need for Pius VII to issue an explicit condemnation of the concordat as the only means to cure the ills of the Church.[100] Peltier also published a long extract from Blanchard's pamphlet *La Vérité proclamé par ses agresseurs*, which argued that, despite their rhetoric, the actions of Milner, Douglass and the Irish bishops showed that they accepted the anti-concordat case.[101] Peltier followed this with allegations that Napoleon intended to separate France from the Holy See altogether, decatholicising her and thus consummating the revolutionary campaign of 'impiété'.[102]

By 1811, however, the whole religious debate was little more than shadow-boxing. The pope would not recant over the concordat, the Napoleonic Church had been firmly established for ten years and death was thinning the ranks of *non-démissionaire* bishops. The last major Blanchardist sally in the *Ambigu*, an anonymous refutation of an anonymous pamphlet entitled *Pie VII vengé, ou le Blanchardisme dans le tombeau*, was greeted with indifference. Its author contended that his adversary's insistence that the émigré schismatics must recant on pain of damnation, thereby accepting the authority of the pope and *concordataire* Church, was tantamount to demanding that the émigrés renounce everything they held dear.[103] Nevertheless, Peltier abandoned publication of the article unfinished, saying readers had complained that theological questions were 'boring'.[104] However, this consideration did not stop him publishing a response to the bishop of

[96] *Ambigu* 237 (30 Oct. 1809), 206; the pope's letters apostolic were published at pp. 193–205.
[97] These two pamphlets, *Déclaration finale de P. L. Blanchard, relativement à M. Milner*, and *Opposition de la déclaration des évêques catholiques d'Irlande du 3 Juillet 1809*, are not listed in Bellenger's bibliography and seem not to survive in pamphlet form.
[98] *Ambigu* 247 (10 Feb. 1810), 301–2.
[99] *Ambigu* 281–3 (20 Jan.–10 Feb. 1811); Maury had repeatedly declared that he would never desert the cause of legitimism. For attacks on Maury see also *Ambigu* 280 (10 Jan. 1811), 22–4. D'Antraigues also attacks Maury, CA 221 (9 June 1807).
[100] *Ambigu* 285 (28 Feb. 1811), 431–6.
[101] *Ambigu* 286 (10 Mar. 1811), 507–30.
[102] Ibid. and *Ambigu* 295 (10 June 1811), 515.
[103] *Ambigu* 327 (30 Apr. 1812), 165–81.
[104] *Ambigu* 329 (20 May 1812), 354n.

Blois contributed by a priest named Thorel, the reflections of a Russian on Napoleon's second concordat and an abusive letter addressed to Cardinal Maury.[105] Nevertheless, by 1814 the religious issue had been reduced to an irrelevance and all but fizzled out.

After the religious issue, the most significant polemics of the émigré journalists after 1803 concerned the French economy. However, none of the anti-Napoleonic writers was an economist, and their economic critique was not pressed home as forcefully as during the 1790s. Peltier and Gérard nevertheless continued to record the works of d'Ivernois.[106] In January 1805 Peltier juxtaposed Napoleon's boast that he had restored regularity in French finances with d'Ivernois's compelling evidence 'that if there has always been a furious activity in the receipts of the French government, there has been neither regularity in its public accounting [dans les exposés], nor order in the [financial] administration'.[107] However, d'Ivernois's economic critique was beginning to lose credibility. Faced with the continuing resilience of 'revolutionary' finances, his annual prophecies of financial collapse began to appear comically predictable and the journalists began to lose patience with his ideas. Unlike Mallet Du Pan, who had seen financial problems at the heart of revolutionary expedients, finances were peripheral to Peltier's interpretation of the revolution. Instead he looked to moral causes. Cupidity, rather than financial crisis, explained revolutionary land seizures, expansionism and persecution.[108] Events inside France were better explained by the 'deficit of justice, of morals, of [respect for] property, of education, and above all . . . of legitimacy' than by the financial deficit.[109] Thus, the Napoleonic government, which saw d'Ivernois as one of the chief writers in the enemy camp, took the financial issue rather more seriously than the émigré pressmen.

Beyond providing figures on the French finances, juxtaposing them with English statistics and presenting the works of d'Ivernois, the émigré press seldom did more than belittle the state of the French economy. Cheap jibes and generalised accounts of French industrial collapse, which bore little relation to reality, were the best that they could offer. In 1803 Regnier compared the position of the French government with that of Figaro, who wrote a tract on money claiming that it was not necessary to have some to write about it.[110] He told his readers that there was never less credit and more insolvency than under Napoleon, attacking him for conspicuous consump-

---

[105] *Ambigu* 340 (10 Sept. 1812), 507–17; 364 (10 May 1813), 209–308; 368 (20 June 1813), 633–57.
[106] See, for example, *Ambigu* 34 (10 Mar. 1804), 296; 65 (20 Jan. 1805), 82–96; *CL* lxxiv/36 (2 Nov. 1813).
[107] *Ambigu* 65 (20 Jan. 1805), 82.
[108] Peltier trivialised the debt crisis as early as *CP* 1 (2 Nov. 1793).
[109] *Ambigu* 65 (20 Jan. 1805), 82.
[110] *CL* liii/23 (22 Mar. 1803).

tion in the midst of poverty.¹¹¹ In 1805 the *Gazette de la Grande-Bretagne* claimed that the French populace blamed the country's financial disarray on a war caused by Napoleon's obstinacy and arrogance.¹¹² The *Courier d'Angleterre* described Bonaparte's financial reports as stories to amuse his companions, which could only be criticised at risk of strangulation by one of his Mamelucks.¹¹³ The supposed impoverishment of France and her empire was juxtaposed with the prosperity and commercial resilience of Great Britain. Accounts of the shortages of colonial goods and medical supplies in French territories contrast with descriptions of the expansion of British commerce and industry in spite, or even as a result, of the continental blockade.¹¹⁴ However, these accounts tended to be crude and unpersuasive, in part due to insufficient data. The exile press failed to realise the full potential of economic propaganda throughout the Napoleonic period.

There were many other polemics for the émigré press after 1802, but from the codification of laws to Napoleon's military abilities, from foreign policy objectives to social policy, all had similar features. They presented Napoleon's regime as a continuation of a revolution based on cupidity, social disorder and the annihilation of property. Moreover, Napoleon was trapped within the revolutionary current: if he tried to escape his revolutionary destiny he would fail.¹¹⁵ Only someone outside the revolution, with a legitimate power base, could master it. This task would not be difficult, for France was tired of revolution and had already acknowledged the need for a single ruler. Thus the most significant political campaigns of the émigré journalists between 1803 and 1814 discussed below focused on the characteristics of the single man at the head of the French government, and his unsuitability for the task.

The first such campaign followed Peltier's trial and was a very personal matter to the journalists involved. Peltier and Regnier were both keen to capitalise on the sympathy and curiosity their confrontation with Napoleon had aroused, both to promote their publications and to reinforce the image of Napoleon as a tyrant who sought to suppress British press freedom. Their efforts began before the trial when Peltier opened a subscription to help with his legal costs, promising subscribers an account of the trial.¹¹⁶ This initiative was backed by d'Artois, who also sponsored publication of Mackintosh's

---

[111] CL liv/22 (12 Sept. 1803); liii/23 (22 Mar. 1803).
[112] GGB 46 (20 Sept. 1805).
[113] CA 249 (30 Aug. 1807).
[114] For this economic critique see CL lxix/2 (4 Jan. 1811); lxxii/37 (6 Nov. 1812); lxxiii/8 (26 Jan. 1813); lxxiv/35 (29 Oct. 1813); *Ambigu* 94 (10 Nov. 1805), 246–68; 98 (20 Dec. 1805), 549–52; 202 (10 Nov. 1808), 236–43; 247 (10 Feb. 1810), 261–73; 293 (20 May 1811), 377–9; GGB 46 (20 Sept. 1805); 69 (10 Dec. 1805); CA 226 (26 June 1807); 300 (11 Mar. 1808).
[115] See, for example, *Ambigu* 185 (20 May 1808), 293–307; 193 (10 Aug. 1808/publ. 22 Aug.), 177–87; 195 (30 Aug. 1808), 396–404; CA 381 (20 Dec. 1808); CL liv/30 (11 Oct. 1803); lvii/16 (22 Feb. 1805); lxvi/1 (4 July 1809).
[116] See CL liii/9 (1 Feb. 1803).

speech.[117] The success of *The trial of John Peltier* was assured by the outbreak of hostilities, which conferred heroic victim status on Peltier and made Mackintosh appear admirably perspicacious.[118]

Meanwhile, Regnier kept the issue in the public eye by attacking the accuracy of Henry Broughton's translation of the *Voeu d'un bon patriote hollandois*, as read in court, concentrating on the meaning of 'apotheosis'.[119] This provoked a reply from Broughton, who argued that the translation was as accurate as possible, and fully conveyed the meaning. Regnier dismissed this reply, accepting Broughton's good faith, but arguing that he had not grasped the 'metaphysical meaning'![120] Simultaneously, he managed to string out coverage of the trial until 8 March by remarking on the reactions of English and French newspapers to the verdict. The *Morning Post* provided the best ammunition, borrowing Peltier's own phrases. It claimed that Napoleon was angry at having had to resort to law, which he believed was for ordinary mortals: as 'God's envoy' he would rather have had Peltier strangled, poisoned, shot or put to death quietly.[121]

When Peltier finally returned to the *Ambigu*, his delight in his notoriety was almost palpable. As a preface to his second volume he offered an adapted version of Lafontaine's fable *Le Lion et le Moucheron*, ending with the observation:

> Cette fable fait voir qu'entre nos ennemis
> Les plus à craindre sont souvent les plus petits.[122]

He also reprinted the *Adresse au public* from his account of the trial to bridge the eight-month gap between numbers and in a poem addressed to Napoleon again suggested that his conviction rested on a mistranslation:

> L'*Ambigu* contre moi tournant mes propres armes,
> Les mots qu'un traducteur renvoyait plus affreux
> Enfin, toute l'horreur d'un débat ténébreux.
> Que pouvait Mackintosh dans ce trouble funeste?
> De mes rares shellins j'ai vu s'enfuir le reste,
> Et je ne dois la vie en ce commun effroi
> Qu'à l'invincible horreur que tu trâme après toi.[123]

---

117 See AAE, CPA 600, fo. 191, report of unnamed agent to Andréossi, Edinburgh, 28 Feb. 1803.
118 In CL liii/48 (17 June 1803), Regnier also promised to print 6,000 copies of a collection of CL articles on Napoleon because his stock of back numbers was exhausted, but I have not found a copy.
119 Ibid. 16 (25 Feb. 1803).
120 Ibid. 18 (4 Mar. 1803).
121 Ibid. 19 (8 Mar. 1803).
122 'This fable demonstrates that among our enemies / those most to be feared are often the smallest.'
123 *Ambigu* 10 (n.d./?June 1803), 13. '*L'Ambigu* turned my own weapons against me / The words that a translator rendered more horrifying / At last, all the horror of a dark debate. /

Peltier's sallies of *esprit* also included a series of letters in which he claimed to be Napoleon's secret agent and most loyal advisor. These letters, masterpieces of satirical exaggeration, offer absurd policy proposals, suggest projects of invasion and dynastic aggrandisement, applaud Bonaparte's tyranny, ruthlessness and bloodthirstiness, denounce the works of his opponents and generally pour scorn on the First Consul through pretended respect and expressions of support.[124] In particular Peltier feigned disappointment at the inexplicable failure of the plan to invade England. This theme also allowed new opportunities to recall his own gallant struggle against Bonaparte in fragments like *Bonaparte et moi*, which is replete with *double entendres*:

> Chacun de nous deux a son lot,
> Chacun de nous fait son complot.
> Toi, le sac d'Albion t'amuse,
> Moi, ta rage exerce ma muse.
> Tu fais des noirs projets:
>   moi, je fais le falot.
> Tu fais des bateaux plats:
>   moi, je fais un brûlot.[125]

However, there were more important subjects of debate, and as public attention passed to other questions, Peltier's energy and *esprit* waned. Never again did the *Ambigu* capture the satirical vigour and triumphant verve of the first dozen numbers following Peltier's trial, though this is partially due to the debilitating grind of producing at least seventy-two pages thrice monthly.

The following year, a new cataclysm struck close to the émigré journalists. On 13 February 1804, the Paris police uncovered a plot to kidnap Bonaparte and restore the Bourbons and began rounding up suspects. They believed, erroneously, on the flimsiest evidence, that a Bourbon prince was involved in the plot. Over the following weeks they arrested General Moreau and General Pichegru, Georges Cadoudal and numerous of his *Chouan* associates in Paris and seized Condé's grandson, the duc d'Enghien, from his refuge in neutral Baden. The police had no direct evidence against d'Enghien, who

---

What could Mackintosh achieve in these sad troubles? / I saw the few shillings remaining to me disappear, / And I owe my very life in this time of terror / Solely to the invincible horror that follows you everywhere.'

[124] They appeared from *Ambigu* 9 (n.d./?late 1802), the last number published before Peltier's trial, until *Ambigu* 28 (10 Jan. 1804).

[125] *Ambigu* 13 (n.d./c. 10 Aug. 1803), 100. 'We two each have our own lot, / We two each nurture our own plot, / You, amuse yourself with the sack of Albion, / Me, my muse practices by [provoking] your rage [read aloud this appears to be a deliberate pun: "ta rage exercée m'amuse" would mean "your practiced anger amuses me". Moreover "la rage" also means "rabies"] / You indulge in shadowy projects / Me, I light the lantern [also means: "I prepare a court martial"] / You build flat bottomed boats [i.e. for the invasion of England; also means "you make poor jokes" and implies Napoleon lacks *esprit*] / Me, I prepare a fireship [also means by implication "I am a firebrand"].'

had been living in innocent and quiet seclusion. Nevertheless, he was taken to Paris secretly, court-martialled before a kangaroo court and shot at Vincennes on 21 March. A fortnight later, on 6 April, Pichegru was found mysteriously strangled in his cell. The French authorities claimed he had strangled himself. The affair provoked a predictable reaction in the émigré press. It was suggested that the charges against Pichegru were trumped-up and an anonymous 'letter to the editor' in the *Courier de Londres* argued that England would never stoop to political assassination. Nor, it was asserted, would Pichegru, Cadoudal or Moreau involve themselves in such a plot.[126] The *Courier de Londres*, denying that it was possible to commit suicide with a tourniquet, styled Pichegru's death murder.[127] Moreover, after so many arrests, Peltier described the plot as the conspiracy 'of three-quarters of France for the restoration of the monarchy'.[128] He claimed that few houses in France would have refused the conspirators hospitality.[129] Once again, he was implying that Bonapartism was not popular in France and that given free expression the nation would pronounce for monarchy. The acquittal of Moreau, who seems to have rebuffed the conspirators' advances, only confirmed the suspicion that Napoleon had used the affair to destroy dangerous rivals.

The kidnapping of d'Enghien had a profound effect on European opinion and was instrumental in turning the tsar against Napoleon. The arrest of the conspirators was a legitimate police operation, but the seizure of d'Enghien was a clear breach of sovereignty and of respect for royalty. Throughout Europe his death was seen as extra-judicial murder. Thus the émigré journalists contributed, as Peltier observed, to a unanimous chorus of disapproval in the London press.[130] Their anguish was acutely personal, but both British and émigré presses stressed common themes. The charges were absurd. D'Enghien could not have been spying against France while on foreign soil. If he had borne arms against France in the past, it was only against those who had driven him from the country. But what did one more crime matter to Napoleon? More pertinently, what did it gain him? Remote from the succession, in retirement, with no army, d'Enghien's murder seemed so pointless that Peltier suggested that it was proof Napoleon had become mentally unbalanced.[131] It was also more culpable than the murder of Louis XVI, who had been allowed a defence and a confessor and had been convicted in open court, by an assembly pressured by the multitude. Louis's last words were public and his last hours and resting place recorded, whereas d'Enghien was tried, shot and buried in secret. Thus Peltier concluded that 'The revolution has regressed to

---

[126] CL lv/25 (27 Mar. 1804).
[127] See ibid. 34 (27 Apr. 1804).
[128] *Ambigu* 35 (20 Mar. 1804), 370.
[129] *Ambigu* 34 (10 Mar. 1804), 293.
[130] *Ambigu* 37 (10 Apr. 1804), 64–6. See also CL lv/28 (6 Apr. 1804).
[131] *Ambigu* 37 (10 Apr. 1804), 51.

the time of Robespierre. What am I saying? It is even more hideous than that epoque', and noted for good measure, 'One can only conclude that honour has suddenly become foreign to France and the French military.'[132]

The émigré journals were not always part of so unanimous a press voice, particularly on foreign policy, where generally they tried to promote, and sometimes to lead, British policy. One such case was the British strike against Denmark in early September 1807 which, according to a French police report, was the result of a conspiracy involving Regnier, d'Antraigues, Puisaye, Fauche-Borel and Danican, who were desperate to re-establish their credit with the ministry. It alleged that the British government was duped by false intelligence concerning the state of Danish military preparations supplied by Danican, who returned to England in August 1807. When the fraud was discovered after the event, the British covered up the whole affair.[133] The report, though incorrect in its details, was apparently based on informed hearsay. The cabinet's decision to attack Denmark was taken in late July, as a direct result of intelligence communicated by d'Antraigues on 21 July of Franco-Russian plans to unite the Russian, Swedish, Dutch and Danish navies, in accordance with the secret articles of the treaty of Tilsit.[134] This would create a North Sea squadron of about sixty ships-of-the-line, and stretch the Royal Navy's resources to breaking-point. The capture of the Danish navy reduced the potential threat by about fifteen ships, and enabled Sweden to continue resisting the French.[135] The readiness of the Danish fleet and magazines was thus of only peripheral concern.

Given Regnier's close relationship with d'Antraigues, the suggestion of the *Courier d'Angleterre* of 24 July that Sweden and Denmark should be reassured rather than worried by the British armament, was probably intended as disinformation.[136] Once the attack had taken place, the émigré journals joined a retrospective campaign to justify Canning's *realpolitik*. The violation of Danish neutrality was denounced in Britain as well as Europe,[137] so when in late August *The Times* published a pre-emptive justification for an attack, Regnier translated it, noting, significantly, that it appeared in an opposition paper.[138] In September he justified the attack by referring to news that Napoleon had demanded the Portuguese fleet, and, like Peltier, countered French protestations at the violation of Danish neutrality by arguing that the conti-

---

[132] Ibid. 50, 35.
[133] See Hauterive, *Police*, iv, para. 524, police bulletin of 29 June 1808.
[134] Duckworth, *D'Antraigues phenomenon*, 292; Peter Dixon, *Canning, politician and statesman*, London 1976, 110. For some of Danican's reports, which are of little importance, see Canning papers, bundle 44.
[135] On policy considerations behind the attack see A. Ryan, 'The causes of the British attack upon Copenhagen in 1807', *EHR* lxviii (1953), 37–55. See also I. R. Christie, *Wars and revolutions*, London 1982, 306–7; Schroeder, *European politics*, 327–30.
[136] CA 234 (24 July 1807).
[137] See J. Clarke, *British diplomacy and foreign policy, 1782–1865*, London 1989, 118.
[138] CA 244 (28 Aug. 1807).

nental blockade had already violated the rights of all neutral powers.[139] Predictably, he also publicised George III's statement that confidential sources had forewarned him of Napoleon's intention to seize the Danish navy.[140] Peltier argued that the Danish fleet must never be returned as it would tip the naval balance in France's favour, alleging that the prince of Denmark's protest against the attack was drafted in Paris.[141] The *Gazette de la Grande-Bretagne* was a little more circumspect, but supported the expedition.[142]

The realignment of European powers after Tilsit naturally caused a shift in the émigré journals' foreign coverage. Previously Russia had been portrayed as the only power capable of saving Europe and Alexander presented as an heroic emperor with the purest of motives.[143] Now both were reduced to an ambiguous position. According to the émigré journals, the tsar was surrounded by wicked advisors. Thus his cause was separated from the cause of the Russian nation, which was portrayed as inimical to peace. According to the *Gazette de la Grande-Bretagne* the Russians realised that France could not offer them the same trade advantages as Britain, but the tsar, misled by base ministers, had deserted the cause and upset most of his nobility in the process.[144] Tilsit had turned Alexander into Napoleon's slave. For Regnier it was 'the most infamous treaty that a great prince has ever made'.[145] Moreover Regnier, who was doubtless privy to d'Antraigues's intelligence, continued to insist on the existence of secret articles.[146] So did Peltier.[147] This was a valuable rhetorical position. The well-founded fear of secret provisions concerning the Baltic and partition of the Ottoman empire was singularly alarming, especially for Austria. The *Gazette de la Grande-Bretagne* was silent on the issue.

The émigré journalists were correct in believing that Tilsit was unpopular with many notables and merchants, but they overlooked the general popularity of peace and the 'considerable fund of anglophobia' existing in Russia.[148] However, their stance was probably not just a rhetorical strategy but a solid conviction based on their secret correspondence with the north

---

139 CA 248 (11 Sept. 1807); 250 (18 Sept. 1807); *Ambigu* 162 (30 Sept. 1807), 671–2.
140 CA 253 (29 Sept. 1807).
141 *Ambigu* 163 (10 Oct. 1807), 41–4.
142 GGB 251–4 (8–18 Sept. 1807).
143 *Ambigu* 98 (20 Dec. 1805), 594; 141 (28 Feb. 1807), 413; GGB 68 (6 Dec. 1805); 73 (24 Dec. 1805); CA 181 (20 Jan. 1807).
144 On these arguments see, for example, GGB 244 (14 Aug. 1807); 259 (6 Oct. 1807); 260 (9 Oct. 1807); CA 242 (21 Aug. 1807); 257 (13 Oct. 1807); 370 (11 Nov. 1808); *Ambigu* 169 (10 Dec. 1807), 501–4.
145 CA 242 (21 Aug. 1807).
146 See CA 244 (28 Aug. 1807); 252 (11 Sept. 1807).
147 See *Ambigu* 178 (10 Mar. 1808), 514–15.
148 Schroeder, *European politics*, 322, 329–32; Madelin, *Consulat et empire*, vi. 340–3. Schroeder notes that Canning and many Britons also believed that Tilsit was unpopular in Russia.

THE CHALLENGE OF BONAPARTE

through d'Antraigues, Pierre-François Fauche and others. In October 1807 Regnier warned Alexander that although he had little reason to fear a national revolution, because opinion could exercise its power in other ways, he ought paradoxically to fear a palace revolution by partisans of his French allies.[149] The warning had serious undertones. Russia's recent history made such alarms sound ominously credible: in fact Alexander feared a palace coup from elements opposed to Tilsit.[150] The disrespectful tone of this article, its suggestive menace, the distinction it drew between the current position of Alexander and the image he had presented, together with suggestions that he had abandoned his people's interest, provoked a permanent rift between Regnier and his Bourbon masters. Flagrant disrespect towards Alexander was not politic at a time when Louis XVIII was trying to win back Russian support in the belief that his hopes lay in Russia and Britain alone.[151] Indeed, such vehement attacks against legitimate sovereigns would probably not have been tolerated by the Bourbons at any time. Certainly, the *Gazette de la Grande-Bretagne* promised that it would never offend the ministers of legitimate sovereigns.[152] Such considerations mattered little to Regnier and d'Antraigues, who had other priorities, nor, one suspects, to Canning, their pragmatic paymaster. Indeed d'Antraigues went so far as to claim that the journal's purpose was to create and foster a national revolutionary consciousness to thwart any pro-French palace coup (see chapter 3). Whether such attacks on Alexander were systematic in the autumn of 1807 is unclear, because only this one edition of the *Courier d'Angleterre* survives from the period, but by early 1808 a yet more abusive attitude to Alexander had set in. For example, the Swedes' enthusiasm to enlist to fight the Russians was attributed to an aversion to Russian 'despotism'. Later, in November, Regnier described how Alexander's alliance with Napoleon forced him into tyranny.[153] However, the most offensive comments were made in an article attacking Napoleon's religious practices, in which Alexander was accused of apostasy.

> It is you, yourself [Alexander], it is your bishops, who by your orders told us that Buonaparté has successively worshipped several gods. Which has he ordered to be adored in Russia? . . . Successively, the timid worshipper of the prostitutes that his predecessor Robespierre raised on the altars – sectary of Mohammed in Egypt – persecutor of Jesus Christ in Europe – cruel and base tyrant over the unfortunate Pontiff that he has dishonoured – what god does Buonaparté worship; what god has this monster ordered you to worship? . . . is his name shrouded in the secret articles of the peace of Tilsit?[154]

---

[149] CA 257 (13 Oct. 1807).
[150] Jean Tulard, *Napoleon, the myth of the saviour*, trans. Teresa Waugh, London 1984, 299.
[151] See Canning papers, bundle 54, d'Avaray to de La Châtre, Gothenburg, 20 Oct. 1807 (copy). Bundle 59b contains a copy of the paper, with the offending article marked.
[152] GGB 160 (24 Oct. 1806).
[153] CA 317 (10 May 1808); 370 (11 Nov. 1808).
[154] CA 317 (10 May 1808).

The anti-Alexandrine rhetoric of the *Courier d'Angleterre* from 1809 to 1810 was scarcely more moderate. The hope that Alexander would return to his senses is combined with dire warnings that he would in time discover 'the full advantages' of French friendship. For the moment, however, Alexander was a lost cause. As the first rumours of Napoleon's proposal for a matrimonial alliance circulated, Regnier commented that he had no doubt that the tsar could neglect his duty to self, family and Russia far enough to offer Bonaparte his sister in marriage.[155] In the following edition Regnier reported, on supposedly good authority, that Alexander had only staved off the long-awaited revolution by dismissing Rumyantsev, his unpopular war minister Arakcheyev and Kuriakin, his pro-French ambassador to Paris.[156] The report was exaggerated, though Arakcheyev was indeed sacked at the end of 1809 and Rumyantsev's influence was on the wane. Despite the Spanish example, it required the invasion of Russia to fulfil Gentz and Regnier's conviction that: 'Europe, lost by her kings, can only be saved by her peoples.'[157]

Between 1807 and 1810 the *Courier de Londres* and the *Ambigu* were more circumspect towards Russia than the *Courier d'Angleterre*, although Peltier did indeed mock the alliance of 'the two friends'. He censured Russia's 'senseless' war with Turkey, but held Rumyantsev responsible.[158] He blamed the war for delaying Russia's rupture with France, but he maintained a long silence for fear of creating or destroying hopes.[159] Intriguingly, this parallels d'Antraigues's silence on Russia (see chapter 2), and may reflect a discrepancy between émigré hopes and ministerial policy.[160] In contrast, Gérard's *Courier de Londres* was full of rumours of rupture between France and Russia throughout early 1811.[161] Once war began in earnest, both Gérard and Peltier were in broad agreement. Russia was too strong and too large for Napoleon to attack successfully.[162] When he attacked regardless, they noted and applauded the tsar's plans to tire Napoleon by constantly retreating, while encouraging the idea that he should fight a 'national war'.[163] The Russian people's enthusiastic support for war, even after the fall of Moscow, and tales of French pillage, rape and destruction were all carefully recorded. Napoleon's bulletins were minutely analysed, contradicted, and supplemented with comments on the probable impact of the climate and supply factors.[164]

---

155 CA 502 (16 Feb. 1810).
156 *Alexey Andreevich Arakcheyev* (1769–1834), minister of war 1807–9; *Prince Alexander Borisovich Kuriakin* (1759–1829), Russian ambassador in Paris 1808–12.
157 Cited CA 370 (11 Nov. 1808). Regnier said the quote came from Gentz's *Etat politique de l'Europe*, which may indicate any one of several similar titles by Gentz.
158 *Ambigu* 263 (20 July 1810), 156–7; 310 (10 Nov. 1811), 302–3.
159 Ibid. 302.
160 PRO, FO 73/69, Regnier to [?Hamilton], 21/23 Aug. 1811.
161 See *CL* lxix/3 (8 Jan. 1811); 18 (1 Mar. 1811); 39 (4 May 1811); 52 (28 June 1811).
162 *CL* lxxi/38 (12 May 1812).
163 *Ambigu* 343 (10 Oct. 1812), 81; *CL* lxxii/5 (17 July 1812).
164 Ibid. 37 (6 Nov. 1812) and passim; *Ambigu* 344–7 (20 Oct.–20 Nov. 1812).

Finally, as the balance of the war swung towards the allies in the spring of 1813 and Alexander reinstated the Hamburg Senate, the *Courier de Londres* assured its readers that restoration, not conquest, was the Russian objective.[165]

Coverage of Spain, Portugal and Sweden followed similar lines to that of Russia, save that there was no subversive intent. Gérard, Regnier and Peltier all followed a similar vigorous policy. Spanish patriotic enthusiasm and religious zeal were marked, praised and recommended as a model for Europe. The generosity of their British allies, especially in urging loyalty in the Spanish colonies, was consistently defended, but Peltier's denunciation of Spanish divisions and the dangers of the Cortes's wartime reform programme, brought hostile fire from some Spanish readers.[166] However, when a council of regency replaced the Supreme Junta, he claimed that his assertions that the Spanish had been hampered by divided, indecisive leadership had been vindicated.[167] The Spanish war was seen from the first as a turning point.[168] It was argued that with total mobilisation and British support, Spain could only be defeated if her people deserted their *patrie*, their religion and their God.[169] Attempts were made to legitimise Spanish atrocities,[170] while denouncing those of the French,[171] and charitable subscriptions for the victims of the rapacious French retreat from Portugal in 1811 were supported enthusiastically.[172] In Sweden, Bernadotte was cultivated and flattered. It was repeatedly emphasised that his tenuous position could only be reinforced by identifying with his people and breaking with France.[173] Moreover, in 1813–14 the Swedish courtier, the comte De La Gardie, in London in a personal capacity, used the *Ambigu* to promote Bernadotte's image.[174]

The political and polemical campaigns of the émigré journalists mainly

---

[165] *CL* lxxiii/28 (6 Apr. 1813).
[166] See, for example, *Ambigu* 271 (10 Oct. 1810), 4–5; 278 (20 Dec. 1810), 644; 294 (30 May 1811), 482.
[167] See *Ambigu* 319 (10 Feb. 1812), 309–10.
[168] See *Ambigu* 190 (10 July 1808), 3–9; *CL* lxiii/47 (10 June 1808); 56 [sic] (12 July 1808); *CA* 325 (7 July 1808).
[169] *CA* 318 (15 May 1808); 341 (2 Aug. 1808); *Ambigu* 190 (10 July 1808), 3–9.
[170] See, for example, *CA* 328 (22 July 1808).
[171] See, for example, *Ambigu* 274 (10 Nov. 1810), 323–4: 290 (20 Apr. 1811), 146–7; *CL* lxix/32 (19 Apr. 1811).
[172] See the free publicity and donations for the Portuguese subscription ibid. 34–7 (26 Apr.–7 May 1811); *Ambigu* 291 (30 Apr. 1811), 267–74. Similar support was given to public subscriptions for Palm's widow in 1806, Russia in 1812 and Germany in 1813.
[173] See especially *CL* lxix/4 (11 Jan. 1811); 15 (19 Feb. 1811); lxxi/12 (11 Feb. 1812); lxxiv/15 (20 Aug. 1813). This last article was identical to that in *Ambigu* 373 (10 Aug. 1813), 264–70 (see next note).
[174] De La Gardie MSS, De La Gardie journal, 9, 22 Jan. 1814. These entries confirm that De La Gardie submitted the letter of Bernadotte to Crown Prince Oscar printed in *Ambigu* 388 (10 Jan. 1814), 95–6; he probably wrote or commissioned articles defending Bernadotte from attacks in the French papers in *Ambigu* 373 (10 Aug. 1813), 264–70, and *Ambigu* 381 (30 Oct. 1813), 249–50. The former article also appeared in *CL* lxxiv/15 (20 Aug. 1813).

addressed the converted, though they might occasionally sway sympathetic neutrals. However, the émigré journals were considerably more dangerous as vectors for potentially explosive information that was not freely or easily available from other sources. The importance of information, whether true or false, as a short-term stimulant to political action and emulation, should not be underestimated. It was vital both to the revolutionary domino effects of 1830, 1848 and 1989 and to the short-lived success of general Malet and his associates, who were able to seize power in Paris for twenty-four hours in 1812 after circulating rumours that Napoleon was dead. In most political decision-making, the link between information and action is impossible to discern, but none the less vital. But after 1803 the limited channels for obtaining fresh political information available to governments and individuals were drying up throughout Europe. As a result of Napoleon's control of the European press and posts, the closure of diplomatic and commercial networks and the unprecedented prevention of foreign travel, the press, private letters, diplomatic channels, merchants' correspondence, travellers' news and even the reports of often venal, self-seeking spies, became increasingly spasmodic and unreliable.

The émigré journalists were well aware that Napoleon was attempting to establish a monopoly over the supply of data upon which executive decisions and 'public opinion' were based.[175] In 1809 Peltier spelt out the danger categorically:

> This man, master of all the presses of the continent save those of Austria, has the greatest means to intercept all news which might reveal his true position to his enemies; and when he tells a diplomatic lie, or proclaims a victory that he has not won, the effect he desires has long been achieved by the time his imposture is discovered.[176]

Thus the French émigré journals worked hard to dissect, interpret and contradict the official *Moniteur* and *Bulletins de la grande armée*, and the *Gazette de la Grande-Bretagne* in its very first number promised that 'We intend to have the glory of delivering those who know no other language than French from the most odious and disastrous tyranny over intelligence and opinion.'[177]

What sort of information was valuable in the propaganda war? Where Napoleon imposed a news blackout, simple factual reporting might suffice. Napoleon's press often failed to report events in Spain for weeks at a time and it remained silent over the Austrian declaration of war in 1813.[178] And Bonaparte imposed a virtual news blackout over the incident Périvier styled

---

[175] See, for example, CA 393 (31 Jan. 1809), which claimed that papers printed in England were the only way to communicate truth to the continent.
[176] *Ambigu* 217 (10 Apr. 1809), 63.
[177] GGB 1 (16 Apr. 1805).
[178] See CA 354 (16 Sept. 1808); CL lxxiv/18 (31 Aug. 1813); 19 (3 Sept. 1813).

'the most sensational event of the age', the kidnapping, trial and execution of d'Enghien. Bonaparte, well aware of the negative impact of the affair, allowed a tiny notice to appear, but only in the *Moniteur*.[179] It is thus no coincidence that the imperial police were very concerned about the circulation of funereal orations to the young prince in pamphlet form inside France, notably that by the abbé Bouvens, formerly *grand-vicaire* at Arras, nor that the British government paid to have them printed.[180] News of Napoleon's excommunication, suppressed by the French government, was also circulated abroad by the émigré journals.

Juxtaposition of military sources was another important means of exploiting politically sensitive information, especially once coalition forces began winning land battles in the Peninsular War. The émigré papers published state papers from the *London Gazette* telling of British victories assiduously, but this was intended to inform their London readers as well as foreign audiences. Journalists drew systematic contrasts between the veracity of official British documents and the propagandist motives behind both Napoleon's dispatches and official documents published in the *Moniteur*. The French reports were so notorious for their mendacity that in 1812 Gérard could ridicule them in a mock decree: 'All the princes of the Confederation of the Rhine, the Senate and the inhabitants of my loyal city of Paris, are ordered to believe the *bulletins de la grande armée*. – [signed] Napoleon.'[181] Mocking Bonaparte's bulletins was also a favourite theme for British caricaturists.[182]

In their factual reporting, it was incumbent upon the journalists to prove that Napoleon exaggerated his strength and his abilities. In military terms they needed to prove that he was not invincible, but was sufficiently strong to require a combined effort if he were to be defeated. Generally, Napoleonic successes were blamed on treachery, good fortune and the incompetence, egotism and short-sighted self-interest of individual courts.[183] This was a delicate line to walk, especially as the journalists risked diplomatic complaints.[184] Thus on one occasion Peltier published a statement that appears to be a retraction. He abandoned the offending tract half-published and offered instead, as a form of apology, a servile and humiliating defence of Prussia's

---

[179] Périvier, *Napoleon journaliste*, 110.
[180] See Hauterive, *Police*, i, paras 97, 1073, 1258; AN, AF^{IV*} 1710, p. 151, no. 293, 'abbé Bouvens'; PRO, FO 27/71, receipt from abbé Bouvens, London, 26 May 1804.
[181] CL lxxii/24 (22 Sept. 1812).
[182] See George Cruickshank's celebrated 'Boney hatching a bulletin or snug winter quarters', which ridicules Napoleon's 27th bulletin (27 Oct. 1812). This print is reproduced in M. Dorothy George, *English political caricature, 1793–1832: a study of opinion and propaganda*, Oxford 1959, plate 53.
[183] See, for example, *Ambigu* 94 (10 Nov. 1805), 269–318, contrasting Nelson's glory at Trafalgar with Mack's treason at Ulm; CA 223 (16 June 1807).
[184] See Peltier's comments on this subject in *Ambigu* 102 (30 Jan. 1806), 183.

record of opposition to the revolution.¹⁸⁵ This was in clear contradiction of his frequent criticisms of the egoism of (unnamed) powers.

Statements on religious matters also worried Napoleon, who took the threat of religious intelligence seriously, writing on 20 June 1809: 'I hear the pope has excommunicated me. He is a raving lunatic who must be shut up.'¹⁸⁶ The émigré press also kept the exiled Bourbons in the public eye, partly to keep their émigré readership in touch with their ostensible leaders, but also for propaganda purposes. Publicity given to the statements and actions of the exiled Bourbons, however trivial, was considered dangerous by the Napoleonic regime. The royal family was only mentioned in the French press when absolutely necessary, as in reporting the Pichegru conspiracy in 1804.¹⁸⁷ The policy seemed to work. In August 1808 the *Courier* reported that French prisoners taken by the Russians were unaware that any Bourbons still survived.¹⁸⁸

Moreover, French agents scoured the *Courier de Londres* and the *Ambigu* for statements from the Bourbon princes and indications of their activities.¹⁸⁹ On 7 November 1804 Fouché informed Napoleon that a recent letter in the *Courier de Londres* 'appears to come from the Cabinet of Calmar' and indicated a change in Bourbon policy. It argued that a restoration need only consist of the return of the Bourbons and not necessarily an integral restoration of the *ancien régime*. Fouché correctly predicted that the letter would be followed by an address to the French people and army.¹⁹⁰ In early 1805 Louis XVIII issued the Declaration of Calmar (dated 2 December 1804) rejecting the reactionary Declaration of Verona (7 July 1795). The émigré press was, therefore, a *dépôt* for Bourbon declarations and sporadic calls for the allies to support a Bourbon restoration. After the retreat from Moscow these pleas became a clamour as the émigré press launched an important, but unsuccessful, campaign for the allies to adopt the restoration of the Bourbons as an explicit war aim.¹⁹¹

Suggestive presentation of information was also used as a weapon. Care continued to be taken to give impartial parliamentary reports. Even on issues such as the slave trade, where several of the journalists had strong views,

---

185 *Ambigu* 89 (20 Sept. 1805), 601n.
186 Tulard, *Napoleon*, 278.
187 Louis XVIII's correspondence with Pichegru appeared in the *Moniteur* on 19 July 1804. It was copied from the *Courier* (30 June), which had transcribed it from *Ambigu* 95 (30 June 1804/publ. 29 June). Peltier's source was J.-G.-M. Roques, comte de Montgaillard, *Mémoire concernant la trahaison de Pichegru dans les années 3, 4 et 5*, Paris germinal an XII, 147, 151. See Hauterive, *Police*, i, para. 27, police bulletin of 30 messidor XII (19 July 1804).
188 Cited in *Ambigu* 193 (10 Aug. 1808/publ. 22 August), 226.
189 Among copies of English papers preserved in Napoleon's daily bulletins on the British press from 1810 to 1812, in AN, AF^{IV} 1569–81, are eleven copies of the CL. This is more than any other title. See also references to both papers in Hauterive, *Police*.
190 CL lvi/31 (16 Oct. 1804); Hauterive, *Police*, i, para. 513, bulletin of 16 brumaire XIII (17 Nov. 1804).
191 See, especially, *Ambigu* 349 (10 Dec. 1812), 585–6; 350 (20 Dec. 1812), 670–4; CL lxxv/4 (14 Jan. 1814); 8 (28 Jan. 1814); 14 (18 Feb. 1814).

strict neutrality was observed. This was intended to prove that England enjoyed a model free constitution, was free from factional strife and had no hidden agenda. This would answer Napoleon's hostile portrayal of British politics and motives and inspire confidence in the stability and reliance that could be placed on the British government. Hence Regnier asked:

> Did Buonaparté, who represents the ever-present struggle of an opposition party against the ministry as the clash of factions tearing England apart, ... really believe the gentle tremors of a free constitution to be the shocks of anarchy, or did he merely wish to embitter certain cabinets, by depicting England as more occupied with her party interests than the destiny of Europe.[192]

Regnier went on to suggest that Talleyrand's portrayal of British parliamentary debates in the *Argus* and *Publiciste* was intended to encourage the British government to stop parliamentary reporting, because Napoleon had just closed his *Tribunat* and feared the comparison of English institutions with French.

Suggestive comment accompanied several other kinds of reporting. When a French paper reported the suicide of a pregnant woman, after first murdering her child, the *Courier de Londres* styled it a 'consequence of the new morality'.[193] Reports of a series of violent crimes in Switzerland, including horrific paedophile abuse and two murders, were given under the title: 'Sad effects of the influence of French manners on the formerly innocent, free and happy Swiss people.'[194] Brigandage, a perennial problem for revolutionary and Napoleonic governments, was said to be rife in France due to the collapse of order and the hypocritical observance of religious forms.[195] Equally, Regnier ran a number of features listing phrases uttered in praise of Bonaparte by officials and literary and public figures under titles such as 'Scenes de bassesse et d'adulation', while the benedictions of his bishops were styled 'Blasphêmes des évêques apostats'.[196]

Perhaps this particular use of suggestion was puerile, but other examples were perceptibly more dangerous. They included a *tableau* of France impoverished; tales of the continued strength of the British economy in the face of the embargo; the military and naval power of Napoleon's enemies; the strength and successes of the Spanish and Portuguese insurrectionists; signs of discontent in Germany; damaging rumours. All were potentially dangerous to morale, and liable perhaps to stimulate resistance.

However, the most enduring contribution of the émigré press in the struggle against Bonapartism was its central role in the evolution and

---

[192] CA 246 (4 Sept. 1807).
[193] CL liv/4 (12 July 1803).
[194] CL lvi/51 (25 Dec. 1804).
[195] CL liii/29 (12 Apr. 1803).
[196] CL lv/3 (11 Jan. 1804); 5 (18 Jan. 1804).

Plate 4. Cryptic vignette from *Ambigu* 10 (n.d. 1803). While the meaning of this illustration is unclear, it is probable that the puppet figure being spun around is intended to be Bonaparte. He is thus a man of many faces and a mere plaything of the Gods rather than the master of his own destiny. These were also common themes in anti-Napoleonic texts.

dissemination of a satirical anti-Napoleonic Black Legend. Anti-Napoleonic satire had a high profile in the émigré press. Often crude, vitriolic and in dubious taste, it must necessarily be defined very widely here. It should include anything intended to make Napoleon and his regime a object of fun, mockery or denigration. Although there are several studies of anti-Napoleonic caricature, the only significant treatments of the written satires of the Black Legend are Jean Tulard's *L'Anti-Napoléon: la légende noire de l'empereur* and John Ashton's *English caricature and satire on Napoleon I*.[197] Ashton's book treats each phase of Napoleon's life, offering a selection of materials in a chronological narrative framework; Tulard's study catalogues the main themes of the Black Legend in a thematic anthology drawn from pamphlets, most of them published in 1813–15. Yet although Ashton notes

---

[197] Jean Tulard, *L'Anti-Napoléon: la légende noire de l'empereur*, Paris 1965; John Ashton, *English caricature and satire on Napoleon I*, London 1888, repr. 1968. On caricature see George, *English caricature*; A. M. Broadley, *Napoleon in caricature, 1795–1821*, London 1911; Catherine Clerc, *La Caricature contre Napoléon*, Paris 1985.

that most British themes were drawn from French sources, neither work considers either the genesis of the anti-Napoleonic legend, nor its European dimension.[198] In both these contexts the émigré press played a vital role, for although a definitive study of the evolution of the Black Legend remains to be written, it is clear that London-based French-language publications were instrumental in two ways. They both passed anti-Napoleonic materials across linguistic frontiers in Europe and America and generated new materials and developed key themes.

The émigré press seems to have led London journalists, pamphleteers and caricaturists in generating new themes and offering anti-Napoleonic materials, especially during and prior to 1803, when, as recent work has highlighted, there was a transformation in the way Napoleon was portrayed in British popular culture. Prior to the peace of Amiens, Napoleon was depicted as a revolutionary general in the British press and popular ephemera, and popular images of Bonaparte were positive, or at least ambiguous.[199] After the cessation of hostilities he enjoyed an enormous wave of popularity, but following the renewal of war there was an unprecedented surge in the output of ephemera, much of it government propaganda, in which Napoleon was portrayed in 'negative and extreme' terms, and as a monstrous military dictator.[200] Allegations of French atrocities were repeated *ad nauseam*.[201] A similar pattern can be seen in the development of British caricature depictions of Napoleon.[202]

With their personal commitment to opposing the revolution, whatever its form, and an audience predisposed to favour this opposition, the émigré journalists had a head start on British propagandists. Thus as early as May 1797 Peltier hinted that Napoleon's younger siblings were the bastard offspring of the French governor of Corsica, the comte de Marboeuf, and in July 1800 he endorsed an assertion in a pamphlet entitled *Mon dernier mot sur Buonaparte* that Marboeuf was also Napoleon's father.[203] The latter allegation is a chronological impossibility, for as the previous article made clear, Napoleon's conception pre-dated Marboeuf's arrival on Corsica. This preoccupation

---

[198] Ashton, *English caricature and satire*, 12, 134. In contrast both issues are treated with regards to caricature in Broadley, *Napoleon in caricature*.
[199] See Philip Gray, 'Revolutionism as revisionism: early British views of Bonaparte, 1796–1803', unpubl. MA thesis, Canterbury, NZ 1995. Stella Cottrell, 'English views of France and the French, 1789–1815', unpubl. DPhil diss. Oxford 1990, 248, argues that in 1801–2 Napoleon was 'metamorphosed into a great leader of admirable qualities', but her view is misleading, since it fails to show the enormous difference between British views of Bonaparte before and after this period.
[200] Cottrell, 'English views', 250.
[201] Ibid. 236, notes that 177 out of 250 pieces in her survey of patriotic literature refer to French atrocities, with 162 referring to Napoleon's campaign in Egypt and Syria, where the notorious massacres and poisonings at Jaffa allegedly occurred.
[202] See George, *English caricature*. See also Broadley, *Napoleon in caricature*; Ashton, *English caricature and satire*.
[203] *Paris* 109 (15 May 1797), 1–3n.; 208 (31 July 1800), 409.

with sexual slander continued a tradition of pornographic libels dating back to the *Gazetier cuirassé* and perpetuated in the anti-Marie-Antoinette pamphlets produced by the revolutionary left and the scurrilous attacks on revolutionary leaders in Peltier's *Actes des apôtres* and exile journals in the 1790s. In exile, Peltier also invented materials concerning Napoleon's siblings, most notably Pauline Borghese, and his libels gave rise to Pauline's enduring reputation as a notorious wanton.[204] He describes her running through Marseilles in 1795 seeking bread, her spirits raised by the news that Napoleon 'has killed lots of Parisians'. In the evening her mother allows her to receive soldiers to distract her from her sufferings, 'in amusements in which innocence might run risks', but which she greatly enjoys. Later, profiting from Napoleon's elevation, she seeks to excel his military conquests by her amorous ones.[205] Elsewhere Peltier claims that she had lesbian passions and Couchery writes of an incestuous affair with Napoleon.[206] Some of the original detail offered by Peltier in 1797–1803 suggests that he had a Corsican informant, almost certainly Pasquale Paoli or one of his small group of followers (see chapter 2), to supply stories of Napoleon's childhood, family and their revolutionary history. Couchery too made an original contribution to the political–pornographic aspect of the Black Legend cycle in 'Le Moniteur secret', but by the time it appeared in the *Ambigu*, British libellists such as Stewarton and Lewis Goldsmith had also developed licentious stories of the Bonaparte clan.[207]

In addition to inventing and developing many themes of the legend, the journals of Regnier, Peltier, Couchery and their collaborators, together with those of Gérard and Heron, were a major mechanism for the translation, transmission and dissemination of the seminal texts of the Black Legend cycle. The works of Stewarton, Robert Wilson, Lewis Goldsmith, Castanos, d'Ivernois, Gentz, d'Antraigues, Sarrazin and many others, whether sober or satirical, grace the pages of the émigré journals, especially the *Ambigu*. Other propagandists then drew upon their anthological arsenal. For example, Peltier and Regnier's use of the title 'envoyé de Dieu' was imitated by British papers such as the *Morning Post*, which referred to Napoleon as 'God's envoy'. The one limitation on the journals, however, was their inability to draw upon British caricature tradition, which was perhaps the best propaganda instrument of all. As Dorothy George has remarked, as the Napoleonic empire finally collapsed and especially after Bonaparte's defeat at Leipzig in the Battle of the Nations, anti-Napoleonic caricatures enjoyed common

---

[204] On this point see Len Ortzen, *Imperial Venus: the story of Pauline Bonaparte Borghese*, London 1974, 41. *Pauline* (1780–1825), Napoleon's sister, married first General Victor Leclerc, and second Prince Camillo Borghese.
[205] *Ambigu* 27 (n.d./Dec. 1803), 221–3.
[206] Ibid. 224; 'Moniteur secret', no. 10, in *Ambigu* 290 (20 Apr. 1811), 175.
[207] See Goldsmith, *Secret history*; H. Stewarton, *The secret history of the court of Saint-Cloud*, London 1806.

Plate 5. Vignette representing the massacre at Jaffa, from *L'Ambigu* 15 (n.d. 1803). The text of the incident refers to a tale told by Robert Wilson in a footnote to his *British expedition to Egypt*, 73, when a French aide-de-camp noticed Napoleon smiling at the remark of a Turkish prisoner and whispered 'He is saved', to his companion, who replied 'You know not Bonaparte, that smile, I speak from experience, does not proceed from the sentiment of benevolence.' The prisoner was duly shot.

currency across Europe, with much copying from country to country.[208] The limitations preventing these caricatures from circulating in the émigré journals were linguistic, technical and economic – the cost of engraved plates remained prohibitive until the 1840s when weekly and monthly illustrated magazines began to address mass markets, especially if translation was required. Thus, ironically, even though British caricature art was in its heyday, Peltier and his colleagues were unable to use it. The only exceptions are the prints that illustrate the first three volumes of the *Ambigu*. These include the famous vignette of Napoleon as sphinx and another, produced by Peltier's printer, in which Napoleon is shown smiling at a Turkish soldier who has provided valuable local information at Jaffa. One of Bonaparte's com-

---

[208] George, *British caricature*, 141, 147–8. On different national caricature styles see Broadley, *Napoleon in caricature*. Clerc, *La Caricature contre Napoléon*, convincingly demonstrates the extensive influence of British, and to a lesser extent other European, caricatures on French caricature art after 1812. However, despite her insistence on the importance of caricature as a new strategy for opposition under Napoleon, no more than 10 of the 178 caricatures she produces predate 1812, and only 18 at most predate Napoleon's fall in 1814.

panions remarks naively that this must mean the man will be spared, but his companion replies sardonically that clearly he does not know the general very well (see plate 5). A second print appears to depict the notorious poisonings at Jaffa (see plate 6 and pp. 216–17 below).

Tulard argues that the Black Legend was originally composed of two strands, a liberal and a reactionary critique, but that the liberal anti-Bonapartism found in France in 1814–15 soon collapsed. The most important factors contributing to its demise were Napoleon's much publicised conversion to liberalism during the Hundred Days; the healing effect of time; and disenchantment with the *ennui* and conservatism of the restoration period and its kings. In consequence, the memory of Napoleon's achievements and military exploits was increasingly romanticised. The desertion of the liberal anti-Bonapartist propagandists left the field clear for the reactionaries. Their legend, a monstrous, exaggerated, repetitious, usually satirical portrayal of Napoleon strangled the liberal and moderate critique of Napoleon at birth but was too extreme and too ephemeral to take root in the popular imagination. It rapidly faded in the face of a positive virile counter-myth of Napoleon the Saviour, skilfully abetted by the hero himself through Las Cases's *Mémorial de Sainte-Helena*. It thus prepared the way for the intellectual and emotional triumph of Bonapartism in France.[209]

The bulk of Tulard's study surveys the main themes of the Black Legend of Napoleon, primarily in the words of the restoration pamphleteers. However, their portrayal of Napoleon, his internal achievements, his abilities, his foreign policy and his family and friends follows a formula developed and popularised in the exile press. The reactionary critique of Bonaparte thus had deeper roots than the liberal strand of the Black Legend even before the restoration.

According to the émigré satirists, Napoleon's character reflected his origins. He was, as all anti-Bonapartist propagandists stressed, 'le Corse':

> Buonaparté is Corsican . . . he was born in a country that Seneca painted in the most odious colours, be it the climate, be it the inhabitants; in a country where the most stoical of philosophers could not console himself for having been exiled. . . . Since the truthful Seneca wrote, Corsica has not changed . . . she has still not yet reached a true state of civilisation . . . the local *mores* are ferocious, vengeance atrocious, and murders far more frequent than in any other part of Europe.[210]

Hence his character 'combines Italian treacherousness, French impetuosity, and the bloody tendencies observed . . . among the Corsicans'.[211]

The circumstances of Bonaparte's birth were also important. When Peltier

---

[209] Tulard, *Anti-Napoléon*. Clerc, *La Caricature contre Napoléon*, stresses similar themes in the history of the Black Legend.
[210] *Ambigu* 138 (30 Jan. 1807), 196.
[211] *Ambigu* 192 (30 July 1808), 134.

imagined a new Bayeux tapestry to celebrate Napoleon's life, the first panel was a nativity scene depicting Marboeuf, 'gazing at him with the tenderness of a father', accompanied by the caption 'Napoleon the legitimate, 15 August 1769'. The second panel showed Marboeuf paying off his lover's husband with letters of nobility and a pension.[212] The story of Marboeuf recurs repeatedly, just as it did in English caricature and satire.[213] When Napoleon published documents concerning the forced abdications of Charles IV and Ferdinand VII of Spain, Regnier, entitled them 'Documents published by Napoleon Buonaparté (son) of Carlo Buonaparté or the comte de Marboeuf, to prove that he was born King of Spain at Ajaccio in Corsica.'[214] Thus the illegitimacy of Napoleon's power was mirrored by the circumstances of his birth. However, the propagators of this often-repeated calumny were inconsistent and appear therefore to have expected their readers to accept it as a humorous allegory. Both Peltier and Regnier offered other versions of Napoleon's unimmaculate conception.[215]

The delineation of Napoleon's character matches Tulard's formula. Peltier defined him in the title of his journal as '*L'Ambigu* [the ambiguous one]'. However, this title was intended to indicate two contrasting pictures of Bonaparte: the claim that he was respected, adored and secure juxtaposed against the ambition, despotism and nepotism by which he prepared all the trappings of a throne.[216] It was not intended to indicate a complex character. The main traits of this portrayal and many others are repeated ceaselessly in the émigré journals. Napoleon's ambition was the most constant theme. Ambition alone was his morality, whether he was chasing a crown, a reputation, or conquest. Thus in 1807 Regnier observed: 'We will see that he has determined to squander the last drop of French blood in order to achieve the chimerical plans of his disordered ambition. He counts as nothing the blood and tears of the French people.'[217]

Napoleon was portrayed as habitually violent, an 'august epileptic', prone to violent fits of rage followed by remorse.[218] Couchery imagined a typical weekly balance-sheet drawn up to explain how much this rage cost him in gifts and compensation to his victims. He records Napoleon punching his Austrian second wife, Marie-Louise, because he took her sighs as expressions of homesickness; sexually assaulting her chambermaid and slapping his secre-

---

[212] *Ambigu* 28 (10 Jan. 1804), 14–15.
[213] On this point see especially Ashton, *English caricature and satire*, 12.
[214] CA 505 (27 Feb. 1810).
[215] See, for example, *Ambigu* 131 (20 Nov. 1806), 336; CL lv/40 (18 May 1804); CA 219 (2 June 1807).
[216] *Ambigu* 2 (n.d. July/Aug. 1802), 25.
[217] CA 207 (21 Apr. 1807).
[218] CA 508 (9 Mar. 1810).

Plate 6. Vignette (presumably) representing the poisoning of French soldiers at Jaffa, from *Ambigu* 14 (n.d. 1803)

tary. He kicks his *aide-de-camp* and calls Maury a hypocrite and Pauline a whore.[219]

But according to the émigré publicists, such viciousness was not just frustration and apoplexy: it was tinged with sadism. Peltier claimed that Napoleon was a secret witness to Moreau's interrogation, Pichegru's fatal torturing and d'Enghien's execution, all of which he enjoyed immensely.[220] Other tales repeated by the émigré press sounded more credible. Robert Wilson's *History of the British campaign in Egypt* provided the standard atrocity stories and was often cited. According to Wilson, Napoleon ordered the massacre of Turkish prisoners at Jaffa and the poisoning of 500 sick French soldiers, to stop the contagion spreading and clear places in the hospital.[221] Both stories may have had a factual basis, but ignored key mitigating factors, notably that Bonaparte was without supplies, his army weakened and desperate to retreat. Since it appears that the Turkish prisoners had been captured under arms for the second time, having previously been released after swearing not to fight against the French again, he acted justifiably, if mercilessly, by the standards of the day. Likewise, critically ill with plague, his troops could expect a worse fate than poisoning if captured by the Turks. In fact it is doubtful that the latter incident occurred, especially on the scale described. Nevertheless, the epithet 'poisoner of Jaffa' was to remain a stock-in-trade for the anti-Napoleonic propagandists.

Napoleon's character was presented as ill-formed to run any empire, let alone a French one. He was ungallant to women and lacked ability and grace when speaking French. But then again he was an Italian islander: hence, after 1802, save for Gérard, the émigré writers always spelt his name Buonaparté. It was also alleged that Napoleon lacked 'esprit':

> Several people are employed to prepare the responses that the Consul will need to improvise during his journey [through Normandy] ... these morsels of erudition will be slipped into the replies to the *conseils généraux*, and are intended to prove to the literary societies in the *départements* that the Consul knows how to read.[222]

The assertion that Napoleon was a charlatan and boorish *parvenu* was designed to de-mystify his regime and to juxtapose the crudeness of his power and hollowness of his glory against the majesty and refinement of Louis XIV. Peltier argued that Napoleon was a greater threat to France than Robespierre because he was boorishly destroying the national character.[223] The émigré

---

[219] 'Moniteur secret', no. 8, in *Ambigu* 287 (20 Mar. 1811). Partially cited in Tulard, *Anti-Napoleon*, 91–2.
[220] *Ambigu* 192 (30 July 1808/publ. 10 Aug.), 134.
[221] Wilson, *British expedition to Egypt*, 72–3. For references to these tales see, for example, *Ambigu* 102 (30 Jan. 1806), 198
[222] CL liii/33 (26 Apr. 1803).
[223] *Ambigu* 192 (30 July 1808/publ. 10 Aug.), 128.

writers charged him with grossness in his language, use of revolutionary terminology, and technical inaccuracies. His speech was 'that of a *parvenu* who uses his native bourgeois idiom and adapts it to his [new] high station'.[224] By implication, he was unfit from birth for higher office.

It was even possible to mock Napoleon's military record, although prior to 1810 morale-boosting ammunition was scant. The retreat from St Jean d'Acre in Syria in 1799 was perennially derided precisely because, other than Napoleon's desertion of his army in Egypt, it was the only example of Napoleon in retreat. Thus Peltier alleged that when Chateaubriand struggled to find a rhyme for 'sacre' in a poem commemorating the 18 Brumaire, his friend Fontanes tentatively suggested 'massacre', 'simulacre' and 'St Jean d'Acre'.[225] The only other ray of hope was France's dismal naval record and the failure of the sea-borne missions to Egypt and Saint-Domingue. Thus in 1803 Regnier reported that Napoleon was generously constructing ships for the British navy at his own expense and in 1807 when Jerome Bonaparte, already an admiral, was appointed a general, he could taunt 'How fortunate Napoléon is to have such a family, composed of amphibious princes.'[226]

Napoleon's religion remained a favourite matter for comment. Far from applauding his enlightened toleration, Peltier styled Napoleon 'the Atheist of the Tuileries', a title which caught on.[227] Likewise, as we have seen, when Alexander I invoked God's blessing for the treaty of Tilsit, Regnier asked to which of Napoleon's many gods he was referring. But Napoleon did believe in something, as Regnier explained: 'He believes above all in omens taken from chance expressions, and from his wife and his favourite fortune-teller; he also places great faith in the auguries of little Ali, son of Madame Leclerc.'[228] Regnier took the myth of Napoleon's providential destiny seriously enough to seek to dispel it by observing that the idea of an 'irresistible destiny' was not unique to Napoleon: 'Almost all the monsters who have exercised boundless military power in this world have had a conviction that they will succeed in everything until the very moment of their downfall.'[229]

Napoleon's family also came under fire. His mother, Madame Mère, was characterised as ignorant and stupid, as well as an adultress. When she withdrew from a convocation of the *Chapître-Général* of the *Soeurs de la Charité*, an order under her presidency, Peltier attributed it to fear of displaying her ignorance and incapacity publicly.[230] Josephine was the butt of racial jibes, both because she originally came from Martinique and because when Peltier labelled the imperial couple 'two august mulattos' he implicitly linked them

---

[224] CA 247 (8 Sept. 1807).
[225] *Ambigu* 5 (n.d./Sept. 1802), 109.
[226] CA 209 (28 Apr. 1807).
[227] *Paris* 195 (15 Jan. 1800), 118.
[228] CA 345 (16 Aug. 1808).
[229] CA 329 (21 June 1808).
[230] *Ambigu* 172 (10 Jan. 1808), 55.

with atrocities committed by the mulattos on Saint-Domingue.[231] She was promiscuous too: 'the chaste Helen whom Bonaparte received from Barras' and 'the widow of the Committee of Public Safety'.[232] It was alleged that the Parisians called her 'the impure actress', a vicious tautology given that 'impures' were prostitutes, as, in the popular imagination, were most actresses.[233] When the *Moniteur* claimed that her return to Paris had brought gaiety back to the city, Regnier said it proved she was still 'a woman of pleasure';[234] when her son Eugène took the title 'de France', Peltier said it was 'to indicate [all] who helped to father him'.[235]

Napoleon's relationship with Josephine was portrayed as stormy. She was an obstacle to his ambitions and thus his family disliked her.[236] Josephine was a liability: she tried to learn etiquette and regal deportment from books, but proved a slow learner.[237] Yet, as Regnier pointed out, Caracalla [sic] had made a horse consul, so why not elevate Josephine?[238] Napoleon's devotion to Josephine was total: he was 'completely enslaved to his wife' and preferred 'her family to his own'.[239] This preference was unmanly and unnatural. Moreover, Napoleon was unable to dominate in his own household: Regnier allows us to eavesdrop on a matrimonial row in which Josephine insists on keeping her *sisebeo* because Napoleon has kept his favourite Mameluke bodyguard.[240] By implication, his inability to command in his own house reflects his incapacity to rule.

Napoleon's inability to control the sexual proclivities of his sister Pauline or to command the respect of his mother; Jérome's choice of wife; the government of Louis in the Low Countries; as well as frequent descriptions of imaginary family rows, were all grist to this mill. In general, attacks on him and his family dominate the Black Legend material. Once the regime was established, few libels were aimed at his courtiers and administrators, who are portrayed *en masse* as cynical time-servers, with no love or loyalty for their master. Rare examples of attacks on his servants included Peltier's vitriol against Maury and Heron's publication of extracts from Stewarton's *Secret history of the court of Saint-Cloud*, which detail Talleyrand's expenditure on his seraglio, and describe the instruction in seduction he gave to female spies.[241] However, direct attacks on the person of the ruler and his family were by

---

[231] *Ambigu* 73 (10 Apr. 1805), 62.
[232] *Ambigu* 58 (10 Nov. 1807), 281.
[233] *Ambigu* 43 (10 June 1804), 438; 46 (10 July 1804), 59.
[234] CA 191 (24 Feb. 1807).
[235] *Ambigu* 102 (6 Jan. 1806), 189.
[236] See, for example, CL liii/27 (5 Apr. 1803).
[237] Ibid. 5 (18 Jan. 1803); 33 (26 Apr. 1803).
[238] Ibid. 28 (1 Apr. 1803). This comment possibly alluded to an earlier 'bon mot' which styled Josephine a mare because she had had a 'beau harnois'.
[239] *Ambigu* 102 (6 Jan. 1806), 189.
[240] CA 245 (1 Sept. 1807).
[241] GGB 31–2 (30 July–2 Aug. 1805).

nature a de-mystification of the usurper: few *libellistes* dared to attack the person of the monarch directly prior to the revolution.

The portrayal of Napoleon's brothers and sisters was probably the most original contribution of the émigré journalists to the Black Legend. Although Pauline was the most notorious, the whole family shared an appetite for sexual debauchery. This was a theme repeated *ad nauseam* by restoration pornographers,[242] but the émigré journalists set the tone. Lucien was so debauched that even Josephine blushed to call on him.[243] An uncle, Cardinal Fesch, was a charitable sort, who on his arrival in Rome repudiated his own mistress in favour of his predecessor's, thus saving her from poverty.[244] It was even suggested that Napoleon's wife and sisters would be keen to help finance Napoleon's coronation by prostituting themselves among his senators. This would also contribute to the re-population of France.[245]

Napoleon's own sexual proclivities were the subject of contradictory defamations. Prior to 1810 he was sometimes accused of impotence.[246] But he was also accused of incest with Josephine's daughter, Hortense, who was also his sister-in-law by virtue of her marriage to Louis Bonaparte. When Hortense's five-year-old son died, Peltier described him as: 'the nephew, the grandson, perhaps even the son of the greatest monarch in the world'.[247] Thus in the greatest breach of faith of all Napoleon cuckolded his brother to ravish his stepdaughter. Later, after his marriage to Marie-Louise, Napoleon began to be portrayed as a sex monster. The act of seizing the daughter of one of the royal houses of Europe by conquest transformed him metaphorically into a rapist. Couchery depicts him visiting Josephine after the marriage, begging to continue their sexual relationship. When neither he nor his religious henchmen, Cardinal Maury and the abbé de Pradt, can overcome her scruples, he takes her by force.[248] Couchery also tells how two maids were mysteriously raped in the Tuileries, in the hope that they could provide a son to substitute in case Marie-Louise produced a daughter.[249] Marie-Louise, of course, was above reproach.

However, the best opportunity to integrate the different strands of the Black Legend was a Bonaparte wedding. These gave the journalists the opportunity to pour out their vitriol and scorn towards the new dynasty and to portray Napoleon at his most monstrous:

> He wishes not only to dethrone kings, to render them his accomplices, to force them to despoil one another, and . . . to force them to carry the effigy of their

---

[242] For examples see Tulard, *Anti-Napoleon*.
[243] CL liv/13 (15 Feb. 1803).
[244] Ibid.
[245] CL lvi/10 (3 Aug. 1804).
[246] See, for example, *Ambigu* 62 (20 Oct. 1807), 593.
[247] *Ambigu* 148 (10 May 1807), 297.
[248] 'Moniteur secret', no. 35, in *Ambigu* 316 (10 Jan. 1812), 84–91.
[249] 'Moniteur secret', no. 31, in *Ambigu* 310 (10 Nov. 1811), 313–26.

tyrant, suspended on a cord stained in the blood of their peoples on their breasts; he wants, moreover, to soil their own blood with the impure mixture of his own, and to menace them with these shameful alliances, in order that their opprobrium would stand the test of events and time, and that the memory of them will be as the torments of Hell, terrible and eternal.... there is no comparable tyranny save that of the Minotaur who used to require six of the most distinguished girls in order to cut their throats: but at least he cut their throats: to see him and to die were at once the torture and the end of the torture.[250]

Though the image is still repulsive it has the strangely ephemeral ring typical of the extremism of the Black Legend. The legend was polluted from its very inception by exaggerated images and a growing irrelevance, which became tedious with repetition. Such denigration of Napoleon had little to offer Restoration France, and contradicted French historic and patriotic aspirations. Though liberal criticisms of Napoleon's militarism, ceaseless bloodletting, relentless conscription, authoritarianism and curbs on civil liberties are found in the émigré journals, they were presented as part of a formula in which the incorporation of satirically exaggerated vitriol and declamation were taken for granted. Thus a realistic critique of the regime was undermined by absurdities. Having adopted a European rationale for resisting Napoleon, having made of him and his regime a tale to terrify foreign children, the Black Legend the émigré journalists created was bound to be stillborn in France. In making Napoleon repulsive, they had rendered their myth unpalatable. Only where a nationalist or liberal input existed as a palliative was their mix digestible. Thus the émigré journalists promoted an anti-Bonapartist sentiment capable of prospering in much of Europe but not in France.

This error was compounded by the failure of the émigré publicists to develop a patriotic rationale or positive programme for Bourbonism. Their entire argument was that restoration would bring peace in Europe through social order in France, but this implicitly abnegated the expansionist traditions of the *ancien régime* and thus denied the Bourbons their patriotic historical mission. The ideological baggage that they brought to the restored regime was almost entirely negative. Thus the émigré press was as much a cause as a symptom of the gaping ideological hole at the centre of the Bourbon restoration.

[250] CA 248 (11 Sept. 1807) on finding a wife for Jérome.

Conclusion

Although émigré journals never matched Linguet's *Annales* or the early *Courier de l'Europe* for circulation or celebrity, the French émigré press enjoyed commercial success on a scale which few, if any, exile media have matched since. This success had both structural and circumstantial causes. The leading émigré journalists were, for the most part, experienced and skilled journalists, but other factors were equally important. The near universality of the French language among the political and social élites of Europe and a tradition of French extra-territorial publishing predisposed readers in their favour. The technological factors that limited the production levels of all newspapers in the period and the taxes that reduced the comparative advantages of domestic British competitors were also important. So, too, was the existence of specialist printers in London, the city's socio-economic importance, the advantages of its geographical position for news-gathering and dissemination and the concentration of the émigré community in England in the capital. Moreover, the almost persistent state of war between Britain and France from early 1793 made the papers increasingly attractive as propaganda vehicles to the British government and her allies. This interest increased as a result of the French government's attempts to control and suppress the exile journals.

The journals were even more successful from a political point of view. This was due not so much to the size of their audience, but its composition and the manner in which the émigré press addressed it. The target audience included royalty, ministers, ambassadors, prominent statesmen and politicians throughout Europe and the Caribbean, as well as propagandists, merchants, émigrés and francophone readers in Europe and its colonies. The exile press offered these people something they could not find easily elsewhere: a regular flow of recent, uncensored information on French, British, European and colonial politics. At the same time, through repetition and continuous suggestion, it promoted the counter-revolutionary ideas of the journalists and their Bourbon, British and other patrons. This explains why Napoleon tried so hard to suppress émigré journals throughout Europe, even to the extent of fatally jeopardising a tactical peace with Britain in the process. Finally, after 1803, the émigré press became the primary means for disseminating information and propaganda to back British policy imperatives to European notables.

Yet despite the importance of their objectives and their relatively small circulations, the émigré papers remained relatively autonomous of their political patrons. In consequence this study concludes that by the late eighteenth century, and possibly earlier, British newspapers were indeed primarily commercial ventures, dependent on subscription levels for direct revenue and to attract advertisers, and hence their relations with patrons were contingent. Newspapers did not need political sponsorship merely to survive and could not afford to pursue an unpopular editorial line. Thus, considering the sums involved, the role of political corruption in the British press in the period seems to have been exaggerated. Even before mechanisation made newspaper production a highly capitalised industry, the British press enjoyed considerable independence.

The propaganda practices of the British and their émigré journalist auxiliaries have interesting ramifications for Habermas's theory of the public sphere, and suggest several useful lines for its further revision. Habermas's theory is, of course, a sociological model, and does not pretend to cover specific historical contingencies, even those as significant as revolutions. Nevertheless, Habermas contends that by the late eighteenth century, a political public sphere was emerging across Europe that had the power to influence political decisions. His political public sphere was a space that was separate and independent from government, and fundamentally 'bourgeois' in that it was sociologically distinct from both the 'people' and the 'court'.[1]

It is clear that the British government propaganda campaign after 1803 did indeed wish to influence a pan-European opinion in order to influence policy. However, this opinion belonged to a very narrow political élite, an 'inner public' of individuals close to the centre of government, who had the power to influence policy directly. If these individuals formed part of a pan-European public sphere, it was far from 'bourgeois'. Indeed, given its constitution, we might almost call it a 'courtly public sphere', although clearly, and significantly, it was not entirely separate from a wider public sphere. While these observations do not invalidate Habermas's contentions, it is surely suggestive that the government of the state that, according to Habermas, had the most advanced public sphere, chose to by-pass 'bourgeois' public opinion and aim its continental propaganda at a 'courtly' public. Nor was this merely an example of traditional thinking by the British government, for as this study has shown, this policy was new in the decade after 1800. Thus the British government perceived a 'bourgeois public sphere' to be of peripheral influence in the formation of 'opinion' and government policy in continental Europe.

Moreover, the independence of the public sphere proved extremely precarious when faced with a hegemonic government intent on suppressing it. The French state was remarkably successful in its attempts to restrict discussion and information flows within the 'public sphere' not only within, but also beyond its borders. The effects of this collapse of the European public sphere and the pan-European information system require urgent consideration by historians and need to be assimilated into conventional accounts of the international politics of the period. Moreover, the ease with which the

---

[1] Habermas, *Structural transformation*.

French government was able to manipulate and control the European information system suggests that the 'public sphere' was very shallowly rooted in much of continental Europe prior to 1815, if it existed at all. It seems therefore that Habermas's chronology for the development of the public sphere in most of continental Europe outside France is in need of revision. In those countries the triumph of a 'bourgeois public sphere', if it occurred at all, came considerably later than he contends, and certainly after the period under discussion in this book. It had not superseded or become wholly separate from a 'courtly' public sphere by the end of the Napoleonic period. Moreover its supremacy was short-lived. Certainly it did not survive the First World War, by which time a third formation, a 'popular' public sphere, a phenomenon produced by mass consumption societies and modern democratic politics, had emerged in many European states.

This study also exposes a number of apparent myths concerning the politics of the counter-revolution and emigration. In particular, it suggests that the antipathy between the *monarchiens* and other émigré groups, especially the princes, in the later 1790s has been exaggerated, and in consequence that the princes have been accused of extreme inflexibility. Harvey Mitchell concluded that the failure of attempts to orchestrate a counter-revolution internally between 1794 and 1797 stemmed from the inability of d'Artois and the *purs* to work effectively with the *monarchiens* and to reassure moderate counter-revolutionaries inside France that a restored Bourbon regime would respect the gains of 1789.[2] After Fructidor 'Britain and her royalist allies reverted to their hopes of overthrowing the Republic by a combination of external military pressure and internal insurrection.'[3] This has remained the consensus view of historians ever since.[4] However, the princes' relations with the émigré press suggest that they did learn some important lessons from Fructidor, and did not abandon hopes of an internal counter-revolution altogether. They appear to have concluded both that they could not succeed by constitutional means without allies in the Executive Directory supported by a majority in the legislative councils and that it was necessary to continue to follow a variety of strategies to achieve a restoration. Thus they did not wholly abandon attempts to achieve internal counter-revolution by constitutional or quasi-constitutional means, side-by-side with efforts for restoration by force. As a result they appear to have been willing to form tactical alliances with the *monarchiens*, who seem to have entertained closer relations with them than either side cared to admit. Unfortunately, this policy came unstuck in the summer of 1799, when Louis XVIII proved unwilling to alienate his *pur* followers by avowing the sentiments expressed in Malouet's article in the *Mercure britannique* (see chapters 3 and 4).

In addition, it appears that in the 1790s the British government did not

---

2   Mitchell, *Underground war*, esp. pp. 244–55.
3   Ibid. 254.
4   See, for example, the synthesis by Roberts, *Counter-revolution*, 13.

have the general preference for the *purs* that has usually been supposed, and that the main source for this belief is the self-serving memoir sources of the *monarchien* circle. Instead, while it used intelligence, advice and services from all comers, the ministry wavered between *purs* and *monarchiens* and could be equally aloof and parsimonious to all. The same *monarchien* sources propagated images of an emigration bitterly divided. It would be perverse to deny that very real ideological differences existed or that different émigré groups blamed one another for many of the events of the revolution – indeed their divisions and recriminations are very evident on the pages of the émigré press. However, since the émigré press was one of the major forums in which they were vented, and disputes in the press were aggravated by Peltier's splenetic prose, it does seem that some of these divisions have been exaggerated.

Nevertheless, the evidence of exile journalism supports previous studies of the counter-revolution in several respects. Certainly there was a general consensus among the émigré journalists that the *ancien régime* was in need of some reform, even if only in practice rather than substance.[5] Moreover, it is clear that the émigré journalists, like their political masters and allies, often fundamentally misunderstood the nature of discontent inside France and motives for internal counter-revolution, and helped to propagate their errors, sometimes with fatal results.

However, the counter-revolutionary views of the émigré journalists were far from static, at least until 1802. Their ideologies and interpretations of the revolution evolved over time in response to events and, in the cases of Peltier, the abbé Calonne and the *monarchien* journalists, underwent significant realignments. By the late 1790s the émigré journalists had developed a range of interpretations of the revolution and its continuing dynamic which conditioned their individual reactions to Napoleon. The *pur* journalists, seeing in Bonaparte's regime nothing more than a continuation of usurpation and disorder, rejected the Napoleonic compromise. In contrast, the *monarchiens* rallied to Napoleon because he seemed to offer effective executive rule through a centralised bureaucratic state; an apparent return to order; and the reversal of revolutionary policies on religion and the social order. This was the message they sold to the émigrés. In consequence this study endorses Robert Griffith's contention that the *monarchiens* were not really anglophiles. Instead, their enthusiasm for Bonaparte stemmed from *étatist* principles.

If this enthusiasm for *étatist* principles is the key to understanding the practical strength of the Napoleonic compromise among the French élite, Napoleon's fundamental achievement was to restore the early revolutionary consensus and realise many of the goals of the monarchic reformers of the *ancien régime*. The early revolutionaries aimed to 'regenerate' France not just politically and economically, but also militarily and even morally: and so '*régénération*' became a key term in the revolutionary lexicon of 1788–9 'in

---

[5] These points have been particularly emphasised by Beik, *French revolution from the right*, Godechot, *Counter-revolution*, and Roberts, *Counter-revolution*.

encapsulating the essential and perceived purpose of the Revolution'.⁶ Once Napoleon recommenced this *'régénération'*, his advocates included constitutional monarchists, because having accepted the principle that the people may consent to their ruler, achievement and political consent become more important than legitimacy.

Moreover, the French exile press provides evidence of the extent to which the acceptance of popular sovereignty as a legitimising force had triumphed in France. For, as we have seen, even Peltier and his fellow *pur* journalists were willing to invoke public opinion when they argued that the revolution was unpopular and had been brought about by a few intriguers. While this usurpation of revolutionary rhetoric may have been largely tactical, the mere fact that they resorted to it indicates the depth to which the new political culture of consent had penetrated, as well, perhaps, as a subconscious acceptance that henceforth the French monarchy would need to inspire popular support. Nevertheless, after 1799 the *purs* developed intellectual frameworks that allowed little space for compromise of any sort, and eventually risked becoming, like the twentieth-century Russian exile press condemned by Edouard Limanov, 'stupidly conservative, with not even rightist views, and every dark superstition available'.⁷ Nor did they ever abandon the crude personality politics that characterised political pornography under the absolute monarchy, continued in the right-wing revolutionary scandal sheets including the *Actes des apôtres* and survived in the subsequent journals of Peltier and Regnier. They thus perpetuated a world-view that revolved around personality and faction rather than interest groups and ideology, and was hence more suited to the *ancien régime* than the restored, constitutional monarchy.

The restoration of the Bourbons in March 1814 ought to have put an end to the labours of the émigré journalists, but unfortunately they did not all receive the recognition they expected from Louis XVIII. The greatest rewards went to Couchery. The circumstances of his *rapprochement* with the Bourbons are unclear, but he was in correspondence with the exile court by January 1813 and in 1814 he was appointed private secretary to Louis XVIII and accompanied him to France.⁸ He was ennobled and awarded the *légion d'honneur*, but died suddenly on 25 October 1814.⁹ In contrast, Peltier's solici-

---

6 Jeremy Whiteman, 'The Constituent Assembly and the problem of French national power', in Michael Adcock, Emily Chester and Jeremy Whiteman (eds), *Revolution, society and the politics of memory: the proceedings of the tenth George Rudé seminar on French history and civilisation*, Melbourne 1996, 170–5 at p. 170. This observation accords with the findings of my study of Morande's early revolutionary journalism: Burrows, 'Exile press', 272.
7 Cited in Michael Glenny and Norman Stone, *The other Russia: the experience of exile*, London 1990, 418.
8 See AAE, mem./docs France 606, fo. 31, Couchery to Blacas (1813); mem./docs France 620, 'Couchery'; Fauche-Borel, *Mémoires*, iv. 209.
9 *Dictionnaire de biographie française*, ix.

CONCLUSION

tations were initially rejected by the Bourbons, a situation he attributed to his service of Christophe of Haiti.[10] He must have been particularly galled therefore to see Malouet accorded the post of Minister of the Navy. After a trip to Paris in 1814, Peltier returned to England pursued by his creditors and resumed publishing the *Ambigu*, offering a vociferous *pur* opposition to Louis XVIII's ministers until 1818.[11] However, he continued to importune rewards from Britain and France and was finally accorded pensions by both the French foreign and interior ministries.[12] Dutheil does not seem to have received significant recompense from the Bourbons.[13] Neither is there evidence that Gérard either received any recognition after the restoration or returned to France, and he may have continued to edit the *Courier de Londres* until it folded in 1826. Regnier, who had so offended the Bourbons, received the full weight of their ire. The *Courier d'Angleterre* was banned from circulating in France, and this probably contributed to its demise.[14] Nevertheless, the French government apparently relented, for in March 1815 the French ambassador supported Regnier's request for a pension from the British government.[15] This, and all his subsequent attempts to solicit a pension or work as a translator from the British government, proved fruitless. His fate after 1819 is unknown. After 1818 French royal governments were never again seriously troubled by French exile journals based in London, although they continued to attempt sporadic actions against the British press.[16]

The émigré press represents virtually the final chapter in the history of the London-based cosmopolitan francophone press that developed in the wake of the Huguenot diaspora and flourished throughout the long eighteenth century. A few last gasp ventures, such as Châteauneuf's attempts to establish a *Chronique de l'Europe* in 1816 and de Châtelain's short-lived weekly *Mercure de Londres*, published in 1826, both opposition journals, were not

---

10 J. W. Croker papers, Peltier to Croker, 3 Apr. 1819.
11 See, for example, *Ambigu* 524 (20 Oct. 1818), 87, attacking Louis XVIII's decision to replace Artois as commander of the National Guard.
12 See BL, MS Egerton 3716, fo. 108, Peltier to the duchesse d'Angoulême, 15 Dec. 1818; J. W. Croker papers, Peltier to Croker, 3 Apr. 1819; Peltier's accounts in ADS, DQ^{10} 1429, dos. 1918.
13 *Nouvelle Biographie générale*, xv, col. 501.
14 See PRO, FO 27/109, Regnier to Foreign Office, 24 Dec. 1814.
15 PRO, FO 27/124, Regnier to Foreign Office, 31 Mar. 1815.
16 AN, F^{18} 18, dos. 32, reveals that in 1818 the prefect of La Manche was instructed to bring pressure to bear to prevent the Guernsey press publishing articles 'in opposition to the French government'; F^{18} 18, dos. 35, records seizures of British newspapers including an incident at Cherbourg when customs officers impounded three old, well-read newspapers discovered among a British ship's papers, but eventually decided not to prosecute their owners. In 1819 the French government considered prosecuting the *New Times* for describing Louis XVIII as 'a poor, imbecile old man on the brink of the grave' until informed they had little chance of success. See PRO, FO 27/202, Charles Stuart to Castlereagh, Paris, 18 Feb. 1819; FO 27/215, Caraman to [Castlereagh], 29 Mar. 1819, and Castlereagh's draft reply, dated 16 Apr. 1819.

successful in the long term.[17] After 1814 the conditions that had made French exile journalism both a successful and an important part of the European cultural and political scene rapidly disappeared. Within months of the first restoration, the economics of newspaper production were revolutionised by the invention of the steam press, which was first used in the production of *The Times* of 29 November 1814.[18] Although the first steam press quadrupled output to 1,100 sheets per hour, within a few years improved models could produce 4,000 an hour, rather than the 250 or so produced by a hand press.[19] As a result outputs and circulation rose, prices fell and margins per unit declined. However, it was not possible for the metropolitan press to address truly mass audiences until the reduction of the stamp duty in 1837, although cheap, illegal, unstamped papers had been addressing popular audiences for some time.[20] In addition, from the 1830s, and especially the 1840s, the European information system was changing, with the advent of railways and the electric telegraph. News information could now be spread more rapidly, and the peripheral ports of London, Hamburg and the Netherlands, the traditional bases for French exile journalists, lost much of their strategic value as centres for news gathering and distribution. As a result of these changes, successful news publishing required large-scale capital investment, large circulations and daily publishing. In addition, the editorial staffing levels of newspapers rose, correspondents became more specialised, and the use of professional foreign correspondents, a complete novelty at the start of the revolution, became more commonplace. By the 1820s, the commercial conditions in which the French exile press had thrived were things of the past.

So, too, were the political and cultural conditions under which they had operated. Under the relatively liberal press regime of the restoration, foreign-based journals did not enjoy the precedence for news in France that they had enjoyed under the *ancien régime*, with its systems of censorship and *privilèges*. Nor did the London-based French-language press have anything fresh to teach the French about political practice. England and its former American colonies had lost their novelty value: they were no longer the only

---

[17] The Bodleian holdings of the *Mercure de Londres* contain the first twelve numbers. It claimed to be a continuation of an earlier journal, *Le Petit Mercure*. Châtelain was presumably the former editor-in-chief of the *Courier français* in late 1802 indicated in AN, 29 AP/91, fo. 149. PRO, FO 27/149, contains the prospectus for Châteauneuf's paper; AN, O³* 767, '1er état des émigrés', records that he wrote articles attacking the French government in an English newspaper and therefore refuses him a pension. It makes no mention of the *Chronique de l'Europe*, and I have found no other traces of it.

[18] Grant, *Newspaper press*, i. 453.

[19] Cranfield, *The press and society*, 152. The figure of 250 sheets per hour is Cranfield's; Grant, *Newspaper press*, i. 453, says 450 was possible.

[20] On the struggle to abolish stamp duty and the unstamped press see Joel H. Weiner, *The war of the unstamped*, Ithaca 1969. The final abolition came in 1855, although the 'final tax on knowledge', the paper tax, was not scrapped until 1860: S. H. Steinberg, *500 years of printing*, 3rd edn, London 1974, 276.

large states with liberal constitutional regimes. France, too, had a liberal constitutional monarchy, and if she had a relatively narrow franchise, at least it was more uniform than in Britain. Moreover, France had tried – and ultimately rejected – a range of alternative political expedients and her unified political élite was frightened of innovation. After a new revolution in 1830, they settled for a change of personnel and minimum changes to the Constitutional Charter. The revolution had also done much to check the French mania for parliamentary oratory *per se*, which so characterised pre-revolutionary comment on the British parliament. Moreover, European readers had less reason to be interested in French affairs after the fall of Napoleon, save perhaps during the revolutionary cataclysms of 1830 and 1848. France was no longer considered a pressing military threat to the rest of Europe, as it had been from the reign of Louis XIV to that of Napoleon and besides, after 1815, Europe experienced almost four decades of peace between the Great Powers. Furthermore, although Paris continued to be seen as the cultural capital of Europe throughout the nineteenth century, her leadership role was more circumscribed because emergent romantic nationalism refocused much of Europe's cultural energy. Nationalism also helped to deal the *coup de grâce* to the pan-European cosmopolitanism that had been a cause of the success and a feature of French extra-territorial journalism in the eighteenth century.

In consequence, after 1814 the London-based French-language press declined quickly, abetted by the policies of French government and the withdrawal of British funding. Nevertheless the French exile press left a significant legacy in other ways. Its most enduring achievement was its role in developing a negative image of the literary and cultural output of the revolutionary era. This view was so hegemonic that until recently it was little remarked or challenged. As a result, counter-revolutionary discourses that described the revolution as a force for cultural and moral decay competed for hegemony with discourses that portrayed the revolution as a force for social and political progress throughout the nineteenth century and beyond. However, in most other ways, the émigré press undermined the goals of its journalists, reinforcing Mallet Du Pan's contention that emigration is the 'least retrievable of political errors'.[21] In the 1790s its quarrels helped to create the image of the émigrés as a divided group that was politically impotent and lacking a clear policy. As a result it intensified uncertainty about the consequences of a Bourbon restoration, to the detriment of *la bonne cause* in both France and Europe. Moreover, after 1803 the émigré papers served their British paymasters by developing a European anti-Napoleonic sentiment in pursuit of short-term goals, rather than developing an ideology or long-term strategy for France. The Black Legend of Napoleon that they had helped to create and disseminate was too ephemeral, extreme and repulsive to appeal inside France, especially after the tyrant's fall. Likewise, the émigré identity

[21] BM 29 (30 Nov. 1799), 263.

they promoted was based on an idealised past rather than present reality, and hence did not acknowledge the need for change. In addition, by making the demand for order virtually their sole imperative, the émigré journalists failed to address more relevant and less ephemeral issues. They therefore failed to create a 'public space' in which the Bourbons and their adherents could discuss and develop a relevant political ideology and effective policies for the Bourbon restoration. Paradoxically the émigré journalists thus contributed both to the intellectual and moral failure of Bourbonism and to the emotional and political triumph of Bonapartism and Napoleon III.

APPENDIX 1

Proprietorship of the Courier de Londres

The proprietorship of the *Courier de Londres* underwent numerous changes. Originally two-thirds of profits went to Samuel Swinton, who provided most, possibly all, of the capital, and one-third to its first editor, Alphonse-Joseph de Serres de La Tour. When Serres de La Tour left the paper at the end of 1783, his share in the proprietorship and profits seems to have reverted to Swinton. By June 1785 Swinton was facing financial difficulties and sold the paper to Radix de Sainte-Foy, treasurer-general of the French navy and a putative former lover of Madame Du Barry. Since the paper's new editor, Charles Théveneau de Morande, was a spy for the French naval ministry, there is reason to think Sainte-Foy was effectively acting as a front man for the French government. Nevertheless, the paper was still a viable financial venture, especially after the onset of the pre-revolutionary crisis, which created an increased demand for news. On 1 January 1788 Swinton bought back the paper, only to sell a 50 per cent stake to John Irving, who was secretly acting as an agent in the purchase for Charles-Alexandre de Calonne, in April 1789 for £2,100.

Calonne sold his share in the paper to his brother, the abbé Calonne, in May 1794. From August 1804 until 1806 the rights attached to the abbé's share seems to have been exercised by the paper's printers John Lewis Cox, Edward Cox and Thomas Baylis who acted as co-proprietors with Swinton's widow. In 1806 the abbé ceded his share to his nephew, the comte de Saint-Morys, to settle debts he had contracted with the comte's father, but by 1812 he had apparently sold his share in the paper to a lawyer called R. A. Routledge.

From December 1795 until March 1796 the paper was published by T. Cicaldi, who had presumably purchased Swinton's share and then sold it back to him. When Swinton died in June 1797, his share passed to his widow Félicité, who seems to have acted as a sleeping partner. Apart from being responsible for certain residual costs, she left all business expenses to others. By 1802 Swinton's son Richard seems to have joined her, for he is also described as the paper's co-proprietor. Nevertheless, a J. F. Swinton, presumably the same Félicité, is referred to as the paper's co-proprietor in both 1804 and 1812. There are no notices between 1812 and 1819 to suggest further changes.

APPENDIX 2

Profiles of Emigré Journals

For details of periodicity, numbers of pages, and format see table 1.

L'Ambigu   July 1802–Nov. 1818

Collections used: Arsenal, Paris, vol. 59; Bodleian Library, Oxford, vols 1–3; British Library, London, vols 26–58; Cambridge University Library, vols 1–25
Editors: Jean-Gabriel Peltier; Jean-Baptiste Couchery = assistant replacement, c. 1810–14
Printers:
  John Lewis Cox, Son & Thomas Baylis, 75 Great Queen Street, 1802–5, nos 1–80
  Paolo Da Ponte, 15 Poland Street, 1805–9, nos 81–97, 100–223
  J. B. G. Vogel, 13 Poland Street, 1805, nos 98–9
  G. Schulze/Schulze & Dean, 15 Poland Street, 1809–18, nos. 224–
Proprietor: Jean-Gabriel Peltier

L'Antidote   occasional, 1804–5, probably only 1–2 numbers published.

Editor/proprietor: François-David Kirwan
Collection used: PRO, FO 27/71 (no. 1 only)

British Mercury, see **Mercure britannique**

Correspondance politique   2 Nov. 1793–2 Aug. 1794
Other titles: *Correspondance française* (1), 2 Nov. 1793

Collection used: British Library, London
Editor/proprietor: Jean-Gabriel Peltier
Printer: [?] Glindon

Courier d'Angleterre   25 April 1805–c. 31 March 1815, c. 1,037 nos

Collections used: Cambridge University Library, 1810; Lund University Library, Sweden, 1807–9; Uppsala University Library, Sweden. 1807–8; West Yorkshire District Archives, Chapeltown, Leeds, no. 257. [None of these collections is complete. The almost complete collection listed in the

British Library Catalogue was destroyed in the blitz; that at Harvard (1810–11) was reported missing in 1975.]
Editor/Proprietor: Jacques Regnier
Printer: Thomas Harper, Jr, to 1812. Thereafter unknown

Courier de l'Europe, see **Courier de Londres**

Courier de Londres 1776–1826. Few copies survive post-1819.
Other titles: *Courier de l'Europe*, 1776–88 (English edition)/1778–92 (continental edition); *Gazette de la Grande Bretagne*, 16 Apr. 1805–29 Dec. 1807

Collections used: Bodleian Library, Oxford, 1789–1819. Miscellaneous others
Editors:
  Alphonse-Joseph Serres de La Tour, 1776–83
  Charles Théveneau de Morande, 20 Jan. 1784–14 May 1791
  [?] Delatouche, [?] Serani, [?] Mercier, 18 May 1791–29 Jan. 1793
  [?Velley], probably 1792–3; possibly chief editor 29 Jan.–Apr. 1793
  [?] Verduisant, Apr.–31 Oct. 1793
  Abbé Jacques-Ladislas-Joseph de Calonne, 1 Nov. 1793–28 Dec. 1798 (co-editor from 1 Aug. 1797).
  Comte de Montlosier, 1 Aug. 1797–c. 20 June 1802 (co-editor with abbé Calonne until end of 1798)
  Jacques Regnier, 22 June 1802–c. 13 Apr. 1805
  Robert Heron, 16 Apr. 1805–Summer 1806
  [?] Gérard, 1806?–26? (named 1809, documented 1810, 1812)
Secondary editors and major collaborators:
  Jacques-Pierre Brissot, Apr.–c. Dec. 1778, 1783 (his role is a matter of dispute)
  Jean-Baptiste Couchery, c. 1802–5
  [?] Goy (dismissed 1783)
  [?] La Corbière, assisted comte de Montlosier
  [?] Lefebvre ? – May 1791–?
  Jean-Gabriel Peltier, 1802–4 (?)
  Joseph Perkins de MacMahon, died 1788
  Jean-Charles Pichegru, c. 1802–4
  [?] Serani, 1789, 1793–? (see above)
  [?] Velley, 1792–3 ? (see above)
Printers and publishers (London edition):
  John Lewis Cox & Son, to 15 Mar. 1803 (probably actually merged with Thomas Baylis in 1802)
  John Lewis Cox, Son & Thomas Baylis, 15 Mar. 1803–Mar. 1808
  John Lewis Cox & Thomas Baylis, 18 Mar. 1808–20+

Shareholding Proprietors:
  Samuel Swinton, 1776–85, 1 Jan. 1788–Dec. 1795, Mar 1796–June 1797
  Radix de Saint-Foy, 1785–1 Jan. 1788
  Charles-Alexandre de Calonne, 17 Apr. 1789–9 May 1794
  T. Cicaldi, c. 8 Dec. 1795–17 Mar. 1796
  Mme J.-F. Swinton, June 1797–?1812+
  R. Swinton ? – 22 June 1802–1804?
  Abbé Jacques-Ladislas-Joseph de Calonne, 9 May 1794–1806
  [?] Saint-Morys, 1806–? (presumably sold share to R. A. Routledge)
  R. A. Routledge (documented 1812)
  John Lewis Cox, 17 Aug. 1804–?
  Edward Cox, 17 Aug. 1804–?
  Thomas Baylis, 17 Aug. 1804–?

Dernier Tableau de Paris Prospectus mentioned 6 Oct. 1792; no. 1 appeared by 18 Oct. 1792, continued into 1793. Several editions and reprints.

Collection used: Wadham College, Oxford
Editor/Proprietor: Jean-Gabriel Peltier
Printed: 'par l'auteur.'
Proprietor: Jean-Gabriel Peltier

Gazette de la Grande Bretagne, see **Courier de Londres**

Histoire de la restauration de la monarchie française, ou la campagne de 1793 March–April 1793, 3 nos [According to Hélène Maspero-Clerc this journal ran to 4 nos, but I have found only 3 and *Ambigu* 397 (10 Apr. 1814), 89, claims only 3 were published.]

Collections used: British Library, London; Cambridge University Library
Editor/Proprietor: Jean-Gabriel Peltier

Impartial, ou Courier de Middlesex 1787, said to exist in 1791

Editors: Pierre Guedon, [?] Guedon and [?] Charton

Note: This journal was identified mistakenly as an émigré journal by Hélène Maspero-Clerc. Although denounced to the French government years later as an outspoken émigré journal and alleged to have appeared in 1791, it was in fact a vitriolic *frondeur* scandal sheet published in 1787, when it brought its authors into conflict with the French embassy. For more information see Burrows, 'Exile press', 40–4.

PROFILES OF EMIGRÉ JOURNALS

Journal de France et d'Angleterre 6 Jan. 1797–22 July 1797

Collection used: Bodleian Library, Oxford
Editor/Proprietor: comte de Montlosier
Printers: W. & C. Spilsbury, Snowhill

Mercure britannique French/English versions dated 24/26 Sept. 1798–25/31 Mar. 1800. There were several reprints and pirate editions as well as an Italian translation.

Collections used: Bodleian Library, Oxford. Vol. ii, second (English) edition, in own possession
Editor/Proprietor: Jacques Mallet Du Pan
Translator: Robert Charles Dallas
Printers: Spilsbury, French edition; English printer not known

Mercure de France 10 Apr. 1800–30 Apr. 1801

Collection used: British Library, London
Editors/Proprietors: 'Une Société de gens de lettres', comprising five unknown persons, both clergymen and 'gentilshommes' and the abbé Jean-Marie de Châteaugiron
Printers: W. & C. Spilsbury, Snowhill

Paris pendant l'année 1795–1802 6 June 1795–30 Dec. 1797; 15 May 1798–15 June 1802

Collections used: British Library, London; Cambridge University Library
Editor: Jean-Gabriel Peltier
Printer: Thomas Baylis
Proprietors: Joseph De Boffe, nos 1–32 (6 June 1795–9 Jan. 1796); Jean-Gabriel Peltier, nos 33–250 (9 Jan. 1796–15 June 1802)

Supplément au Rédacteur June–July 1799. 4 nos? Prospectus early June, 4 nos by 19 July 1799

Collection used: PRO, FO 27/54
Editor: Nicolas Dutheil
Printer: not given

Tableau de l'Europe 10 Aug. 1794–early 1795; last number and tables issued from Fleet Prison, 2 June 1795

Collection used: Cambridge University Library
Editor/Proprietor: Jean-Gabriel Peltier
Printer: W. Glindon, Coventry Court, Haymarket

Bibliography

Unpublished primary sources

CANADA

Trois-Rivières, Archives des Ursulines
Documents and copies of documents concerning the abbé Calonne
II–B–6–11, II–B–6–19, II–B–6–24, II–B–6–25, II–B–6–30, II–B–6–31, II–B–6–39, II–B–6–84, II–B–6–112, II–B–6–118, II–B–6–139, II–B–6–163, II–B–6–171

FRANCE

Chantilly, Archives Condé
Série Z papiers de Condé, correspondance générale
Tomes CXV, CXXV, CXXX

Grenoble, Archives Départementales d'Isère
Série L époque révolutionnaire
L. 113, 120

Nantes, Archives Départementales de la Loire Atlantique
F1192, F1225, IIc2055, 4E2/2111

Nantes, Bibliothèque Municipale
MS 659, pièces 142–3
MS 672, pièce 202
MS 675, pièces 214–15

Paris, Archives Départementales de la Seine
DC^6 31
DQ^{10} c.614, dos. 1677
DQ^{10} 1429, dos. 1918

Paris, Archives du Ministère des Affaires Etrangères

Correspondance politique, Angleterre
Vols 567–70, 576–90, 592–7, 600–4, 606

Correspondance politique, Angleterre, supplément
Vols 17, 21–3, 29–31

Mémoires et documents, Amérique
Vol. 15

Mémoires et documents, Angleterre
  Vol. 103

Mémoires et documents, France
  Vols 594–5, 600, 604–7, 614–15, 620, 630–1, 633, 635–6, 639, 641–4, 658, 1773–5, 1891

Dossiers de personnel
  Vol. 52, dos. Montlosier

Paris, Archives Nationales

Archives privées (Série AP)
  29AP/91 Roederer papers
  297AP/1–2 Calonne papers
  306AP/32, 33bis Castries papers
  419AP D'Antraigues papers
  446AP/1–4, 13 Brissot papers

Imprimerie et librairie (F18)
  F^{18} 12, F^{18} 18

Maison du roi (O3)
  O^3 614, O^{3*} 767, O^{3*} 769, O^3 777, O^3 2594, O^3 2602

Miscellaneous
  AB XIX 3353, dos. 3

Police générale (F7)
  F^{7*} 105, F^7 3367, F^7 3418, F^7 3444, F^7 3701–5, F^7 3762, F^7 4336^A, dos. 3–5, F^7 5790, F^7 6068, F^7 6139 (33BP), F^7 6240, F^7 6286, dos. 5841, F^7 6286, dos. 5846, F^7 6330, dos. 6959, F^7 6330, dos. 6980, F^7 6415 (8341 BP), F^7 6445, no. 9892, F^7 6480–2, F^7 6888, no. 6333, F^7 7849, dos. 7608

Secretairerie d'etat imperiale (AF^{IV})
  AF^{IV} 1469, AF^{IV} 1490, AF^{IV} 1494, AF^{IV} 1521, AF^{IV} 1569–81, AF^{IV*} 1710

Paris, Archives de la Préfecture de la Police
  Aa 165, pièces 80–1
  Aa 169, pièces 128–9
  Aa 202, pièces 255–63,
  Aa 311, pièces 3, 6, 68, 78, 101, 228

Paris, Bibliothèque Historique de la Ville de Paris
  MSS 722–8 Journaux bibliographie

BIBLIOGRAPHY

GREAT BRITAIN

Durham, University Library
Papers of the Second Earl Grey
Correspondence with d'Antraigues

Leeds, West Yorkshire District Archives, Chapeltown
George Canning papers
Bundles 38a, 42, 44, 54–6, 56a, 58a, 59, 59a, 59b

London, British Library
MS Add. 8073 Puisaye papers
MSS Add. 27473–81 Notebooks of *Courier de Londres* reports
MSS Add. 27482–4 Commonplace books attributed [erroneously] to the abbé Calonne
MSS Add. 33109–11, 33115, 33117, 33121, 33124 Pelham papers
MS Add. 37290 Wellesley papers
MS Add. 37356 Liverpool papers
MSS Add. 37853, 37855, 37858–9, 37861, 37870, 37872, 37905 Windham papers
MSS Add. 38229, 38232, 38245, 38357 Liverpool papers
MSS Add. 38734–6, 38764, 38769 Huskisson papers
MS Add. 39978 Banks papers
MS Add. 48413 Paget papers
MSS Add. 51463–4, 51653, 51820 Holland House papers
MS Add. 52451^B Mackintosh papers
MS Add. 57537 Vansittart papers
MS Add. 59035 Dropmore papers

MS Egerton 3716.

MS Loan
Loan 57/4
Loan 57/20 Bathurst papers

London, National Register of Archives
NRA 18,862 Typescript descriptive list of Mallet papers sold at Sothebys, lot 58, 8 November 1977

London, Public Record Office, Kew

Bankruptcy papers
B.3.3894 Peltier, 1811

Foreign Office correspondence
Diplomatic correspondence, Denmark, FO 22 series
FO 22/57–8

Diplomatic correspondence, France, FO 27 series
FO 27/41–4, 47–8, 51–4, 56–8, 62–7, 69–71, 75–6, 80–1, 85–8, 90–2, 94, 102, 105–9, 124, 127, 144, 147, 149, 202, 215, 219

Diplomatic correspondence, Portugal, FO 63 series
FO 63/118

Diplomatic correspondence, Spain, FO 72 series
FO 72/121, 54

Diplomatic correspondence, Sweden, FO 73 series
FO 73/37, 63, 69

Diplomatic correspondence, supplementary, bundles, FO 95 series
FO 95/2/4, 5; FO 95/3/1, 3, 4; FO 95/8/13 France
FO 95/630–2 Calonne papers
FO 95/636 D'Antraigues papers
FO 95/637–8 Copies of intercepted Bourbon correspondence
FO 323/4 Whitworth papers

Home Office papers
HO 1/6
HO 5/5
HO 42/22–4
HO 42/67–71

Privy Council papers
PC 1/124–31 Calonne papers

Public Record Office series
PRO 30/8/165 Chatham papers

Treasury Solicitor's papers
TS 11/429

War Office papers
WO 1/68

Oxford, Balliol College
Mallet Family papers, Jacques Mallet Du Pan papers
Folders #3, #6, #7, #8, #10, #13, #14, #15, #20, #22, #25, #26, #30

Winchester, Hampshire Record Office
Wickham papers 38M49/1/79/1–29

SWEDEN

Lund, Universitetsbibliotek
De La Gardie MSS
Typescript translation of passages from De La Gardie's 'Journal under en resa til England, Frankrike, Spanien, åren 1813–1815', trans. into English by Jan-Olof Friström, assistant librarian
Correspondence of Peltier and Mme Peltier with De La Gardie

Stockholm, Riksarkivet
Hovkanslerns arkiv, vol. 60 Correspondence of P.-F. Fauche

SWITZERLAND

Geneva, Bibliothèque Publique et Universitaire
MS. Fr. 212; MS. Fr. 1269/1; MS. Fr. 1269/2; MS. Suppl. 866; MS. Suppl. 976; 1947/19; 1956/27; 1968/28 D.O.; 1973/1 D.O.

UNITED STATES

Durham, North Carolina, Perkins Library, Duke University
Acomb papers
Croker papers
Dundas papers
Wilberforce papers

Primary printed sources

Periodicals and newspapers
Actes des apôtres
Ambigu
Année littéraire
Annual Register
Antidote
Argus patriote
British Mercury
Bulletin des lois
Correspondance politique
Correspondenten
Cosmopolite
Courier d'Angleterre
Courier de Londres
Courier de Londres et de Paris
Décade philosophique
Dernier Tableau de Paris
Gazette de la Grande-Bretagne
Gentleman's Magazine
Histoire de la restauration de la monarchie française
Journal de l'Europe
Journal de France et d'Angleterre
Journal de Londres
Journal de Middlesex
London Chronicle
Mercure britannique
Mercure de France (London)
Il Mercurio britannico
Moniteur

National Register
Observer
Paris pendant l'année
Patriote françois
Phare politique et littéraire
Précis des événements militaires
Rédacteur
Spectateur du nord
Supplément au Rédacteur
Tableau de l'Europe
The Times
Traddução do Correio de Londres

Books and pamphlets

André, Michel (ed.), *Correspondance inédite de Mallet du Pan avec la cour de Vienne*, Paris 1884

Barras, J.-N.-P.-F., *Mémoires*, Paris 1829

Barruel, Augustin de, *Mémoires pour servir à l'histoire du jacobinisme françois*, London 1797–8

Boosey, Thomas, *Piscatorial reminiscences and gleanings by an old angler and bibliopolist, to which is added a catalogue of books on angling*, London 1835

Bourrienne, L.-A. Fauvelet de, *Mémoires*, 3rd edn, Paris 1830

Brissot de Warville, Jacques-Pierre, *Mémoires*, ed. Claude Perroud, Paris 1910

Browning, Oscar (ed.), *The despatches of Lord Gower*, Cambridge 1885

Burke, Edmund, *The correspondance of Edmund Burke*, Chicago–Cambridge 1958–70

────── *Reflections on the revolution in France*, ed. Conor Cruise O'Brien, London 1968

[Cadet de Gassicourt, Charles-Louis], *Le Tombeau de Jacques Molai, ou le secret des conspirations à ceux qui veulent tout savoir: oeuvre posthume de C. L. C. G. D. L. S. D. M. B. C. D. V.*, Paris an IV [?1796]

Calonne, Charles Alexandre de, *Le Tableau de l'Europe en novembre 1795; et pensées sur ce qu'on a fait et qu'on n'aurait pas dû faire*, London 1796

Catalogue alphabétique d'une partie des livres français qui se trouvent chez J. C. De Boffe, No. 10, Nassau Street, Soho, à Londres, London 1813

Catalogue général, methodique et raisonné des livres françois, italiens, espagnols, portugais &c. &c. qui se trouvent chez A. B. Dulau & co., Soho Square. London Jan. 1813

Caudrillier, H., *La Traihison de Pichegru*, Paris 1908

Chapuisat, E. (ed.), *La Correspondance de Mallet Du Pan et le maréchal de Castries*, Geneva 1948

Chateaubriand, François-René de, *Mémoires d'outre-tombe*, Paris 1973 (Livre de Poche edn, Librairie générale française)

Concluyen las noticias del exercito Ingles, no. 9, n.p. n.d. [?Spain 1809]

Couchery, Jean-Baptiste, *Le Moniteur secret*, Paris 1814

Dumas, Mathieu, *An epitome of military events*, London 1798–9

Fauche-Borel, Louis, *Exposition of the persecutions which Louis Fauche-Borel has experienced from MM. d'Antraigues et de Puisaye in consequence of the zeal he has manifested in the service of England and in the cause of legitimacy*, London 1812

―――― *Mémoires*, Paris 1829
Goldsmith, Louis, *Secret history of the cabinet of Bonaparte*, London 1810
Hansard, *Journals of the House of Commons*
Hauterive, E. d' (ed.), *La Police secrète du premier empire*, Paris 1908–68
HMC, *Report on the manuscripts of J. B. Fortescue, esq., preserved at Dropmore*, London 1892–1927
Ivernois, Francis d', *Coup d'oeil sur les assignats*, London 1795
―――― *Réflexions sur la guerre*, London 1795
Jephson, R., *Confessions of Jean-Baptiste Couteau, citizen of France, written by himself and translated by Mr Jephson*, London 1794
La Motte, Jeanne de, *An address to the public explaining the motives which have hitherto delayed the publication of the memoirs of the countess de Valois de La Motte which contains a justification of her conduct; and exposing the various artifices which have been used for the suppression of their appearance*, London 1789
Lally-Tollendal, T.-G. de, *Première Lettre au rédacteur du Courier de Londres; et au correspondant, auteur de la notice insérée dans le no. [i.e. vol.] 50 de ce journal sur le bref du pape aux évêques français*, London 1801
―――― *Seconde Lettre au rédacteur du Courier de Londres précédée d'une traduction du bref du S. S. avec l'original à côté*, London 1801
―――― *Troisième Lettre au rédacteur du Courier de Londres sur cette question: la religion catholique est-elle à rétablir en France?*, London 1801
―――― *Quatrième et Dernière Lettre sur les questions relatives aux affaires ecclésiastiques de France*, London 1801
Las Cases, E. de, *Memorial of Saint-Helena*, London 1823
Mackintosh, James, *Vindiciae gallicae: a defence of the French revolution and its English admirers against the accusations of the Right Hon. Edmund Burke*, London 1791
Mallet, John-Lewis, *An autobiographical retrospective of the first twenty-five years of his life*, privately printed, Windsor 1890
Mallet Du Pan, Jacques, *Compte rendu de la défense des citoyens-bourgeois de Genève, adressé aux commissaires des représentants, par un citoyen natif*, Geneva 1771
―――― *Considérations sur la Révolution de France et sur les causes qui en prolongent la durée*, London [actually Brussels] 1793
―――― *Correspondance politique pour servir à l'histoire du républicanisme française*, Hamburg 1796
Malouet, P. V., *Mémoires de Malouet*, 2nd edn, Paris 1874
Mehée de la Touche, J.-C.-H., *Alliance des Jacobins français avec le ministère anglais*, Paris germinal an XII (1804)
Milner, J., *A pastoral letter addressed by the Right Rev. J. Milner, bishop of Castabala, vicar apostolic, &c. to the Roman Catholic clergy of his district in England shewing the dangerous tendencies of various pamphlets, lately published in the French language by certain emigrants; and more particularly cautioning the faithful of the Midland district under his spiritual jurisdiction, against the schismatic and heretical principles advanced in two publications by the Abbé Blanchard and M. Gaschet, parish priests in France, previous to the revolution; with a full refutation of their charges against his Holiness Pius VII*, Dublin 1808
Montgaillard, J.-G.-M. Roques, comte de, *Mémoire concernant la trahaison de Pichegru dans les années 3, 4 et 5*, Paris germinal an XII (1804)

Montyon, A.-J.-B.-R. Auget de, *Rapport fait à sa majesté, Louis XVIII (sur le livre intitulé Tableau de l'Europe)*, Constance 1796

Peltier, Jean-Gabriel, *Avis du rédacteur du Tableau de l'Europe à ses souscripteurs en Angleterre*, Fleet Prison 2 June 1795 (bound with *Paris*, vol. i in CUL)

—— *Les Campagnes de Portugal, 1810–1811*, London 1811

—— *Le Coup d'equinoxe d'octobre 1789: lettre de M. P... de Paris à M. M... son ami négociant de Nantes*, Paris 1789

—— *Domine, salvum fac regem*, Paris 1789

—— *Tableau des massacres des ministres et des martyrs de l'honneur exécutés dans le couvent des Carmes et à l'abbaye de St Germain*, Paris–Lyon 1797

—— (ed.), *The trial of John Peltier esq., for a libel against Napoleon Buonaparté, First Consul of the French Republic, at the Court of King's Bench, Middlesex, on Monday 21st February 1803, taken in short-hand by Mr. Adams and the defence revised by Mr. Mackintosh*, London 1803

Pins, J. de (ed.), 'La Correspondance de Mallet Du Pan avec la cour de Lisbonne', AHRF xxxvi (1964), 469–77; xxxvii (1965), 468–84; xxxviii (1966), 84–94

Portalis, Roger (ed.), *H. P. Danloux: peintre des portraits et son journal durant l'émigration*, Paris 1910

Regnier, Jacques, *Lettre d'un colon de Saint Domingue à M. Malouet*, London 1798

—— *Seconde Lettre d'un colon de Saint-Domingue à M. Malouet*, London 1798

—— *Troisième Lettre d'un colon de Saint-Domingue à M. Malouet*, London 1798

Reynaud de Montlosier, François-Dominique, *Essai sur la théorie des volcans d'Auvergne*, n.p. 1788

—— *Mémoires sur la révolution française, le consulat, l'empire, la restauration et les principaux événements qui l'ont suivie*, Paris 1829

—— *Observations sur le projet du code civil présenté par la commissaire nommé par le gouvernement le 24 thermidor an VIII*, Paris 1801

—— *Souvenirs d'un émigré (1791–1798)*, ed. le comte de Larouzière-Montlosier and E. d'Hauterive, Paris 1951

Roche, Eugenius, *London in one thousand years, with other poems*, London 1830

Sayous, A. (ed.), *Mémoires et correspondance de Mallet Du Pan pour servir à l'histoire de la révolution française*, Paris 1851

Serres de La Tour, A. de, *Appel au bon sens dans lequel M. de La Tour soumet à ce juge infaillible les détails de sa conduite relativement à une affaire qui fait quelque bruit dans le monde*, London 1788

Stewarton, H., *The secret history of the court of Saint-Cloud*, London 1806

Théveneau de Morande, Charles, *Réplique de Charles Théveneau Morande à Jacques-Pierre Brissot sur les erreurs, les infidélités, et les calomnies de sa réponse*, Paris 1791

Traduccion del numéro 237 del Ambigu, en que se incertan las letras Apostolicas . . . en 10 de Junio de 1809, Mexico City 1810

Turreau, Louis-Marie, *Memoirs for the history of the war in the Vendée*, London 1796

Watkins, J. and F. Shoberl, *A biographical dictionary of authors*, n.p. 1816

Wilson, Robert T., *History of the British expedition to Egypt*, London 1802

BIBLIOGRAPHY

Works of reference

Biographie universelle, ancienne et moderne, Paris 1811–65
British biographical archive: a one alphabet accumulation of 324 of the most important English language biographical reference works originally published between 1601 and 1929, London–New York–Paris–Munich 1990 (microform)
Dictionary of Canadian biography, 1966–
Dictionnaire de biographie française, 1966–
Nouvelle Biographie générale, depuis les temps les plus reculés jusqu'a nos jours, Paris 1852–66

Balleine, G. R., *A biographical dictionary of Jersey*, London n.d.
Caron, A., *Manuel practique pour l'étude de la révolution française*, Paris 1947
Chambers, R., *A biographical dictionary of eminent Scotsmen*, new edn, London 1855.
Emsley, Clive, *The Longman companion to Napoleonic Europe*, London–New York 1993
Jones, Colin, *The Longman companion to the French revolution*, London–New York 1988
Palmer, Alan, *An encyclopaedia of Napoleon's Europe*, New York 1984
Rétat, Pierre, *Les Journaux de 1789: bibliographie critique*, Paris 1988
Sgard, Jean (ed.), *Dictionnaire de journaux*, Paris 1991
―――― (ed.), *Dictionnaire des journalistes*, 1st edn, Grenoble 1976; suppléments i–iv (1981–5)
Tourneux, Maurice, *Les Sources bibliographiques de l'histoire de la révolution française*, Paris 1898
Walker, David M., *The Oxford companion to law*, Oxford 1980

Secondary sources

Acomb, Frances, *Mallet Du Pan (1749–1800): a career in political journalism*, Durham, NC 1973
Adcock, Michael, Emily Chester and Jeremy Whiteman (eds), *Revolution, society and the politics of memory: the proceedings of the tenth George Rudé seminar on French history and civilisation*, Melbourne 1996
Armbruster, Carol (ed.), *Publishing and readership in revolutionary France and America*, Westport, Conn. 1993
Ashton, John, *English caricature and satire on Napoleon I*, London 1888, repr. 1968
Aspinall, Arthur, *Politics and the press, c. 1780–1850*, Brighton 1973
Baker, Keith Michael, *Inventing the French revolution: essays on French political culture in the eighteenth century*, Cambridge 1990
Baldensperger, Fernand, *Le Mouvement des idées pendant l'émigration*, Paris 1914
Bardoux, A., *Le Comte de Montlosier et les constitutionnels pendant l'émigration, d'après des documents inédits*, Paris 1879
―――― *Le Comte de Montlosier et le gallicanisme*, Paris 1881
Barker, Hannah, *Press, politics and public opinion in late eighteenth-century England*, Oxford 1998
Baruch, Daniel, *Simon-Nicolas-Henri Linguet ou l'irrécupérable*, Paris 1991

Beik, P. H., *The French revolution seen from the right: social theories in motion*, Philadelphia 1956
Bellanger, Claude, Jacques Godechot, Pierre Guiral and Fernard Terrou (eds), *Histoire générale de la presse française*, Paris 1969
Bellenger, Dominic Aidan, *The French exiled clergy in the British Isles after 1789: a historical introduction and working list*, Downside 1986
Bertaud, J.-P., *Les Amis du roi: journaux et journalistes royalistes en France de 1789 à 1792*, Paris 1984
Biron, Hervé, 'Un Ami de Beaumarchais aux Trois-Rivières', *Le Nouvelliste* (Trois-Rivières), 12 Dec. 1949
Black, Jeremy, *The English press in the eighteenth century*, London 1987
Blanc, Olivier, *Les Espions de la révolution et de l'empire*, Paris 1995
Boosey, Jeremy, 'Beethoven, Bellini, ballads and bands', in *Boosey and Hawkes 150th anniversary*, 2–4
Boosey and Hawkes 150th anniversary, London 1966
Brewer, John and Roy Porter (eds), *Consumption and the world of goods*, London 1993
Broadley, A. M., *Napoleon in caricature, 1795–1821*, London 1911
Brugerette, A., *Le Comte de Montlosier et son temps (1755–1838)*, Aurillac 1931
Burrows, Simon, 'British propaganda for Russia in the Napoleonic Wars: the *Courier d'Angleterre*', *New Zealand Slavonic Journal* (1993), 85–100
—— 'The cultural politics of exile: French émigré literary journalism in London, 1793–1814', *Journal of European Studies* xxix (1999), 157–77
—— 'Culture and misperception: the law and the press in the outbreak of war in 1803', *International History Review* xviii (1996), 793–818
—— 'A literary low-life reassessed: Charles Théveneau de Morande in London, 1769–1791', *Eighteenth Century Life* xxii (1998), 76–94
—— 'The struggle for European opinion in the Napoleonic wars: British francophone propaganda, 1803–1814', *French History* xi (1997), 29–53
Cabanis, André, *La Presse sous le consulat et l'empire*, Paris 1975
Carpenter, Kirsty, *Refugees of the French revolution: émigrés in London, 1789–1799*, Basingstoke 1999
—— and Philip Mansel (eds), *The French émigrés in Europe and the struggle against the revolution, 1789–1814*, Basingstoke 1999
Censer, Jack R., 'English politics in the *Courrier d'Avignon*', in Censer and Popkin, *Press and politics*, 170–203
—— *The French press in the age of enlightenment*, London 1994
—— *Prelude to power: the Parisian radical press, 1789–1791*, Baltimore 1976
—— and Jeremy D. Popkin (eds), *Press and politics in pre-revolutionary France*, Berkeley–Los Angeles 1987
Chapuisat, E. (ed.), *La Correspondance de Mallet Du Pan et le maréchal de Castries*, Geneva 1948
Chartier, Roger, 'Book markets and reading in France at the end of the old regime', in Armbruster, *Publishing and readership*, 117–36
—— *The cultural origins of the French revolution*, Durham, NC 1991
Chisick, Harvey, 'Politics and journalism in the French revolution: the readership of the *Journal de la Montagne* and the Jacobin clubs', *French History* v (1991), 345–72
—— (ed.), *The press in the French revolution*, Oxford 1991

Christie, I. R., *Wars and revolutions*, London 1982
Clarke, J., *British diplomacy and foreign policy, 1782–1865*, London 1989
Clerc, Catherine, *La Caricature contre Napoléon*, Paris 1985
Cranfield, G. A., *The press and society from Caxton to Northcliffe*, London 1978
Cruppi, Jean, *Un Avocat-journaliste au XVIIIe siècle: Linguet*, Paris 1895
Darnton, Robert, *The business of enlightenment: a publishing history of the Encyclopédie*, Cambridge, Mass. 1979
—— *The corpus of clandestine literature in France, 1769–1789*, London–New York 1995
—— *The forbidden best-sellers of pre-revolutionary France*, London–New York 1996
—— 'The high enlightenment and the low-life of literature in pre-revolutionary France', *Past and Present* li (1971), 81–115, repr. in his *Literary underground*, 1–40
—— *The literary underground of the old regime*, Cambridge, Mass. 1982
—— *Mesmerism and the end of enlightenment in France*, Cambridge, Mass. 1968
—— and Daniel Roche (eds), *Revolution in print: the press in France, 1775–1800*, Berkeley 1989
Daudet, E., *Histoire de l'émigration pendant la révolution française*, Paris 1905–7
Dixon, Peter, *Canning, politician and statesman*, London 1976
Doyle, William, *The Oxford history of the French revolution*, Oxford 1989
—— and H. T. Mason (eds), *The impact of the French revolution on European consciousness*, Gloucester 1989
Duckworth, Colin, *The d'Antraigues phenomenon: the making and breaking of a revolutionary royalist espionage agent*, Newcastle-upon-Tyne 1986
Duranton, Henri, Claude Labrosse and Pierre Rétat (eds), *Les Gazettes européennes de langue française (XVIIe et XVIIIe siècles)*, St Etienne 1992
Durey, Michael, 'The British secret service and the escape of Sir Sidney Smith from Paris in 1798', *History* lxxxiv (1999), 437–57
Ebbinghaus, T., *England, Napoleon, und die Presse*, Munich–Berlin 1914
Eisenstein, Elizabeth L., *Grub Street abroad: aspects of the French cosmopolitan press from the age of Louis XIV to the French revolution*, Oxford 1992
—— *The printing press as an agent of change*, Cambridge 1979
—— *The printing revolution in early modern Europe*, Cambridge 1983
Farge, Arlette, *Dire et mal dire: l'opinion publique au XVIIIe siècle*, Paris 1992
—— *Subversive words: public opinion in eighteenth-century France*, trans. Rosemary Morris, Cambridge 1994
Ferdinand, Christine, 'Selling it to the provinces: news and commerce around eighteenth-century Salisbury', in Brewer and Porter, *Consumption and the world of goods*, 393–411
Feyel, Gilles, 'Les Frais d'impression et de diffusion de la presse Parisienne entre 1789 et 1792', in Rétat, *La Révolution du journal*, 77–99
Flieschmann, Hector, *Marie-Antoinette libertine*, Paris 1911
Forneron, H., *Histoire générale des emigrés*, Paris 1884–90
Fryer, W. R., *Republic or restoration in France? 1794–1797*, Manchester 1965
Geggus, David, 'The Anglo-French conflict in the Caribbean in the 1790's', in Jones, *Britain and revolutionary France*, 27–39
—— *Slavery, war and revolution: the British occupation of Saint Domingue, 1793–1798*, Oxford 1982

Gelbart, Nina Rattner, *Feminine and opposition journalism in old regime France: Le Journal des dames*, Berkeley 1987
George, M. Dorothy, *English political caricature, 1793–1832: a study of opinion and propaganda*, Oxford 1959
Gill, Conrad, 'The relations between England and France in 1802', *EHR* xxiv (1909), 61–78
Glenny, Michael and Norman Stone, *The other Russia: the experience of exile*, London 1990
Godechot, Jacques, *Le Comte d'Antraigues*, Paris 1986
—— *The counter-revolution: doctrine and action, 1789–1804*, trans. Salvator Athanasio, Princeton 1971
Goodman, Dena, 'Public sphere and private life: towards a synthesis of current historical approaches to the old regime', *History and Theory* xxxi (1992), 1–20
Gough, Hugh, *The newspaper press in the French revolution*, London 1988
Grant, James, *The newspaper press, its origin – progress – and present position*, London 1871
Greer, Donald, *The incidence of the emigration during the French revolution*, Cambridge, Mass. 1951
Griffiths, Robert, *Le Centre perdu: Malouet et les monarchiens dans la révolution française*, Grenoble 1988
Grimsted, P. K., *The foreign ministers of Alexander I: political attitudes and the conduct of foreign policy, 1801–1825*, Berkeley 1969
Habermas, Jürgen, *The structural transformation of the public sphere: an inquiry into a category of bourgeois society*, Cambridge, Mass. 1991
Haig, Robert L., *The Gazeteer: 1735–1797: a study in the eighteenth-century English newspaper*, Carbondale, Ill. 1960
Hammett, B. R., 'Spanish constitutionalism and the impact of the French revolution, 1808–1814', in Doyle and Mason, *Impact of the French revolution*, 64–80
Harris, Bob, *Politics and the rise of the press: Britain and France, 1620–1800*, London–New York 1996
Hatin, E., *Les Gazettes de Hollande et la presse clandestine au xviie et xviiie siècles*, Paris 1865
Hazard, Paul, 'Le Spectateur du nord', *RHLF* (1906), 26–50
Hesse, Carla, *Publishing and cultural politics in revolutionary Paris, 1789–1810*, Berkeley 1991
Hindle, W., *The Morning Post*, London 1937
Holtman, Robert B., *Napoleonic propaganda*, Baton Rouge 1950
Houston, R. A., *Literacy in early modern Europe: culture and education, 1500–1800*, London 1988
Hunt, Lynn (ed.), *Eroticism and the body politic*, Baltimore–London 1991.
—— 'The many bodies of Marie-Antoinette: political pornography and the problem of the feminine in the French revolution', in Hunt, *Eroticism*, 108–130
Hutt, Maurice, *Chouannerie and counter-revolution: Puisaye, the princes and the British government in the 1790s*, Cambridge 1983
Ingram, Edward, 'The geo-politics of the first British expedition to Egypt, IV: Occupation and withdrawal, 1801–1803', *Middle Eastern Studies* xxxi (1995), 317–46
Jervis, Robert, *Perception and misperception in international politics*, Princeton 1976

Jones, Colin (ed.), *Britain and revolutionary France: conflict, subversion and propaganda*, Exeter 1983
Karmin, Otto, *Sir Francis d'Ivernois (1757–1842): Sa vie, son oeuvre et son temps*, Geneva 1920
Klaits, Joseph, *Printed propaganda under Louis XIV: absolute monarchy and public opinion*, Princeton 1976
Kukiel, M., *Czartoryski and European unity, 1770–1861*, Princeton 1955
La Croix, R. G. M. de (duc de Castries), *Les Emigrés*, Paris 1962
Labadie, E., *La Presse à Bordeaux pendant la révolution*, Bordeaux 1910
Lacour-Gayet, R., *Calonne, financier, réformateur, contre-révolutionnaire, 1734–1802*, Paris 1963
Landes, Joan, *Women and the public sphere in the age of the French revolution*, Ithaca, NY 1988
Laski, P., *The trial and execution of Madame Du Barry*, London 1969
Lebow, Richard Ned, *Between peace and war: the nature of international crisis*, Baltimore 1981
Lenôtre, G., *Two royalist spies of the French revolution*, London 1924.
Levy, Darlene Gay, *The ideas and careers of Simon-Nicolas-Henri-Linguet: a study in eighteenth-century French politics*, Urbana–Chicago–London 1980
Luna, Frederick A. de, 'The Dean Street style of revolution: J.-P. Brissot, jeune philosophe', *French Historical Studies* xvii (1991), 159–90
Lyons, Martyn, *Napoleon Bonaparte and the legacy of the French revolution*, London 1994
McCalman, Iain, 'Queen and courtesan: gender, scandal and the public sphere in pre-revolutionary London and Paris', in Martin Fitzpatrick and Iain McCalman (eds), *Enlightenment, Religion and Science*, special issue of *Enlightenment and Dissent*, forthcoming
Madelin, Louis, *Le Consulat et l'empire*, Paris 1937–54
Mallet, Bernard, *Mallet Du Pan and the French revolution*, London 1892
Mallet, Charles Edward, *Family records*, privately printed, London 1917
Mansel, Philip, *Louis XVIII*, London 1981
Marguerite-Marie, Sr, OSU [attrib.], *Vie de l'abbé Calonne: mort en odeur de sainteté aux Trois-Rivières (Octobre 1822)*, Trois-Rivières 1892
Maspero-Clerc, Hélène, 'Une Gazette anglo-française pendant la Guerre d'Amérique, *Le Courier de l'Europe*, 1776–1788', *AHRF* xliv (1976), 572–94
—— *Un Journaliste contre-révolutionnaire: Jean-Gabriel Peltier (1760–1825)*, Paris 1973
—— 'Un Journaliste émigré jugé à Londres pour diffamation du Premier Consul', *Revue d'histoire moderne et contemporaine* xviii (1971), 261–81
—— 'Journaux d'émigrés à Londres (1792–1818)', *BHESRF* années 1972–3 (1974), 67–79
—— 'Montlosier, journaliste de l'émigration', *BHESRF* année 1975 (1977), 81–103
—— 'Samuel Swinton, éditeur du *Courier de l'Europe* à Boulogne-sur-Mer (1778–1783) et agent secret du gouvernement britannique', *AHRF* lvii (1985), 527–31
—— 'Vicissitudes des *Actes des apôtres*', *AHRF* xxxix (1967), 481–9
Matteuchi, N., *Jacques Mallet du Pan*, Naples 1957

Maxted, I., *The London book trades, 1775–1800: a preliminary checklist of members*, Woking 1977
Maza, Sara, 'The diamond necklace affair revisited: the case of the missing queen', in Hunt, *Eroticism*, 63–89
—— *Private lives and public affairs: the causes célèbres of pre-revolutionary France*, Berkeley–Los Angeles 1993
Middleton, C. R., *The administration of British foreign policy, 1782–1856*, Durham, NC 1977
Mitchell, Harvey, *The underground war against revolutionary France: the missions of William Wickham, 1794–1800*, Oxford 1965
Mori, Jennifer, 'The British government and the Bourbon restoration: the occupation of Toulon, 1793', *Historical Journal* xl (1997), 699–719
Morton, J. B., *Camille Desmoulins and other studies of the French revolution*, London 1950.
Mossiker, Frances, *The queen's necklace*, London 1961
Murphy, Martin, *Blanco White: self-banished Spaniard*, New Haven, Conn. 1989
Murray, W. J., *The right-wing press in the French revolution*, Woodbridge 1986
Nathans, Benjamin, 'Habermas's "public sphere" in the era of the French revolution', *French Historical Studies* xvi (1990), 620–44
O'Leary, P., *Sir James Mackintosh: the Whig Cicero*, Aberdeen 1989
Ortzen, Len, *Imperial Venus: the story of Pauline Bonaparte Borghese*, London 1974
Osen, James, *Royalist political thought during the French revolution*, Westport, Conn. 1995
Ozouf, Mona, 'Public opinion at the end of the *ancien régime*', *Journal of Modern History* lx, supplement (1988), S1–S21
Parkinson, Wenda, *This gilded African: Toussaint L'Ouverture*, London 1978
Périvier, A., *Napoléon journaliste*, Paris 1918
Polnay, Peter de, *Napoleon's police*, London 1970
Popkin, Jeremy D., 'The business of political enlightenment in France, 1770–1800', in Brewer and Porter, *Consumption and the world of goods*, 412–36
—— *News and politics in the age of revolution: Jean Luzac's 'Gazette de Leyde'*, Ithaca, NY 1989
—— 'Pamphlet journalism at the end of the old regime', *Eighteenth-Century Studies* xxii (1989), 351–67
—— 'The pre-revolutionary origins of political journalism', in Keith Michael Baker (ed.), *The political culture of the old regime*, Oxford 1987
—— *Revolutionary news: the press in France, 1789–1799*, Durham, NC–London 1990, 16–34
—— *The right-wing press in France, 1792–1800*, Chapel Hill, NC 1980, 3–53
Proschwitz, Gunnar von and Mavis von Proschwitz, *Beaumarchais et le Courier de l'Europe: documents inédits ou peu connus*, Oxford 1990
Rétat, Pierre (ed.), *La Révolution du journal, 1788–1794*, Paris 1989.
Richardson, James L., *Crisis diplomacy: the great powers since the mid-nineteenth century*, Cambridge 1994
Roberts, James, *The counter revolution in France, 1787–1830*, London 1990
Robiquet, Paul, *Théveneau de Morande: étude sur le XVIIIe siècle*, Paris 1882.
Rodger, A. B., *The war of the second coalition, 1798–1801: a strategic commentary*, Oxford 1964

Ryan, A., 'The causes of the British attack upon Copenhagen in 1807', *EHR* lxviii (1953), 37–55

Saugier, B., *Pichegru: histoire d'un suicide*, n.p. 1992

Saul, Norman E., *Russia and the Mediterranean, 1797–1807*, Chicago 1970

Schroeder, Paul W., *The transformation of European politics, 1763–1848*, Oxford 1994

Schweizer, Karl and Rebecca Klein, 'The French revolution and developments in the London daily press to 1793', in Schweizer and Black, *Politics and the press*, 171–86

—— and Jeremy Black (eds), *Politics and the press in Hanoverian Britain*, Lewiston 1989.

Sgard, Jean, 'On dit', in Harvey Chisick (ed.), *The press in the French revolution*, Oxford 1991, 25–32

Slavin, Morris, *The Hébertistes to the guillotine: anatomy of a 'conspiracy' in revolutionary France*, Baton Rouge 1994

Smith, Anthony, *The newspaper: an international history*, London 1979

Sorel, A., *L'Europe et la révolution française*, Paris 1885–1905

Sourdeval, C. de, 'Le Journal d'un Nantais à Londres pendant la Terreur', *Revue de Bretagne et de Vendée* xxv (1869), 5–25

Steinberg, S. H., *500 years of printing*, 3rd edn, London 1974

Thomson, Oliver, *Mass persuasion in history: an historical analysis of the development of propaganda techniques*, Edinburgh 1977

Thrasher, Peter Adam, *Pasquale Paoli: an enlightened hero, 1725–1807*, London 1970

Tulard, Jean, *L'Anti-Napoléon: la légende noire de l'empereur*, Paris 1965

—— *Napoleon, the myth of the saviour*, trans. Teresa Waugh, London 1984

van Caenegem, R. C., *Judges, legislators and professors: chapters in European legal history*, Cambridge 1987

Vidalenc, J., *Les Emigrés français, 1789–1825*, Caen 1963

Vogne, Marcel, *La Presse périodique en Franche-Comté des origines à 1870*, Paris 1977–8

Wagner, Peter, *Eros revived: erotica of the enlightenment in England and America*, London 1990

Weiner, Margery, *The French exiles, 1789–1815*, London 1960

Werkmeister, Lucyle, *The London daily press, 1772–1792*, Lincoln, Neb. 1963

Whiteman, Jeremy, 'The Constituent Assembly and the problem of French national power', in Adcock, Chester and Whiteman, *Revolution, society and the politics of memory*, 170–5

Wiener, Joel H., *The war of the unstamped*, Ithaca 1969

Woolf, Stuart, *Napoleon's integration of Europe*, London 1991

Zawadzki, Adam, *A man of honour: Adam Czartoryski, minister of Russia and Poland*, Oxford 1993

Ziegler, Philip, *Addington: a life of Henry Addington, first Viscount Sidmouth*, London 1965

Unpublished sources

Barker, Hannah, 'The freedom of the press: political manipulation and the role of subsidy in late eighteenth-century newspapers', paper given at Colloquium on British History, London, 2 Jan. 1992
────── 'Politicians and the press', seminar paper, Lincoln College, Oxford, 15 Oct. 1991
Brown, Christopher, 'Anti-slavery petitions: origins of the anti-slavery movement in the 1780s', seminar paper, Lincoln College, Oxford, Feb. 1992
Burrows, Simon, 'The French exile press in London, 1789–1814', DPhil. diss. Oxford 1992
Carpenter, Kirsty, 'Les Emigrés à Londres, 1793–1797', doctorat du nouveau régime, Paris I 1993
Cottrell, Stella, 'English views of France and the French, 1789–1815', DPhil. diss. Oxford 1990
Gray, Philip, 'Revolutionism as revisionism: early British views of Bonaparte, 1796–1803', MA diss. Canterbury, NZ 1995
Griffiths, Robert, 'Pierre-Victor Malouet and the *monarchiens* in the French revolution and counter-revolution', PhD diss. British Columbia 1975
Marino, Samuel Joseph, 'The French-refugee newspapers and periodicals in the United States, 1789–1825', PhD diss. Michigan 1962
Miramon-Fitzjames, H., 'Le Comte de Montlosier pendant la révolution et l'empire', PhD diss. Aix-en-Provence 1944
Mori, Jennifer, 'The impact of the French revolution on the ideas and policies of William Pitt', DPhil. diss. Oxford 1992
Wilkinson, E. M., 'French émigrés in England, 1789–1802, their reception and impact on English life', BLitt. diss. Oxford 1952

Index

Page references in italics refer to content of tables.

Abeille, 128
abolitionists: and *Ambigu*, 74; and *Courier de Londres*, 74, 87–8; and Malouet, 173; and Peltier, 74, 131–2, 171, 176; and Swinton, 74, 87–8, 169. See also *Amis des noirs*, Brissot, Montlosier, Théveneau de Morande
absolutism, 158, 167. See also abbé Calonne
Act of Mediation, 120
Actes des apôtres: conception, 37; contributors, 21, 37, 38, 41, 44; and pornographic libels, 212
Addington, Henry, 1st viscount Sidmouth: on Alien Act, 112; and Malta, 126; formation of ministry, 188; and Otto, 114, 119; and outbreak of war (1803), 108–27 passim
Addington, Hiley, 119
advertising, see newspapers
Agricultural Magazine, 37
Alexander I, tsar of Russia: and Czartoryski, 137; fears coup, 136, 203; and Napoleonic alliance, 137, 203; treatment after Tilsit, 202–3. See also Antraigues, *Courier d'Angleterre*
Alexandria, 125
Alien Act: and émigré journalists, 90; Franco-British interpretations, 109, 112; French invoke, 116. See also Addington, Pelham
Alopeus, David, 137
Alopeus, Maximilien, 131
Ambigu: and Auckland, 77; and Bernadotte, 205; and caricature art, 213–14; and Castlereagh, 128; and Henri Christophe, 139; *Les Evêques d'Irlande et M. Milner réfutés . . . de Pie VII*, 195; and Louis XVIII, 131; *Oraison funèbre du duc d'Enghien*, 141; and Peltier's trial, 16, 122–4; *Pie VII vengé*, 195; *Réclamations canoniques*, 141; on Russia, 204; *Vérité proclamé par ses agresseurs*, 195. See also abolitionists, Antraigues, 'Black Legend', British government, circulation, Couchery, De Boffe, Gentz, Germany, Hamburg, Ivernois, *Ode atribuée à Chénier*, periodicals, printers, *Voeu d'un bon patriote hollandois*
Ami du Roi, 38, 95
Amiens, peace of, 108–16 passim, 121, 125, 185, 186, 211
Amis des noirs, Société des, 171, 175
Andoe, Anne (Mme. Peltier): at Bordeaux, 120; family background, 48
André de Montluel, [?], 71, See also collaborators, correspondents
Andréossi, Antoine-François: on *Courier de Londres*, 179; instructions from Talleyrand, 125; misinterprets British motives, 126; and Regnier, 120
Angely, François-Marie and son, barons d', 128
anglophobia, see Russia
Annales politiques, civiles et littéraires du dix-huitième siècle, 37, 222
Annales politiques du dix-neuvième siècle, 128n., 134
Antidote, see Kirwan, periodicals, 'propaganda journals'
Anti-Gallican Monitor, 93
Anti-Jacobin Review, 85
Antraigues, Louis-Henri-Alexandre de Launai, comte d': and Alexander I, 136; and *Ambigu*, 68n., 212; and Armfeldt, 137; background, 29, 39, 44; at Berlin, 140; and 'Black Legend', 207; and brochures, 140; and Canning, 53, 91, 92, 131, 135; and Castanos, 91; and Castlereagh, 53; correspondence, 91; and Confederation of the Rhine, 134; and *Courier d'Angleterre*, 29, 31, 53, 82, 91, 134–40 passim; and Czartoryski, 136, 137; and Dalberg, 134; and Danish expedition, 201; death, 51; and Grenville, 134; and Henri-Larivière, 29; intelligence network, 72; and

253

Maury, 195n.; and middle ground, 184; and Panin, 136; and Pichegru, 5; and Regnier, 29, 72, 82, 91, 92, 131, 135, 140, 201, 202; and Russia, 68n., 82, 91, 134–8 passim, 202–4 passim; and Sweden, 82, 135, 201; and Talavera, 92; and Tilsit, 135–6. *See also* British government, collaborators, embezzlement, pensions, police
Arakcheyev, Alexey Andreevich, 204
Argus, 90n., 114, 209
Armfeldt, Gustave Maurice, 137, 138
Arras, bishop of, *see* Conzie
Artois, comte d' (later king Charles X): and Bertin d'Antilly, 107; character, 12, 14; and Conzie (Arras), 103, 111; and Mackintosh, 197–8; Mallet on, 103; and Mallet Du Pan, 60, 103, 105; and Malouet, 103, 104; and Mesmont, 107; and Montlosier, 50, 105; and Napoleon, 110; and *Paris pendant l'année*, 102; and Peltier, 72, 87, 102, 104, 111, 125, 131, 197; and Regnier, 72. *See also* Bourbons, *purs*
Aspinall, Arthur, 89
assignats: 149, 178; forged, 52. See also *Coup d'oeil sur les assignats*
atrocities: French, 144, 168, 211; at Jaffa, 126n., 211n., 217; on Saint-Domingue (Haiti), 219; in Spanish war, 205; in Switzerland, 168, 209
Auckland, *see* Eden
Auerstadt, battle of, 134
Auerweck, Louis d', baron de Steillenfels, 31, 32, 40, 41, 51, 53, 54. *See also* collaborators
Auget de Montyon, A.-J.-B.-R., 47n., 102n., 159
Austria: and Brunswick manifesto, 47; and *Cosmopolite*, 44n.; Mainz surrendered, 99; and Malta, 121; press, 206; and Tilsit, 202; and Venetia, 99; and war (1813), 206
Avaray, Antoine-Louis-François de Bésiade, comte d', 130–1, 132
Axtell, bookseller, 67

Badini, Carl Francis, 90, 107
Bagot, Sir Charles, 92
Baker, Keith Michael, 4
Barentin, Charles-Louis-François de Paule de, 103
Barker, Hannah, 90
Barras, Jean-Nicolas-Paul-François: and Bourbons, 104; *Mémoires*, 104n.; resignation, 180. *See also* Josephine de Beauharnais, Montlosier
Barruel, Augustin, abbé de: 36n., 60n.; and counter-revolutionary theory, 143, 148; *Mémoires pour servir à l'histoire du jacobinisme françois*, 146
Batavian Republic, 133
battles, *see* Auerstadt, Danish expedition, Jena, Nations, Talavera
Baudus, Jean-Louis-Amable de, 106
Baylis, Thomas, 33, 66
Beauharnais, Eugène de, 219
Beauharnais, Josephine de, 218–20 passim
Beaumarchais, Pierre-Augustin Caron de, 45
Bédée brothers, [?], *l'aîné* and *jeune*, 31, 32, 38. *See also* collaborators
Béhague, Jean-Pierre-Antoine, comte de, *see* collaborators, pensions
Belgium, 24, 83. *See also* distribution
Bellenger, Dominic Aidan, 11, 13
Bell's Weekly Messenger, 85, 90n.
Bentabole, Pierre-Louis, 150
Bérardier, priest, 149
Bernadotte, Jean-Baptiste-Jules, 92, 205
Berne, 27, 58, 71
Bertin d'Antilly, Louis-Auguste, 107
Bertrand de Moleville, Antoine-François, comte de, 155n.
bishops, 189–90, 191–5 passim, 203, 209. *See also* bishops (*non-démissionnaires*), Peltier
bishops (*non-démissionnaires*): and concordat, 189–91, 195; and *Controverse pacifique* 191; declining numbers, 195. *See also* Lally-Tollendal, Montlosier
'Black Legend', 25–6, 152, 210–21 passim
blackmail, 86, 113
Blanchard, Pierre-Louis: and concordat, 191–5 passim; condemnation, 193; *Controverse pacifique*, 191; *Les Evêques d'Irlande et M. Milner réfutés . . .*, 195; and Maury, 195; and Milner, 194; and Peltier, 193, 194, 195; *Pie VII vengé . . .*, 195; and Pius VII, 192, 195; *Réclamations canoniques*, 141; and Regnier, 193; *Vérité proclamé par ses agresseurs*, 195
blockade: continental, 73, 197, 201–2; of Saint-Domingue (Haiti), 176
Boffe, Joseph De, *see* De Boffe

INDEX

Bonald, Louis-Gabriel-Amboise, vicomte de, 147, 148
Bonaparte, Jérome, 218, 219
Bonaparte, Joseph, 112
Bonaparte, Laetitia, *see* Ramolino
Bonaparte, Louis, 220
Bonaparte, Lucien, 188, 219, 220
Bonaparte, Marie-Louise, 220
Bonaparte, Napoleon: and Bourbons, 110, 208; in British press, 211; rendered as Buonaparté, 217; and concordat, 189; and Egypt, 121, 126; and Enghien, 207; and English papers, 70n.; excommunication, 194, 207, 208; bans foreign travel, 206; and Ivernois, 196; and Jaffa, 213–14, 217; kidnap plot, 199–200; on libels, 127; and Ottoman Empire, 121; annexation of papal states, 194; and Portugese fleet, 201; press control, 106–7, 206, 207; and propaganda, 105–6, 110, 116, 134, 206, 207; and religious affairs, 208; and war (1803); 108, 118. *See also* 'Black Legend', Couchery, Gérard, Las Cases, Mallet Du Pan, Montlosier, *Paris pendant l'année*, Peltier, press, Regnier
Bonaparte, Pauline, *see* Borghese
bookseller-publishers, French, in London, 61n., 66–8
Boosey and Hawkes, 68
Boosey, John, 68
Boosey, Thomas, 61, 67, 68
Borghese, Pauline, *née* Bonaparte, 212, 217, 219, 220
Bourbons: and allies, 167; and Auerweck, 41; and abbé Calonne, 168; and Canning, 203; and Couchery, 44, 132, 182, 226; and *Courier de Londres*, 133, 148, 155, 157–8; and Dutheil, 103, 111, 227; and émigré press, 44, 101–5 passim, 130–3 passim, 141; expansionism, 116; and Fauche-Borel, 104; and Gérard, 133, 182, 227; hopes of restoration, 104, 208; and Mallet, 103; and Mallet Du Pan, 46, 87, 102–5 passim, 185; and Malouet, 103, 104, 163; and *monarchiens*; 102–3; and Montlosier, 50, 87, 105, 106, 186, 187; and Napoleon, 110, 208; and Paul I, 104; and Peltier, 45, 101–11 passim, 131, 132, 182, 227; policy dichotomy (1799), 104; and Regnier, 87, 110, 111, 131, 182, 203, 227, 203; war aims, 165–7. *See also* Barras, British government, Foreign Office, *Mercure britannique*, Pichegru
Bourgevin de Vialart, Charles-Etienne de, comte de Saint-Morys, 55, 81, 231
Bourgevin de Vialart, Charles-Paul-Jean-Baptiste de, comte de Saint-Morys, 55, 231
Bourrienne, Louis-Antoine Fauvalet de, 108
Bouvens, abbé Charles de, 207
Brabant, 89, 99
Brazil, and *Essai historique sur . . . la liberté hélvetique*, 99. *See also* circulation
Bréard, [?], 172–3
bribery, of press, 86, 90, 106, 133
Brienne, Etienne-Charles Lomenie de, 153
brigandage, in France, 209
Brissot de Warville, Jacques-Pierre: and abolitionism, 171: and *Amis des noirs*, 175; execution, 150; and factional conflict, 145; journalistic background, 8–9, 16, 145; on readers per copy, 75. *See also* circulation, *Courier de l'Europe*, *Courier de Londres*, *Patriote françois*, Peltier
British Critic, 85
British government: and *Ambigu*, 83, 84, 87, 129; and Antraigues, 91, 201; and Bernadotte, 92; and Bourbons, 118; and Conzie (Arras), 118; and *Courier d'Angleterre*, 29, 82, 87, 92, 129, 130, 135, 141; and *Courier de Londres*, 81, 87, 99–100, 129, 130, 141; and Dutheil, 100–2, passim, 109; and émigré press, 90–4, 141; and *Gazette de la Grande-Bretagne*, 92; and Heron, 92, 130; and Mallet Du Pan, 60–1, 92, 100; and *monarchiens*, 100–1; and Montlosier, 105; and newspaper propaganda, 28–30, 129; and Peltier, 86, 92, 100, 129; and Regnier, 81, 91, 92, 129, 130; and Swinton, 92, 99–100. *See also* Foreign Office
British Mercury, see *Mercure britannique*
British Press, 37
Brittany: communications, 73; Peltier's sources, 53, and *Supplément au Rédacteur*, 28; Verduisant proposes invasion, 166. *See also* Chouans, Quiberon
Broughton, Henry, 198
Broval, [?], chevalier de: and Peltier, 131; and Regnier, 72

Brumaire: impact on emigré press, 179–96 passim
Brunswick, Charles William Ferdinand, duke of: and Mallet Du Pan, 71, 99; and *Mercure brittanique*, 64. See also Brunswick manifesto
Brunswick manifesto, 47, 64n., 104
Budberg, Andrei, 136
Bulletins de la grande armée, 206, 207
Burke, Edmund, 95, 143, 144
Butet, [?], 71. See also collaborators

Cabarrus, Thérèse, 150, 151
Cadell and Davies, 62, 67
Cadet de Gassicourt, Charles-Louis, 146
Cadoudal, Georges: arrest, 199; France demands deportation, 114, 125, British reaction, 116, 118; and *Moniteur*, 117; and Pichegru, 52
Caen, Claude Gilles de, see Gilles de Caen
Calais, 68, 73, 98, 105
Calmar, Declaration of, 208
Calonne brothers, means of differentiation in text, p. xv
Calonne, Charles-Alexandre de: on *assignats*, 176–7; fears for British political stability, 165; and abbé Calonne, 158; and *Courier de Londres*, 19, 31, 32, 81, 88, 95, 154; and Cristin, 153; and De Boffe, 176–7n.; and Dumouriez,157; family background, 39; on French constitutional position, 159; and Ivernois, 176–7; and Malouet, 157; on *mandats territaux*, 177; and moderates, 157; and Pitt, 166; and propaganda, 39, 95–6, 176–7; break with *purs*, 159; and Quiberon, 166; on revolutionary finances, 176–7; and Routledge, 88; and Swinton, 88–9, 154; and Théveneau de Morande, 88; and Verduisant, 88–9, 89. See also collaborators, diamond necklace affair, proprietors, *Tableau de l'Europe en novembre 1795*, *The Times*
Calonne, Jacques-Ladislas-Joseph de, abbé: and absolutism, 158; background, 39, 41; and Beaumarchais, 45; on Bourbon restoration, 168; and C.-A. de Calonne, 158; in Canada, 36; character, 36, 39; at Coblenz, 46; on Constitution (of Year III), 157; and *Courier de Londres*, 19, 21, 38, 55, 66, 81, 88; on Danton, 169; and 'divine judgement', 148; emigration, 47; and émigré clergy, 161; on French constitutional position, 159; on Jacobins, 150; and Lally-Tollendal, 158; and Mallet Du Pan, 157, 162; attacks moderates, 158; moderation of stance, 157, 158; on monarchy, 159; and Montlosier, 27, 36, 158–60; peace (argues for), 168; and Peltier, 157; break with *purs*, 159; and Quiberon, 52, 100, 166; and restoration, 148; on slavery, 170n.; on Tallien, 151; on Thermidoreans, 156, 160; on Two-Thirds Decree, 156; and Verduisant, 36, 158; on war aims, 168, 177; and Windham, 100. See also journalists (major).
Canada: abbé Calonne and, 36, 55; *Ambigu's* influence in, 139
Canning, George: and Antraigues, 53, 91, 92, 131, 135; and Bourbons, 203; and Castlereagh, 53; and Danish expedition, 201; and propaganda warfare, 135; and Regnier, 53, 82, 135; and Talavera, 92
Cardo, [?], comte de, 96
Caribbean, and war; 168–76. See also French West Indies, Grenada, Guadeloupe, Jamaica, Martinique, Saint-Domingue (Haiti)
caricature, see *Ambigu*, satire
Carnot, Lazare-Nicholas-Marguerite, 152
Carpenter, Kirsty, 11, 13
Carrier, Jean-Baptiste, 151, 155
Castanos, Francisco Xavier de, 91, 212
Castlereagh, Robert Stewart, 2nd viscount, 53, 128
Castres, Sabatier de, see Sabatier de Castres
Castries, Charles-Eugène-Gabriel, marquis de; and Mallet Du Pan, 71, 103, 104–5; and Malouet, 103, 104
Cavendish-Bentinck, William Henry, 3rd duke of Portland, 60, 118
Cazalès, Jacques-Antoine-Marie de, 159
Censer, Jack, 8
Censeur, 107
censorship and confiscation, in France, 5–6, 7–8, 97, 106, 117, 141. See also Napoleon, *Journal des dames*, Peltier
Channel Islands, 140. See also Jersey
Charette de la Contrie, François-Athanase, 24, 166
Charles IV, king of Spain, 215
Charles X, king of France, see Artois

INDEX

Charles XIII, king of Sweden, 136
Charmilly, *see* Vénault de Charmilly
Châsteaugiron, *see* Châteaugiron
Chateaubriand, Armand de, 52, 53
Chateaubriand, François-René, vicomte de: on circulation, 83; on De Boffe, 61; and émigré critics, 147; and Fontanes, 218; and Peltier, 33–4, 69, 218
Châteaugiron, Jean-Marie de, 39. *See also* journalists (minor)
Châteauneuf, [?], de, 227
Châtelain, Jean-Baptiste-François-Ernest de, 227, 228n.
Chauvelin, Bernard-François, marquis de, 89
Chénier, Marie-Joseph, 124, 147. *See also* Mallet Du Pan, *Ode atribuée à Chénier*
Chouans: arrests in Paris, 199; and Auerweck, 51; and Dutheil, 28; and Jersey, 116, 118; and Peltier, 70, 124, 167; and Puisaye, 166; religious background, 192; and La Roberie, 166
Christin, Ferdinand, 89, 153
Christophe, *see* Henri Christophe
Chronique de l'Europe, 227
Cicaldi, T., 231
circulation: 19, 74–85 passim; Brissot's estimates, 75; Heron's estimates, 85; émigré journals, in Americas, 139, in Brabant, 99, in Brazil, 78, 138, in England, 68, 77–9 passim, in France, 78, 79, 97, 98, in Germany, 99, 133, in Grenada, 171, in Holland, 141, in Italy, 79, 99, in Martinique, 140, in Mexico, 138, 139, in Portugal, 138, in Russia, 82, 134–8 passim, in Saint-Domingue (Haiti), 78, in Spain, 138, in Spanish colonies, 138, in Sweden, 82, 135–9 passim, in USA, 79, 139–40, in West Indies, 83, 139; of domestic newspapers in Britain and France, 84–5; of news sheets in Germany, 85; on number of readers per copy, 75; of royalist journals, 98n.
Citoyen français, 187
Clef du cabinet, 187
Clousier brothers, Parisian printers, 98
coalitions: Czartoryski and, 137; Kirwan proposes, 28–9; Mallet Du Pan proposes, 162; Paul I targeted, 99; and Peninsular War, 207
Cobbett, William, 110, 115, 120n., 124n.
Coblenz: émigré army at, 14; journalists at, 46; 'press releases' from, 89, 95, 96, 153

'collaborators': definition, 31; finances, 48; functional details, 31–2; journalistic experience, 38, 39; nationalities, 40–1; political activity, 32, 44; social status, 39. *See also* counter-revolution, families, pensions
colons, 25, 72, 168–76 passim
Conchy, [?], de, bookseller, 67
concordat, 116, 189–96 passim
Condorcet, Jean-Antoine-Nicolas de Caritat, marquis de, 146, 171
Confederation of the Rhine, 134, 207
confiscation, *see* censorship and confiscation
Constantinople, 31, 71
constitution: British, 116, 117, 118, 188, 209; French, general, 47, 119, 158, 159, 162, 178, 183, 184, *ancienne*, 105, 159, of 1791, 161, 167, 183, of Year I (1793), 161, of Year III (1795), 156–7, 161, 180, of Year VIII (1799), 179, 183–6 passim; of Roman Catholic Church, 191. *See also* C.-A. de Calonne, abbé Calonne, Louis XVIII, Mallet Du Pan, *monarchiens*, Montlosier, Peltier
constitutional monarchy, 19, 47, 179, 183
continental blockade, *see* blockade
Convention: membership, 156; and press control, 16; press reports, 24, 25, 149, 150, 157, 169; and slavery, 169–70
conventionnels, 150n., 156, 157, 161, 164, 184n.
Conzie, Louis-François-Marc-Hilaire de, bishop of Arras: alleged role in distribution of seditious papers, 118 and Artois, 103, 111; and Dutheil, 111; and Mallet Du Pan, 103; and Malouet, 103; and Otto, 114; and Peltier, 111; and Regnier, 111–12. *See also* British government
Copenhagen, battle of, *see* Danish expedition
Corbière, *see* La Corbière
Cornwallis, Charles, 1st marquess, 112
Correspondance française ou tableau de l'Europe, *see* *Correspondance politique*
Correspondance politique: back issues, 76; collapse, 23–4; economic propaganda, 177–8; and Quiberon, 166; and victims of revolutionary tribunal, 155. *See also* circulation, Germany, Italy, newspapers, Peltier

257

Correspondance politique pour servir à l'histoire du républicanisme français, 62
Correspondenten, (*Correspondant de Hambourg*), 63, 85n.
correspondents, 31, 71–2
Cosmopolite, 37, 44, 45
Couchery, Jean-Baptiste: and *Ambigu*, 30, 38; background, 41; and 'Black Legend', 212; and Bonapartism, 51; on Pauline Borghese, 212; character, 35; and *Courier de Londres* 30, 38; emigration, 47; and Fauche-Borel, 35n., 131; in French government records, 128; and Jacobins, 42; on legitimacy, 182; and Louis XVI, 44; on Napoleon, 215–17, 220; and Peltier, 132; and Pichegru, 47, 54; and satire, 179, 215–17; and Terror, 45. *See also* Bourbons, embezzlement, journalists (major), pensions
Couchery, Victor, 54
counter-revolutionary activities: journalistic, 32; non-journalistic, 32, 36, 51–4 passim; British reaction, 144; historiography, 224; ideology, 143–8 passim, 180–2; publicity, 143–4. *See also* cultural issues
Coup d'oeil sur les assignats, 176n.
Courier, 84, 124n., 132
Courier d'Angleterre: and Alexander I, 130, 137, 203–4, 205, 218; background, 29–30; banned in restoration France, 227; brochure format, 140; and Danish expedition, 201; and Louis XVIII, 130–1; merger, 18, 29, 93; promotes nationalism, 137; on Napoleonic finances, 197; Spanish translations, 138. *See also* D. Alopeus, Antraigues, British government, circulation, Gentz, Germany, Henri-Larivière, newspapers, Regnier
Courier du Bas-Rhin (subsequently *Provinciale Zeytung*), 95, 97n.
Courier de l'Europe (subsequently *Courier de Londres*): back issues, 76; and Brissot, 8, 75; and 'opposition', 8; and parliamentary reporting, 164; readers per copy, 75. *See also Courier de Londres*, Peltier, Théveneau de Morande
Courier français, 228n.
Courier de Londres: *Avis à tous les négociants de l'Europe*, 177; banned in Batavian Republic, 133, in France, 81, 97, at Hamburg, 133, in Saxony, 133, in Switzerland, 97; on Brissot, 150; capitalisation, 231; and concordat, 190; and Directory, 107; editorship, 19, 106, 187n.; financial news, 77; finances, 80–1; foundation, 18; foreign correspondents, 31, 71; and Granada, 171; on Jacobins, 154; on Louis XVI, 154, 155; on Louis XVIII, 132; mergers, 18, 29, 159; motto, 155; on 'natural equality', 154–5; and Peltier's trial, 125; and *philosophes*, 145; on Pichegru's death, 200; policy shifts, 19, 130, 153, 155; Portuguese edition, 138; on prison massacres, 154; propaganda, economic, 177–8, general, 209; on Saint-Domingue (Haiti) 169; readers per copy, 75; on *Royal proclamation on the war*, 167; on Russia, 204; production, 69; on republicanism, 154; *Table des faits . . . dans le Courier de Londres*, 76; and Calonne's *Tableau de l'Europe en novembre 1795*, 159; on war aims, 167, 205. *See also* abolitionists, Andréossi, Bourbons, British government, C.-A. de Calonne, abbé Calonne, circulation, J.-B. Couchery, *Courier de l'Europe*, Directory, Fauche-Borel, Fouché, *Gazette de la Grande-Bretagne*, Gérard, Germany, Heron, Malouet, Montlosier, newspapers, proprietors, Regnier, Swinton
Courier de Middlesex, see *Impartial ou Courier de Middlesex*
Courrier d'Avignon, 8
Courrier de Londres et de Paris, 50, 189
Courvoisier, Jean-Baptiste, 96
Cox [Edward] and Son, 66
Critical Review, 85
cultural issues, 147–8; historiographical consequences, 148
Czartoryski, prince Adam, 136, 137

Dalberg, Karl Theodore von, 134
Dallas, Robert Charles, 62, 64. *See also* collaborators
Danican, Auguste, 53, 201
Danish expedition, 189, 201–2
Danloux, Henri-Pierre, on Peltier, 34, 76
Danou, *see* Daunou
Danton, Georges, 16, 148, 152, 169, 177
Dantonists, 156
Darnton, Robert: on booktrade, 6–7; on *Encyclopédie*, 56, 71n.; on

INDEX

enlightenment, 45n., 56; on mesmerism, 35n.; on Montlosier, 35n.
Da Souza-Coutinho, Don Roderigo, 71, 99
Daunou, Pierre-Claude-François, 184
Davis, George, 140
De Boffe, Joseph: and *Ambigu*, 67, 68, 83; background, 67n.; and back issues, 76; and C.-A. de Calonne, 176–7n.; Chateaubriand on, 61; merger, 67; and imports, 77; and Liverpool, 70; and Mallets, 61, 62, 68; and Peltier, 25, 66–7, 87, 100; and Serres de La Tour, 66n.; and Talleyrand, 67. *See also Essai historique sur . . . la liberté hélvetique*, *Paris pendant l'année*, proprietors
De La Gardie, Jacob-Gustaf, comte, 87n., 205
Debrett, John, 67
Décade philosophique, 17, 84, 90n.
Dechasteaugiron, *see* Châteaugiron
Défense des émigrés, 102
Delatouche, [?], 90
Delille, Jacques, abbé, 71, 111, 147
Denmark, *see* Antraigues, Danish expedition, League of Armed Neutrality
Dernier Tableau de Paris: abbreviated versions, 97; back issues, 76–7; confiscations, 97; content, 144, 146; counter-revolutionary publicity, 143–4; and French government, 96; alleged inaccuracies, 34; objective, 21–3; prospectus, 96; seizures, 97; on Saint-Domingue (Haiti), 169; and September massacres, 21–3; sources, 23; style, 23. *See also* circulation, periodicals
Desmoulins, Camille, 16, 46n., 152, 159n. *See also* Peltier
Dessarts, [?], syndic of Geneva, 71
diamond necklace affair, 5, 7, 88
Diderot, Denis, 146
Directory: and *Courier de Londres*, 107; and Dutheil, 28, 102; imperialism under, 168; Mallet Du Pan on, 58, 162, 184; and Montlosier, 151, 161; and Peltier, 157, 161, 163; and press control, 16, 97. *See also* atrocities
distribution, *see* circulation, press
Douglass, John, 193–4, 194
Drouin, [?], 101
Du Barry, Jeanne, comtesse, 97, 156
Du Bouchet, *see* Sandillaud Du Bouchet
Dulau, A. B., 61, 67, 76, 83

Dumas, Gabriel-Mathieu, 76
Dumouriez, Charles-François Du Périer, 157–8
Durfort-Boissières, Alphonse, 51, 110. *See also* collaborators
Dutheil, Nicolas: agents, 110; background, 28, 32, 48n., 51; and Durfort-Boissières, 51; French demand expulsion, 109; and Hawkesbury, 109, 110; and rue Niçaise, 109; and Otto, 83, 113; and Peltier, 51, 101, 110, 111; and Regnier, 51, 54, 110, 111; and Saint-Domingue, 114. *See also* Bourbons, British government, Directory, journalists (minor), *Paris pendant l'année*, police, 'propaganda journals', *Supplément au Rédacteur*
duties, *see* taxes

East India Company, 73–4
Eden, William, Lord Auckland, 77
editor-proprietors, *see* abbé Calonne, Châteaugiron, Kirwan, Mallet Du Pan, Montlosier, Peltier, Regnier
Edwards, Bryan, 174–5
Egypt: British misperceptions, 126; correspondents in, 71; Mallet Du Pan on, 184; Sébastiani's mission to, 121. *See also* Alexandria
Eisenstein, Elizabeth L., 2–3
elections: (1795), 156–7; (1797), 168; (1799), 104
Elgin, Thomas, 7th Earl, 52
Ellenborough, *see* Law
embezzlement: by Antraigues and Regnier, 82, 135; by Couchery (alleged), 54; by Sonthonax (alleged), 172
emigration patterns, 12. *See also* collaborators, émigrés, journalists (major), journalists (minor)
émigré(s): usage, p. xv; amnesty of 1802, 50, 179; demography, 13; clergy and laity, 12; finances 13, 74; historiography, 10–13; influence in Britain, 12; invited back (1797), 161; political profiles, 13; return to France, 13, 179; social life, 74, 75. *See also* Coblenz
Encyclopédie, 56, 71n.
endorsements, 85–6
Enghien, Louis-Antoine-Henri de Bourbon-Condé, duc d': kidnap, 199, 200–1, 207; murder, 28–9, 200–1, 207; obituary, 101. *See also Ambigu*

Enlightenment: 145–7 passim; Darnton on, 45n., 56
Erskine, Charles, Cardinal, papal legate in London, 189–90
Essai historique sur . . . la liberté helvétique: and De Boffe, 68; publication, 63, 64, 79; in Paris, 98; pirate editions, 80; Portuguese translation, 80, 99
Este, Charles, 96
European Magazine, 85
'exile(s)', defined p. xv. *See also* émigré(s)
extortion, *see* bribery, embezzlement

families (wives, consorts and children) of journalists, 48–9. *See also* individual names for family backgrounds
Fauche and Lamaisonfort, 62, 63, 68, 99. *See also* under names of the individual partners
Fauche, Pierre-François: background, 39, 40, 62; and *Courier d'Angleterre*, 31, 32, 135; and Mallet Du Pan, 62, 63, 64; and Sweden, 135, 136; and Tilsit, 202–3. *See also* Foreign Office, collaborators, pensions
Fauche, Samuel, 62
Fauche-Borel, Louis: background, 39, 40, 51, 53; and Couchery, 35n., 131; and *Courier d'Angleterre*, 31, 32; and *Courier de Londres*, 141; and Danish expedition, 201; *Mémoires*, 101, 141; and Peltier, 131; and Pichegru, 51, 104. *See also* Bourbons, collaborators, Foreign Office, pensions
Ferdinand VII, king of Spain, 215
Fesch, Guiseppe, Cardinal, 220
Fesch, Laetitia, *see* Ramolino, Maria Laetizia
Fiévée, Joseph, 106
financial analysis: impact on allied strategy, 176–7. *See also* propaganda
Flint, Charles, 60
Foedon, Noël, 171
Fontanai, abbé Louis-Antoine-Bonafous de, 75n., 95
Fontanes, Louis de: background, 49n., 50n.; and Chateaubriand, 218; and émigré critics, 147; and *Paris pendant l'année*, 102; and Peltier, 102
Fontassy, [?], Russian consul in Gothenburg, 136
Foreign Office; and *Ambigu*, 141; and Antraigues, 131, 134; and Bourbons, 102; and *Courier d'Angleterre*, 82, 130, 135; and *Courier de Londres*, 141; and Dutheil, 102; and Fauche, 135; and Fauche-Borel, 141; and *London Gazette*, 140; and Malouet, 101; and Mauritius, 139; and Peltier, 86; and propaganda, 129, 140, 142; and Regnier, 91, 130, 131; and Russia, 135, 138; and Sweden, 135, 138; understaffing, 91, 93, 101; and West Indies, 139
Foreign Post Office, 68, 91, 133n., 138
Foster, Sir Augustus John, 138
Fouché, Joseph; and amnesty (1802), 50; and atrocities, 151; background, 43n.; and *Courier de Londres*, 208; education, 42, 43n.; and Montlosier, 190; and Otto, 114; and Peltier, 43n., 114, 125
Fouquier-Tinville, Antoine-Quentin, 151, 155
Freeling, [?], British consul in Gothenburg, 82, 136
Freeling, Francis, secretary of the Post Office, 118
freemasons, 146
French West Indies, 101
Frouillé, [?], marquis de, 72, 175, 176
Fructidor: and Carnot, 152; and clampdown on journalists, 31, 46, 95; impact on journalists, 161–3, 168; and Pichegru, 41–2

Gallatin, Pierre, chevalier de, 64, 71, 99
Garat, Dominique-Joseph, 152, 184
Gaschet, abbé François, 194
Gassicourt, *see* Cadet de Gassicourt
Gazeteer, 81, 84
Gazetier cuirassé, 6, 212
'gazette', definition, p. xv
Gazette de Cologne, 95
Gazette française, 172
Gazette de France, 5–6
Gazette de la Grande-Bretagne, (previously and subsequently the *Courier de Londres*): on Danish expedition, 202; editorial approach, 203; on Napoleonic finances, 197; objectives, 206; relaunch, 19; on Russia, 202. *See also* British government, Heron, newspapers
Gazette de Jersey, 120, 125
Gazette de Leyde, 97n.
Gazette de Paris, 15n., 95
Gazette prussienne, 97n.
'general will', *see* public opinion
Gentleman's Magazine, 85

Gentz, Frederich von: and *Ambigu*, 212; and *Courier d'Angleterre*, 136; and counter-revolutionary theory, 143, 204n.; and Mallet Du Pan, 63, 71, 73; and *Mercure britannique*, 63; and Peltier, 93; and Regnier, 93, 204n.
George III, king of Britain, 202
Gérard, [?]: background, 41; character, 34–5; and *Courier de Londres*, 227; and Ivernois, 196; on legitimacy, 182; on Napoleon, 207; on Portugal, 205; Routledge on, 35; and satire, 207; on Spain, 205; on Sweden, 205; on war (Franco-Russian), 204–5. See also Bourbons, journalists (major), pensions, police
Germany: agents in, 64; and *Ambigu*, 133; and *Correspondance politique*, 24, 99; and *Courier d'Angleterre*, 134; and *Courier de Londres*, 133; and emigration, 62; francophone élite in, 57; and francophone papers, 77; French press control, 133–4, 140; and Paoli de Chagny, 128, 133; and propaganda warfare; 133–4, 140. See also circulation, Confederation of the Rhine, Hamburg, Mallet Du Pan, Swabia
Gilles de Caen, Claude, 141
Girondins, 150
Glindon, printer, 66
Globe, 37
Goldsmith, Lewis, 33, 93, 212
Gothenburg, 73, 82, 135–8 passim
Gourie [Gourlier?], Marguerite Suzanne, 98
Grenada, 171
Grenville, William Wyndham, 1st baron, 28, 134, 176
Grey, Charles, 2nd earl Howick, 93
Griffiths, Robert, 183–4, 225
Guadeloupe, 68, 170, 171
Gustave III, king of Sweden, 167
Gustave IV, king of Sweden, 136

Habeas corpus, 117
Habermas, Jürgen, 3–4, 141, 223–4
Haiti, see Saint-Domingue
Hamburg: and *Ambigu*, 133; distribution centre, 73, 76, 99; and emigration, 62; co-operation with Napoleon, 107, 134; printing centre, 62; Senate restored, 205
Hamilton, William Richard, 141

Hammond, George: and Kirwan, 29; and Regnier, 34, 130
Hampshire Chronicle, 85
Harcourt, Marie-François, duc d', 103
Hardenburg, Karl Auguste von, 71, 99
Harper, Thomas, 66, 82
Hawksbury, 1st baron, see Jenkinson, Charles
Hawkesbury, Lord, see Jenkinson, Robert Banks
Hébert, Jacques-René, 16, 150
Hébertists, 44, 156
Hénin, Adélaïde-Félicité-Henriette de Montconseil, princesse d', 65
Henri Christophe, king of Haiti, 87, 131, 139
Henri-Larivière, Pierre-François-Joachim: and Antraigues, 29; and *Courier d'Angleterre*, 29, 31, 32; background, 52; in French government records, 128; and Regnier, 29. See also collaborators, pensions
Heriot, John, 119
Heron, Robert: background, 37–42 passim, 66n.; character, 35–6; and *Courier de Londres*, 81, 130; and *Gazette de la Grande-Bretagne*, 19, 21, 92; interests, 37; and Regnier, 130; and Talleyrand, 219. See also British government, circulation, journalists (major)
Herries, Charles, 89, 154
Histoire de la restauration française, see Peltier, periodicals
Historical Magazine, 37
Historical survey of the island of St. Domingo, 174–5
History of the British campaign in Egypt, 217
Holland: Addington demands French withdrawal, 126; annexation rumours, 189; communications, 73; invasion, 25, 99; provisioning for France, 177; and *Tableau de l'Europe*, 99, and war (1803), 126. See also Batavian Republic, Brabant, circulation, Montlosier
Holy Roman Empire, see Austria, Germany
Hood, Samuel, 1st viscount, 167
Howick, Lord see Grey
Hugues, Victor, 170, 171
Hyde de Neuville, Jean-Guillaume, 128

Ile de France, see Mauritius
Impartial ou Courier de Middlesex, 234

Imperial Review, 85
India: comparative value as colony, 175–6; news reports from, 17; Peltier's agent in, 69. *See also* East India Company
information: journalists' sources, 53, 64, 69–73, passim, 76, 89, 177; political role of, 206
Irving, John, 88, 89, 154, 231
Italy: and *Correspondance politique*, 24, 99; information from, 72, 89. *See also* circulation, papal states, Piedmont, Sardinia, Venetia, Verona
Ivernois, François d': and *Ambigu*, 212; and C.-A. de Calonne, 176–7; and French government, 196; and Gérard, 196; and Mallet Du Pan, 176; and Peltier, 196; and Pitt, 176; on revolutionary finances, 176, 196

Jacobins: and Couchery, 42; and Montlosier, 161, 168, 185; and Peltier, 86, 151, 155, 181; and Thermidor, 157. *See also* abbé Calonne, Mallet Du Pan
Jaffa, 213, 214, 217
Jamaica, 139, 174, 175
Jena, battle of, 134
Jenkinson, Charles, 1st baron Hawkesbury (1783–96) thereafter 1st Earl of Liverpool, 59–60, 70, 100
Jenkinson, Robert Banks, Lord Hawesbury (later 2nd Earl of Liverpool): and Dutheil, 109, 110; and French attacks on Peltier, 114–21 passim; and Malta, 121; and Otto, 110–21 passim
Jephson, Robert, 150
Jersey, 98, 115, 116, 118, 125, 140. *See also Gazette de Jersey*
Jourgniac de St Méard, François de, 23
'journal', defined, p. xv. *See also* newspapers, periodicals, press
Journal de Bruxelles, 6
Journal des dames (1–Paris, pre-revolution), 6n.
Journal des dames (2–New York), 128
Journal des dames et des modes, 84
Journal de l'Europe, 66n.
Journal de France et d'Angleterre: back issues, 76; distribution, 99; failure, 27, 56, 65; finances, 65, 78; on Malouet and St. Domingue, 172; merger, 18; and *monarchiens*, 26, 27; explanation of revolution, 160; staffing, 65; on Thermidoreans, 160. *See also*

circulation, Mallet, Montlosier, periodicals, printers, taxes
Journal de Francfort, 63, 97n.
Journal général, 75n., 95
Journal de Hambourg 9, 97n.
Journal hélvetique, 37
Journal de Paris, 5
Journal des princes, 96
Journal de Ratisbonne see Mercure universel
Journal des savants, 5
Journal of Voyages and Travel, 85
journalists (émigré): religious status, 39–40; historiography, 10; intimidation, 45–6; nationalities, 40; political activity, 32, 43–5; social status, 39, 41. *See also* collaborators, information, journalists (major), journalists (minor), press
journalists (major): pre-existing acquaintanceships, 37; ages, 42; and Alien Act, 90, 109, 112, 116, 119; alienation of, 47–8; and colonial trade, 41; editorial activities, 38; education, 42–3; emigration, 46–7; financial position, pre-emigration, 41–3 passim, on arrival, 48, thereafter, 48, 54–5, 71; pre-emigration journalistic experience, 37–8; and Jacobins, 44; professional backgrounds, 41; rejection of revolution, 44–5; work-load, 69. *See also* counter-revolution, families, information, and under names of individual journalists
journalists (minor): journalistic experience, 38. *See also* counter-revolution, families information, and under names of individual journalists
Julien, [?], citoyen, 98

Karamzin, Nicholas Mikhailovich, 137–8
Kirwan, François-David, 29, 38, 40, 46. *See also* periodicals, 'propaganda journals', journalists (minor).
Knights of St John, 120–1. *See also* Malta
Kuriakin, prince Alexander Borisovich, 204

La Bintinaye, Agathon-Marie-René, chevalier de, 95n., 153
La Corbière, [?], 48n. 107, 187n. *See also* collaborators
Lacretelle, Jean-Charles-Dominique, 158n.

INDEX

Ladies Magazine, 85
La Gardie *see* De La Gardie
La Harpe, Jean-François de, 158n.
Lally-Tollendal, Trophime-Gérard de: and abbé Calonne, 158; and bishops (*non-démissionnaires*), 190, 192; and *monarchiens*, 43; and Montlosier, 190; argues for peace, 168n.; and Peltier, 102, 192; and princesse d'Hénin, 65n.; and Verduisant,158. *See also Défense des émigrés, Lettres au rédacteur du Courier de Londres*
Lamaisonfort, Antoine-François-Philippe Du Bois des Cours, marquis de, 62, 63, 64
La Marche, Jean-François de, bishop of Saint-Pol de Léon, 114, 118
Lamballe, Marie-Thérèse-Louise de Savoie-Grignan, princesse de, 7
Lambert, [?], Parisian bookseller, 98
Lameth, Alexandre-Théodore-Victor de, 145
La Motte, Jeanne de Saint-Rémy de Valois de, comtesse de, *see* diamond necklace affair
La Roberie, Pierre de, 24, 166
Las Cases, Emmanuel-Auguste Dieudonné, comte de, 70n., 214
law, *see* legal systems
Law, Edward, 1st baron Ellenborough, 125
League of Armed Neutrality, 188
Lebrun, Pierre-Henri-Hélène-Marie, 96
Leclerc, Pauline *see* Borghese
Leclerc, Victor-Emmanuel, 174, 212n.
Lefèvre, Félicité, *see* Swinton
legal systems: British and French contrasted, 109. *See also* libel laws
Legendre, Louis, 150
Leipzig, 212
Lettres au rédacteur du Courier de Londres, 192
Lettres d'un colon, 41n., 173
Lezay de Marnésia, Adrien, 25
libel: laws, British and French contrasted, 109; French views on; 113–16 passim; Mackintosh on, 124
libelles, 6–7, 141
Lille, comte de, *see* Provence
Linguet, Simon-Nicolas-Henri, 37, 222
Lisbon, 138
literary issues, *see* cultural issues
Liverpool, 1st Earl, *see* Jenkinson, Charles
Liverpool, 2nd Earl, *see* Jenkinson, Robert Banks

Lloyds Evening Post, 37
London Gazette: extracts, 17; information source, 92; as propaganda, 140, 207; translations, 87
Louis XIV, king of France: comment on, 160, 186, 217
Louis XV, king of France: comment on, 160
Louis XVI, king of France: and Auerweck, 41; comment on, 144, 148, 154, 155, 187, 200; and Couchery, 44; and Mme. Du Barry, 156; and Mallet Du Pan, 46–7
Louis XVII, king of France: 14, 167
Louis XVIII, king of France, *see* Provence
Louis-Philippe, *see* Orléans
loyal opposition, 164–5
Luillacs, [?], comte de, 74–5, 77
Luneville, treaty of, 108
Lyon, 24, 97, 151, 177

Macaulay, Zachary, 83
Mackintosh, James: agent for Peltier, 69; and Artois, 197–8; counsel for Peltier, 124–5; and *Trial of John Peltier*, 198. *See also* libel
MacPherson, Sir John, 188
Madrid, 138
Mainz, 99
Maistre, Joseph de, 148
Malet, Claude-François, 206
Mallet, Jean-Louis [John Lewis]: change of name, p. xv; autobiography, 10n.; on Bourbons, 103; British civil servant, 86, 100; family background, 40, and *see also* Mallet Du Pan; on French booksellers, 61–2; historiographical consequences, 100–1; and *Journal de France et d'Angleterre*, 32; and Mallet Du Pan, 31; and *Mercure britannique*, 31, 32; and *monarchien* memoirs, 100–1; and Montlosier, 31; naturalisation, 86; mission to Paris, 58; on Pitt, 60. *See also* circulation, collaborators
Mallet-Butigny, François, 98
'Mallet dit Crecy', *see* Mallet-Butigny
Mallet Du Pan, Jacques: on Artois, 103; background, 27, 37, 38, 40–2 passim, 44; biography, 100; and Bonapartism, 50–1, 184, 185–6; and Brumaire, 184–5; and Brunswick, 71, 99; and abbé Calonne, 157, 162; on Carnot, 152; and Castries, 71, 103, 104–5;

263

character, 35, 48; on Chénier, 131; on coalitions, 162; on Concordet, 146; on constitution(s), 162, of 1795, 184, 185; and Conzie (Arras), 103; on Danton, 152; on Daunou, 184; and De Boffe, 61, 62, 68; on Desmoulins, 152; on Diderot, 146; and Dumas, 76; emigration, 47; on emigration, 229; and European audience; 99; expulsion from Berne, 58; and Fauche, 62, 63, 64; on Garat, 152, 184; flight from Geneva, 42; and Gentz, 63, 71, 73; German contacts, 71; health, 69; and Ivernois 176; on Jacobinism, 184–5; and Lamaisonfort, 62–3; and Liverpool, 100; and Louis XVI, 46–7; and Louis XVIII, 103, 105, 164, 185; and Luillacs, 74–5; and Mallet, 31; and Malouet, 60, 103, 163, 168; and dispute between Malouet and Peltier, 163–4; and *Mercure Britannique*, 26, 27–8, 38, 58–64; and *Mercure de France* (2), 43; and J.-F. Michaud, 70; on moderation in war, 162; and *monarchiens*, 26; and Montlosier, 60, 100n., 162; on masonic conspiracy theories, 146; on Napoleon, 148–9, 152–3, 184, 185; at Neuchâtel, 62; and Peltier, 99, 102, 103, 163–4; and Pitt, 86, 101; and Portalis, 71n.; and *Quotidienne*, 58; on peace or war, 161–2; political consultancy, 52–3; readership, 99; and Reeves, 58–9, 100; on 'rights of man in society', 162; on Rousseau, 146; on royalism, 185; on Siéyès, 184; on Swiss Confederation, 27; on Voltaire, 146; on war aims, 185; and Wickham, 53, 58, 62; and Windham, 59, 60, 100. *See also* Bourbons, British government, Directory, Egypt, *Essai historique sur . . . la liberté helvétique*, journalists (major), pensions

Malouet, Pierre-Victor: autobiography, 10n., 101n.; on Bréard, 172–3; and C.-A. de Calonne, 157; and Castries, 103, 104; *colon* representative, 168–72 passim; and Conzie (Arras), 103; and *Courier de Londres*, 157–8; proposes leniency, 163; on Louis XVIII, 163; and Mallet Du Pan, 60, 103, 163, 168; manifesto for Bourbon restoration, 103, 104, 163; and *Mercure britannique*, 28, 32, 186n.; Minister of the Navy, 227; and Montlosier, 172–6 passim; and

Peltier, 102, 103, 163; and Regnier, 41, 173; and Saint-Domingue (Haiti), 41, 52, 168–176 passim; on slavery, 172, 173; and Vénault de Charmilly, 174. *See also* abolitionists, Bourbons, collaborators, Foreign Office
Malta, 118, 120–1, 125, 126
Mansel, Philip, 11
Manzon, Jean, 95
Marat, Jean-Paul, 16, 23n., 146, 151
Marboeuf, Louis-Charles-René, comte de, 211, 215
Marie-Antoinette, queen of France 53, 212. *See also* diamond necklace affair
Marseilles, 144, 177, 212
Martinique, 140, 218
masons, *see* freemasons
Maspero-Clerc, Hélène, 10, 102, 187
massacres, *see* atrocities, *Dernier Tableau de Paris*
Mauritius, 139
Maury, Cardinal Joseph-Siffrein, 195, 196, 217, 219, 220
Medical and Physical Journal, 85
Méhée de la Touche, Jean-Claude-Hippolyte, 30n., 49
Mémoire, see bishops (non-démissionnaires)
Mémoires pour servir à l'histoire du jacobinisme françois, *see* Barruel
Mercure britannique: treatment of quotations, p. xvi; back issues, 76; and Bourbon propaganda, 103; clandestine production in Paris, 98, in Hamburg, 99, in Rouen, 97–8; establishment, 27, 58–64; financial affairs, 58–65 passim; foreign language editions, 79–80; and Luillacs, 74–5; and *monarchiens*, 26; pirated editions, 80; production difficulties, 64; translations, 27, 62. *See also* Brunswick, circulation, Directory, *Essai historique sur . . . la liberté helvétique*, Gentz, Mallet, Mallet Du Pan, Malouet, periodicals, Paul I, Pitt, police, printers
Mercure de France (1–London): and Bonapartism, 51, 181–2; and Brumaire, 181; editors, 26, 31; failure, 26, 56, 179; financing, 65; and Hamburg, 99; on legitimacy, 182; and Louis XVIII, 181–2; and *monarchiens*, 26; on non-interference, 182; on peace or war, 181–2. *See also* circulation, periodicals, printers

Mercure de France (2–Paris), 17, 43, 84
Mercure galant, 5
Mercure de Londres, 227
Mercure universel ou Journal de Ratisbonne, 97n.
Merry, Anthony, 116, 117
mesmerism, 35n.
Mesmont, Germain-Hyacinthe de Romance, marquis de, 107
Mexico, 138, 139
Michaud, François, 71n.
Michaud, Joseph-F., 58, 70
Milner, John, bishop of Castabala, 193–5
Mirabeau, Honoré-Gabriel Riquetti, comte de, 16, 19, 45, 149
Moleville, *see* Bertrand de Molleville, 155n.
Monaco, Louise-Félicité-Victoire d'Aumont, princesse de, 133
monarchiens: definition, 13n.; and Bourbons, 102–3; and British government, 100–1; constitutional programme, 45; historiography of memoirs, 33, 100–1; and war, 168. *See also* British government, Mallet, Mallet Du Pan, Malouet, Montlosier
Moniteur, 72, 99, 112–21 passim, 127, 206, 207, 208n., 219
Moniteur secret, 212
Montesquieu, Charles-Louis Secondat, baron de, 184
Monthion, *see* Auget de Montyon
Monthly Magazine, 85
Monthly Mirror, 85
Monthly Review, 85
Montlosier, François-Dominique Reynaud, comte de: on abolitionists, 174; and *Actes des apôtres*, 37; and Amiens, 186; and amnesty of 1802, 50; and André de Montluel, 31, 71; on anti-clericalism, 187; anti-revolutionary proposals, military, 162, moral force, 163; autobiographical works, 10n., 100n., 101n.; background, 37, 39, 41; on Barras, 152; and bishops (*non-démissionnaires*), 189–91; and Bonapartism, 50, 106, 185–91 passim; on Lucien Bonaparte, 188; and Bréard, 172–3; fears for British political stability, 165; reaction to Brumaire, 179–91 passim; and Butet, 71; and abbé Calonne, 27, 36, 158–60; character, 35, 174; and *Citoyen français*, 187; and *Clef du cabinet*, 187; on Code Civil, 189; emigration, 47; and émigré clergy, 189–90; at Coblenz, 46; and concordat, 190; constitutional proposals and analysis, 21, 183–4, 185, 186–7; and *Courier de Londres*, 21, 27, 38, 81, 190; and *Courrier de Londres et de Paris*, 50, 189; Darnton on, 35n.; on equality, 160; on the family, 189; family background, 38, 41; and Fouché, 190; visits France, 186, 189; returns to France, 50, 179–80; reaction to Fructidor, 162; future hopes and fears, 160–1, 187–8; on Gallican Church, 190; on government, 186–7; on Holland, 189; interests, 35, 37, 39, 42; on 'intermediary power', 184, 185; on jacobinism, 161, 168, 185; on Jamaica, 174; and *Journal de France et d'Angleterre*, 26–7, 54; journalistic style, 35; and Lally-Tollendal, 190; and League of Armed Neutrality, 188; on Louis XIV, 160; on Louis XV, 160; on Louis XVI, 187; on Louis XVIII, 187; on 'loyal opposition', 164–5; and Mallet, 31; and Mallet Du Pan, 60, 100n., 162; on Malouet and Saint-Domingue, 172–6 passim; and masonic conspiracy theories, 146; and J.-F. Michaud, 70; military activity, 46; on *monarchie limitée*, 183–4; and *monarchiens*, 27, 45; and Napoleon, 105, 106, 183, 187–8, 191; on 'the nation', 160; and Otto, 50n., 186–7; and *Paris pendant l'année*, 27; argues for peace, 168; on peace negotiations (1801), 191; and Peltier, 102; on *le peuple*, 160; on Portugal, 189; on property rights, 160, 186; on public opinion, 160–1; and Regnier, 34; on causes of revolution, 146, 160–1; on Siéyès, 183; on slavery, 173–4; on the state, 186–7; and Félicité Swinton, 106, 186; and Talleyrand, 50, 187; on Thermidor, 151, 160; and Tromelin, 31, 71; on Vendémiaire, 160. *See also* Bourbons, British government, Directory, journalists (major), patronage
Montluel, *see* André de Montluel
Montyon, *see* Auget de Montyon
Morande, *see* Théveneau de Morande
Morbihan, Gulf of, 166. *See also* Quiberon
Moreau, Jean-Victor, 180, 199, 200, 217
Morning Chronicle, 37, 99, 113, 153

Morning Post, 90n., 120, 124n., 198, 212
Mourant, Philip, 125
Mulgrave, see Phipps, Henry

Nancrède, Joseph, 80
Nantes, 42, 70, 151, 155, 177, 187
Napoleon I, see Bonaparte
National Register, 55
Nations, Battle of, 212
Necker, Jacques, 43, 45, 153
'newspapers': defined, p. xv; and advertising, 17, 67, 73; content, 17–24 passim; financial structures, 58–65; formats, 17–18, 140; periodicity, 17–18; in revolutionary France, 16–17. See also circulation, editors, information, journalists, parliamentary reporting, press, printers, individual titles
Nicholson's Journal, 85
Noailles, Louis-Marie de, vicomte, 23
Noël, François, 96

Ode atribuée à Chénier . . ., see Chénier
'opposition', 8. See also loyal opposition
Oracle, 37
Oraison funèbre du duc d'Enghien, see *Ambigu*
Orléans, Louis-Philippe, duc d', 72, 131
Orléans, Philippe, duc d' (Philippe-Egalité), 146, 148
Osterwald, Samuel-Frédéric, 37, 62
Otto, Louis: and Addington, 114, 119; amnesty proposals, 188n.; arrives in London, 96; and Conzie (Arras), 114; and Dutheil, 83, 113; and Fouché, 114; and Hawkesbury, 110–21 passim; and Montlosier, 50n., 186–7; and action against Peltier, 109–27 passim
Ottoman empire, 121, 202. See also Constantinople

Paget, Sir Arthur, 69
Palm, Johann Philip, 134
Panckoucke, Charles-Joseph, 5–6, 46, 65.
Panin, count Nikita [the younger], 136, 137
Paoli, Pasquale: and Bonapartes, 72n.; and Peltier, 72, 212
Paoli de Chagny, François-Etienne-Auguste, comte de, 128, 133, 134
papal states, 194
'paper', definition, p. xv. See also journalists, newspapers, periodicals

Paraguay, 139
Paris pendant l'année: and *Amis des noirs*, 171; and Artois, 102; and Auckland, 77; background, 21; back issues, 76; ceases publication, 111; and De Boffe, 25, 66, 87; distribution, 99; and Dutheil, 83, 102, 114; financing, 102; and Hamburg, 99; inauguration, 25; and Napoleon, 110; resumes publication, 102; on Saint-Domingue, 175–6; sharing of copies, 75. See also Artois, circulation, Fontanes, Montlosier, Peltier, Pitt, periodicals, police, printers
parliamentary reporting, 17, 23–4, 25, 30, 164, 173, 208, 209
parodies, see satire
Pas-de-Calais, see Calais
Patriote françois, 8–9
patronage: and British press, 89–90; and émigré press, 57, 58, 85, 90–4 passim, 187; historiography, 89–90
Paul I, tsar of Russia: coup of 1801, 137, 189; and *Mercure britannique*, 64, 99; proposals for Bourbon restoration, 104
peace treaties: draft of 1806, 127. See also Amiens
Pelham, Thomas, Lord: and Peltier, 113–19 passim; on Alien Act, 119
'Pelletier', see Peltier, Jean-Gabriel
Peltier, Anne, see Andoe
Peltier, Jean-Gabriel: *Adresse au public*, 198; agents, 68–9, 139; and *Ambigu*, 25–6, 33, 198–9, 215, 227; and *Amis des noirs*, 171, 175; and Artois, 72, 87, 104, 111, 125, 131, 197; and Auerweck, 41; *Avis à toutes les villes riches du monde*, 177; background, 41; bankruptcies; 41, 54, 83; on Du Barry, 156; on Eugène de Beauharnais, 219; and bishops (*démissionnaires*), 192; and 'Black Legend', 26, 210–21 passim; and Blanchardism, 192–6 passim; and Bonapartism, 26, 51; on Laetitia Bonaparte, 218; on Pauline Bonaparte (Borghese), 212; in book trade, 67; on Brissot, 145, 175; and Broval, 131; on Brumaire, 180–1; and abbé Calonne, 157; on Carrier, 155; character, 32–3, 34, 48–9; and Charette de la Contrie, 24n.; and Chateaubriand, 33–4, 69, 218; on Church, 194; and *colons*, 72, 175; on concordat, 192, 193; on Constitution of Year III, 156–7, 180;

INDEX

on continental blockade, 202; and Conzie (Arras), 111; and *Correspondance politique*, 23; and Couchery, 132; on *Courier de l'Europe*, 164; counter-revolutionary publicity, 143–4; and De Boffe, 25, 66–7, 87, 100; on decatholicisation, 195; on deChristianisation, 150; on Danish expedition, 201–2; and De La Gardie, 87n.; on Desmoulins, 149; diplomatic appointments, 72, 87, 92, 131–2, 176; and 'divine judgement', 148; and Douglass, 194; and Drouin, 101; and Dumas, 76; and Durfort-Boissières, 51, 110; and Dutheil, 51, 101, 110, 111; and economic propaganda, 177–8, 196; and Edwards, 174–5; emigration, 47; and Enghien, 200–1; on English press, 155, 200; family background, 41; and Fauche-Borel, 131; and Fontanes, 102; and Fouché, 43n., 114, 125; on Fouquier-Tinville, 155; on French censorship, 145; on Frouillé, 176; on Fructidor, 161; and *Gazette française*, 172; and Gentz, 93; on Girondins, 150; and *Histoire de la restauration française*, 23; imprisoned, 24, 25; and Ivernois, 196; and Jacobins, 86, 151, 155, 183; on Josephine de Beauharnais, 218–19; knighthood, 76; and Lally-Tollendal, 102, 192; on legitimacy, 156, 181, 182; and literary criticism, 147; on Louis XVI, 144; and Louis-Philippe, 131; and Mackintosh, 69, 124–5; and Mallet Du Pan, 99, 102, 103, 163–4; and Malouet, 102, 103, 163; and Marboeuf, 211, 215; and Mauritius 139; on Maury, 219; and J.-F. Michaud, 70; and Milner, 194–5; deserts *monarchiens*, 102; and *Morning Post*, 212; Méhée de la Touche on, 49; and Montlosier, 102; and Napoleon, 72, 110, 112, 180–1, 192–220 passim; on naval balance, 202; and *Oraison funèbre du duc d'Enghien*, 141; alleges Orléanist plot, 146; and Paoli, 72, 212; and *Paris pendant l'année*, 25, 66, 69; on parliamentary government, 164; and Pelham, 113–19 passim; on *philosophes*, 145–6; and Pitt, 70, 99, 100; and Pius VII, 92, 193, 194; on plebiscites, 145; and pornographic libels, 212; on Portugal, 86n., 205; and Portuguese legation, 132; on Prussia, 207–8; and Quiberon, 166, 167; readership, 99; and *Réclamations canoniques*, 141; and Regnier, 30, 33, 34, 92–3, 198; on religion, 144; and Rieder, 96; on revolution, character of revolutionaries, 149–51 passim, explanations, 144–6, resulting immorality in France, 149; on Rewbell, 149; on Russia, 204; and Saint-Domingue (Haiti), 41, 72, 92, 132, 168–76 passim; and satire, 150–1, 179–80, 192, 199; on Siéyès, 145; on slavery, 169, 175; on Sonthonax, 172; on Spain, 205; and Spanish language documents, 138; and sphinx vignette, 26, 123; on Sweden, 205; and Swedish legation, 132; and Swinton, 19–20; and *Tableau de l'Europe*, 24–5; on Talleyrand, 149; on Tallien, 150; on Terror, 155–6, 161; on theatre, 147; on Thermidoreans, 151, 156; on Tilsit, 202; and *The Times*, 113; titles of journals, 21–6; translation work, 86, 87, 100; trial background, 112–21 passim; trial, 67, 121–5, 126, 197; on Two-Thirds Decree, 156–7; on ultramontanism, 194, 195; u-turn, 207–8; and Vénault de Charmilly, 72, 169–70, 174–5; on Vendémiaire, 157; on conduct of war, 165; on French war motives, 145; on war (Franco-Russian), 204–5; and Windham, 99. *See also* abolitionists, *Ambigu*, *Actes des apôtres*, atrocities, blackmail, Bourbons, British government, *Chouans*, *colons*, *Correspondance française*, *Correspondance politique*, *Dernier Tableau de Paris*, Directory, *Histoire de la restauration française*, information, journalists (major), *Ode atribuée à Chénier*, Otto, *Paris pendant l'année*, patronage, pensions, police, printers, *Tableau de l'Europe*, *Trial of John Peltier*, *Voeu d'un bon patriote hollandois*

Peninsular war, 138–9, 207
pensions (for journalists and families), 50, 54, 86, 91, 101, 129n., 132, 141
Perceval, Spencer, 134
'periodicals': definition, p. xv; content 17–18, 21–30 passim; formats, 17–30 passim; periodicity, 17–18, 21–30 passim; style, 17. *See also* circulation, parliamentary reporting, press, 'propaganda journals'
Petit Mercure, 228n.

Philippe-Egalité, *see* Orléans
philosophes, 145, 146
Philosophical Review, 85
Phipps, Henry, 3rd baron Mulgrave, 29n., 130
Pichegru, Jean-Charles: agent of Bourbons, 51–2, 104; and Antraigues, 51; arrest, 199; and Cadoudal, 52; and Couchery, 47, 54; death, 52, 200; and Fauche-Borel, 51, 104; and French press, 208; legacy (financial), 131; political background, 39, 44. *See also* collaborators, Fructidor, pensions
Piedmont, 120. *See also* Sardinia
Pitt, William: and C.-A. de Calonne, 166; and Ivernois, 176; Mallet on, 60; and Mallet du Pan, 86, 101; and *Mercure britannique*, 60; and *Paris pendant l'année*, 77; and Peltier, 70, 99, 100; and Quiberon, 166; and Regnier, 120
Pius VII, pope: and annexation of papal states, 194; and Blanchard, 192, 195; and concordat, 189–90, 195; excommunicates Napoleon, 194; and Peltier, 192, 193, 194; and Regnier, 193
pluralism, political: and France, 16
Poland, 24, 76n.
police, French, observation: of Antraigues, 201; of Dutheil, 110; of Gérard, 128, 133; of *Mercure britannique*, 97–8, 107; of *Paris pendant l'année*, 107; of Peltier, 128
politics, *see* collaborators, journalists (minor), journalists (major), pluralism
Ponte, Paolo da, 66
Porcupine, 37, 110
pornography, *see Actes des apôtres*, 'Black Legend', *Gazetier cuirassé*, Peltier
Portalis, Jean-Etienne-Marie de, 71, 189n.
Portland, *see* Cavendish-Bentinck
Portugal: correspondents, 71n.; coverage, 205; French ambitions, 189; invasion, 138; regent, 99; resistance, 193. *See also* circulation, Gérard, Lisbon, Montlosier, Napoleon, Peltier
Pour et le contre, 128n
Pradel, [?], *see* collaborators
Pradt, Dominique Dufour de, abbé, 71
Précis des événemens militaires, 76
press, British: on Enghien's murder, 200; on Napoleon, 211. *See also* bribery, circulation, patronage
press, émigré: background, 17; and British caricature tradition, 212–14; and British government, 90–4; decline, 229; dilemma of Brumaire 179–96 passim; business administration, 65–9; distribution, 66–7, 68; economics, 56–94 passim, esp. 73–87; historiography, 10, 229; readership, Francophone, 78, in general, 74–80; and Spanish press, 139; staffing, 65; and outbreak of war (1803), 107–28 passim; and war, 128. *See also* Bourbons, bribery, censorship, circulation, collaborators, information, journalists (major), journalists (minor), patronage, printers, proprietors
press, French: domestic, 2–9 passim, 15–17, 56; extra-territorial, 7–8, 9; Napoleonic, 206–8 passim. *See also* censorship, circulation
press, Spanish, 139
pressmen: definition, 32. *See also* journalists (émigré), journalists (major), journalists (minor)
printers: London, 66, 67, 69; Paris, 98
Proly, Pierre-Jean-Berthold, comte de, 37, 44, 45
propaganda: Bourbon, 103; economic, 176–8, 196–7; 'propaganda journals', 28–30; propaganda warfare, and British government, 95, 99–100, 133–4, 135, 140, 142, 207, and C.-A. de Calonne, 95–6, and Napoleon, 95, 142n., phases of, 95
proprietors (non-editorial), 66, 87–94 passim, 155, 231, 235. *See also* editor-proprietors
Proschwitz, Gunnar von, 8
Proschwitz, Mavis von, 8
Provence, comte d' (Louis XVIII): and Alexander I, 130, 203; and *ancienne constitution*, 105; assassination attempt, 33; and *Courier d'Angleterre*, 130–1; and *Courier de Londres*, 132; diplomatic designation, 14; journalistic comment on, 29, 163, 181–2, 185, 187; and *Mercure de France*, 181–2; and Peltier, 103, 111, 131, 141, 164, 227; peregrinations, 14; policy, 104; 'regent', 14; and Regnier, 29, 66, 130–1, 203; restoration negotiations, 104; 'succession', 14, 167; and Sweden, 167. *See also Ambigu*, Bourbons, Calmar, Mallet Du Pan, Malouet, *Rapport à Louis XVIII*, Verona
Provinciale Zeytung see Courier du Bas-Rhin

Prussia: and Auerweck, 51n.; and Brunswick manifesto, 47, 64n.; and Gentz, 63n.; and Hardenburg, 71n.; and League of Armed Neutrality, 188n.; and Malta, 121. *See also* Peltier
Public Advertiser, 96n.
Publiciste, 209
'public opinion': abbé Calonne on, 158; British attempts to influence, 140, 142; British, on revolution, 96; contrast with 'popular opinion', 4; in France, 4–5; Malouet on, 163; Montlosier on, 160–1; and Napoleon, 206; Peltier on, 145, 206; as political arbiter, 3–5, 145, 226
publishing, *see* press
Puisaye, Joseph-Geneviève, comte de, 53, 166, 201
purs: and abbé Calonne, 21, 157–9; and Artois, 14; attacked by Malouet and Mallet Du Pan, 163–4; attacks on *monarchiens*, 13; as audience for journals, 179, 180; and Black Legend, 183, 224; and British government, 101, 224; and compromise, 226; and constitution, 13, 178; and *Courier de Londres*, 155; defined, 13; disdain for revolutionaries, 152; and failure of counter-revolution, 224; and Louis XVIII, 104, 224, 227; and Mallet Du Pan, 56, 163; and masonic conspiracy theories, 146; and Peltier, 45, 104, 164; and public opinion, 226; role in emigration, 13; and war aims, 185. *See also* abbé Calonne, C.-A. de Calonne, Artois, royalists

Quatremère de Quincy, Antoine-Chrysostôme, 71
Quiberon, 52, 100, 166–7. *See also* Brittany, C.-A. de Calonne, abbé Calonne, Peltier, Verduisant
Quotidienne, 58, 152

Radix de Sainte-Foy, Pierre-Maximilien, 231
Rapport à Louis XVIII, 159
Ramolino, Maria Laetizia, (*Madame Mère*), 218
Réclamations canoniques, see *Ambigu*, Blanchard
Rédacteur, 28
Reeves, John, 58–60, 100
Regnier, 'Mme. Jacques', 49, 120

Regnier, Jacques: and Alexander I, 202–4 passim; and Andréossi, 120; and Antraigues, 29, 72, 82, 91, 92, 131, 135, 140, 201, 202; and Artois, 72; background, 40, 41; and Blanchard, 193; and Bonapartism, 51; on Jérome Bonaparte, 218; and Bourbons, 87, 110, 111, 131, 182, 203, 227; and British government, 81, 91, 129–31 passim; and Broughton, 198; and Broval, 72; and Canning, 53, 82, 135; character, 34, 48; and *colons*, 72; on continental blockade, 202; and Conzie (Arras), 111–12; and *Cosmopolite*, 44; and *Courier d'Angleterre*, 21, 29–30, 81–2; and *Courier de Londres*, 29, 33, 81, 88, 130; and Danish expedition, 201–2; and Durfort-Boissières, 51; and Dutheil, 51, 54, 110, 111; emigration, 47; finances, 65–6, 82; and French government records, 128; and Gentz, 93, 204n.; and Grey, 93; and Hammond, 34, 130; health, 69; and Henri-Larivière, 29; and Heron, 130; imprisoned, 44; on Josephine de Beauharnais, 219; journalistic style, 29–30; on legitimacy, 182; and *Lettres d'un colon*, 173; and Louis XVIII, 29, 130; and Malouet, 41, 173; in Manchester, 55; and Marboeuf, 215; and Montlosier, 34; and *Morning Post*, 212; on Napoleon, 56, 92, 193–219 passim; on Napoleon's destiny, 218; and *National Register*, 55; naturalisation, 47; and Peltier, 30, 33, 34, 92–3, 198; and Pitt, 120; and Pius VII, 193; on Portugal, 205; and Routledge, 34, 35, 88; and Russia, 91; and satire, 179; and *Semānario patriotico*, 72, 139; on Spain, 205; on Sweden, 205; and Talavera, 92; on Talleyrand, 209; on Tilsit, 202; and *The Times*, 201; translation work, 87; and Vénault de Charmilly, 44n., 173; and *Voeu d'un bon patriote hollandois*, 198. *See also* Bourbons, British government, *colons*, embezzlement, journalists (major), pensions and Saint-Domingue
retail distribution, *see* press
Reventlow, Christian Ditlev Frederick, comte de, 99
Rewbell, Jean-François, 149
Richer-Sérizy, Jean-Thomas-Elisabeth, 158–9n.

Rieder, bookseller, 96
Rivarol, Antoine, 34
Roberie, *see* La Roberie
Robespierre, Maximilien, 16, 44, 149, 151, 177
Rochambeau, Donatien-Marie-Joseph de Vimeur, vicomte de, 171
Rolleston, [Stephen or Henry John], 69n.
Ross, James Tyrell, 91, 136
Rosslyn, 1st Earl of, *see* Wedderburn, Alexander
Rouen, 98
'Rouen chieftain', *see* Mallet-Butigny
Rousseau, Jean-Jacques, 19, 146
Routledge, R. A.: and *Courier de Londres*, 88, 231; on Gérard, 35; and Regnier, 34, 35, 88; and Félicité Swinton, 88
royalism: abbé Calonne on, 47; C.-A. de Calonne on, 47; Mallet Du Pan on, 162, 164, 184–5; Montlosier on, 187
royalists: army, in Brittany, 166; allies and, 158; agents, 51–2, 54, 62, 98; cipher, 111; and British support, 167; and elections (1795), 157, 158; journalists, 25, 38, 153, 165; loss of middle ground, 184; and Napoleon, 184; papers, 38, 141, 145; sympathisers in France, 159. See also *purs*
Royal proclamation on the war, 167
Royou, [Louis or Jacques-Corentin?], *see* collaborators
Royou, Thomas-Marie, 95. *See also* collaborators
Rumbold, George, 128n
Rumyantsev, Nicholas Petrovich, 137, 204
Russia: anglophobia in, 202; army advances on France, 104, 163; and Artois, 107; conquest of Sweden by, 137n.; and *Courier d'Angleterre*, 136–8; coup (1801), 137; émigré perceptions, 202; Francophone élite in, 78; and Hamburg, 107; and League of Armed Neutrality, 188n.; and Malta, 121; and Ottoman Empire, 121; policy shifts, 136–7. *See also* Alexander I, Antraigues, circulation, Foreign Office, Paul I, Peltier, Regnier, St. Petersburg, Tilsit

Sabatier de Castres, abbé Antoine, 128, 133
Saint-Domingue (Haiti), 168–76 passim; and *Ambigu* 139; and *Dernier Tableau de Paris*, 169; and French *commissaires*, 171; economy, 169–70; and Malouet, 41, 52, 168; British and French military involvement, 114, 171; and *Paris pendant l'année*, 83; and Peltier, 41, 72, 92, 132, 168–76 passim; and Regnier, 41, 45; slave revolt, 168; and Vénault de Charmilly, 169–70. *See also* atrocities, blockade, Caribbean, circulation, Henri Christophe, Peltier
Saint-Just, Louis-Antoine-Léon de, 149, 156
Saint-Morys, *see* Bourgevin de Vialart
St. Petersburg, 120, 138
Saint-Pol de Léon, bishop of, *see* La Marche
Sainte-Aldegonde, [?], 103
Sainte-Foy, *see* Radix de Sainte-Foy
Salisbury Journal, 85n.
Salopian Journal, 85
Sardinia, 161. *See also* Piedmont
Sarrazin, general Charles, 212
satire: 150–1, 210; and *Actes des Apôtres*, 21; and *Ambigu*, 21; and British caricature tradition, 212–14; and *Courier de Londres*, 21. *See also* 'Black Legend', Couchery, Peltier, Regnier
Sayous, A., 100
Saxony, 134
Schulze, George and Company, 66
Sébastiani, Horace-François, 121, 126
Semānario patriotico, 72, 139
September massacres, *see Dernier Tableau de Paris*
Serani, [?], *see* collaborators
Serres de La Tour, Alphonse-Joseph de, 18, 19, 66n., 231
Sicily, 139
Sidmouth, 1st viscount, *see* Addington, Henry
Siéyès, Emmanuel-Joseph, abbé, 63n., 145, 183, 184
slavery, 168–70 passim, 208–9. *See also* abbé Calonne, abolitionists, Convention, Malouet, Montlosier, Peltier, Vénault de Charmilly
smuggling, 54, 73, 98, 140
Sonthonax, Léger-Félicité, 171, 172. *See also* embezzlement
Souza-Coutinho, Don Rodrigo Da, *see* Da Souza-Coutinho
Spain: abdications, 215; and *Courier d'Angleterre*, 138, 139; coverage, 205; Francophone élite in, 78; and Napoleonic press, 206; and Peltier 205;

war, 205; resistance, 193. *See also* atrocities, circulation, Gérard, Madrid, Talavera
Spectateur du nord, 62, 76, 97n., 106
sphinx, *see* Peltier
Spilsbury, printer, 66
Staël-Holstein, Germaine, baronne de, 147
stamp duty, see taxes
steam press, *see The Times*
Steillenfels, Louis d'Auerweck, baron de, *see* Auerweck
Stewart, Robert, *see* Castlereagh
Stewarton, H., 212, 219
Street, T. G., 132
Stuart, Daniel, 124n.
Suleau, François, 46, 95–6
Sun, 118, 119n.
Supplément au Rédacteur, 18, 28, 98, 101, 129. *See also* periodicals, 'propaganda journals'
Swabia, 133
Sweden: and Danish expedition, 201; Francophone élite in, 78; and League of Armed Neutrality, 188n.; coup, 136; Russian conquest, 137n.; war with Britain, 136. *See also* Antraigues, circulation, Fauche (P.-F.), Foreign Office, Gérard, Gothenburg, Peltier
Swinton, Félicité: and *Courier de Londres*, 20, 66, 87, 88, 231; and French agents, 106–7; and Montlosier, 106, 186; and Regnier, 88, 106; and Routledge, 88, 231
Swinton, Richard, 20, 231
Swinton, Samuel: and C.-A. de Calonne, 88–9, 154; character, 18, 19; and *Courier de Londres*, 18, 154, 155; and French agents, 106–7; and Peltier, 19–20; and Théveneau de Morande, 19, 88. *See also* abolitionists, British government, collaborators, diamond necklace affair, *Gazette de la Grande-Bretagne*, patronage, proprietors
Switzerland: and *Courier de Londres*, 97; correspondents, 71–2; and Wickham, 62. *See also* Act of Mediation, atrocities, Berne, Mallet Du Pan
Syria, 71, 218

Tableau de l'Europe, 24–5, 76, 99, 155
Tableau de l'Europe en novembre 1795, 159, 176
Talavera, battle of, 92

Talleyrand-Périgord, Charles-Maurice de: and Christin, 89; and De Boffe, 67; and Heron, 219; instructions to Andréossi, 125; Mirabeau on, 149; and Montlosier, 50, 187; and outbreak of war (1803), 108–27 passim; Peltier on, 149; Regnier on, 209; seraglio, 219
Tallien, Jean-Lambert, 150, 151
taxes, 57–8, 75, 228
Terror, 144–59 passim; and Couchery, 45; Peltier on, 161; and press, 95, 177; and *Tableau de l'Europe*, 25
Thermidor, *see* abbé Calonne, Ivernois, *Journal de France et d'Angleterre*, Montlosier, Peltier
Thermidorians, *see* Thermidor
Théveneau de Morande, Charles-Claude: and C.-A. de Calonne, 88; and *Courier de l'Europe*, 86; and *Courier de Londres*, 19, 38, 74, 88, 153, 231; and *Gazetier cuirassé*, 6; and Swinton, 19, 88. *See also* abolitionists, blackmail, diamond necklace affair
Tilly, Alexandre, comte de, *see* collaborators
Tilsit, treaty, 91, 136, 201–3 passim
The Times: and Bourbons, 89; and C.-A. de Calonne, 95; and Danish expedition, 201; and Napoleon, 109; and Peltier, 113; and steam press, 228
Tinseau d'Amondans de Besançon, Charles-M.-T.-L. de, 52. *See also* collaborators, pensions
Toulon, 24, 167
Toussaint L'Ouverture, François-Dominique, 174
treaties, *see* Amiens, Luneville, peace, Tilsit
Trial of John Peltier, 123, 125, 198
Tribunat, 209
Tromelin, Jacques-Jean-Marie-François Boudin de, 52, 71. *See also* collaborators
True Briton, 118, 119
Tuer n'est pas assassiner, 93
Tulard, Jean, 210, 214, 215
Two-Thirds Decree, 156–7

Universal Magazine, 85
United States of America, 79, 139–40

Vansittart, Nicholas, 113
Vaudreuil, Joseph, comte de, 103
Vedette, 37–8

Velley, [?], and *Courier de Londres*, 31, 32, 153. *See also* journalists (minor)
Vénault de Charmilly, P.-F: and Edwards, 175; and Malouet, 174; and Peltier, 72, 169–70, 174–5; and Regnier, 44n., 173; and Saint-Domingue (Haiti), 72, 169–75 passim; on slavery, 175; and *Tableau de l'Europe*, 25
Vendée, 24, 53, 70
Vendémiaire, 157, 160, 180n.
Venetia, 99
Verduisant, [?]: background, 39, 41, 42; and abbé Calonne, 36, 158; and C.-A. de Calonne, 88–9, 89; and *Courier de Londres*, 38, 167n.; and 'divine judgement', 148; emigration, 47; and Lally-Tollendal, 158; attacks moderates, 158; remuneration, 65; on Terror, 155–6. *See also* Brittany, journalists (major)
Verona, Declaration of, 208
Vimeur de Rochambeau, *see* Rochambeau
Vindiciae Gallicae, 124
violence, *see* atrocities, brigandage, intimidation
Voeu d'un bon patriote hollandois, 122, 124–5, 198
Volkonski, prince Paul, 137
Voltaire, 146

Warville, Jacques-Pierre Brissot de, *see* Brissot de Warville
Wedderburn, Alexander, 1st Earl of Rosslyn, 60
Weekly Messenger see Bells Weekly Messenger
Wellesley, Arthur, 1st duke of Wellington, 92, 132
Wellington, 1st duke of, *see* Wellesley
West Indies: and *Ambigu*, 139; and *Paris pendant l'année*, 83. *See also* circulation, French West Indies, Guadeloupe, Jamaica, Martinique, Saint-Domingue
Whitworth, Charles, baron, 108, 121, 125, 126
Wickham, William, 53, 58, 62
Wilberforce, William, 74, 131–2. *See also* abolitionists
Wilson, Robert T., 26n., 212, 217
Windham, William: and abbé Calonne, 100; and Mallet Du Pan, 59, 60, 100; and Peltier, 99
wives, of émigré journalists, *see* families
World, 96n.

Yorke, Henry Redhead, 119
Yvernois, *see* Ivernois

O U... IBRARY
... as you have